Child Custody Made Simple

Understanding the Laws of Child Custody and Child Support

D1308267

Writer's DIGEST

1st Place

National Competition, 1st Place, Nonfiction

"Webster Watnik has addressed two of the most important and enduring issues involving children and parents, and made a great contribution to understanding and properly dealing with the legal, emotional and financial complexities of child custody and child support.

"He explains the many aspects and problems with wonderful clarity and simplicity, and writes with compassion, insight, sensitivity, ease and humor. He supports his comments, descriptions and advice with a substantial foundation of information and research, making his book perhaps the most comprehensive on the market.

"This book is enormously valuable for all single parents, whether separated, divorced or never married."

—Paul D. Mitchell, Senior Consulting Editor, HarperCollins, Writer's Digest National Competition Judge

PMA Benjamin Franklin Awards™

Parenting (Family Issues/Child Care)

WINNER
Child Custody Made Simple, Single Parent Press
FINALISTS
Our Family Has Cancer, Too!, Pfeifer-Hamilton Publishers
Seeds of Love, Folio One Publishing

Benjamin Franklin Award, 1st Place, Parenting

What People Are Saying...

"*Child Custody Made Simple* is an excellent starting point. Each chapter is chock full of both basic information and detailed examples that walk you through the child custody process."
—*David L. Levy, President, Children's Rights Council*

"*Child Custody Made Simple* offers a detailed chronology of what happens during a divorce plus state-by-state guidelines. I recommend it."
—*Andrea Engber, National Organization of Single Mothers*

"One of the best guides about child custody matters that I have seen."
—*Joseph A. McMillen, Attorney, National Congress for Fathers and Children*

"The power of this book rests in Watnik's understanding of the complex interactions and negotiations that drive child custody... an excellent book."
—*Margorie L. Engel, Author, The Divorce Decisions Workbook*

"Packed with family court case examples, tips on the legal system, and plenty of practical examples."
—*Midwest Book Review*

"This comprehensive legal guide to child custody... is a must-read for the uninitiated. I highly recommend it."
—*Ralph Warner, Publisher, Nolo Press*

"I was so impressed with the breadth of material that I suggest a more appropriate title might be *Child Custody: The Ultimate Reference Manual!*"
—*Michael L. Oddenino, Attorney, Children's Rights Council*

"Watnik is a divorced parent inspired by his own custody fight to compile information on how the law says parenting shall be conducted when a marriage dissolves. He begins by explaining the laws and court structures that affect custody decisions. Watnik recommends creating parenting plans that allow former partners to avoid the expense, time, and agony of court battles, and he provides a checklist for drawing up such a plan. Typical living arrangements and schedules are discussed and augmented with graphs that show how time can be divided between parents. The chapters on going to court and working with lawyers explain procedures and prepare readers for situations in which support and custody cannot be settled amicably. A worthy addition to family law collections.
—*Library Journal,* Joan Pedzich, Harris, Beach & Wilcox, Rochester, N.Y.

"*Child Custody Made Simple* is one of the best books on custody and support issues. Webster Watnik, the author, presents a huge amount of information with accuracy, clarity, and simplicity. His writing is lucid and use of graphics effective. Watnik makes an overwhelming experience manageable. He offers tips on choosing a lawyer, explains legal terms, describes options, and how to get what you want and need. Watnik wrote the book after he tried "buying a good book on the subject," during his custody battle, but could not find one, so he wrote his own. Watnik is a professional writer, not a lawyer, who surpasses many lawyers in explaining the law."
—*Family Law Advisor,* The Divorce, Alimony, and Custody Reporter

"Thank you, for writing the book *Child Custody Made Simple.* I have been divorced for a little over eight years and am now going through another custody battle. There are things in your book I wish both my present husband and I knew about eight years ago. If we did we might not be going through all of this now. Your book was written so that anybody could understand it. I'm getting ready to pass it on to a friend who would like to read it. I'm sure she will enjoy it as I did."
—*Debbie Dietrich,* countr1275@aol.com

Child Custody Made Simple

Understanding the Laws of Child Custody and Child Support

Webster Watnik

Cover design and illustration (c) 1997, 2003 by Lightbourne Images.

Grateful acknowledgment is made for permission to reprint excerpts
from CALIFORNIA DIVORCE HANDBOOK: HOW TO DISSOLVE
YOUR MARRIAGE WITHOUT FINANCIAL DISASTER, by Judge James
W. Stewart. Copyright (c) 1990 by Judge James W. Stewart.
Reprinted by permission of Prima Publishing, Rocklin, CA.

Grateful acknowledgment is made for permission to reprint excerpts
from DIVIDING THE CHILD: SOCIAL AND LEGAL DILEMMAS OF
CUSTODY, by Eleanor E. Maccoby and Robert H. Mnookin.
Copyright (c) 1992 by the President and Fellows of Harvard College.
Reprinted by permission of Harvard University Press.

Library of Congress Control Number (LCCN): 2002115134

Publisher's Cataloging in Publication

Watnik, Webster.
      Child custody made simple: understanding the laws of child
custody and child support / by Webster Watnik. —
2nd ed.
        p. cm.
        Includes index, appendix, glossary.
        ISBN 0-9649404-3-4
        1. Custody of children--popular works. 2. Child support--
popular works. I. Title
KF547.Z9W38   2003
346.7301'7   QBI95-20814

Single Parent Press
P.O. Box 1298
Claremont, CA 91711
(909) 624-6058 phone
(909) 624-2208 fax
www.SingleParentPress.com

This book is dedicated to Wyeth

Table of Contents

Child Support

Negotiating a Parenting Plan

Hiring a Lawyer

Representing Yourself

How Courts Work

Difficult Problems

Acknowledgments

For this latest edition, I want to thank all of my friends and others who were kind enough to help.

Thanks to Brad and Jeanne Weiner for their solid support during a long custody battle. Thanks also to Joe Feka, Michael Lindsay, and Charlie Dietz for endless encouragement.

Thanks to the first edition team, Stephanie Sharf, editor, and Gaylene Hatch, indexer.

And finally, thanks to Shannon Bodie, a highly talented designer.

In memory of my parents, Bud and Bette.

Introduction

"Of course it'll work. She'll be the 'wife' and I'll be the 'husband.' What could go wrong?"

Chapter 1

What Happens When You Divorce With Children

✓ If you work out an agreement with the other parent, then child custody is simple. But if you cannot work out an agreement, then child custody can be difficult, time-consuming, and expensive.

✓ When you were married or living together, you shared custody of your children, but when you separated or divorced, the government took over the role of deciding what is best for your children.

✓ Most parents negotiate a custody arrangement privately or use a mediator or psychologist to help them.

✓ Few parents battle for custody in court, and even fewer have high-conflict battles that involve sexual abuse, kidnapping, or violence.

Who Gets The Children?

When you divorce with children, that's the first question everyone asks. Depending on your situation, the answer can be simple or complex.

If you agree on an arrangement, then child custody is simple.

For example, Paul and Susan have two children. After six years of marriage, they decide to split up. During the marriage, Paul traveled on business while Susan worked part-time so she could stay home for the children. Paul and Susan separate on a cordial, friendly basis. They agree the children will stay with Susan during the weekdays and go to Paul's house on weekends.

That's it. Paul and Susan don't need lawyers, they don't need to go to court, and they don't need court orders. They can start following the schedule they created. For this couple, the answer is simple.

But suppose you don't agree on a custody arrangement. Then the answer can be complex.

 When Woody Allen and Mia Farrow began dating in 1980, Mia already had six children, including Soon-Yi. Five years later, after Mia and Woody had been unsuccessful in having a baby, they adopted Dylan. But before the adoption was finished, Mia became pregnant with their daughter, Satchel. By 1991, however, Mia and Woody grew emotionally apart, Soon-Yi enrolled in college, and Woody and Soon-Yi became lovers. Mia discovered the affair when she found erotic pictures of Soon-Yi taken by Woody. Mia took Woody to court. She complained about Woody having sex with Soon-Yi, she accused Woody of sexually abusing Dylan, and she asked for custody of their children. The court granted her requests, and gave Woody limited, supervised visitation with the children. Woody appealed, but lost. *Woody Allen v. Mia Farrow* (1994) 611 N.Y.S.2d 859, 197 A.D.2d 327.

Imagine LeAnn and Robert have one child. They never married. LeAnn wants child support from Robert, but Robert denies the child is his. LeAnn hires a lawyer, who prepares court papers and sends a copy to Robert. The court sets a hearing date, and LeAnn, her lawyer, and Robert show up. The judge orders Robert to submit to a paternity test. Robert cooperates, and the results come back that state with 99% certainty the child is his.

Robert then hires a lawyer and demands custody of the child. LeAnn doesn't want Robert to have custody, but she still wants child support. They have a short custody trial. At the end of the trial, the judge awards LeAnn custody and orders Robert to pay child support. However, Robert's lawyer appeals, and the decision awarding LeAnn custody is reversed. The case is sent back to the trial court for a second trial.

By now, LeAnn has run out of money and her lawyer drops her. At the second trial, she is forced to represent herself. This time, the judge decides the parents should have joint custody. Now, LeAnn and Robert are both unhappy, and they return to court criticizing each other. The judge orders them to attend co-parenting classes. They come back to court again. LeAnn accuses Robert of abusing the child. Robert denies it. The judge orders everyone to be evaluated by a psychologist and appoints a lawyer to represent the child. A social worker investigates. More hearings, more trials, and more custody orders follow.

See how it can become complex? Once LeAnn and Robert began going to court, they had to wait for their turn to voice their complaints. And even after the judge made a decision, neither parent liked it, and they returned to court again. All of this took time, a lot of money, and never brought the dispute to an end.

If there is one thing you learn from this book, here it is:

If you work out an agreement with the other parent, then child custody is simple. But if you cannot work out an agreement, then child custody can be complex.

There is another subject involving children that is not covered in this book. *Dependency law* or *juvenile law* involves people who have committed serious offenses. Not only is this a different area of law, but these cases are usually heard in a different court. For that reason, this book is limited to the more common problems that occur in *divorce court* or *family court.*

Child Custody Laws Protect Children

You may not have known this, but when you were married you shared custody of your children. The law gave you wide deference in how you raised them. Unless your children were being abused, you could raise them as you saw fit.

But once you separated or divorced, you were no longer an intact family. And because you were no longer an intact family, the government decided it must pay extra attention to your children. The government decided that children of separated or divorced parents are at risk.

And because children of divorce are at extra risk, there is a whole group of laws that protect children when their parents split up. These are the laws of *child custody* and *child support.*

This book discusses the laws of child custody, child support, and many more topics, including preparing court papers, hiring a lawyer, and using a mediator.

As you read, feel free to skip around. Because every family is different, you won't need to read the entire book. Just remember that there may be parts you might need to know. So flip through what seems relevant and keep the book handy.

If this book helps you make wise, informed decisions during and after your divorce, then reading this book was time well spent!

Divorce With Children Roadmap

Though every family is different, here are some common milestones you may experience.

Divorce With Children Roadmap

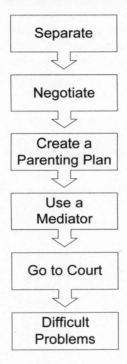

Separate
If you were living together—whether married or not—the process of divorce began when you *separated*. It can get complicated if you were not married and the father does not admit he is the father, or the father is unknown. But generally, most divorces begin when one parent moves out.

Negotiate
At first, you will try talking with your former spouse. *Negotiation* is common, and many parents never hire a lawyer but instead resolve custody and support issues all on their own. Though you may have heard about high-conflict custody battles, those are rare. The most common result is

that you and the other parent will discuss what you need to discuss and somehow work it out.

Create a parenting plan

While many people agree to a vague, flexible arrangement, you may want to write out the details on a piece of paper. This is called a *parenting plan*. If you create a formal parenting plan, you can insert all of the issues you want to address. Keep in mind, though, that if you plan on asking a court to turn your parenting plan into a formal order, the court is not required to adopt everything you say, and can accept or reject the terms you create.

Use a mediator

If you want to work out issues with a third-party, you can always work with a *mediator, family counselor,* or *psychologist.* In some states, the judge will order you to meet with a mediator before the judge will listen your case. Of course, there is nothing stopping you from finding a professional on your own. Many parents choose to work our their differences in mediation.

Hire a lawyer

Because custody and support are legal issues, when you need help, you will need to talk to a *lawyer.* While it's common in divorce cases for one, or both, parents to represent themselves, it's hard for a non-lawyer to know what to do. So if you have a legal problem, you may need to hire a lawyer.

Go to court

If you cannot come to an agreement, you have to go to *court.* The court will address the disagreement you have. The judge who handles custody and support has the authority to make all kinds of orders. The important thing to remember is that resolving disagreements in court can be slow, expensive, and frustrating. For those reasons, only a small percentage of parents end up having a judge decide their custody disputes.

Difficult problems

Finally, for a very small group of parents, *serious custody issues* develop. These are the extreme cases where sexual abuse, domestic violence, kidnapping, and so on, are alleged or occur. Unfortunately, some divorces become a battle where

Divorce Books

The Complete Idiot's Guide to Surviving Divorce, Pamela Weintraub, Terry Hillman, Elayne Kesselman, Alpha Books, $16.95. This easy-to-read book covers everything you need to know about divorce.

Crazy Time, Abigail Trafford, HarperPerennial, $13.00. Trafford weaves her own life experiences with well-written insights and observations about the "process" of divorce.

Divorce Busting, Michele Weiner-Davis, Simon and Schuster, $12.00. Weiner-Davis offers straightforward advice on how couples can work together to save a troubled marriage.

The Divorce Decisions Workbook, Margorie L. Engle, Diana Gould, McGraw-Hill, $27.95. Filled with tear-out forms, this is a great book to get your life organized.

Divorce for Dummies, John Ventura, Mary Reed, IDG Books Worldwide, $19.99. This very readable and comprehensive book covers most of the issues you'll need to know

Divorcing, Melvin Belli, Mel Krantzler, St. Martins, $6.99. Co-written by Belli, a legendary trial attorney, this book offers excellent legal advice, as well as coping with the emotional side of divorce.

Getting Divorced Without Ruining Your Life, Sam Margulies, $9.00. Written by a divorce lawyer, here's a friendly and sensible book on getting divorced without being chewed up by the legal system.

Joint Custody With a Jerk, Julia A. Ross, Judy Corcoran (Contributor), St. Martin's Press, $13.95. A straight-from-the-hip, dead-on discussion of sharing custody with an "immature" ex-spouse.

the children become pawns and the parents fight endlessly. If it happens to you, keep in mind that these high-conflict cases are rare.

This roadmap is too simple to describe what will happen in your situation, but there is one thing you should know. After the divorce, you'll be doing just what you did before the divorce, somehow raising your children and trying to get along with your ex.

 "Contested custody proceedings account annually for approximately 7 percent of the more than one million divorces occurring in America." Melvin Belli, *Divorcing*

Child Custody and Visitation

*"I'm also available as an expert witness
in custody battles."*

Chapter 2

The Laws of Child Custody

- ✓ Custody is the right to raise your children. You share custody of your children when you stay together, but when you separate or divorce, you divide up custody.

- ✓ Depending on the laws in your state, custody may be divided between *legal custody,* which is the right to make major decisions about the children, and *physical custody,* which is the right to raise the children day-to-day.

- ✓ Many states allow each custody component to be divided between *sole* and *joint.* Sole gives one parent full and exclusive rights, while joint shares those rights between parents.

- ✓ If one parent is awarded sole custody, the other parent is almost always allowed *visitation.* Visitation is when the noncustodial parent may see the children.

- ✓ Visitation can take many forms, including *reasonable visitation,* which does not specify exact days and times, and *scheduled visitation,* which is more precise.

- ✓ The court loses authority to make custody orders when the children reach the age of majority or become emancipated.

Child Custody and Visitation

When you first separate, you must decide how to share your children. If you agree, you can begin living the new arrangement. But if you do not agree, a judge will decide for you. And when the judge decides, he will be guided by the laws of child custody and visitation.

Types of Custody

Responsibilities for children are usually divided into two categories: legal and physical.

Legal custody is the right to make major decisions about your child. *Physical custody* is the right to have your child live with you.

In addition, legal and physical custody are each divided into two more categories: sole and joint. *Sole* assigns the right to one parent exclusively, while *joint* shares the right between the parents.

Types of Custody

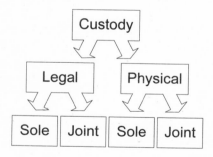

Legal Custody

Legal custody is the right to make major decisions about the child. The parent granted legal custody is the guardian of the child and will make the important decisions about the child's health, education, and welfare.

The rights of legal custody can include making decisions about:
- What schools the children will attend.
- What medical and dental care they will receive.
- What religion they will be raised in.

The right to makes these decisions can be assigned to one parent exclusively, or shared between the parents.

> If you want custody of your children, do not move out of the family home. If you leave, you abandon the children to the other parent, who may be granted temporary custody.

Sole Legal Custody

Sole legal custody entitles one parent—and one parent alone—the right to make all major decisions in a child's life. That parent becomes the sole legal guardian, with the exclusive right to decide what is best for the child.

The advantage of sole legal custody is that it may reduce parental conflict by clearly establishing who has authority to make decisions. The disadvantage is that by making one parent solely responsible for the child, the other parent is reduced to being a visitor, prevented from having a meaningful say in the child's life.

Sole legal custody may be appropriate when one parent prefers to relinquish his or her involvement with the children, or when a parent is too unstable to make basic decisions for the children.

Joint Legal Custody

Joint legal custody shares the authority to make child-raising decisions between the two parents.

Under joint legal custody, the parents must share information and must consult and agree on issues regarding the children's health, education, and welfare. The scope of issues may be stated in the custody order, or may be left undetermined.

When Heaven Rideout was a sixteen-year-old high school student, unmarried, and living with her parents, she gave birth to a baby girl, Keiko. Over the next six years, she married and divorced one man, married and separated from another, moved several times, and had two more children, Roman and Mariah. Each time she broke up, she returned to live with her parents, Rose and Chelsey. After Heaven returned home once again, Rose contacted the Department of Human Services and complained about Heaven's parenting. Rose also filed a petition to adopt Keiko. Heaven then took her three children and moved back in with her second husband. She also terminated all contact between Rose, Chelsey and the children. Rose and Chelsey asked for court-ordered visitation pursuant to the Maine Grandparents Visitation Act, but the court denied their request. *Rideout v. Riendeau* (2000) 761 A.2d 291, 2000 ME 198.

Typically, joint custodians are required to consult each other on:
- Education.
- Religion.
- Nonemergency medical care.

Joint legal custody requires the parents to cooperate, and may create conflict when they cannot resolve even the simplest child-rearing issues. However, if a conflict arises under this arrangement, the parents may agree to consult a friend, attempt mediation, or take the issue to court.

Physical Custody

Physical custody is the right to care for the children on a daily basis. The parent granted physical custody is the caretaker who provides day-to-day nurturance for the child

The rights of physical custody can include:
- In whose home the children will live.
- Who will make day-to-day child care decisions.

As with legal custody, physical custody can also be assigned solely to one parent, or shared between them.

Sole Physical Custody

Sole physical custody—also known as *primary physical custody* or *residential custody*—assigns the day-to-day child care responsibilities to one parent. Sole physical custody usually means the children live primarily with one parent, and that parent is solely responsible for supervising their daily activities.

Joint Physical Custody

Joint physical custody, also called *joint parenting* or *shared parenting,* shares the day-to-day child care decisions between the parents. Under joint physical custody, both parents typically spend a more equal amount of time with their children than under sole custody arrangements.

An order of joint physical custody does not automatically determine how much time the children will spend with each parent. Some joint physical custody awards divide the children's time evenly, while others do not. For example, one joint arrangement might require the children to live with one parent during one week, and the other parent during the next. Or, the children might spend one-half of all non-school days with one parent, and the remainder with the other.

The advantages to joint physical custody are that because one parent is no longer burdened with the entire obligation to raise the children, each has more time to go back to school, pursue a more demanding job, build a new family, and so on. Also, because joint physical custody assures that the parents will have frequent contact with their children, it more closely approximates the relationship the children had with their

 Joint physical custody may influence the amount of child support ordered. Under joint physical custody, parents are supposed to share the daily child-rearing responsibilities and costs more evenly, which may result in each parent paying his or her expenses directly.

Divorce Sites

There are many divorce sites out there, but some are better than others. The following are some of the best on the web.

Divorce Net
www.divorcenet.com
This major site has plenty of articles, resources, bulletin boards, child support calculators, and more. Because this site has been around for a long time, the resources are very extensive.

Divorce Source
www.divorcesource.com
An excellent divorce site with a concise summary of divorce laws in all states, articles, chat rooms, summaries of cases by subject, and more.

Divorce Support
www.divorcesupport.com
A sister site to *Divorce Source.* If you want to start a divorce or create a separation agreement, you can download forms here.

Divorce Magazine
www.divorcemag.com
Plenty of well-written articles make this site worthwhile. You can read about custody, support, relationships, mediation, budgeting, taxes, and much more.

Divorce Info
www.divorceinfo.com
Another site with divorce articles, the home page claims there are more than 100,000 pages on the site. Good site to wander around.

Divorce Central
www.divorcecentral.com
Active bulletin boards make this site worth visiting. This online community is organized into four areas: legal, financial, emotional (called Lifeline), and parenting.

parents when everyone was together. And finally, this arrangement allows the children to grow up with both male and female role models.

The disadvantage to joint physical custody is that since each parent is assured of regular contact with their children, they will also have regular contact with each other. While some parents may be able to resolve differences peacefully, others may not. Also, joint physical custody may cost more money, since each parent will have to maintain a complete family household.

Many states have statutes referring to joint custody. Some states make joint custody a presumption or preference, which means that it will be ordered unless someone proves that it would not be best for the child. Other states make it an option the parents can ask for or the judge can order. Some states allow the judge to award joint custody even over the objection of one of the parents.

Joint physical custody is appropriate when the parents can cooperate, and when they live close enough so that the children can maintain consistency in their school and friends.

Other Forms of Custody

Because individual circumstances vary, a variety of custodial arrangements have evolved. Here are some other ones:

Bird's Nest Custody
In *bird's nest custody,* the children do not go back-and-forth from one parent's house to the other, but instead, the parents move in-and-out. This schedule minimizes the disruption to the children's lives, and forces the parents to cope with the upheaval of regular moves. A common arrangement calls for the children to stay in the family home, and the parents to move in-and-out from a separate apartment.

Alternating Custody
Also known as *serial custody,* this arrangement calls for the children to live a long time with one parent, and then switch and live a long time with the other parent. While the amount of time can vary, one example would be if the children lived

with one parent for a year, and then moved in with the other parent for a year. This differs from joint custody in that each parent assumes sole authority over the children while they are with them. Generally, parents choose this custody arrangement when they live too far apart—such as in different states or countries—to make other arrangements practical.

Split Custody

Custodial terms can be confusing, but generally *split custody* refers to the decision to split up the children by having one or more live with one parent while one or more of the children lives with the other parent. Split custody has the appearance of fairness, since each parent is granted custody of a child.

Parents who choose split custody do so because it eliminates the need for the children to routinely move back and forth. Also, it is a way to separate siblings who don't get along with each other or with a new mate.

Split custody has been criticized because it is believed that when siblings are separated from one another, they are also severed from the emotional support they gain by having brothers or sisters. This forced separation may only compound the distress they are experiencing from the divorce.

 When Tammy was unable to care for her child and needed to find work in another city, she left her daughter with Judith and Gordon Knopp, her aunt and uncle. Before she left, she appointed the Knopps temporary guardians. Three month later, with Tammy out of town, the Knopp's asked a district court to award them custody, and the court gave them temporary custody. When Tammy returned, she discovered she was barred from picking up her daughter. Tammy asked the district court to deny the Knopp's request for permanent custody, arguing that the court did not have the authority to award custody to a non-parent until the natural parent's rights have been terminated. The court agreed, and Tammy was given her child. *Knopp v. Knopp* (2001) 305 Mont. 351, 27 P.3d 953, 2001 MT 120.

If the custodial parent dies, custody of the children will go to the noncustodial parent. If the noncustodial parent cannot care for the children, a third party—such as a grandparent—may be appointed guardian. If no third party is available, another adult will be appointed guardian.

In some cases, however, the damage to the children from split custody can be reduced by arranging visitation so that the children are together at least every other weekend.

Third-Party Custody
In some families, the children do not remain with either natural parent, but instead, are awarded to a third person. This is known as *third-party custody*. Third-party custody occurs when the biological parents either do not want the children or are incapable of caring for them. Third parties can include grandparents, stepparents, family friends, or foster homes.

Third-party custody disputes typically arise when the parents have voluntarily relinquished their children, or when a judge deems both parents unfit. While there is no absolute rule regarding third-party disputes, case law has established that biological parents have a "natural" right to their children superior to the claims of third parties.

Voluntary Relinquishment. Sometimes, parents agree to let another adult raise the children. If either parent later changes his or her mind, he or she can seek custody.

Unfit Parents. Because the court retains authority over the children, it can award custody to another adult if the biological parents appear unfit. Reasons that could cause a parent to be declared unfit include:
- Child abuse or neglect.
- Substance abuse.
- Deliberate abandonment of the children.
- Inability to provide the minimum income necessary to raise the children.

Social Theories about Child Custody

There is no consensus regarding which custody arrangement is best. Various psychologists and social theorists have speculated about how to share the children, but they do not agree. Here are some common beliefs:

Sole Custody

	Legal	Physical
Parent A	✓	✓
Parent B		

Proponents of sole custody argue that children need to belong to one family unit. Firm boundaries need to be drawn around the custodial parent and the child, and the noncustodial parent should be relegated to the role of an "outside" visitor. They believe that continuing contact with conflicting parents is more harmful to the children than the loss of one parent.

Opponents of sole custody acknowledge that parental conflict hurts the children, but point out that few families are that high-conflict. Also, they believe that the loss of the noncustodial parent is much more harmful to the children, noting the grief and sense of abandonment children experience when they lose a parent. Additionally, they argue that a source of conflict in sole custody situations comes from the custodial parent's having power to control or deny visitation. And finally, they point out that relegating one parent to "visitor" status is the main reason why so many noncustodial parents fail to visit their children or pay support.

In *California Divorce Handbook,* Judge Stewart offers one reason why many judges resolve custody disputes by awarding sole custody to one parent: "Designing a structured custody order requires compulsive attention to details—judges are often mind—boggled by such potential work and may unfortunately give in to a misbelief that if they order sole custody and traditional visitation, such structure and detail is less necessary."

Joint Legal and Sole Physical Custody

	Legal	Physical
Parent A	✓	✓
Parent B	✓	

Proponents of joint legal and sole physical custody believe that this arrangement eliminates many of the problems of sole custody. They argue that it does not isolate the visiting parent as much as sole custody does, primarily because he or she still retains legal authority over the child. Also, if the parents do not cooperate, the judge can add highly detailed schedules that resolve most day-to-day disputes. This arrangement also gives the child the stability of having one primary home.

Opponents agree that this custody offers certain advantages, but state that it does not go far enough. For all practical purposes, the noncustodial parent is still cut-off from having a meaningful say in the children's lives. And if the parents are truly high-conflict, the arrangement still exposes the children to parental disputes.

Joint Custody

	Legal	Physical
Parent A	✓	✓
Parent B	✓	✓

Those who argue for joint legal and physical custody point out that the children are the ones who suffer the most when parents divorce. By sharing child care responsibilities more evenly, joint custody reduces the day-to-day stress put on sole custodial parents—which helps the children. Also, joint custody protects the children by preventing either parent from controlling the other's access to them. And finally, they point to studies that show that parents with joint custody are much more likely to spend time with their children and pay child support. Put simply, they say, two parents are better than one.

Opponents of joint custody believe that it harms the children. They believe that joint custody forces the children to remain in the middle of the conflict, which can only inflict more emotional damage. They also argue that children who bounce back and forth from one home to another cannot develop a stable home life.

Visitation

Even if one parent is awarded physical custody of the children, the other parent still has a legal right to see them. The time the noncustodial parent is allowed to spend with the children is called *visitation*.

Visitation lets the parents share the children but still protects the authority of the custodial parent to make child care decisions. For all practical purposes, visitation time is the parenting time for the noncustodial parent.

Types of Visitation

There are several kinds of visitation orders:

Reasonable Visitation
Reasonable visitation allows the parents to create their own visitation schedule. It does not specify days and times, but rather, gives the parents flexibility to work out their own schedule. The noncustodial parent is allowed to see the children upon "reasonable notice" to the custodial parent.

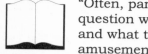

"Often, parents not living with their children question where they should take the children and what they should plan in the way of amusement for them, particularly if the children are young. Activities may add to the pleasure of the time together, but most important is the parent's involvement with the children. A giving of self is more important than whatever material things they may get."
Parents Are Forever, Association of Family and Conciliation Courts

United States Supreme Court Custody Cases

Troxel v. Granville (2000) 530 U.S. 57, decided that a Washington state law giving grandparents broad visitation rights was unconstitutional because it infringed on the fundamental rights of parents to raise their children.

M.L.B. v. S.L.J., (1996) 519 U.S. 102, decided that a state cannot prevent an indigent parent from appealing an order terminating parental rights because he or she cannot afford the fees to prepare the trial record.

Michael H. et al. v. Gerald D. (1989) 491 U.S. 110, decided that if a woman has a child while she is married, and the father is a different man, the biological father has no standing to establish his parental rights.

Palmore v. Sidoti (1984) 466 U.S. 429, decided that awarding custody based on race was a violation of the fourteenth amendment to the United States Constitution.

Santosky v. Kramer (1982) 455 U.S. 745, decided that a court cannot terminate parental rights unless the court has met the higher, more stringent legal standard of "clear and convincing evidence."

Stanley v. Illinois (1972) 405 U.S. 645, decided that parents are "constitutionally entitled to a hearing on their fitness before children are removed from their custody."

Because reasonable is vague and undefined, it gives the custodial parent the authority to approve or deny visitation. Reasonable visitation is best suited when everyone cooperates. Reasonable visitation is not appropriate when parents disagree about how to raise the children.

Fixed-Schedule Visitation
Fixed-schedule or *court-scheduled visitation* specifies exactly which days and times the parents have the children. The orders are very detailed, and can include which parent will transport the children, the exchange location, etc.

During their three year marriage, Gwendolyn and John had two sons, Mitchell and Jonah. When they divorced, Gwendolyn was given primary custody of Mitchell, and John was allowed limited visitation. There was no order about Jonah. Six years later, after Gwendolyn's new husband spanked Mitchell, John filed a petition to modify the order for Mitchell and to establish custody for Jonah. Initially, the court said the children should live with Gwendolyn, but John refused to return the children. Gwendolyn then obtained an order forcing John to return the children. John complied. After more hearings and motions, the trial court finally designated John the domiciliary parent, and ordered that Mitchell and Jonah live with him. By way of explanation, the district court said that Gwendolyn "abdicates her authority over the boys to her husband and other male members of her family; and the boys are... subjected to many different rules... and personalities." *Greene v. Taylor* (2002) 809 So.2d 1187.

A fixed schedule minimizes the need for negotiation between the parents, which makes it appropriate when parents argue and their continued contact puts the children at risk.

A fixed schedule is also useful if the noncustodial parent anticipates that the custodial parent will interfere with his or her visitation. The detailed schedule allows the judge to determine fault in the event of a disagreement.

Supervised Visitation

Another type of visitation is *supervised visitation*. Supervised visitation is when a neutral third-party remains present during the visit in order to protect the children from dangerous behavior by the noncustodial parent. The court must approve the adult who supervises, and if the parents don't agree on who this should be, the court will appoint someone.

A judge may order supervised visitation when he wants to allow visitation, but is convinced the behavior of the noncustodial parent poses a threat to the child.

For example, supervised visitation may be ordered if a parent:
- Has been convicted of child abuse or drunk driving.
- Abuses alcohol or drugs.
- Has attempted suicide.
- Has a history of violence or domestic abuse.

Additionally, if the noncustodial parent has not seen the children for a long time, that parent may be awarded supervised visitation until he or she demonstrates ability to care for the children.

Third-Party Visitation

After divorce, other family members have the right to continue their relationship with the child. Thus, most states allow some visitation by third-parties, including:
- Grandparents.
- Great-grandparents.
- Stepparents.
- Foster parents.
- Siblings.

Also, some states expand the definition of third parties beyond family members to allow visitation by "any other person having an interest in the welfare of the child."

Third-party custody disputes typically occur when the parents of the noncustodial parent are prevented from seeing their grandchildren.

Third parties can join in any lawsuit filed by the parents, or can initiate their own. However, if a third party seeks visitation over the objections of the parents, there is no guarantee the court will grant it.

Fatherless America, by David Blankenhorn, eloquently expresses the noncustodial parent's experience, "A great many visiting fathers, angered and ultimately defeated by the realization that they are reduced to becoming visitors in their children's lives, simply give up the effort and withdraw completely from their children's lives."

When Child Custody Ends

Generally, the authority of the court to decide custody ends
when the child reaches the age of majority or is emancipated.

Emancipation occurs when a child demonstrates freedom from
parental control. For a child to become emancipated, the
court must order it, or a significant act must occur, such as
when the child:
- Gets married.
- Joins the military.
- Moves out and becomes self-supporting.

Parents cannot simply declare a child emancipated, but must
bring a special proceeding to have the child declared
emancipated. The child can also seek to be emancipated.
One exception occurs when a child reaches adulthood, but is
incapable of managing his or her own affairs. In that
situation, the parent or a third-party may be appointed
guardian.

 Matt and Kim were married four years and had
two children when Kim was in an automobile
accident and became paralyzed from the arms
down. As a result, Kim became severely obese,
lost motor control below her shoulders, relied on a
motorized wheelchair, and needed daily assistance to
perform routine tasks and bodily functions. A few years
later, Matt and Kim divorced. Even though the divorce
decree gave them joint custody, Matt moved out and left
the children with Kim. The following year, the children
went to Matt's house for spring break, and Matt refused
to return them. Kim asked the district court for physical
custody of the children, and Matt responded by also
asking for physical custody. The court gave custody to
Kim. However, Matt appealed the decision, and the Court
of Appeals reversed, explaining that "Kim's physical
condition seriously impacts her ability to minister
effectively to the daily needs of her two children." *In re
Marriage of Shook* (2002) Iowa No. 1-830 / 00-1806.

Chapter 3

The Reality of Child Custody

- ✓ Don't be surprised if you feel differently about the children. The fact is, most mothers want sole custody and most fathers don't.

- ✓ Even if you disagree on custody, you probably won't fight. About 80% of all parents decide custody on their own.

- ✓ If you go to court, you'll settle long before trial. Less than 2% of all custody decisions are made by a judge.

- ✓ If a judge does make the decision, there's a good chance it will be in favor of joint custody. At the end of a trial, joint custody is ordered 40% of the time.

- ✓ Divorce often means the children stop seeing one parent. After parents separate or divorce, more than 20% of all children have no visitation with the other parent.

Who Wants the Children

The best study for illustrating custody negotiations is *The Stanford Custody Project,* a survey of 1,123 divorcing California families by Eleanor Maccoby and Robert Mnookin.[1]

When Maccoby and Mnookin asked divorcing parents what custodial arrangement they wanted, here's what they found:

What Mothers Want[2]

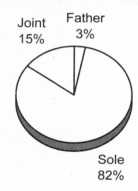

Joint
15%

Father
3%

Sole
82%

Among separated or divorced mothers, 82% wanted sole custody, 15% wanted joint, and 3% wanted the father to have custody.

What Fathers Want[3]

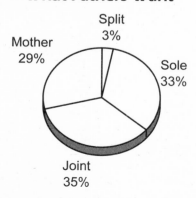

Split
3%

Mother
29%

Sole
33%

Joint
35%

On the other hand, fathers only wanted sole custody 33% of the time, 35% wanted joint, and 29% wanted the mother to have custody.

To explain the difference, Maccoby and Mnookin offered
several reasons. First, many parents may have felt the
mother was more experienced in the care of the children, and
decided it was impractical for the father to suddenly assume
the extra burdens. Still others may have believed the mother
was naturally better suited to raising the children. And a
third group may have disagreed, but the father deferred to the
mother in the face of her strong desire for custody.

Since most mothers wanted the children, and most fathers
were flexible, the parents should have been able to agree
much of the time... and that's just what they did.

How Custody Is Decided

When Maccoby and Mnookin tracked how the parents decided
custody, here's what they found:

How Custody is Decided[4]

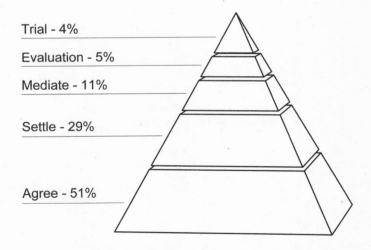

Trial - 4%

Evaluation - 5%

Mediate - 11%

Settle - 29%

Agree - 51%

In their study, 51% of the parents completely agreed on
custody, 29% settled their differences without any third-party
involvement, 11% decided custody during mediation, 5%
resolved their differences after a custody evaluation, and only
a small portion—4% of all parents who disputed custody of
the children—made it to trial.

As they reported in *Dividing the Child,* "The common perception of widespread conflict is a myth: most parents resolve the custody and money issues without substantial conflict, and it is extremely uncommon for disputes to require resolution by a judge."

When Parents Agree

When parents agreed on custody, they overwhelmingly decided to give custody to Mom. Here's what they did:

Who Gets Custody When Parents Agree[5]

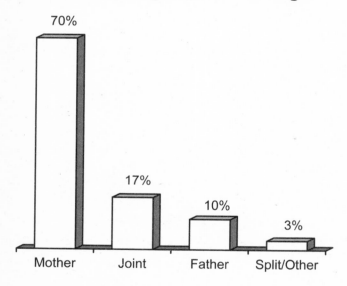

Parents agreed to give custody to the mother 70% of the time, custody to the father 10%, and they settled on joint custody of the children 17% of the time.

In explaining these results, Maccoby and Mnookin hypothesized that many parents held a traditional view of parenting—meaning that mothers should be the primary caretakers. Also, when the parents first separated, the children remained with the mother 67% of the time.[6] This *initial residence* of the children was important to parents who wanted to avoid disturbing the status quo of the living arrangements.

Not all parents agreed on custody, however, and when they didn't, things changed.

When Parents Settle

Of the total number of parents who faced a custody decision, about half disagreed. Of those, many managed to settle their differences on their own. Here's what they decided:

Who Gets Custody When Parents Settle[7]

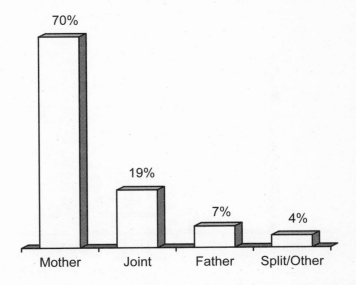

When parents settled on their own, they gave custody to Mom 70% of the time, custody to Dad about 7% of the time, and decided on joint custody 19% of the time. These results were not very different from those of the parents who agreed on custody.

Among the many reasons why these parents settled, some may have been bargaining in the *shadow of the law*. That meant they wanted to decide custody as closely as possible to what they believed would happen in court—without actually going to court. They chose to resolve their dispute without the time and money involved in litigation.

Of course, many parents could not resolve their incompatible custody desires, and they entered the legal system.

When Parents Mediate

The remaining 20% of the parents in the study could not resolve custody on their own. They were "assisted" by a third party—often a court-appointed mediator. Here's what happened:

Who Gets Custody When Parents Mediate[8]

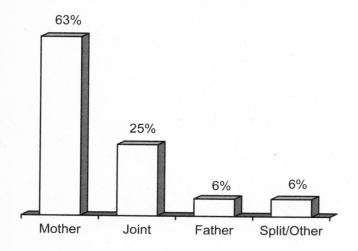

When parents took their first step into the legal system— court-assisted mediation—they ended up agreeing to give custody to Mom 63% of the time, custody to Dad 6% of the time, and settled on joint custody 25% of the time.

In the California counties where the study took place, mediation is court-ordered, and parents face a mediator who can make a custody recommendation to the judge. Because judges often adopt the mediator's recommendation, this authority is a powerful deterrent to parents who cannot resolve their custody dispute, and many parents settled at this point.

But some did not.

When Parents Go to Evaluation or Trial

The final two groups doggedly pursued their dispute to the very end of the line. These two groups—parents who settled after a custody evaluation and parents who actually went to trial—were so small that Maccoby and Mnookin combined their custody results into one table.

Here's what happened:

Who Gets Custody When Parents Go To Evaluation or Trial[9]

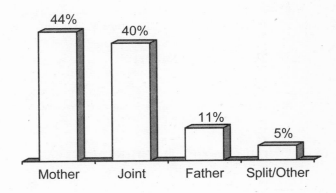

As the study revealed, something interesting happened when the parents pursued their custody dispute.

At this stage, Mom got custody 44% of the time, Dad got custody 11% of the time, and the parents ended up with joint custody 40% of the time.

In other words, when the conflict reached the end of the legal system, the odds of a mother getting custody dropped to 44%, and the odds of joint custody being awarded increased to 40%.

Maccoby and Mnookin found that—despite what happens in the movies—very few parents actually finished a trial. Of the 4% that made it to trial, only 1.5% completed it. A number of parents decided to settle "either on the courthouse steps or during the trial itself."

This means that only a tiny fraction of all divorcing parents actually have the custody of their children decided by a judge.

The *Stanford Custody Project* also illustrated who "wins" a custody dispute by measuring which parent achieved what they sought.

Mothers "won" more than twice as often as fathers.

In custody disputes, mothers prevailed 59% of the time, fathers prevailed 26% of the time, and neither side prevailed 15% of the time. When neither side prevailed, typically each parent sought sole custody, and the result was joint custody.

Final Custody Arrangements

When Maccoby and Mnookin added up all the custody decisions from the families in their study, here's what they found:

Final Custody Arrangements[10]

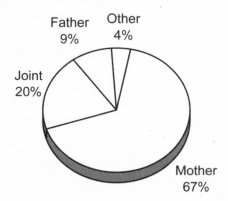

In the custody orders, mothers got custody of the children about 67% of the time, fathers got custody about 9% of the time, the parents ended up with joint custody 20% of the time, and the remaining 4% of the families reached a different arrangement.

The results of the *Stanford Custody Project* were very similar to those in a national study. *The National Center for Health Statistics* reported that 71% of children of divorce were living with their mothers, 15.5% were shared by their parents, 8.5% were living with their fathers, and 5% were living with other relatives. *Advance Report of Final Divorce Statistics,* National Center for Health Statistics.

Visitation

After custody is decided, the amount of visitation must be determined. Here's what the families in the study did:

How the Children's Time Was Divided[11]

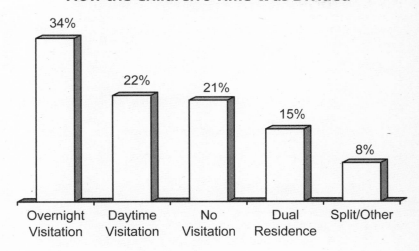

When the children lived primarily with one parent, about 34% had overnight visitation and 22% had daytime visitation with the other parent. In the study, visitation was defined as less than four overnight visits in a two-week period. Typically, this meant the children lived with one parent and visited the other on alternate weekends.

Another 21% of the children had no visitation with the other parent at all, while 15% of the children had just the opposite experience—they had two homes. Dual residence meant that the children spent as few as four, but as many as 10, overnights in a two-week period with the other parent.

The last group of children either lived in a split situation or were in some other arrangement. Interestingly, for many of these children, the parents were divorcing but still lived together.

The Facts of Child Custody

Dividing the Child: Social and Legal Dilemmas of Custody, Eleanor Maccoby and Robert Mnookin, Harvard University Press, $12.95.

Results from a survey of over 1,100 California families. A terrific work that contains fascinating insights into the unique problems of child custody. Be forewarned, though, some sections will make you wish you had stayed awake in statistics class.

---

1 *Dividing the Child,* Eleanor Maccoby and Robert Mnookin, Harvard University Press, 1992.
2 Ibid. Custody requested in divorce petition (table 5.1, page 99).
3 Ibid.
4 Ibid. Conflict pyramid for custody and visitation issues (figure 7.2, page 137).
5 Ibid. Physical custody outcomes by mode of resolution (figure 7.6, page 151).
6 Ibid. De facto residence of children and visitation patterns at time 1 (table 4.1, page 74).
7 Ibid. Physical custody outcomes by mode of resolution (figure 7.6, page 151).
8 Ibid.
9 Ibid.
10 Ibid. Distribution of custodial decrees (table 5.3, page 113).
11 Ibid. De facto residence of children and visitation patterns at Time 1 (table 4.1, page 74).

Chapter 4

Deciding Child Custody

✓ The legal standard for deciding child custody is known as the *best interests of the child.*

✓ When first deciding custody, the judge considers many factors, such as abuse or violence, or which parent has the closer emotional bond to the children.

✓ The children may be interviewed, but the desires of the children are usually important only when they are older.

✓ Some courts use a psychologist to evaluate the parents. The psychologist may use tests or interview family members to gather information for a custody recommendation.

✓ After deciding custody, it is likely the arrangement will change. Events in the lives of the parents—or just the children getting older—may require a change to the custody schedule.

✓ The legal standard to change an existing custody order is known as a *significant change of circumstances.*

Best Interests of the Child

When deciding custody, the judge must follow a legal standard to make the decision. This standard is called the *best interests of the child.*

Because parents are more than parents, and custody disputes often involve charges and counter-charges that have little to do with actual parenting skills, the judge must find a way to sift through the debris of the failed relationship and reach a decision.

That's why the custody decision is based on the best interests of the child. By doing what is best for the child—and not what is best for either parent—the judge focuses on the important issues and eliminates the unimportant ones.

Deciding what is best for the child sounds good, but it's actually vague and open-ended. It often results in judicial bias—custody decisions that vary from one judge to the next.

Proponents of the standard, however, insist that it cannot be different. If the qualifications for custody were more specific— say, a series of tests a parent must pass to get their children—then the government would be in the business of deciding the "perfect" family.

 When Carrie divorced Leonard after their eight year marriage, she asked for custody of their son, Anthony, but Leonard objected. At trial, Leonard's daughter from his first marriage, Cori, testified that Carrie smoked marijuana around her when Cori was a fourteen-year old high school freshman, and gave alcohol and marijuana to Cori and her friends when Cori was fifteen. Another witness, Diana, testified that she personally saw Carrie use marijuana on a daily basis at work, in a car with Anthony, and in front of Cori. And Carrie herself admitted to getting high while Anthony was home and smoking marijuana in front of Cori. The court gave Leonard physical care of Anthony. *In re Marriage of Fazio* (2002) Iowa No. 2-203 / 01-1045.

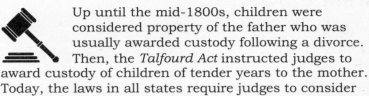
Up until the mid-1800s, children were considered property of the father who was usually awarded custody following a divorce. Then, the *Talfourd Act* instructed judges to award custody of children of tender years to the mother. Today, the laws in all states require judges to consider what is in the best interests of the child when making a custody decision.

Regardless of its flaws, the best interests standard is one that will be followed when a judge decides custody.

Factors That Influence Custody

When deciding what is best for the child, the judge must consider a long list of factors.

Some factors are negative, such as things that might harm the child, while others are positive, such as things that will help. Some are based on past behaviors, while others are predictive of the future.

Primary Caretaker
When a judge decides custody, the judge tries to determine which parent has been the child's primary caretaker. The primary caretaker is the parent who cared for the child day-to-day. This includes such activities as making the child's meals, taking the child to-and-from school, bringing the child to the doctor, helping with homework, and so on.

Generally, the parent who has been the primary caretaker is favored for custody. This reflects the belief that whoever has been raising the child may not only be more committed, but is more experienced.

Established Residence
Normally, judges want to maintain the *status quo*—or established living pattern—in a child's life. This means keeping the child in the same home, the same school, the same church, the same community, and so on. The parent who can provide continuity may be favored for custody.

Where the children live matters. In their study of California families, Maccoby and Mnookin found that custody was awarded to the parent with whom the children were living 77% of the time.[1] As they stated in *Dividing the Child,* "In cases where parents had conflicting requests, physical custody was more likely to be awarded to the parent with whom the children were living at the time of initial separation— in other words, 'possession' was 'nine tenths of the law.'"

Logistics

Judges may also consider the logistics of parenting. Logistics typically include which parent has more free time or a more suitable work schedule, or which parent lives closer to the child's school or day care facilities, or how much driving each parent has to do. The parent in a more favorable position has an advantage.

Religion

Under normal circumstances, a parent's religion should not influence custody. However, if a child has been raised in a particular religion, that may be a reason to maintain continuity in the child's life. But if a parent subscribes to a nontraditional or unconventional religion, the judge must decide if the religion will threaten the health or well-being of the child. If so, it may be a factor. For example, a judge may decide that a religion that advocates avoiding doctors may put the child's health at risk.

Remarriage

If one of the biological parents has remarried, it may influence custody. This is based on the belief that two adults can more easily raise a child than one. The remarriage may also create an issue when the morals or behaviors of the new mate are questioned.

Sex

This factor is vague, but generally, only behavior that affects the child is relevant. This factor can either be positive or negative. For example, when a parent becomes involved with a new partner, it can demonstrate a positive, healthy relationship. In other cases, the sexual activities of the parent and the new partner may place the child in an embarrassing, stressful situation. However, if the parent takes a new partner who is of the same sex, that will influence custody. A number of conservative family courts will deny custody to a homosexual parent, based upon the reasoning that children of gay parents will be harmed.

Drinking and Drugs

When a parent abuses alcohol or drugs, this behavior creates a dangerous environment for the child and it will influence custody. Be aware, however, that some judges believe that if one parent uses drugs, the other parent probably does, also.

Abuse and Violence

When deciding custody, judges must consider whether either parent has been violent or abusive.

Violence. While domestic violence usually influences custody, there are some judges who believe that spousal battering is not relevant to the decision. However, if a parent has battered the children, they may be denied visitation, or be restricted to supervised visitation.

Four Factors That Do Not Influence Custody

1. *Gender.* There is no legal preference for awarding custody to either parent based on sex. Mothers and fathers have an equal right to custody.

2. *Race.* Judges may not use race as the sole basis for making a custody decision.

3. *Physical Disability.* A judge cannot base a custody decision solely on a parent's handicap that only affects his or her ability to play with the children in physical activities.

4. *Not Married.* Custody cannot be denied to either parent because they were unmarried when the child was born.

Special Interest Support Groups

In the area of child custody, many advocacy groups exist. Here are some support groups with a point of view:

National Congress for Fathers and Children
9454 Wilshire Blvd., Suite 907
Beverly Hills, CA 90212
(310) 247-6051
www.ncfc.org

American Coalition for Fathers and Children
1718 Main Street NW, Suite 187
Washington, DC 20036
(800) 978-3237
www.acfc.org

National Organization for Women
733 15th Street NW, 2nd floor
Washington, D.C. 20005
(202) 628-8669
www.now.org

National Organization of Single Mothers
P.O. Box 68
Midland, NC 28107
(704) 888-KIDS
www.singlemothers.org

Children's Rights Council
6200 Editors Park Dr., Suite 103
Hyattsville, MD 20782
(301) 559-3120
www.gocrc.com

Joint Custody Association
10606 Wilkins Avenue
Los Angeles, CA 90024
310-475-5352
www.jointcustody.org

Child Abuse. Child abuse is any behavior that harms a child. Physical abuse is physically hurting the child, and includes punishments that bruise or burn the child. Emotional abuse is speech intended to humiliate, or to lower the child's self-esteem. Sexual abuse is any behavior by an adult directed toward a child for the adult's sexual gratification. All forms of child abuse will influence custody.

Work and Income

In theory, your work and income shouldn't influence custody. In reality, they might. Some judges may feel that the parent with more money can take better care of the children. The reasoning is that this parent can afford a better house in a better school district. This penalizes the lower-income parent, who may have chosen a less demanding—and less rewarding—career in order to devote more time to the children. In either case, children require parents who have time for them, and a parent with an involving, time-consuming job is at a disadvantage.

School

Since children spend most of their awake hours at school, the educational opportunities each parent offers may be a factor. School issues can include curriculum differences, such as which school has an enriched or specialized program, or pupil performance, such as which school has a higher-scoring student population. School may also become a factor when the child has perfect attendance while living with one parent, but a record of tardiness and absences when residing with the other.

Children's Wishes

Sometimes, children's wishes are a factor. When a child expresses a preference, the judge must decide if the child is mature enough to make a choice. This usually means the child is a teenager, though some judges have listened to children as young as seven.

In addition to hearing the stated preference, the judge must assess the child's insight and ability to reason. For example, if a child wants to be with the parent who will let him do "whatever he wants," the judge may not approve. Or, if a child's preference for one parent seems rehearsed and

Native American Custody

If you are Native American, there are special federal laws about child custody that affect you. These laws are found in the United States Code, Title 25, Chapter 21, Subchapter I.

For example, Section 1911(a) grants Native American tribes jurisdiction over child custody. The federal law says "An Indian tribe shall have jurisdiction exclusive as to any State over any child custody proceeding involving an Indian child who resides or is domiciled within the reservation of such tribe, except where such jurisdiction is otherwise vested in the State by existing Federal law. Where an Indian child is a ward of a tribal court, the Indian tribe shall retain exclusive jurisdiction, notwithstanding the residence or domicile of the child."

There are a number of sections in the federal subchapter. To find them—as well as to read opinions that interpret the laws—you can search on many legal websites, including www.findlaw.com or www.law.cornell.edu.

artificial, the judge may decide the child was coached, and discount the statements. On the other hand, if a child genuinely feels closer to one parent, this preference may be respected.

Interviewing the Children

Asking children what they want poses problems.

The children are harmed because they are forced to take sides. This makes them feel trapped, or that they are pawns, or that if they tell the truth they will hurt one of their parents.

The professionals who interview the children also have difficulties, because they know children have a natural instinct for survival, and will say whatever they must to appease their parents.

Nevertheless, children are routinely asked their preference. One way they can be asked—by taking the stand as a witness in open court—is rarely used. Instead, judges rely on the following methods to learn the child's views on custody:

Judge

Sometimes the judge will talk to the child *in camera*—in the judge's chambers. This is a private meeting between the child and the judge. The lawyers may be allowed to attend, and either parent can request that a court reporter make a record.

In the meeting, the judge may want to hear the child's wishes first-hand, or might want to give the child a chance to express an opinion so that he or she doesn't feel left out. Or, perhaps the judge wants to explain why the child will not be granted his or her already-expressed preference.

Mental Health Professional

If the judge has appointed a mental health professional to make a custody evaluation, the report may include the child's custody preference.

When Melanie was sixteen, she wanted to move from her mother's house to her father's house. Walter, her father, asked family court to change custody, and attached several letters from Melanie stating her preference. Charlotte, her mother, disputed most of what Walter said, but did not deny that Melanie wanted to live with Walter. Family court denied Walter's request without even a hearing. In the decision, the judge said, "I did not find any compelling reasons to have Melanie leave her present situation. And I just did not want to place her in the middle of choosing between her father and her mother... I did not order a hearing because the hearing would basically come down to Melanie having again to testify against her mother as to why she should live with her father." Walter appealed the decision, pointing out that family court was required to consider what Melanie wanted, and the appellate court reversed the decision by family court. *Mackowski v. Mackowski* (1998) 317 N.J. Super. 8, 721 A.2d 12.

Attorney
If the judge has appointed an advocate to represent the child, the advocate may convey the child's wishes.

Judicial Bias

In addition to the factors mentioned above, there are other elements that may play a role in the custody decision. One element is *judicial bias.*

When deciding custody, a judge is supposed to base the decision on the facts. He or she plays the role of an impartial arbiter who listens to each side and then makes a decision.

 Custody disputes are as old as time. The story of Solomon: two women came to King Solomon, each claiming they were the mother of a baby. To settle the dispute, Solomon ordered the baby cut in half and divided between them. One woman screamed, "No, give the child to her!" Solomon knew only the real mother would give away her child rather than let it be harmed. He gave her the baby.

In reality, it is quite different. Most judges award custody to the mother and order the father to pay support. There are exceptions, of course, but in the day-to-day business of the court, the judge will consistently display bias.

Because the legal standard that judges must follow—the best interests of the child—allows plenty of discretion in deciding custody, judicial bias is an unavoidable part of family law.

Custody Evaluations

When parents dispute custody, it's quite possible the judge will order a *custody evaluation.* A custody evaluation is a report used by the judge to help with the custody decision.

Judges order custody evaluations to help them make the custody decision. They also order evaluations when one parent accuses the other parent of harming the child.

The Evaluator

The custody evaluation will usually be made by a *mental health professional*—typically a licensed psychiatrist, psychologist, or social worker. These mental health professionals may also specialize in child psychology.

The choice of evaluator is crucial, because there is a wide range of ability. Some evaluators are extremely competent, and possess uncanny insight into the families they analyze. Others are utterly incompetent, and will make a devastating evaluation that defies all common sense. Because the quality of the evaluation is critical, the choice of who will do the evaluation plays a significant role in the final custody decision.

 "The judge follows the recommendation of the custody evaluator at least 86 percent of the time in permanent custody disputes, and 99.9 percent of the time in temporary awards of custody pending settlement or trial of the case."
California Divorce Handbook

Gathering the Information

The purpose of the evaluation is to assess each parent's ability to be a parent. To do that, the evaluator has many ways to gather information, including:

Conducting Interviews. The evaluator may interview everyone who is relevant to the custody decision, including:
- Parents.
- Children.
- Grandparents.
- Stepparents.
- Teachers.
- Neighbors.
- Doctor.

Reviewing Documents. The evaluator may review all appropriate papers, including documents related to work or financial matters, medical records, and school reports.

Administrating Psychological Tests. The evaluator may give psychological tests to the parents and interpret the results. One such test, the *Minnesota Multiphasic Personality Inventory (MMPI-II),* is composed of hundreds of questions. The MMPI uses a technique called forced-choice, where the test-taker must choose between two answers. The results supposedly reveal various personality traits. Interestingly, the tests used in custody evaluations do not test parenting skills, but instead, measure personality characteristics assumed to be associated with parenting.

Writing the Report

Once the evaluator has gathered the information, he or she must write the report. Depending on the purpose of the report, it may be limited it to the child, one parent, or all family members.

The report will be detailed, and may include a custody recommendation. The recommendation will be based on the evaluator's own opinions—a combination of interpretations from the psychological tests and impressions from interviews and observations. In the recommendation, the evaluator may suggest which parent should be granted custody, as well as how much time the noncustodial parent should be allowed for visitation. If the report does not contain a custody recommendation, the evaluator has decided to leave that decision to the judge.

Using the Report

The custody report will be given to the judge, and copies will be supplied to the attorneys for both parents.

Recommendations from custody evaluations are routinely adopted by the court. This is because the report is considered an unbiased report by an objective, neutral expert. Even if the expert is wrong, the opinion is important. Also the judge appointed the evaluator to help reach a decision. It doesn't help to ignore the advice that was sought. And finally, when a judge rejects a recommendation from an evaluator, lawyers take notice. The judge knows that—by rejecting the recommendation—he or she encourages other lawyers to challenge future evaluations.

Guidelines for Child Custody Evaluations

If you want to know more about custody evaluations, the *American Psychological Association* has created *Guidelines for Child Custody Evaluations in Divorce Proceedings*. You can find the complete guidelines at www.apa.org/practice/childcustody.html. Here are some highlights:

- The primary purpose of the evaluation is to assess the best interests of the child.

- The evaluation focuses on parenting capacity, the needs of the child, and the resulting fit.

- Parents are evaluated for their ability to plan for the child's future needs, capacity to provide a stable and loving home, and any potential for inappropriate behavior or misconduct that might negatively influence the child.

- The psychologist must avoid conducting an evaluation when the psychologist has served in a therapeutic role for the child or his or her immediate family.

- The psychologist is not required to evaluate all parties. The psychologist can make a recommendation after evaluating only the child, or after evaluating only one parent and the child.

- The psychologist may conduct clinical interviews, conduct observations, administer psychological assessments, and review reports from schools, health care providers, child care providers, etc. The psychologist may also interview extended family, friends, and other individuals.

- The psychologist does not give any opinion regarding the psychological functioning of any individual who has not been personally evaluated. However, the psychologist can report what an evaluated individual—such as the parent or child—has stated.

In November, 1999, Elian Gonzales' mother fled Cuba with Elian on a small boat to illegally enter the United States. She died on the journey, but the six year-old boy was rescued by two fisherman. The INS temporarily placed Elian with his great-uncle, Lazaro. Lazaro petitioned for Elian's asylum in the U.S., but the INS spoke to Elian's father, Juan Gonzales-Quintana, in Cuba, and learned that he opposed asylum. The INS rejected Lazaro's petition. Lazaro then asked a state circuit court in Miami-Dade County, Florida, for custody of Elian, claiming the boy would suffer harm to his "mental health" and "emotional well-being" if he were returned to Cuba. The circuit judge gave Lazaro temporary custody. At this point, the case became an international event, with the global news media covering it. In state court, the case was reassigned to another judge, who decided that Elian was a Cuban national, and thus, Florida did not have jurisdiction. Lazaro was denied custody of Elian. An undaunted Lazaro, however, filed a lawsuit in the United States District Court for the Southern District of Florida, a federal court, asking to overturn the INS decision denying Elian asylum. The court dismissed his lawsuit. Lazaro then appealed to the Eleventh Circuit Court of Appeals, a federal appeals court, seeking to overturn the federal district court. Lazaro asked for a temporary order preventing Elian's "physical removal from the jurisdiction of the United States during the pendency of this appeal." The order was granted. But before the federal court could decide the appeal, the INS stormed into Lazaro's house and physically removed Elian. Elian was then reunited with Juan, who had traveled from Cuba to get his son. Soon after, the federal court denied Lazaro's appeal, and Juan and Elian returned to Cuba. *Gonzalez v. Reno* (2000) 212 F.3d 1338

After submitting the report to the court, the evaluator is considered an expert witness—someone with special training—who can be cross-examined under oath by either attorney.

Influencing a Custody Evaluation

Despite the intent of the evaluator to make a neutral report, in reality, bias and prejudice play a major role in the outcome.

Custody evaluators always bring their own opinions and pre-formed judgments to the process. If you do not present yourself well in the short time you have with the evaluator, the long-term results can be devastating.

Here are some suggestions for creating the best possible outcome when going through a custody evaluation.

When being interviewed by the evaluator, make steady eye contact and listen carefully to what is said. If you disagree with something, do not argue. Instead, state your opinion as, "I understand what you are saying, but..." or "You make a good point, however..."

When discussing your situation, don't assume the evaluator understands your background or culture. You will have to bridge the gap and speak in the language of the evaluator. That means putting everything in "the best interests of the child."

For example, when complaining about the other parent, it's not enough to say that he or she drinks. You must also show how that behavior affects the children. Instead of saying, "My husband is an alcoholic," you might say, "My husband drinks

"Family court judges... have limited access and resources to examine the key components of family functioning. As a result, many family court judges now regularly appoint mental health professionals... to evaluate the family dynamics and patterns, with a specific focus on protecting the physical and psychological well being of children." G. Andrew H. Benjamin and Jackie K. Gollan, *Family Evaluation in Custody Litigation: Reducing Risks of Ethical Infractions and Malpractice*

in front of our children and neglects them." Or, if you want to complain about a new mate, don't just say, "My wife has a new boyfriend," say "My wife spends all her time with her new boyfriend and ignores our children."

If you have documents or other evidence that supports what you say, bring it with you and show the evaluator. You want to demonstrate that you are being open and honest, and you do that by confirming what you say. Relevant records include daycare or school documents that show you have been consistently involved with the children, or medical records that show you have been responsible for the children.

Finally, if the evaluator wants to observe you and your children together, remember that you are being monitored for certain parenting behaviors—such as how you discipline your children and how your children react to you. When you are in that situation, try to avoid scolding or disciplining your children, and instead, do some activity that you and your children like to do together.

Changing Child Custody

No matter how detailed your custody arrangements are, things are bound to change.

One parent might want to remarry and start a new family, or the other parent might want to move away. Or either parent might start a new job and work different hours.

And even if the parents don't change, the children will change. As they grow older, they will find new hobbies, interests, and activities. School, friends, and sports will all evolve as the children grow. The schedule that worked one year won't work the next.

When change occurs gradually—such as the children growing older—simple inertia may prevent you from renegotiating custody. But when a distinct event occurs—such as a residential move or a remarriage—it may be time to update the arrangement.

Gender Wars

Books for Women

Cutting Loose, Ashton Applewhite, HarperCollins, $13.00. An upbeat and inspiring book that debunks the myth that divorce causes emotional and economic ruin.

Suddenly Single, Kerry Hannon, John Wiley and Sons, $14.95. A financial writer tells women how to handle money for the first time.

What Every Woman Should Know About Divorce and Custody, Gayle Rosenwald Smith, Berkley Publishing Group, $14.00. Crucial advice from judges, lawyers, and therapists on how women can protect themselves in prolonged divorce or custody proceedings.

Books for Men

Divorced Dads, Sanford L. Braver, Diane O'Connell, Putnam, $24.95. A psychology professor dispels the popular myths about divorce, including that men abandon their children.

Fatherless America, David Blankenhorn, HarperPerennial, $14.00. A thoroughly researched book that argues that many problems in families are caused by the lack of active, involved fathers.

Fathers' Rights, Jeffery Leving, Kenneth A. Dachman, Basic Books, $12.50. Fathers' Rights accurately describes the legal system from a man's point-of-view. A must-read for men who go to court for custody of their children.

Screw the Bitch, Dick Hart, Victor Santoro, Loompanics Unlimited, $17.95. Despite an awful cover, this book contains solid advice for men who want to "get lost" and not be found.

Significant Change of Circumstances

Because custody modifications disrupt a child's life, many judges are reluctant to change the arrangements. This reluctance is intended to promote stability and discourage parents from constantly returning to court. To successfully modify custody, the parent seeking the change must show that a *significant change of circumstances* has occurred.

A significant change of circumstances is some event or change that has such a profound impact on the child that a change in the custody order is necessary.

When custody is first decided, the judge assumes both parents are equally fit. But once custody is settled, and one parent is deemed to be more fit, it becomes the responsibility of the other parent to prove that something has occurred that alters the basis for the original decision.

Factors That Influence a Custody Modification

When considering a request to change custody, the judge will look to see if there has been a significant change of circumstances.

What constitutes a change of circumstances is different in each state. Generally, however, the judge follows the same standard in deciding whether to change custody as he did in setting custody the first time—the best interests of the child.

The parent seeking the change must usually demonstrate that something has occurred that has resulted in the child's present environment endangering his or her physical, mental, moral, or emotional health.

 A modification usually becomes effective on the day the judge signs the order. However, the judge can also make the effective date retroactive to when the motion was filed. If child support is involved, this can create an immediate arrearage for the paying parent.

The more things change. In their study of divorcing families, Maccoby and Mnookin found that 28% of the children switched homes within three years after the divorce, and 45% changed the amount of visitation with the noncustodial parent—about two-thirds decreasing the amount of time and the rest increasing it. *Dividing the Child*

In addition to all of the factors a judge considers during an initial award of custody, here are some additional factors a judge may consider when deciding whether to modify custody:

Moveaway

When parents move, they often force a change in the court orders. That's because a residential move may require that a new schedule be created. If the custodial parent wants to move, and the new home is so far away that the noncustodial parent is prevented from seeing the children during the school year, the judge will have to change the custody orders.

Also called a long-distance move, generally the move must force the other parent to drive an hour to see the children.

In resolving a moveaway dispute, a judge has many options. One alternative is to award the noncustodial parent more time with the children over the summer and during the holidays as compensation for the time lost during the school year. If a judge chooses this option, he may also require that the moving parent pay for all additional transportation costs so the children can visit the noncustodial parent. Another option is to switch custody completely from one parent to the other. A third option is to bar the custodial parent from moving away beyond a given distance—say fifteen miles. This restriction maintains the capability of both parents to continue seeing their children.

The flip side to a moveaway is that the same restrictions against moving away placed on the custodial parent are not placed on the noncustodial parent. That's because—if the noncustodial parent seeks to move away—it does not interfere with the custodial parent's access to the children.

Parental Alienation Syndrome

Parental Alienation Syndrome is a psychological theory
that describes brainwashing by one parent to make the
children hate the other parent. PAS does not refer to
genuine complaints of poor parenting, but rather, the
conduct of a parent who creates or distorts complaints so
much that the children believe the complaints and grow
to hate the other parent.

According to Dr. Richard Gardner, PAS "arises almost
exclusively in the context of child-custody disputes."
Here are some signs of parenting behavior that may be
parental alienation syndrome:

- Blaming the other parent for personal and financial
  problems, such as dating breakups or job problems.

- Telling the children everything about the divorce—all
  in the name of "being honest."

- Reacting with hurt or sadness when the children say
  they have a good time with the other parent.

- Refusing to be flexible with the visitation schedule
  when it ignores the children's needs.

- Using the children as spies to gather information
  about the other parent, or questioning the children
  when they return from the other parent.

- Letting the children decide for themselves to visit
  when the court order says there is no choice. This
  places the noncustodial parent in a "no-win"
  situation.

- Denying the noncustodial parent access to the
  children's school, extracurricular activities, and
  medical information.

- Scheduling activities for the children that conflict with
  the visitation schedule.

Destabilized Household

Any significant event that destabilizes the household of either parent may affect custody. If the custodial parent's home is destabilized, the noncustodial parent may be awarded custody. If the noncustodial parent's home is destabilized, the custodial parent may seek to have visitation restricted or prevented. Destabilizing events include any devastating event, such as:

- Death of a household member.
- Arrest of the parent for a crime.
- Parental desertion of the children.

Custodial Interference

If the custodial parent interferes with the noncustodial parent's efforts to visit the children, the judge can respond by awarding custody to the noncustodial parent.

Children's Wishes

Finally, since children's wishes almost always play a part in custody decisions, if a child wishes to change custody, that may constitute a change of circumstances. However, a judge still has to evaluate if the child is of sufficient age and capacity to reason to make a choice, and there is no guarantee that will happen.

Reluctance to Change Custody

When it comes to the children's living arrangements, judges are typically conservative and try to avoid making frequent changes. They do this for the following reasons:

Stability

Judges know that a divorce unsettles the children, and they try to promote stability by maintaining the residential status quo. By avoiding constant changes in the living arrangements, the judge tries to minimize the harm to the child's emotional development.

Avoiding Litigation

Judges know that some parents will fight no matter what they put in custody orders. They recognize that custody of the children is not the real issue, but rather, the parents have an underlying, hidden agenda for the dispute.

For these parents, the judge wants to discourage the endless litigation that simply uses up valuable court time without genuinely resolving the conflict. Thus, the judge avoids changing custody to discourage the parents from initiating endless lawsuits.

Modifying Visitation

In addition to changing custody, parents may also need to change visitation.

As with custody, visitation can be modified any time there is a significant change of circumstances. When deciding whether to change visitation, a judge will use the same standard to make his decision—what is in the best interests of the child. Here are some common reasons to modify visitation:

- The custodial parent is interfering with the reasonable visitation of the noncustodial parent.
- The noncustodial parent is harming or endangering the child during his or her visitation.
- The children wish to see more—or less—of the other parent.

Custodial Interference

When the custody order calls for the noncustodial parent to have reasonable visitation, it may not specify the exact days and times when visitation will occur. While the intent is to let the parents work out the schedule themselves, this may create conflict when they cannot agree on what is reasonable. Thus, there may be times when the noncustodial parent is frustrated in his or her attempt to see the children.

Under these circumstances, the noncustodial parent may seek visitation orders that secure more reliable access to the children. This means asking the judge to create a detailed schedule—one with the exact days and times for visitation spelled out.

When a judge is convinced a threat exists, he can take many steps to protect the child. Among other things, he can order the noncustodial parent be allowed only supervised visitation—which means a neutral third-party must be present during the entire visitation period. Or, the judge can

Parenting Books

"Does Wednesday Mean Mom's House or Dad's?", Marc J. Ackerman, John Wiley and Sons, $16.95. Written by a clinical psychologist, this is a good primer for understanding the reality of custody and the legal system.

Families Apart, Melinda Blau, Perigee, $12.00. A well-written book that explains how to overcome the animosity in divorce and cooperate "for the sake of the kids."

The Good Divorce, Constance Ahrons, Basic Books, $14.00. Written by a social scientist, this book focuses on the relationship between ex-spouses after divorce.

Helping Your Kids Cope With Divorce the Sandcastles Way, M. Gary Neuman, Patricia Romanowski, Times Books, $25.00. An excellent book that describes the Sandcastles program, a national divorce program for children.

Mom's House, Dad's House, Isolina Ricci, $13.00. This classic book describes co-parenting in a way that is clear, so straightforward, and so balanced—it's routinely used in divorce classes.

Second Chances, Judith S. Wallerstein, Sandra Blakeslee, Houghton Mifflin, $12.95. Another classic, this book is full of insights about the long-term effects of divorce.

Vicki Lansky's Divorce Book for Parents, Vicki Lansky, Book Peddlers, $5.99. A very book that reminds parents to pay attention to how divorce affects the children.

terminate companionship, which means the noncustodial parent is barred completely from seeing his or her children.

However, because custody law encourages contact between children and their parents, even in the case of genuine endangerment, it's possible the noncustodial parent will be allowed to seek counseling or take other steps before a judge permanently bars him or her from seeing the children.

Judith Seider, a psychologist, met with a mother about possible sexual abuse of her four-year-old son. Two months later, the mother terminated the relationship. Seider then entered into a professional relationship with the father, and disclosed to him his son had been, and continued to be, sexually abused. Seider entered into the relationship with the father without the mother's knowledge or consent, and Seider also released confidential information about the mother to the father. A custody dispute then ensued, and in support of the father, Seider provided an affidavit disclosing confidential information about the mother. Even though Seider failed to report her suspicions to the Department of Human Services, DHS began an investigation, and issued an investigative subpoena to Seider, requesting "[a]ny and all notes, records, and evaluations, regarding [the daughter, the father, the mother, and the son]." Seider, however, went further, and wrote a 51 page report that divulged confidential information about the mother. The mother complained to the *Board of Examiners of Psychologists* stating that Seider had breached her obligations of confidentiality. The Board found Seider had 12 violations of the *American Psychological Association Ethical Principles of Psychologists and Code of Conduct,* and three violations of the *American Association of State Psychology Boards Code of Conduct.* *Seider v. Board of Examiners of Psychologists* (2000) 762 A.2d 551, 2000 ME 206.

Child's Wishes

A final reason to change visitation is when the children want to. When a child expresses a preference, the judge must evaluate the child's ability to understand the choice and consider whether the child is making the choice of his or her own free will or is being coerced by a determined parent. Also, the judge is more likely to grant the preferences of an older child over a younger one.

---

1 *Dividing the Child,* Correspondence of actual residence at time 1 and time 3 with physical custody decrees (table 8.1, page 166).

Child Support

"I got custody of the money."

Chapter 5

The Laws of Child Support

✓ When one parent has primary responsibility for the children, the other parent is expected to pay *child support*. Child support is the money one parent pays the other to help care for the children.

✓ Usually, the noncustodial parent pays the custodial parent. That's because—while both parents are responsible for the children—the custodial parent is already meeting the obligation through the act of custody. The noncustodial parent meets the obligation by paying child support.

✓ When setting the amount of child support to pay, the two parents can agree on their own. If they don't agree, the amount will be set by a judge.

✓ Child support orders can arise from a number of circumstances, including: divorce, legal separation, annulment, or a paternity action.

Types of Child Support

There are several types of child support:

Temporary Child Support
When parents first separate or file for divorce, the judge may order that one parent pay *temporary child support.* The amount set will be based on preliminary information available to the judge, and may be raised or lowered when the divorce is complete.

Permanent Child Support
When a final court order is issued that includes child support, the support is called *permanent child support.* This means that the obligation remains until some specific event occurs. Calling this permanent may be misleading, because any orders regarding the child—including support—can be changed if circumstances change.

Family Support
Some states allow parents to combine alimony and child support into one payment called *family support.* Unlike child support, family support is taxable income to the receiving parent and a deduction for the paying parent. When the paying parent earns much more than the receiving parent, paying family support can save money in taxes because it shifts income to the parent with the lower tax rate. Family support arrearages, however, cannot be enforced with the same collection tools as child support arrearages.

Child Support Guidelines

When deciding how much support should be paid, judges must use *child support guidelines.* These are minimum amounts that are either listed in tables or are calculated with a mathematical formula.

 Child support has no effect on your federal income tax return. The payments are not taxable income to the receiving parent and are not a deduction for the paying parent.

When Paula and Robert divorced, a circuit court gave Robert custody of their son. The judge then calculated Paula's income as a medical receptionist at $1,086, and Robert's income as the owner of a service station at $3,063. Based on these figures, the judge did not order Paula to pay any child support, but did order Robert to pay Paula $500 per month in maintenance because Paula "cannot maintain herself anywhere near the standard of living enjoyed by the parties during the course of their marriage without indefinite maintenance." *In re Marriage of Minear* (1998) 181 Ill.2d 552, 693 N.E.2d 379, 230 Ill.Dec. 250.

The guidelines are not set by judges, but rather, by lawmakers in each state who create the laws. Lawmakers use standard tables or formulas in order to be fair and impose the same child support award on parents in similar economic circumstances.

After determining the guideline amount, the judge can then add or subtract money based on several other factors. These other factors account for specific and unusual circumstances, such as special needs of the child, special hardships of the parents, and so on.

The guideline amounts are also called the *presumed correct* figure. This is the amount presumed to be the correct amount of support, and a judge can award less only if there are special circumstances. If less is awarded, the reasons must be stated by the judge on the record.

While child support guidelines are the same within a state, they can vary considerably between states. That's because the lawmakers in each state can choose what's important when setting child support.

Some states think that only the net income of the two parents is important, while other states consider the additional income of a new mate if either parent has remarried or has begun living with someone. And still other states consider how much time each parent spends with the child.

While judges have the authority to reject an agreement between the parents, that doesn't mean they will. Judges recognize that an agreement is the result of bargaining, and may resist disturbing the arrangement unless there is clear evidence that the best interests of the child are not being served.

However child support is decided, the goal remains the same.

The goal of child support is to provide for the economic needs of the child.

How the Guideline Amounts Are Determined

The guideline amounts are not chosen arbitrarily, but are designed to meet the costs of raising children at various standards of living. Generally, the guideline amounts are based on:

Needs of the Child

Child support payments are an attempt to meet the minimum economic needs of the child. The guideline amounts only cover the minimum expenses of raising a child—basically food, clothing, and shelter. Because children almost always need much more, all states allow additional expenses to be considered when setting child support.

Parent's Ability to Pay

Each parent must support the children according to his or her ability to pay. Ability to pay is usually what a parent earns— gross income minus some allowable expenses.

Allowable expenses vary from state to state. Some states only allow mandatory expenses to be subtracted from gross income. Mandatory expenses include: income taxes, social security, health insurance, and required union dues. Expenses that are not mandatory are excluded because—if they were included—a parent might artificially reduce income by taking numerous deductions, and then pay less support.

Some states also allow a deduction for support paid for children from another relationship. This allows all children to be treated equally, so that each has an equal claim to the parent's earnings. Also, many states allow a child care expense deduction for a custodial parent who pays for child care expenses in order to work or attend school.

Standard of Living

When parents divorce, they must create two homes where there was one. Two homes cost more, which means a decrease in the standard of living. A goal of child support is to maintain and balance the standard of living of the child.

Maintain the standard of living. Had the parents stayed together, the child would have enjoyed a certain standard of living. Child support guidelines try to maintain the child's former standard of living, while at the same time realistically reflecting the increased costs of maintaining two households.

Balance the standard of living. When one parent earns much more than the other, the child may go back-and-forth between two homes of vastly different economic circumstances. Child support can be used to transfer wealth from the higher-earning parent to the lower-earning parent.

When the standard of living of the lower-earning parent is improved, the child is then sharing in the standard of living of both parents. This is a goal of child support, and it is why a parent can spend support on things not related to the child. The custodial parent and the child share the same standard of living, thus what benefits the parent benefits the child.

 Ability to pay is different from *ability to earn.* Ability to pay is based on your income. Ability to earn is what a judge thinks you are capable of earning, whether you're actually earning it or not. This can happen when a parent works less than 40 hours, or when he or she quits work and refuses to find another job. If this economic misconduct occurs, a judge may set support based on a parent's potential to earn rather than actual earnings.

When a Judge Can Depart from the Guideline

In divorce, you lose certain rights over your children and the judge takes over. This legal authority allows the judge to:

Depart from the Presumed Correct Figure

Judges have the last word on child support, so a judge can always depart from the guideline. To depart from the presumed correct amount, a judge must find that it is unjust or inappropriate due to special circumstances.

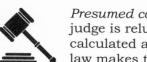 *Presumed correct.* There is a reason why your judge is reluctant to deviate from the calculated amount of child support. Federal law makes the calculated amount presumed correct. 42 U.S.C. § 667 states, in part: "Each State, as a condition for having its State plan approved under this part, must establish guidelines for child support award amounts within the State... There shall be a rebuttable presumption for the award of child support, that the amount of the award which would result from the application of such guidelines is the correct amount of child support to be awarded. A written finding or specific finding on the record that the application of the guidelines would be unjust or inappropriate in a particular case, as determined under criteria established by the State, shall be sufficient to rebut the presumption in that case."

There are specific factors a judge can consider, and—as stated earlier—if a judge awards less than the guideline amount, he or she must state the facts that justify the departure.

Overrule the Agreement between the Parents

Because the court has final authority over all child support decisions, the judge can overrule any agreement between the parents. This safeguard prevents a parent from bargaining away the right to receive child support. If an agreement does not provide for the support of the children, the judge may approve it anyway if the custodial parent has sufficient resources to support the children.

Paying Child Support

After the amount to be paid is set, the next question is how the support will be paid. This is not an easy question to answer, since many parents fail to pay some or all of their child support.

Here are some methods for routine, on-time payment:

Sending a Check to the Receiving Parent
In some states, the paying parent can send a monthly check to the receiving parent. This method is best suited when the paying parent has been paying support, and has a record of full, on-time payments. Because new or modified support orders routinely include a wage assignment, parents who choose this method have to *stay* the wage assignment.

Wage Assignment
Also called *wage withholding,* a wage assignment is when the child support is automatically deducted from the paycheck of the paying parent and sent to the receiving parent. Wage assignments are appropriate when the paying parent earns a salary or has another regular source of income, such as payments from a pension, annuity, retirement fund, or disability. Basically, for a wage assignment to work, there must be a payment administrator on whom to serve the wage assignment. Wage assignments do not work when the paying parent is self-employed or does not receive regular income.

Wage assignments are automatically initiated on new or modified orders. Typically, the court sends a copy of the orders to the paying parent's employer, who waits ten days before deducting the money, giving the parent time to contest the assignment.

 A *wage assignment* stays in effect until the paying parent's employment ends, the support obligation ends or is modified, or the parent succeeds with a *motion to quash* the assignment.

Since wage assignments are automatic, if you do not want one, you must ask the judge to stay the service on the employer. Some judges will be more agreeable to doing this than others.

Paying an Officer of the Court

A third way to pay child support is for the paying parent to send a check to an officer of the court—usually the court clerk or a court trustee. When the officer receives the check, a payment is sent to the receiving parent. Some states allow payments to be sent to the child enforcement agency or some other state agency. An advantage to this method is that if the paying parent misses some payments, collection procedures begin automatically.

This method is the best approach when the paying parent is self-employed or doesn't receive regular income.

 When child support orders are being drafted, try to synchronize the receipt of the money with the bills you'll be paying. If you can't influence when the checks arrive, try asking your creditors to change the dates when they get paid.

Other Payment Elements

In addition to deciding how support will be paid, parents may add the following elements to an agreement:

Insurance

If something happens to the paying parent, the children's support will be at risk. To secure future payments, support orders may require an irrevocable life insurance policy on the paying parent, with the children as the beneficiaries.

Security Deposit

Another way to secure support is to require the paying parent to deposit money into a security account. When the paying parent misses some payments, the receiving parent withdraws money from the fund and the paying parent has to replace it. The security deposit can be as much as two years of support.

Late Payment Fees

Late fees are useful when the support is paid directly—not through wage withholding. Late fees are justified if the support is being used to pay creditors who themselves charge late fees for missed payments.

COLA Clause

COLA, or *Cost of Living Adjustment,* is a clause used to automatically increase child support when the cost of living increases. Generally, this increase is based on some common index, such as the *Consumer Price Index.* The advantage of a COLA clause is that—as inflation reduces the buying power of child support—the receiving parent gets an increase without returning to court.

Five Ways to Prevent
Child Support Payment Problems

1. Have payments sent to an officer of the court.

2. Include a late-payment fee.

3. Require a security deposit.

4. Include a Cost of Living Adjustment (COLA) clause.

5. Keep wage assignments up to date.

When Child Support Ends

Generally, child support ends when your child reaches the age of majority or when certain circumstances occur, such as:

- You gain custody.
- A court orders your child support to end.
- A court declares your child emancipated.
- Your child gets married.
- Your child joins the military.
- Your child moves out of the house to live independently.
- Your child is adopted.
- Your child dies.

When Ronald and Sharon divorced, Sharon was given custody of their two daughters, Eva and Alicia, and Ronald was ordered to pay $1,000 per month in child support "until said child attains legal age, marries, dies, becomes self sustaining, or until further order of the court." After Eva turned 18 and left for college, Ronald voluntarily paid her college tuition, room and board, and stopped paying Sharon child support for Eva. Ronald also asked the court to terminate his child support obligation for Eva. Sharon objected, saying that even though Eva was attending college full-time, her legal residence was still with her. The court denied Ronald's requests to terminate child support before Eva reached the age of majority in Nebraska, 19. The court also refused to credit Ronald any money he voluntarily paid for Eva's college expenses against his child support obligation. *Palagi v. Palagi* (2001) 10 Neb.App. 231, 627 N.W.2d 765.

However, child support can end later when certain things happen.

Child support may end later if:
- Your state requires you to support your child until he or she completes high school or turns 19, whichever comes first.
- Your state requires you to support your child until he or she completes college or turns 21 or 23, whichever comes first.
- Your child is disabled.
- You agree to continue paying support (for whatever reason).

Also, child support may earlier if your child becomes *emancipated*. Emancipation is when a child demonstrates freedom from parental control. For a child to become emancipated, the court must order it. This usually happens because a significant act occurred, such as the child getting married, joining the military, or moving away from the custodial parent and becoming self-supporting.

Parents cannot simply declare their children emancipated, but must bring a special proceeding to have the child declared emancipated.

Child support may end later if you live in a state that requires you to assist your child through school. For example, in some states, divorced parents may be required to continue child support until the child turns 23 so long as the child remains in college. Also, a court may require a parent to continue paying support if the child is physically or mentally disabled.

 Unpaid support. In 2000, nearly 10 million noncustodial parents owed a total of $84 billion in child support arrearages, with arrears per parent ranging from approximately $4,000 in Louisiana to $16,000 in Alaska. Of the $84 billion owed, only $6 billion was collected, *or less than 7%.*[1]

1 U.S. Department of Health and Human Services, *Annual Statistical Report for Fiscal Years 1999 and 2000,* Administration for Children and Families, Office of Child Support Enforcement

Chapter 6

The Reality of Child Support

- ✓ While the goals of child support are to provide support for the child, the reality of child support is quite different.

- ✓ Child support is almost always awarded to mothers.

- ✓ However, only about half of all mothers get a full payment on time, and about one quarter receive nothing at all.

- ✓ Despite efforts to increase awards, the average amount received is less than half of what it costs to raise a child.

- ✓ Because support is usually very little, total income for single mothers is dramatically less than for any other family group.

Who Gets Child Support Awards

Child support is almost always awarded to the mother because of *custody* and *income.*

Custody

When custody is decided, the mother is much more likely to be the custodial parent. This outcome is vital in determining support because the guidelines used to set child support assume that support will be awarded to the custodial parent.

Here are the results of one study of divorced families:

Custody Arrangements[1]

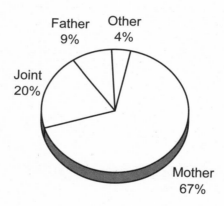

In their study, Maccoby and Mnookin found that mothers had sole or primary custody about 67% of the time, fathers had sole or primary custody about 9% of the time, the parents shared custody about 20% of the time, and the rest had a different arrangement.

Income

Generally, the higher-earning parent pays child support to the lower-earning parent. This usually means fathers pay mothers, because fathers typically earn almost twice as much as mothers. Disparity in income is so important in deciding who pays and how much that it can lead to a lower-earning noncustodial parent paying child support to a higher-earning custodial parent, or even a custodial parent paying child support to a noncustodial parent!

By the way, even though the mother is the parent most likely to get a support award, that doesn't mean that all mothers get one. According to the Census Bureau, in one year, only 81% of the mothers who wanted a child support award actually received one.[2]

But even when mothers receive a child support award, it still doesn't guarantee they will get paid...

What Percentage They Collect

As many parents have already found out—getting an award is one thing, getting a check is something else.

As the Census Bureau has reported, only about half of all mothers who are owed child support received the full amount. The other mothers received less than they were owed—or nothing at all. Here's an illustration:

Child Support Collections[3]

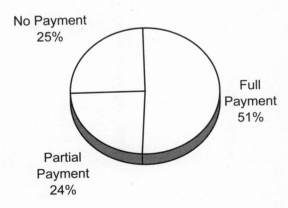

No Payment
25%

Full
Payment
51%

Partial
Payment
24%

This is the statistic, by the way, that generates all the headlines about deadbeat dads. As the Census Bureau reported, in one year, mothers received only 68.7% of the money they were due.

Many people have offered reasons for this, and many have offered suggestions about how to improve it. What seems likely is that the problem won't be going away for a long time.[4]

If you are a receiving parent, be aware that your odds of receiving your full child support check are only about 50-50.

What Amount They Collect

Even when mothers receive their child support check, the amount is not very much. Again, according to the Census Bureau, the average amount received by all mothers was $2,995.

That's not very much, but what is more important is that the average figure disguises a critical distinction:

If the mother never married the children's father, she received much less support than if she divorced the children's father.

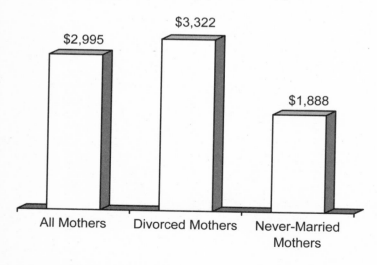

Annual Child Support Receipts[5]

This is particularly bad news for never-married mothers. According to Census Bureau data, never-married mothers received an average of $1,434 less per year than divorced mothers.

Now, take a look at what it costs to raise a child...

What It Costs to Raise a Child

If you've been dragged into a Toys R Us recently, you know that it costs a ton to raise a child. But the government has actually calculated an average per year.

Here's the chart:

Annual Costs to Raise a Child[6]

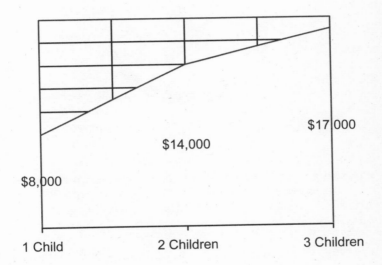

Interestingly enough, these estimates are probably low, as they only represent the direct costs of raising a child. They exclude such hidden costs as taking time off work to care for the children when they're sick, or working at a lower-paying job so that you can be with them more, and so on.

And they completely omit the single biggest expense that most parents face—college!

Now, combine the cost of raising the children with the average child support received, and you get...

The Child Support Gap

The child support gap is the difference between what the children cost, and what the parent receives.

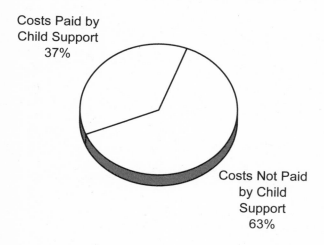

The Child Support Gap

Costs Paid by
Child Support
37%

Costs Not Paid
by Child
Support
63%

As you can see, for the average parent, child support just doesn't cut it. In fact, typical mothers receive only 37% of what it costs to raise one child, and the percentage goes way, way down when there are more children.

By the way, this figure is highly simplified, since custodial parents can take advantage of the head of household filing status, the dependency exemptions for the children, and other child care tax credits to help reduce the child support gap. Still, don't be unduly surprised to discover that the child costs much more than the child support pays.

This subject generates endless books and articles. Some relevant books include: *Fatherless America,* by David Blankenhorn, *Growing Up With a Single Parent,* by Sara McLanahan and Gary Sandefur, and *Marriage, Divorce, Remarriage,* by Andrew J. Cherlin.

For many receiving parents, this means that they will simply live on less; much less as it turns out, than any other family group.

Single Parent Family Income

Single mothers earn dramatically less than any other family group.

Specifically, the Census Bureau calculated that all other family groups had greater total income than single mothers. In some cases—much more. For example, married couples brought in $28,168 a year more than single mothers, and even single women managed to collect $7,494 a year more than single mothers!

Annual Family Income[7]

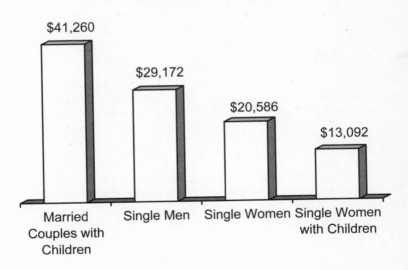

Why is this? Again, there's no shortage of people suggesting reasons. In one classic book, Lenore J. Weitzman in *The Divorce Revolution* argued that "...on the average, divorced women and the minor children in their households experience a 73 percent decline in their standard of living in the first year after divorce. Their former husbands, in contrast, experience a 42 percent rise in their standard of living."

Years later, Andrew J. Cherlin in *Marriage, Divorce, Remarriage,* updated those numbers with this response "... separated and divorced women suffered an average drop of about 30 percent in their standard of living in the year following a marital break-up. Men, in contrast, experienced a rise of 10 to 15 percent..."

Whichever sets of numbers you believe, it seems likely that—after divorce—the living standard of women and children declines.

---

1 *Dividing the Child,* Eleanor Maccoby and Robert Mnookin.
2 U.S. Bureau of the Census, Current Population Reports, series P-60, no. 173, *Child Support and Alimony: 1989.* The primary reason given why the mothers couldn't get an award was that they were unable to locate the father.
3 Ibid.
4 One theory that seeks to explain the lack of compliance considers the status of fathers. By including large numbers of incarcerated men who owe child support, as well as the homeless and indigent, it's possible to conclude that most able-bodied fathers are already paying support. For mothers who don't receive support, it may be because the father is in jail, destitute, or dead.
5 U.S. Bureau of the Census, Current Population Reports, series P-60, no. 173, *Child Support and Alimony: 1989.*
6 U.S. Department of Agriculture, Family Economics Research Group, *Expenditures on a Child by Husband-Wife Families: 1990.* You should know that these estimates were for a two-parent middle-income family, but it seems reasonable to use them for all families-two-parent or not.
7 U.S. Bureau of the Census, Consumer Income, series P-60, no. 174, *Money Income of Households, Families, and Persons in the United States: 1990.*

Chapter 7

Calculating Child Support

- ✓ All states calculate child support based on a mathematical table or formula. The most common methods are *Shared Income* and *Percent of Income*.

- ✓ The support formula is based on what each parent earns, not expenses. However, child care expenses may be added.

- ✓ The support formula creates an amount that is presumed to be the correct amount of child support.

- ✓ If a judge believes a parent is earning below his or her ability, the judge can assume income at a higher level.

- ✓ There are inherent problems with using standard formulas. For example, wealthy people would pay too much, while poor people cannot pay the minimum.

- ✓ The judge has authority to depart from the presumed correct amount if the result would be unfair.

- ✓ No matter what amount of child support is initially ordered, you will probably return to court to change it.

What Financial Information the Court Needs

When you go to court for child support, you must supply your financial information. Generally, this means completing forms that ask for income and expense information. Along with the forms, you may have to attach copies of various pay stubs, tax returns, financial statements, loan applications, and so on.

These financial statements allow the judge to construct an accurate picture of each parent's finances.

Income

Because child support is based on ability to pay, the court must know the income of each parent. In some states, this means gross income, and in others, it means adjusted gross or net income. Whether it is before- or after-tax income is an important part of the calculations.

Gross Income	Every dollar you received...
- Expenses	Minus some expenses allowed by the court...
Adjusted Gross	Is your AGI.
– Deductions	Minus more deductions allowed by the court...
Net Income	Is your net income.

Gross Income
Gross income is everything you receive, including wages, interest, capital gains, and so on. Gross income usually excludes support you receive for children from a previous relationship, and certain public assistance payments. If your state uses gross income as the base for calculating child support, no deductions are allowed prior to calculation of the guideline amount. Only a few states use gross income.

Adjusted Gross Income

If the income base in your child support formula is *adjusted gross,* you can usually deduct certain expenses. Depending on your state, these expenses may include court-ordered support for children from a previous relationship, as well as health insurance for current children. Many states base support on adjusted gross.

Net Income

If your state calculates support on *net income,* you can deduct certain other expenses from your gross income. Though it varies, deductions are usually the mandatory payments you must make, such as:

- Federal and state withholding.
- Social Security.
- Mandatory disability or unemployment tax.
- Mandatory union dues.
- Mandatory retirement contributions.

In addition, some states allow you to deduct support to children from a previous relationship.

Disposable income to a judge is different from *net income* to a banker. That's because a judge is not interested in whether you can repay a car loan, he wants to know *your ability to pay child support.*

Imputing Income

If there is reason to believe that a parent is intentionally unemployed or underemployed, the judge can calculate that parent's potential income and set child support accordingly. When a judge calculates theoretical income, it is called *imputing income.*

The need to impute income can happen when a parent with a history of steady employment suddenly loses a job and does not return to work, insisting that he or she cannot find another job. Or a parent with a history of steadily increasing

After seven years of marriage to Robert, Margaret took their two children, Matthew and Michael, and moved to New Jersey. Robert stayed in Virginia. Before she moved away, Margaret and Robert signed a divorce agreement. The agreement gave physical custody to Margaret and gave Robert alternate weekend visitation. It also said that as long as Robert remained unemployed or was earning less than $25,000 per year, "Margaret shall make no claim for payment to her of any amount for support and maintenance of the [children]." The agreement was ratified by the Virginia circuit court, with the additional language that "due to [Robert's] current unemployment the child support amount is No/100 dollars as agreed by the parties." A few months later, Robert asked a New Jersey family court to register and enforce the divorce agreement. Margaret asked the New Jersey court to modify the agreement and order Robert to pay child support. At the time, Margaret's annual income was $387,000, and Robert's annual income was estimated to be $30,000. The New Jersey court ordered Robert to pay $531 in child support and calculated his back-due child support at $2,541. The New Jersey judge also ordered Robert to pay Margaret's legal fees of $4,500. Robert appealed the decision, and it was reversed. *Whitfield v. Whitfield* (1998) 315 N.J.Super. 1, 716 A.2d 533.

wages may suddenly go to work for a different company at lower pay, insisting that he or she cannot return to the former level of earnings.

Whatever the reason, whether it is deemed *willful suppression of income,* or *failure to earn to capacity,* all states allow the judge to consider a parent's capacity to earn—rather than actual earnings—when setting child support.

Of course, some parents always believe that a former spouse is earning below ability. However, others point out that a parent does not have to maximize economic wealth. Indeed, rising and falling wages reflect the natural career movement that all adults experience—whether married or not.

If imputed income becomes an issue in the calculations, the judge will have to weigh more factors, including the number of hours the parent works, prevailing wages in the area, recent work history, and even the parent's personal assets—such as a car, real estate, etc.

Expenses

In addition to your ability to pay, the judge needs to know the expenses involved in raising the children. These include direct expenditures on the children, and in some cases, may include expenses of the parent.

Expenses fall into two groups:

Children's Expenses
In setting child support, the judge wants to provide for the child. To do that, he must know all the child-related expenses.

Here's a checklist of typical expenses:
- Insurance: health and dental premiums.
- Medical: uninsured health care costs.
- Child Care: day care, after school care, baby-sitting.
- Education: tuition, room and board, books, tutors, fees.
- Extracurricular: sports lessons, uniforms, equipment, hobbies.

Parent's Expenses
As appealing as it may seem, there is little to gain by going into court and telling the judge about your bills. In truth, many of the parent's expenses are not relevant in setting child support. For your expenses to be considered, they must establish your standard of living or be a special circumstance.

 The judge knows how much you're supposed to have withheld from your paycheck. If you jack up your withholding to make it look like you earn less, the judge will simply recompute your proper withholding.

Some expenses that may be relevant include:

- Housing: rent or mortgage, utilities, telephone, repairs.
- Food: groceries, meals outside the home.
- Transportation: gas, repairs, parking, public transportation.
- Insurance: life, health, dental, disability, homeowner's, auto.
- Medical: uninsured health care costs.
- Debts: credit cards, charge accounts, auto loans, personal loans.
- Other: clothing, entertainment, gifts, memberships.

To get a copy of your state's child support guidelines, you have many choices. The easiest is to make an appointment with a family lawyer. Generally, they offer an initial consultation for $50 or less. Other choices include calling the district attorney, the local child support enforcement office, the court clerk, or going online and searching the internet. They should all have the same information.

Determining the Guideline Amount

Once the financial information is in front of the judge, he or she will determine the *guideline amount*. Since there is no national child support formula, it is done differently in each state.

Some states use formulas, others use tables. Some consider the earnings of both parents, others include only the income of the noncustodial parent. Some use net income, others use gross or adjusted gross.

The only thing that all states have in common is that they provide a mathematical formula for calculating base child support, and they all allow for adjustments for special circumstances.

Here are the common child support models.

Dependency exemption. Generally, only the custodial parent can claim exemptions for the children. However, that parent can transfer the exemptions to the noncustodial parent so that both parents can share the tax savings.

Shared Income Model

The most common model for calculating child support is called the *shared income* model. In this method, the income of the two parents is first added together—giving a total family income. Then, the judge either uses a table or a formula to determine how much of this money should be spent on the child. Finally, the support is calculated by splitting the amount owed in proportion to each parent's income.

This model is based on the belief that children should not suffer when their parents break up. It requires both parents to share in the cost of supporting their children. It also incorporates a sliding scale that decreases the percentage of family income spent as total income increases. This prevents children of high-earning parents from receiving much more money than they could possibly use.

Example of Shared Income

Here's an example of a child support calculation based on shared income.

Suppose a mother has primary physical custody of her two children. She earns $1,000 per month, and the noncustodial father earns $3,000 per month. To keep it simple, all these amounts are net amounts, and there are no other factors

In *California Divorce Handbook,* Judge Stewart estimates that the guideline amount is awarded over 90% of the time.

(such as the percentage of visitation time). In a typical state, here's what might happen.

First, the judge adds the parents' incomes together:

Mom's Earnings	$1,000
Dad's Earnings	+$3,000
Combined Earnings	$4,000

Then, the judge consults a large chart or inputs the numbers into a computer program. This helps determine the total amount of support:

	1 child	2 children	3 children	4 children	5+ children
$2,000	427	662	831	936	1,020
$2,500	526	816	1,023	1,152	1,255
$3,000	561	872	1,092	1,232	1,340
$3,500	575	894	1,119	1,264	1,375
$4,000	609	946	1,185	1,336	1,455
$4,500	677	1,050	1,314	1,484	1,615
$5,000	738	1,148	1,437	1,616	1,765

In the example, the total child support is $946 per month.

Next, the judge calculates each parent's share of the total family income:

Mom's Earnings	$1,000	25%
Dad's Earnings	+$3,000	75%
Combined Earnings	$4,000	100%

Then, the total support is split between the two parents in proportion to their income:

Mom's Share	~~$236.50~~	25%
Dad's Share	+$709.50	75%
Total Family Support	$946.00	100%

Finally, the judge orders the father to pay 75%—or $709.50 per month—to the mother. Because the mother has custody, she's assumed to be already paying her share.

This is the method used in a majority of the states, but it is by no means universal. There are several other child support models in use.

Percent of Income Model

A second method for calculating child support is the *percent of income* model. In this model, child support is based on either a fixed or varying percent of the noncustodial parent's income. This method assumes that the custodial parent is already providing for the child by virtue of having custody, and that the noncustodial parent should contribute financially.

The *fixed percent of income* model calculates child support as a fixed percentage of the noncustodial parent's income. Thus, a noncustodial parent with two children will pay a standard percent—say 25%—of his or her income in child support, no matter how much is earned. Some states use the parent's gross income in the calculations, others use adjusted gross or net income.

In one year, of all parents who were awarded child support, 51% received full payment, 24% received partial payment, and 25% received no payment at all.[1]

The *varying percent of income* model works the same way as the fixed percent, except the percent changes based on the income of the noncustodial parent.

Thus, a noncustodial parent who earns more will pay more in child support, but the overall percent of income diverted to child support will decrease.

Example of Percent of Income

Here's an example of a child support calculation based on the fixed percent of income model.

In this model, the only two factors that are considered are the income of the noncustodial parent and the number of children. In this case, there are two children, the mother is the custodial parent, and the father earns $3,000 per month. Here's how the child support might be computed:

First, the judge looks up the percent from the support guidelines:

Children	% of Net Income
1	20%
2	25%
3	32%
4	40%
5	45%
6+	50%

Then, the judge applies that percent to the noncustodial parent's income:

Dad's income	$3,000
% of income	x 25%
Child support	$750

Finally, the judge orders the father to pay $750 per month in child support.

By excluding the income of the custodial parent, this model makes it easier to calculate support, but it also ignores whether the custodial parent is contributing anything towards the care of his or her children.

 Barry Bonds (yes, the famous baseball player) met Sunny in the summer of 1987. After living together for a few months, they decided to marry. Before the Las Vegas wedding, they entered into a written premarital agreement that each party waived any interest in the earnings and acquisitions of the other party during the marriage. At the time, Barry was earning $106,000 a year for the Pittsburgh Pirates. Six years later, when Barry was earnings millions, they divorced. Sunny requested custody of their two children, child and spousal support, and that the premarital agreement be thrown out because she had not signed it voluntarily. The Superior Court upheld the premarital agreement, the Court of Appeals reversed, but the California Supreme Court reversed the appellate court, finding that Sunny had entered into the agreement "free from the taint of fraud, coercion and undue influence." *Bonds v. Bonds* (2000) 24 Cal.4th 1, 5 P.3d 815, 99 Cal. Rptr.2d 252.

Melson Model

A final child support model is called the *Melson* formula. This model considers many more factors than the other models, and thus is more complicated.

Basically, the model computes the minimum amount of support needed by the child. Then, the support obligation is divided between the parents based on ability to pay. Next, a standard of living allowance is applied, and finally, child-care expenses are added in.

While this model is much more comprehensive than the others, it is also more difficult to implement, and only three states currently use it: Delaware, Hawaii, and Montana.

Problems with Child Support Models

No generalized table or formula can possibly account for the differences in child-rearing between households, which leads many skeptics to criticize the shortcomings of the current models.

For example, many guidelines are based on a set of assumptions. While these assumptions reflect the majority of parents, they don't reflect everyone, and in some cases, the assumptions will be wrong and the guidelines will recommend an inappropriate amount.

Here are a few typical assumptions built into some guidelines:

"Traditional" Custody

Often, the custodial parent has physical custody of the children about 80% of the time, and the noncustodial parent has visitation 20% of the time. This 80-20 split means that the custodial parent is shouldering most of the costs of raising the children. However, when parents devise a different schedule, say a 50-50 or 60-40 division of the children's time, some guidelines don't account for the more equitable sharing of the child rearing costs.

Income Differential

Because many custodial parents earn less than many noncustodial parents, some guidelines assume that the custodial parent earns about 25% less. This assumption is embedded in the amounts the guidelines recommend as presumed correct. When it's not true—such as when the custodial parent earns more than the noncustodial parent—the guidelines will be inappropriate.

 "The guidelines do seem to be working. Support awards are higher and more equitable, and the entire process takes less court time. In addition, more cases are settled and those that are litigated are often narrowed in scope."
When Your Ex Won't Pay

Child Support Calculation Web Sites

The internet has plenty of useful information about child support. Here are some sites worth a visit:

Support Guidelines
www.supportguidelines.com
A comprehensive website operated by Laura Morgan—a nationally recognized family law attorney—with links to the support guidelines in all states, on-line support calculators, state bar associations, divorce web sites, and more.

Divorce Source
www.divorcesource.com
This most heavily visited divorce sites will charge you $39.95 for a comprehensive report explaining child support amounts, calculations, state guidelines and income adjustments.

All Law
www.alllaw.com
This general legal site has a set of simple, on-line calculators by state. The calculators will yield a general guess-timate of support, and you can get a more precise calculation on one of the other sites.

Divorce Headquarters
www.divorcehq.com
This exhaustive divorce website also has simple, on-line calculators for each state. As with *All Law,* use these calculators for a general estimate of your support.

High and Low Income

Very low or very high wage earners have something in common—they make it difficult to set child support by a mathematical formula. That's because either they cannot pay for the most basic costs of raising children, or they can pay so much the children can't possibly use all the money.

Troy and Daphne had one child during their three-year marriage. When they divorced, the dissolution stated that Troy would pay $80 per week in child support, but he would get a "10% visitation credit of $9.33 for 'regular visitation' and another $3.98 reduction to defray [his] portion of the travel expenses." When Troy didn't pay any child support for 25 weeks, Daphne asked the court to hold him in contempt. Troy argued that he was entitled to a "100% abatement," and thus had amassed a child visitation credit of over $3,000. The court held him in contempt. *In re Marriage of Cohoon* (2002) Indiana No. 49A04-0109-CV-400.

Standard of Living

Many guidelines seek to maintain the child's standard of living at pre-divorce levels. Unfortunately, this ignores the reality of divorce in that two households must be supported where there formerly was one. This results in less income overall, forcing the families to lower their standard of living. Unfortunately, some guidelines do not consider that fact, forcing the parents to maintain previously higher levels.

Noncustodial Costs

And finally, because the guidelines focus on the parent's income—and not the actual costs of raising children—expenses incurred by the noncustodial parent are often overlooked. This may include a bed, clothes, toys, books, etc., that children require when they "visit."

Departing from the Guideline Amount

After determining the guideline amount, the judge can then adjust it up or down. To do this, he or she must find that the award is unjust or inappropriate.

The factors that can be considered when adjusting support vary by state. In addition, some states have mandatory add-ons that must be shared by both parents.

Factors That May Affect Child Support

Most factors that influence child support either increase or decrease it, depending on which parent is affected. Factors that increase support involve additional expenses for raising the children, or make more income available to the paying parent. Factors that decrease support reflect decreases in the cost of raising the children, or increase the income to the receiving parent.

Here are some typical factors that influence the guidelines:

Medical Expenses
Most group health plans require you to pay a small deductible or copayment, but if the children have allergies, asthma, or other chronic conditions, the costs can really climb. If the receiving parent pays—or anticipates paying—the children's unreimbursed health care costs, the judge can increase the award. Alternatively, if the paying parent pays those costs, the judge can decrease the award. Quite often, the judge will order the cost of health care not covered by insurance to be paid equally or prorated based on income.

Medical Insurance
Whichever parent pays the premiums for the children's health insurance can get the savings. If the receiving parent pays, child support can be increased. If the paying parent pays, child support can be lowered. Many states require the paying

How likely is it the judge will depart from the guideline amount? Not very. In *California Divorce Handbook,* Judge Stewart reasoned that for a judge to deviate from the guideline he "...must state in writing or on the record the facts and circumstances underlying the rebuttal factor, the value of the factor, and the length of time the factor will be in effect." Practically speaking, this is not feasible in many overworked courts, because "The time it will take to make all the findings necessary to justify such a factor will seem like a lifetime to a busy judge."

parent to include the children under his or her health and
dental plan—if a plan is available through work or at a low
cost. If insurance isn't available that way, either parent can
buy the insurance, and the cost may be divided.

Life Insurance

In order to provide security for the children, the paying parent
may be ordered to maintain a life insurance policy naming the
children as irrevocable beneficiaries until the support order
ceases. The paying parent may get a reduction in child
support to pay for the premiums for this policy, or—if the
receiving parent has to pay for the policy—he or she may get
an increase in support.

Children from Previous Relationships

Parents have a duty to support all of their children. Thus, if a
receiving parent pays support to children from a previous
relationship, he or she has less available, and the judge may
increase the support. Likewise, if the paying parent supports
children from a previous relationship, support may be
lowered. These payments must be required, and are usually
limited to the amount dictated by the guidelines.

Children from Subsequent Relationships

If the children are from a subsequent relationship—that is,
the parent had them after support was established—it may
not have the same effect. That's because most guidelines do
not explicitly address this issue, leaving it up to the judge to
use his discretion. In real life, some judges have accounted
for the extra children in the support award, while others have
insisted that the children have no effect on the support.

New Mate

In a few states, if a new mate enters the picture, child support
can be adjusted. That's because a new mate usually—though
not always—adds income to the household of the parent
involved. Thus, if the receiving parent has a new mate, the
judge can decrease the amount of support. Alternatively, if
the paying parent has a new mate, more money is available
for the children, and the judge can increase the award. The
amount of the new mate's income that can be taken into
account varies. Some judges may decide that all of the new
mate's income is available to the parent, while others may

Uniform Interstate Family Support Act (UIFSA)

In 1998, this uniform law was adopted by all states, replacing the existing interstate child support laws, the *Uniform Reciprocal Enforcement of Support Act* (URESA) and its revised version, RURESA. UIFSA solves common interstate child support problems such as:

Conflicting child support orders
This uniform law grants "continuing and exclusive jurisdiction" to one state to create or modify a child support award. By giving only one state this authority, UIFSA prevents two courts from making simultaneous—and conflicting—support orders.

Modifying an out-of-state support order
By granting only one state the authority to enter a support order, this law prevents a court in a second state from modifying a support order made by a court in the first state. As the UIFSA states: "The role of the responding State is limited to enforcing that order except in the very limited circumstances under which modification is permitted."

Enforcing an out-of-state support order
UIFSA also allows a child support-receiving parent to enforce a support order by contacting the paying parent's employer directly. The receiving parent is not required to *register* the support order in a court in the paying parent's state in order to initiate wage witholding. As the UIFSA states: "An income-withholding order issued in another State may be sent by or on behalf of the obligee, or by the support enforcement agency, to the person or entity defined as the obligor's employer under [the income-withholding law of this State] without first filing a [petition] or comparable pleading or registering the order with a tribunal of this State."

The guiding principle of the UIFSA is to prevent problems with enforcing existing orders across state lines, as well as to ensure there is only "one order at a time."

that as little as 25% of the income should be
.dered. And, of course, still other judges will decide that
.e of it is available.

"Non-Traditional" Custody

Some states include the percentage of time with the child in
their support calculations. This means that an award will be
raised or lowered based on how much time the parent spends
with the child. For example, if the receiving parent has the
child 80% of the time, and the paying parent has the child
20% of the time, a typical award may be for $500. But if the
parents change the schedule, giving the receiving parent the
child 60% of the time, and the paying parent 40% of the time,
child support can be decreased. This reflects the reality that
the more time a paying parent spends caring for the child, the
less he should pay in support to a receiving parent. And the
more time a receiving parent spends with the child, the more
support the paying parent should pay. To calculate
percentage of time with the child, add up all the hours in an
entire year each parent spends with the child.

When James and Twila divorced, they agreed
to share custody of their nine-year old
daughter, Shannon. James had custody of
Shannon every other weekend from Friday
after school until Monday morning, and Wednesday after
school until Thursday morning. In addition, James had
custody of Shannon an additional Friday night each
month plus an extra day every month. All non-school
time was divided evenly. When it came time to calculate
child support, James submitted a joint custody worksheet
to the district court, calculating his time with his
daughter from 32.88 to 39.45 percent of the time. Twila
used a sole custody worksheet. The court found that
since James had less than 40 percent of the time with his
daughter, he did not have joint custody, but rather, Twila
had sole custody and he had visitation. The court used
the sole custody worksheet in calculating his child
support. *Heesacker v. Heesacker* (2001) 262 Neb. 179,
629 N.W.2d 558.

Till death do we part. If the child support order is properly written, it will remain as a claim against the estate of a paying parent who suddenly dies. In addition, the paying parent may be required to carry life insurance with the children named as beneficiaries.

Hardship

If the receiving parent suffers an extreme financial hardship due to uninsured catastrophic losses, the judge can increase child support. Likewise, if the paying parent suffers a financial hardship due to catastrophic losses, the judge can decrease the child support.

High Income

If the paying parent earns a great deal of money, the formula may indicate an amount greater than what the children realistically need. If that's the case, the judge can lower the support to a more reasonable amount. High income is subjective, but generally, if the paying parent earns more than $200,000 a year, the guideline will indicate more support than is needed. Most schedules begin to lose their usefulness when either parent's earnings reach high levels.

Low Income

The opposite of high income is low income. If the paying parent would be left with too little to live on, child support may be lowered. Low income is subjective, but generally, if the paying parent keeps less than 40% of net income after paying child support, he or she no longer has an incentive to continue working.

Child Care

Child care costs include both day care and after-school care. In some states, the costs are automatically prorated, while in others, accounting for this expense is entirely at the discretion of the judge. Typically, the receiving parent must pay child care costs in order to work or go to school, and the judge will increase the support in kind. By the way, child care is one of the few costs that actually decrease as the children grow older.

After an eight-year marriage, Kristi left Michael and took their three children with her. Kristi worked in a day care center, and Michael worked as general manager for a Pizza Hut. In her divorce papers, Kristi asked for sole custody of their three children. It was granted. The circuit court then went on and said that Michael had "voluntarily impoverished" himself because he had been fired by Pizza Hut for falsifying documents, and calculated his child support based on his salary from a job he no longer had. Michael appealed. The Court of Appeals reversed the decision of the trial court regarding Michael's voluntary impoverishment, stating that "[Michael's] intent that led to his being discharged was not to avoid child support." *Stull v. Stull* (2002) Maryland No. 878.

Travel Costs

This issue comes up when one parent moves away, and the children have to take long trips by plane, train, or car. If the receiving parent pays the travel costs for visitation, the judge can increase child support. If the paying parent pays visitation costs, support can be lowered. By the way, in some states it doesn't matter who moved away—the judge isn't allowed to give that issue any weight when setting support.

Job Expenses

If the paying parent must maintain a car or special work clothes for his or her job, the judge may lower the child support award.

School

School costs include tuition, fees, books, room and board, and so on. If the receiving parent pays these costs, he or she can ask to have child support increased. Alternatively, a paying parent who pays these costs can ask to have child support lowered.

Children's Income

In a few states, if the children have independent income, the paying parent may be able to lower the amount of child support.

Bargain Housing

When the receiving parent remains in the family residence and pays a much lower mortgage than what rent would be, the judge can lower child support. The reason is that the receiving parent is getting a financial break, and thus has more income available for the children.

Other

Finally, if an expense doesn't fit another other category, but the judge believes it's appropriate, the judge can adjust the award. Costs in this category might include summer camp, religious training, and so on. The parent who pays the costs may be entitled to an adjustment in the child support.

Modifying Child Support

As children grow, their lives change. Perhaps a child takes up music, and now needs an instrument and lessons. Or maybe the child needs braces, and the costs aren't covered by insurance.

Or maybe it's not the children who change, but the parents. Suppose one parent gets a big raise, and now has a higher standard of living. Or the other parent remarries, and has another child. Whatever the cause, child support can be modified anytime there is a *change of circumstances*.

What constitutes a change of circumstance varies from state to state. In some states, a 10% difference in payments justifies a return to court. But in others, the amount must be more.

If you can agree on the amount to change, you can write up your own agreement. But if you cannot agree, you will have to go to court.

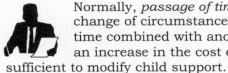 Normally, *passage of time* is not considered a change of circumstances. However, passage of time combined with another reason—such as an increase in the cost of living—may be sufficient to modify child support.

Full Faith and Credit for Child Support Orders Act (FFCCSOA)

Along with the *Uniform Interstate Family Support Act (UIFSA)*, which has been adopted by all states, there is a federal law that requires one state to enforce the child support orders made by another state. This law is known as the *Full Faith and Credit for Child Support Orders Act (FFCCSOA)* 28 U.S.C. § 1738B.

This federal law addresses the problem of courts in different states making competing child support orders by granting *continuing, exclusive jurisdiction* to the first court to make an order.

Under the FFCCSOA, jurisdiction belongs to the court in the state where the child lives or where either parent lives. As the law states: "A court of a State that has made a child support order consistently with this section has continuing, exclusive jurisdiction over the order if the State is the child's State or the residence of any individual contestant..."

This law then requires any subsequent court to enforce the order, and not modify it, unless certain requirements are met. Specifically, a state can only modify a support order from another state if the second state has jurisdiction and the first state no longer has jurisdiction.

As the law says: "A court of a State may modify a child support order issued by a court of another State if (1) the court has jurisdiction to make such a child support order pursuant to subsection (i); and (2)(A) the court of the other State no longer has continuing, exclusive jurisdiction of the child support order because that State no longer is the child's State or the residence of any individual contestant; or (B) each individual contestant has filed written consent with the State of continuing, exclusive jurisdiction for a court of another State to modify the order and assume continuing, exclusive jurisdiction over the order."

Standards for Modification

While it varies from state to state, most states require that the new support being sought is at least 10% different from the old support. If the difference is less the modification may be denied.

Other states set the threshold even higher, such as 25% or 30%. And a few states simply ignore the amount and consider a modification after two years have passed since the prior order.

Types of Modifications

These are the various types of modifications:

Temporary Modification
Child support can be modified *temporarily.* This might occur when a parent suddenly loses a job, or is injured, or when the child's needs change—but only for a definite period of time. The modification can be structured to last only for a specific period and then revert back to the prior terms.

Permanent Modification
Child support can be modified *permanently.* This happens when the support changes from a certain point forward for an indefinite period of time. Though nothing about child support is ever permanent, the orders remain until a judge changes them or they end.

Retroactive Modification
As a general rule, child support is not modified *retroactively.* That's to prevent a parent who owes a large amount of back support from going into court and arguing that the past-due payments were too large, and thus, the debt should be erased.

However, there are times when child support is modified from an earlier date. A judge may set support back to the date when the motion was filed, even if it was months—or years— earlier. And if a mother is establishing paternity, the court may order support back to the child's date of birth. Finally, support may be modified retroactively when the receiving parent is guilty of snatching or concealing the child, or when a parent supplied fraudulent income and expense information to the court.

It's not easy to modify child support. You have to submit detailed financial statements, elicit financial information from the other parent, and then sit though a lengthy court hearing. A better bet? Anticipate future reasons for a modification and bring them to the attention of the judge, who can add them to the original court order.

Factors That May Modify Child Support

All kinds of events can trigger a modification. In fact, many of the same factors that cause child support to be adjusted initially can also cause it to be modified. For example:

Income
When either parent's ability to pay has changed, child support can be changed. That's because children are entitled to the same standard of living as their parents. Thus, depending on which parent's income is affected and how it's affected, child support can either be raised or lowered. For example, support can be raised if the paying parent has more income, or if the receiving parent has less income. And the reverse is true, too. Child support can go down if the paying parent experiences a drop in income or if the receiving parent has an increase in income.

Hardship
If either parent suffers an extreme financial hardship, support can be modified. A receiving parent who is suddenly burdened with huge financial losses can seek to have child support increased. Conversely, if the paying parent suffers a financial emergency, he or she can ask that support be decreased. By the way, if a hardship that was incorporated into a prior child support award has now ended, that constitutes a change of circumstance, and either parent can file a motion to modify.

Health Care

If the children have a medical emergency, the parents will have to pay the bills. If the receiving parent has a health emergency and cannot work, the paying parent may have to pay additional support. If the paying parent has a medical crisis and cannot work, the receiving parent may have to accept less support. If the problem is temporary, the judge may grant a temporary change in support, but when a problem is permanent, such as a disability, support may be permanently modified.

School

If a child changes from private to public school, that may be a cost that justifies changing child support. However, if a child changes from public to private school, the parent insisting on the change may have to foot the entire bill. Other examples include the child needing a tutor, or the child joining a team and requiring money for uniforms and equipment.

New Children

If either parent gains a new child, that may be a reason to modify child support. In this case, however, the parent must be legally obligated to support the child. Because stepparents do not have the same legal obligations as biological parents, gaining a stepchild through remarriage may not be a reason

 After thirteen years of marriage, Dorothy divorced Bradley. The decree granted Dorothy physical custody of their two children with Bradley "receiving up to one-half of the time with both children during any calendar month." Bradley was also ordered to pay Dorothy $5,070 per month in child support. One month later, Bradley changed his mind and sought sole custody of the children and a recalculation of his child support, but the court dismissed his request. Then, ten months later, Bradley again asked for custody and a recalculation of his child support "based on the sudden, unforeseen halving of his net salary." The court did not change custody, but reduced his child support to $3,890 per month. *Hall v. Hall* (2001) 96 Haw. 105, 26 P.3d 594.

to change the support. An adoption, on the other hand, is often considered a reason to change because it represents a genuine legal obligation.

New Mate

The new mate that comes along with a remarriage may well represent a change of circumstances. The new mate may represent additional available income, and in some states the judge can include that income in the calculations. If the receiving parent gets the new mate, child support can be decreased, and if the paying parent gains the new mate, child support may be raised.

Percentage of Time with the Child

One reason to change support occurs if the parents change the visitation schedule. In states where percentage of time is included in child support calculations, whichever parent starts spending more time with the child will benefit. Thus, if the paying parent gets more time with the child, he or she will qualify for less child support. If the receiving parent gets more time, the opposite occurs.

Change in Law

Interestingly enough, there is one change that has nothing to do with the parents—the laws change! When child support laws are revised, or new ones are passed, that's considered a change of circumstance all by itself. When that happens, parents can file without having to prove anything has changed.

Cost of Living

A final possible reason to change support occurs when inflation has eroded the value of the child support. Either parent may seek to increase the support award.

---

1 U.S. Bureau of the Census, Current Population Reports, series P-60, no. 173, *Child Support and Alimony: 1989*

Counting On Your Support

Child Support Survival Guide, Bonnie M. White, Douglas Pipes, Career Press, $12.99. This book is an excellent guide to understanding how child support works and how to deal with the federal Child Support Enforcement (CSE) agencies.

Divorce and Money, Violet Woodhouse, Victoria F. Collins, Robin Leonard, M.C. Blakeman, Nolo Press, $26.95. This excellent book on the money side of divorce includes extremely detailed discussions of marital property, retirement benefits, insurance, taxes, business assets, debts, and spousal and child support.

The Dollars and Sense of Divorce, Judith Briles, Carol Ann Wilson, Dearborn Financial Publishing, $17.95. An informative guide to divorce issues, including dividing property, retirement plans, etc. It includes a list of helpful organizations.

Don't Settle For Less, Beverly Pekala, Doubleday, $12.95. Written by a lawyer who advocates women's rights, this book offers a step-by-step explanation of how women can keep from being economically victimized by divorce and custody settlements.

How to Collect Child Support, Geraldine Jensen with Katina Z. Jones, The Association for Children for Enforcement of Support, Inc. (ACES), Longmeadow Press, $7.95. An accurate and very easy-to-follow guide to enforcing support orders.

The Single Parent's Money Guide, Emily W. Card, Macmillan, $14.95. Written by a lawyer and a single parent, this book explains alimony and child support, insurance coverage, budgeting for emergencies, and other financial decisions.

When Your Ex Won't Pay, Nancy S. Palmer and Ana Tangel-Rodriguez, Pinon Press, $12.00. Co-written by the Chair of the Florida Family Law Bar, this book explains the laws and various methods for collecting support.

Chapter 8

Child Support Worksheet

✓ This worksheet will give you a rough estimate of your child support.

✓ If you want a really simple estimate, use the following guide:

Number of Children	Percent of Noncustodial Parent's Gross Income
1	22%
2	34%
3	42%
4	47%
5+	50%

✓ To get a more accurate calculation, use the worksheet, talk to a local lawyer, or ask the court clerk for more information.

Step 1. Preliminary Information

The following worksheet will approximate the amount of child support likely to be awarded. Remember, there is no national child support formula. Not only do different states use different formulas, but judges can deviate from the formula— so the resulting calculation is a rough estimate only.

To complete the worksheet, you'll need the following information for both parents:
- Pay stubs.
- Last year's tax return.
- Adjustment expenses.

If you don't have this information handy, you can still complete the worksheet. Just keep in mind that the more accurately you guess, the more reliable the estimate will be.

Some of this information isn't strictly necessary, but completing it will help you get all your information in one place—which you'll need to do for court anyway.

Number of children. The number of children eligible for child support. This may be different from the number of dependents you claim on your tax return.

Tax filing status. Your choices are: single, head of household, married filing jointly, married filing separately, or widow(er).

Number of dependents. The number of people you claim as dependents, adding one for yourself.

Percentage of time with the children. The annual percentage of time each parent spends with the children. If you have more than one child, and the schedule is different for each child, use an average of the total time.

Step 2. Monthly Income

In this section you determine your *net monthly income.* Your *net monthly income* is your *gross monthly income* minus your *deductions.*

Step 1. Preliminary Information

Paying Parent

Name   _____

Occupation   _____

Employer   _____

Address of employer   _____

Tax filing status   _____

Number of children   _____

Number of dependents   _____

Percentage of time with children   _____

Receiving Parent

Name   _____

Occupation   _____

Employer   _____

Address of employer   _____

Tax filing status   _____

Number of children   _____

Number of dependents   _____

Percentage of time with children   _____

Everything in the worksheet will be based on monthly averages, so if you're not paid monthly (or if your income varies from month-to-month), calculate the monthly amounts by taking the annual amount and divide by 12.

Earnings. Your gross pay before any deductions are taken out.

Investment Income. The average monthly amounts you receive in interest, dividends, etc. These amounts should be your best guess for the next year.

Other Income. Include most kinds of income, including net income from self-employment, rentals, alimony from a previous marriage, and job-related reimbursements. Do not include child support.

Taxes. This is the average monthly amount you pay, not the average monthly amount withheld. If you pay other taxes, include those under *Other Deductions.*

Mandatory pension or retirement. This applies only if you are required to make a pension or retirement fund contribution. If your contributions are not mandatory, do not enter them.

Mandatory union dues. This only applies if union dues are required for all employees working under the same job classification for the same employer. If joining the union is not required, don't enter anything.

Children's health insurance premiums. Only enter the amount paid to insure the children. Do not include insurance costs for the parent.

Income. Subtract *Total Monthly Deductions* from *Total Gross Monthly Income.*

Step 3. Combined Income

In this step, you combine the net earnings of each parent.

Combined Income. Add *Paying Parent's Income* to *Receiving Parent's Income.*

Step 2a. Monthly Income (Paying Parent)

Gross Monthly Income

Earnings

Wages, salary	$
Bonuses	$
Commissions	$

Investment Income

Interest	$
Dividends	$
Capital Gains	$
Retirement plan distributions	$
Annuities	$

Other Income

Business net income	$
Rentals net income	$
Royalties	$
Pensions and Trusts	$
Social Security	$
Disability	$
Unemployment	$
Military basic allowance for quarters	$
Alimony	$
Other income	$

Total Gross Monthly Income	$

Monthly Deductions

Federal income tax	$
State and local income tax	$
Social Security (FICA)	$
State Disability Insurance (SDI)	$
Self-employment tax	$
Mandatory pension or retirement	$
Mandatory union dues	$
Children's health insurance	$
Other deductions	$

Minus (-)

Total Monthly Deductions	$

Equals (=)

Paying Parent's Income	$

Step 4. Minimum Child Support

This step uses the parents' combined income to calculate the minimum child support amount.

Minimum Child Support. Copy *Combined Income* from Step 3. Then, look up *Percent of Income* in the table below and copy it to the worksheet column. Now, multiply *Percent of Income* by *Combined Income.*

Number of Children	Percent of Income
1	.22
2	.34
3	.42
4	.47
5+	.50

Please note this is a general formula with an error factor of about ±2%. If you want to try to reduce the error to ±1%, do the following. If *Combined Income* is less than $1,500, add .1 to *Percent of Income.* If *Combined Income* is more than $2,500, subtract .1 from *Percent of Income.* If *Combined Income* is more than $3,500, subtract .2 from *Percent of Income.*

What does this mean? It means that the more you earn, the smaller the percentage of your total earnings you spend on your children.

Step 5. Paying Parent's Portion

Here, you determine the amount of child support attributable to the paying parent.

First, copy *Paying Parent's Income* from Step 2a and *Combined Income* from Step 3.

Then, divide *Paying Parent's Income* by *Combined Income.* This gives you *Paying Parent's Percentage.* This is the portion of the combined income the paying parent contributes.

Step 2b. Monthly Income (Receiving Parent)

Gross Monthly Income

Earnings

Wages, salary	$
Bonuses	$
Commissions	$

Investment Income

Interest	$
Dividends	$
Capital Gains	$
Retirement plan distributions	$
Annuities	$

Other Income

Business net income	$
Rentals net income	$
Royalties	$
Pensions and Trusts	$
Social Security	$
Disability	$
Unemployment	$
Military basic allowance for quarters	$
Alimony	$
Other income	$

Total Gross Monthly Income $

Monthly Deductions

Federal income tax	$
State and local income tax	$
Social Security (FICA)	$
State Disability Insurance (SDI)	$
Self-employment tax	$
Mandatory pension or retirement	$
Mandatory union dues	$
Children's health insurance	$
Other deductions	$

Minus (-)

Total Monthly Deductions $

Equals (=)

Receiving Parent's Income $

Finally, multiply *Paying Parent's Percentage* by *Minimum Child Support* to get *Paying Parent's Portion.* This is the portion of the child support the paying parent should pay.

Step 6. Adjustments

In this step, you enter any adjustments for special circumstances. The list of possible adjustments is lengthy, but a few may apply to you. Try to use known amounts whenever possible.

To make adjustments for special circumstances:

Add (+) for factors that increase child support:
- Receiving parent suffers extreme hardship.
- Receiving parent pays travel costs for visitation.
- Receiving parent pays children's uninsured health care costs.
- Receiving parent pays for children's educational or other needs.
- Paying parent has income available from a new mate.
- Paying parent has less than 20% visitation.

Subtract (-) for factors that decrease child support
- Paying parent suffers extreme hardship.
- Paying parent pays travel costs for visitation.
- Paying parent supports children from previous or subsequent relationships.
- Paying parent has an unusually high income, and the formula calculates an amount greater than what the children need.
- Paying parent would be left with an unreasonably low amount of money to live on.
- Paying parent has more than 20% visitation.
- Receiving parent has income available from a new mate.
- Receiving parent resides in the family residence and has a much lower mortgage payment compared to fair rent.

To make adjustments, you need to know which factors are relevant in your state. The factors most likely to affect support include: percentage of time with the children, support paid for children from previous relationships, child care costs,

Step 3. Combined Income

Paying Parent's Income (*from 2a*) $ _____

Plus (+)

Receiving Parent's Income (*from 2b*) $ _____

Equals (=)

Combined Income $ _____

Step 4. Minimum Child Support

Combined Income (*from 3*) $ _____

Times (x)

Percent of Income (*see instructions*) $ _____

Equals (=)

Minimum Child Support $ _____

Step 5. Paying Parent's Portion

Paying Parent's Income (*from 2a*) $ _____

Divided (/)

Combined Income (*from 3*) $ _____

Equals (=)

Paying Parent's Percentage $ _____

Times (x)

Minimum Child Support (*from 4*) $ _____

Equals (=)

Paying Parent's Portion $ _____

Step 6. Adjustments

Adjustments

_____ $ _____ (+ or -)

_____ $ _____ (+ or -)

_____ $ _____ (+ or -)

Total Adjustments $ _____

Step 7. Child Support

Child Support $ _____

health insurance premiums for the children, and new mate income.

When adjusting support, keep in mind that the presumed correct figure is awarded an estimated 90% of the time.

Step 7. Child Support

In this step you add (or subtract) your adjustments to the minimum child support amount, and you've finished.

Compute *Child Support* by adding or subtracting *Total Adjustments* to *Paying Parent's Portion*.

Congratulations! You did it.

You now have an approximation of the support likely to be awarded. Remember, the estimate is based on a number of assumptions about both parents' future income and expenses. Don't assume it's absolute. Instead, use it as a guide for approximating your support order.

Negotiating a Parenting Plan

Chapter 9

Negotiating With the Other Parent

✓ When you disagree over custody of your
   children, you don't have to hire a lawyer and
   go to court. You can also resolve your
   disagreement by *negotiating a settlement.*

✓ Negotiation has many advantages—such as
   lessening the hostilities, but it also has some
   disadvantages—such as allowing a parent
   drag out the dispute.

✓ When you prepare to negotiate, you have to
   decide which issues to negotiate and who will
   do the negotiating—you or a third party.

✓ You also have to identify your *leverage*—
   bargaining factors that favor your side. And
   you'll have to choose a negotiating *strategy*—
   position-based or interest-based.

✓ Despite your best efforts, the negotiations
   may fail, and if they do, you'll have to resort to
   go to other forms of dispute resolution.

Settling

If you disagree with the other parent, you don't automatically have to go to court. You can also *negotiate a settlement.*

A settlement is any agreement you work out with the other parent. You can negotiate a settlement before you file a lawsuit, during the pretrial phase, or even during the trial itself.

You don't have to settle everything. You can agree on some issues and leave the rest for a judge to decide. In order for the agreement to be binding, however, you have to file it with the court, which means a judge will approve or reject it.

Negotiating a settlement is common, with many courts actually encouraging the parents to negotiate. Lawmakers realize that *private ordering*—where parents work out their own problems—is better than having a judge decide everything.

 "The art of negotiation is the ability to perceive and use these leverage factors to obtain concessions. Since both sides usually have something the other side wants, these factors are traded like chips. The side with more leverage can obtain more concessions in the trading process. The end result of the trades and compromises is the settlement." Eleanor Maccoby and Robert Mnookin, *Dividing the Child*

Advantages of Negotiation

Decreases the Conflict
If you think about it, there may be no better way to increase the conflict than to litigate. By litigating, you are attacking the other parent's rights and position and forcing them to attack yours. Negotiation, on the other hand, encourages the parents to talk to each other, which allows them to immediately identify and address a problem before it becomes any bigger.

Saves Time and Money

Negotiation lets you quickly and efficiently resolve a disagreement. By negotiating, you don't have to spend endless hours filing motions, waiting for a hearing date, and sitting in court. You also don't have to spend your life savings on legal fees.

Improves the Outcome

If you litigate, you put the final decision in the hands of someone else. If you negotiate, you don't. Negotiation not only gives you more control over the outcome, but also reduces the possibility that an inept third party—such as a poorly trained evaluator or biased judge—will make a bad decision. Negotiation also allows you to get the details right—tailoring the agreement to your specific needs.

 It's easy to get sidetracked when negotiating with the other parent. Anger, hurt, bitterness, revenge—all are feelings that can interfere with negotiations. Your best bet? Stick to one issue and don't talk in front of the children.

Disadvantages of Negotiation

Doesn't Equalize Positions

If one parent wants to sabotage the negotiations by bluffing, threatening, or lying, negotiating will not place the other parent on an equal footing. For negotiation to work, both parents must have equal negotiating skill, equal knowledge, and equal power.

Doesn't Force a Resolution

Since there's no practical time limit to negotiating, a parent who wants to delay can stall almost indefinitely. Negotiation may not be best when the parents are operating under a deadline and need a definite resolution.

Doesn't Guarantee a Fair Outcome

There's nothing inherent about negotiating that guarantees an agreement will be fair to both sides. Even if attorneys review the agreement, it's possible a judge would have ruled differently. Also, if you agree but later on don't like the agreement—you can't appeal a negotiated settlement.

 During their 11 year marriage, Terry and Teresa had three children: Chad, Tony, and Joshua. When the marriage ended, Teresa was awarded custody of the children and Terry was ordered to pay $75 per week in child support. Eight years later, they agreed that Teresa would have custody of Joshua and Terry would have custody of Tony, and they would have joint custody of Chad. Then, one year later, five days before he turned nineteen, Chad filed a motion for child support, complaining that Terry and Teresa had abandoned him in 1997 and had failed to provide him with any income or support. In response, Terry filed a petition to emancipate Chad and terminate support. The superior court found that Chad had lived with his aunt since he was fifteen, and granted Terry's motion to emancipate Chad because Chad had not been under the care or control of either parent. The Court of Appeals agreed, but the Indiana Supreme Court reversed. *Dunson v. Dunson* (2002) Indiana No. 34S02-0108-CV-370.

Preparing to Negotiate

If you plan to give negotiation a try, you will benefit by *preparing.* The amount of preparation you do depends on the type of negotiation. For a quick chat with the other parent, you don't need to do anything. But if you're planning on elaborate and time-consuming bargaining, you need to do a lot.

As you prepare to negotiate, you'll need to make several decisions.

Who Will Negotiate?
One of the first questions is who will be doing the negotiating—you or a third party, such as an attorney or a friend. If you negotiate for yourself, you can be much more flexible in responding to the other side, and you can save a

substantial amount of money—usually on legal fees. That's the good news. The bad news is that you are probably not a skilled negotiator, which means that you won't know how to assess the strengths and weaknesses of your position. You also won't know how to handle the *negotiator's dilemma*—the inescapable conflict between cooperating with the other side to forge an agreement, while competing with them to secure your personal gains.

What Will You Negotiate?
Next, you must select the issues to negotiate. While there's a natural tendency to limit the bargaining to a few specific items, inevitably that will leave loose ends that can come back to haunt you. Also, if you hire a third party to handle the negotiations, you'll not only have to tell that person what you want, but also all of the facts that bear upon those issues.

When Will You Negotiate?
Finally, you'll have to decide when to negotiate. If you're not ready, or if the other side isn't ready, you won't accomplish anything. Even worse, you may compromise your position by showing your cards too soon. Experienced negotiators know that timing is crucial to success.

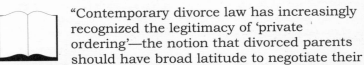

"Contemporary divorce law has increasingly recognized the legitimacy of 'private ordering'—the notion that divorced parents should have broad latitude to negotiate their own financial and custodial arrangements... The judiciary functions primarily not to regulate the lives of divorcing families, but instead to resolve those legal difficulties that divorcing parents cannot work out." Eleanor Maccoby and Robert Mnookin, *Dividing the Child*

Leverage

In addition to making some decisions, you'll also have to assemble information. Because bargaining depends on your ability to pressure the other side into making concessions, you'll need to identify the factors that you can use for *leverage*.

There are many types of leverage, but they generally fall into two categories—legal and psychological.

Legal Leverage

Legal leverage concerns the legal norms, that is, what would happen to you if the negotiations fail and you go to court. You don't necessarily have to go to court—just the mere possibility of it influences the negotiations. This is called bargaining in the *shadow of the law,* and parents negotiate custody of their children well aware of how courts have ruled in the past. A parent who seeks a traditional or typical custodial arrangement gains a significant bargaining endowment that pushes the negotiations in his or her favor.

Five Ways to Deal with the Other Parent

1. *Be reasonable.* Don't expect to get your way more than half the time—if that.

2. *Be flexible.* If you think your kids require flexibility, wait until you start dealing with your ex.

3. *Be kind.* Of course your ex-spouse is not perfect—but you had a child with him or her anyway.

4. *Be reliable.* Do what you'll say you'll do.

5. *Be quiet.* If you don't have to talk—don't. Less is more.

Psychological Leverage

Psychological leverage has nothing to do with the law, and everything to do with how the parents feel. If one parent is angry or selfish, or the other parent feels guilty, the emotions can dramatically influence the negotiations. It's not unusual for a "burned" ex-spouse to try to punish a former mate by battling over custody. And even if strong emotions aren't involved, the personal preferences of the parents will play a role. For example, if one parent genuinely wants to raise the children and the other doesn't, that will shift the negotiations. In addition, because a judge's decision is never a sure thing, the amount of risk each parent is willing to take is a factor. Some parents will simply be more willing to take their chances in court, while others will be risk-adverse—disturbed by the mere possibility of losing.

 When Michelle and Jarrod separated, they signed a separation agreement that Michelle would have physical custody of their three year-old son. The separation agreement was incorporated into the divorce judgment. A month later, Jarrod changed his mind and asked the court to set aside the judgment. After a hearing, the court awarded custody to Jarrod, citing Michelle's marital adultery and lack of child care support. *Headrick v. Headrick* (2002) Alabama No. 2001196.

How to Negotiate

Negotiation can be simple and straightforward, or elaborate and complex. It can stay between the parents, or include third parties. It can take a few moments, or last several months. There's no right or wrong way to negotiate, only what works for you.

If the issue is simple and communication is good, try talking. "Why don't I take the kids on Saturday?" "Sure." For many decisions, the simpler the better.

If the issue is more complex, or communication is poor, consider writing a letter. In the letter explain the problem and what you propose to do about it. Writing a letter will help you organize your thoughts, and may be a better approach. You can even indicate a response date so the problem isn't ignored. And if the negotiations fail, you'll have the letter as documentation for court.

If the other parent ignores your offer, you can also suggest a face-to-face meeting. This can be a private meeting, or it can include third parties—such as lawyers. And if the parent refuses to meet, you will also have evidence of that refusal for court.

In fact, document all communications you have with the other parent. And if your lawyer sends or receives letters for you, insist on being given copies.

Finally, if you do reach an agreement, be sure to put it in writing and have everyone sign it. A written record of the agreement will avoid future confusion over what was agreed to.

 Richard A. Gardner, M.D., the author of dozens of divorce-related books including books on false abuse allegations and *Parental Alienation Syndrome (PAS)*, has a website where you can order his books—www.rgardner.com. The website also contains links to scholarly articles about PAS.

Negotiating Strategies

However you approach the other parent, you'll be pursuing a *negotiating strategy*. This strategy will dictate what you do and when you do it.

When negotiating, you should know that there are several theories of negotiation. One theory divides strategies into two categories:
- Position-based negotiation.
- Interest-based negotiation.

Position-Based Negotiation
In *position-based negotiation,* you immediately adopt an extreme position and then refuse to budge. As the bargaining proceeds, you demand everything, concede nothing, and threaten retaliation if you don't get your way. To get what you want, you bluff, threaten, lie, posture, and bully your opponent into submission. Position-based negotiation is hardball, where you attack and intimidate your adversary in order to win.

The main advantage of this negotiating style is that it works. The parent who can bargain for children by threatening and stonewalling gains an enormous strategic advantage.

The main disadvantage is that this style dramatically increases the hostilities. A "scorched earth" approach leaves little of the good will necessary for parents to continue a relationship afterwards.

Position-based negotiation is often adopted by parents who view custody as a zero-sum game, where one person's gain must necessarily be the other's loss.

Negotiating Strategies

Position-Based	vs.	Interest-Based
"win-lose"		"win-win"
hardball		softball
competitive		cooperative
extreme position		mutual interests
threaten, bluff, lie, posture, stonewall		honest, genuine, flexible, constructive
zero-sum		non zero-sum

Interest-Based Negotiation

In *interest-based negotiation,* you strive to change a "win-lose" result into "win-win." With this strategy, you immediately disclose all relevant information, fully explain your reasons, and then genuinely listen to the other parent as you search for an agreement that satisfies both your interests. This type of negotiation is cooperative, with each side offering constructive suggestions on how to solve the problem.

The main advantage of interest-based negotiation is that it dramatically lowers the conflict, allowing the parents to cooperatively work together in the future.

The main disadvantage is that both parents must genuinely want to participate. If one parent cooperates and the other one doesn't, the cooperative parent is vulnerable to being bullied or coerced by the non-cooperative parent.

Interest-based negotiation is an attempt to turn custody into a non zero-sum game, where parents create additional value by cooperative trading. In a sense, this strategy seeks not just to divide up the pie, but to actually make the pie bigger, and then to share the increase.

If Negotiation Fails

If negotiation fails, you have reached an *impasse*. An impasse is when you cannot come to an agreement.

Negotiation can fail for many reasons. Perhaps you approached the negotiations in good faith, but the other parent had a hidden agenda—such as wanting to hurt you or to live better at your expense. Or maybe one of you was too emotional to negotiate—letting feelings of insecurity or jealousy get in the way. Or maybe one of you is simply a litigious ex-spouse, viewing any negotiated agreement as a "giving in" or "surrendering" to the other parent.

Whatever the reason, if you still need a resolution, you will have to use another dispute resolution method. These include forms of alternative dispute resolution—such as mediation, arbitration, and conciliation—and litigation.

 Sheree and Keith had two children when they divorced, Ethan, age four, and Katherine, age two. The Arkansas divorce decree specified that Sheree have primary physical custody, but the parents shared the children equally until Ethan entered kindergarten. Sheree then remarried, and announced she was moving to Tennessee. Keith responded by asking for custody of the children. The Chancery Court awarded him custody, but the Court of Appeals reversed, finding that "children belong to a different family unit than they did when their parents lived together. The new family unit consists of the children and the custodial parent, and what is advantageous to the unit's members as a whole, to each of its members individually, and to the way they relate to each other and function together is in the best interests of the children." *Hollandsworth v. Knyzewski* (2002) Arkansas No. CA 01-982.

Mental Health Resources

If you need some advice, these official sites all feature solid information and links to other sites:

American Academy of Child and Adolescent Psychiatry
www.aacap.org
Click on "Facts for Families" for more information.

National Institute of Mental Health
www.nimh.nih.gov
This site has good information "For the Public."

U.S. Department of Health and Human Services, Substance Abuse and Mental Health Services Administration
www.mentalhealth.org
To select a topic, enter it in the search box.

American Psychological Association Consumer Help
helping.apa.org
This "consumer" site gives short information, free brochures, and a toll-free number to find a psychologist.

Substance Abuse and Mental Health Services Administration
www.samhsa.gov
Click on "Publications" for access to directories, help lines, publications, and more.

Chapter 10

Using a Mediator

✓ If you choose to negotiate, you don't have to go it alone. You can go into mediation where you discuss issues in a structured, formal process.

✓ *Mediation* has many advantages over litigation, but if the other parent does not cooperate, then mediation may not work.

✓ If you decide to go with mediation, choose the mediator with care. The skills of the mediator will influence the outcome.

✓ Besides mediation, other forms of *alternative dispute resolution* include *conciliation* and *arbitration,* though those forms are rarely used in custody disputes.

✓ If you need to resolve a dispute, but do not want your case to be tried by a public judge, you can opt out of the legal system entirely by hiring a private judge, who can resolve the case more quickly and privately.

Using a Mediator

If you cannot agree on custody of your children, you can try to resolve your dispute through *mediation.*

Mediation, or assisted negotiation, is one way to settle your dispute. In mediation, you meet with a third party, or mediator, who helps you discuss the issues and create a mutually acceptable agreement.

A mediator does not take sides or make a decision for the parents. Instead, the mediator helps you and the other parent find your own solution. If you come to an agreement during mediation, the agreement is written up and filed with the court—making it an official court order. If you do not agree, you can continue with the dispute by reverting to traditional litigation.

 "The bottom line is that a fair settlement agreement produced by mediation will save you money. This is the reason that mediation as a form of dispute resolution has become so popular and becomes more so each year." Judge Stewart, *California Divorce Handbook*

Advantages of Mediation

Mediation offers you the opportunity to:

Save Time and Money
Compared to full-blown litigation, mediation saves everyone time and money. Gone are the costs and delays associated with the adversarial system—discovery, hearings, motions, and trial. Instead, you meet quietly and privately with the mediator to discuss the situation. This informal approach avoids the interminable delays of waiting for an open courtroom, and relegates the lawyers to the limited—and much less expensive role—of an advisor. Mediation lets you reach an agreement sooner and keep more of your money.

Create a Better Agreement
Mediation can also lead to better agreements. When a judge
imposes a decision, you or the other parent are much less
likely to obey it than when you create the agreement yourself.
This higher rate of compliance results in less conflict
afterwards. Also, when you create your agreement, you can
customize it to fit your situation. In reality, most judges will
never get all the details right. And finally, when you make
your own agreement, you may be able to find a "win-win"
situation where you and the other parent each gets what is
most important.

Learn Problem-Solving Skills
By resolving the dispute through mediation, you also learn
valuable problem-solving skills. When custody is in dispute,
you do not just resolve the disagreement and move on. In
fact, you'll have to interact with the other parent for many
years afterwards. This makes it crucial that you and the
other parent learn how to settle future disagreements.
Mediation teaches a new model for communication that helps
avoid disputes and offers techniques for resolving problems
that are disputed.

 In 2001, 69% of American children lived with
two parents, 22% lived with only their mothers,
4% lived with only their fathers, and 4% lived
with neither of their parents. *America's
Children: Key National Indicators of Well-Being, 2002*

Disadvantages of Mediation

Unfortunately, mediation isn't for everyone, and it has several
disadvantages. Here's the downside:

The Other Parent May Not Cooperate
In mediation you cannot force the other side to participate. If
one parent refuses to participate, or if one parent does show
up but takes a completely unreasonable position; it won't
work. Mediators do not have the power to compel someone to
cooperate, and they cannot impose a decision. If the

Five years after Terry and Douglas married, they entered into a marital settlement agreement that Terry would have primary residential custody of their two children. Five months later, Douglas changed his mind, and asked the Circuit Court for custody. His petition was granted. Terry appealed, and the Court of Appeal reversed. *Wyckoff v. Wyckoff* (2002) Florida No. 2D00-5342.

mediation sessions don't result in an agreement, nothing tangible is accomplished.

The Other Parent May Dominate

One of the reasons why you may hire a lawyer is to equalize the relative bargaining positions. If one parent is exceptionally domineering or manipulative, the lawyers can help to offset the imbalance. But when the lawyers are removed—as in mediation—you and the other parent are right back to your former roles. This lets someone who lies or hides information effectively sabotage the negotiations, or bring about a result that would not have occurred otherwise. The lack of extensive pretrial discovery is one reason why mediation costs less, but discovery is also an important check-and-balance in the adversarial system.

The Other Parent May Scare You

In mediation, a parent who has been victimized by prior acts of abuse or violence will lose some protection. Because mediation usually brings the parents together in the same room, a parent who is afraid for his or her own safety may be intimidated and unable to fully participate in the process. Because of this, some states allow the parents to be excused from court-required mediation, while others allow each parent to meet with the mediator privately.

What Happens When You Mediate

You typically get involved in mediation when the court orders you to go, or when you and the other parent agree to give it a try. Either way, the process is usually the same.

Preparation

Before attending the first session, you want to decide the issues to negotiate and the obstacles to reaching a settlement. Preparation includes choosing what you consider the best result, the next best result, and your bottom-line position. You also want to consider the strengths and weaknesses of your arguments.

Preliminary Meeting

At the first meeting, the mediator needs to get everyone organized. This is usually a joint session where the mediator describes the process. The mediator will explain that his or her role is to keep the debate civilized, moderate discussions, keep the negotiations going, and bring the process to a close. The mediator may also gather basic information from each parent.

You may be asked for a brief statement of your position and a summary of your arguments supporting your position. At this point, the mediator will begin to focus the issues down to specific questions that need to be addressed. A good mediator will take control of the process and not let the discussion disintegrate into squabbling and name-calling.

Joint Sessions

After the preliminary meeting, you may return to the mediator's office for a series of joint sessions. Depending on the mediator, these sessions may last as little as 30 minutes,

"Consider letting your children participate in at least one of your sessions, if you are not locked in battle. It will allay their fears about what is going on and will give them a chance to speak, be heard, and thereby gain a sense of control over their lives. My children were surprised at the orderliness of mediation. They had envisioned a long table where we sparred verbally with mediators trying to control us. They were surprised about the small room, the informal setting, and the fact that the mediator was in charge." Vicki Lansky, *Vicki Lansky's Divorce Book for Parents*

or as long as two hours. And they may conclude within a few weeks, or stretch out over several months.

In these sessions, you will discuss the problems. Usually, each parent is allowed to talk without interruption and is given a chance to express concerns. Every issue is on the table during the meetings, including school involvement, discipline techniques, medical needs, and more. By letting you and the other parent talk, the mediator seeks to help you understand each other and reach a satisfactory agreement.

How to Decide If Mediation Is Right For You

1. You are both willing to participate.

2. You are both willing to compromise.

3. You are both able to clearly communicate your goals.

4. Neither of you can dominate the other.

5. Neither of you is too emotional to participate.

Private Sessions
You may also have private sessions with the mediator. These sessions allow you to talk privately and to "sound out" a possible settlement offer without revealing the plan to the other parent. If necessary, the mediator can shuttle back-and-forth with the offers until an agreement is reached.

Agreement
If you and the other parent can reach an agreement, the mediator will write it down in a *memorandum*. This document is then submitted to the judge, who generally approves it and enters it into the court record—making it an official order. Because this document is so important, you may wish to ask an attorney to review it prior to signing it.

Impasse or Court Recommendation
If you cannot reach an agreement, you have reached an *impasse*. If the mediation is private, you can pursue other

Henry and Marjorie married in North Carolina then moved to Maine, where their daughter was born. When the baby was seven months old, Marjorie took her to North Carolina and did not return. The next year, Henry filed for divorce in Maine. Two years later, when their divorce was final, Marjorie was granted primary physical residence of their daughter, and Henry's visitation was sent to binding arbitration. Marjorie and Henry also agreed that Maine would keep jurisdiction. The next year, Marjorie asked a North Carolina district court to assume jurisdiction and to amend the Maine visitation order. She said the visitation schedule interfered with her daughter's schooling in North Carolina. Henry moved to dismiss Marjorie's motion. The North Carolina judge wrote to the Maine judge and suggested that North Carolina had jurisdiction to modify the Maine visitation order. The Maine judge disagreed, insisting that Maine continued to have jurisdiction. North Carolina then denied Henry's motion to dismiss, and declared that it had jurisdiction to enter custody and visitation orders. Back in Maine, Henry filed a motion to clarify the visitation schedule and Marjorie responded by asking the court to decline jurisdiction and defer all future hearings to North Carolina. The Maine court concluded that "North Carolina is the more convenient and more appropriate forum to determine [visitation]." *Shanoski v. Miller* (2001) 2001 Me. 139, 780 A.2d 275, 2001 ME 139.

approaches—such as litigation. But if the mediation is court-ordered, several things may happen.

In some states, the mediation is confidential, and you will then proceed with litigation. In other states, the mediator is asked by the judge to make a *recommendation,* and this recommendation will influence the judge's final decision. In still other states, the mediator can be called to the witness stand and asked to testify about the case. If you are in a court where the mediation is not truly confidential, you are in *muscle mediation,* where the mediator can coerce an agreement if the parents can't agree on their own.

Types of Mediation

When you engage in mediation, you can choose between two types.

Facilitative mediation

Facilitative mediation gives you maximum control over the outcome. In this type of mediation, the mediator's role is limited to ensuring that all relevant information is exchanged between you and the other parent and that settlement offers are transmitted back-and-forth. The mediator may suggest solutions if you and the other parent seem to be stuck over an issue.

Mediation withdrawal. Many states allow parents to be excused from mediation if there has been a history of abuse or violence, or if mediation is deemed inappropriate under the circumstances.

Evaluative mediation

Evaluative mediation is more structured, with the mediator actively inserting his or her own opinion in the negotiations. This type of aggressive mediation often occurs when you and the other parent are deeply entrenched and have widely different custodial views. In this process, the mediator may "push" you to settle by pointing out the flaws in your position.

Choosing a Mediator

Whoever mediates your dispute is important. Because you and the other parent cannot agree, you are looking to a mediator for help in reaching an agreement. This makes the skills and abilities of the mediator crucial to your success.

If your state requires mediation, you may end up with a court-appointed mediator. If your state does not require mediation, or if you choose to move your dispute away from court, you can hire a private mediator to help you.

Court-Appointed Mediators
Court-appointed mediators sometimes work right in the courthouse, and you may be able to see one by just walking down the hall. These mediators typically are limited to giving you only a few hours of time, and to only mediating the most basic issues of custody and visitation.

Because court-appointed mediators rarely charge more than a small fee, you can save a lot of money with them. Unfortunately, in some states, the mediator may be asked to make a recommendation, which will put pressure on the parents to reach an agreement during the sessions.

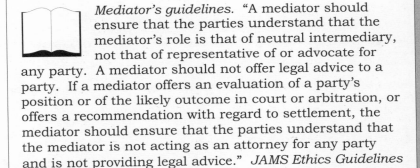

Mediator's guidelines. "A mediator should ensure that the parties understand that the mediator's role is that of neutral intermediary, not that of representative of or advocate for any party. A mediator should not offer legal advice to a party. If a mediator offers an evaluation of a party's position or of the likely outcome in court or arbitration, or offers a recommendation with regard to settlement, the mediator should ensure that the parties understand that the mediator is not acting as an attorney for any party and is not providing legal advice." *JAMS Ethics Guidelines for Mediators*

Private Mediators
Private mediators are not limited to helping you with just the basic agreement. You can hire a private mediator who will spend as long as you need, and who will see you at your convenience. Also, a private mediator is not going to be asked by the court to make a custody recommendation, so your mediation sessions will stay private.

When you hire a mediator, you have many choices. Therapists often deal better with the emotional aspects, while attorneys or former judges will usually know current family law. If you can't find one person who does both, you can hire an attorney-therapist team.

Questions to Ask a Mediator

If you have a choice in mediators, there are some questions you should ask:

Experience. How much experience does the mediator have with the issues you will be negotiating?

Success rate. How many disputes has the mediator resolved successfully, and how many have not been settled in mediation?

Style. Does the mediator step back and let the parents work it out, or does the mediator actively insert himself into the process?

Prior contacts. Has the mediator worked with any of the parties before, including any of the attorneys hired by either parent?

How the mediator answers these questions will reveal whether he or she is the right mediator for you.

What Mediation Costs

Generally, mediation costs between $200 to $300 per hour. The overall cost will depend on many things, including the style of mediation and how long you spend in mediation.

If you and the other parent prepare well and use the mediation process efficiently, you can reach an agreement in less than an hour. On the other hand, if you arrive at the mediator's office unprepared and do not try to bring the dispute to an end, you could spend 15 hours or more before reaching an impasse.

 Court-appointed mediators often charge a minimum amount—about $35 per hour. Private mediators charge more and often base their fees on their professional background. For example, a therapist or counselor may cost $75 to $100 per hour, while an attorney might bill at $150 to $250 per hour.

When Edward and Barbara divorced, Barbara was granted physical custody of their three year-old child. Two years later, Edward sought to modify custody, and a court-appointed evaluator recommended that Edward be given physical custody. Instead, the court increased his visitation. Nine months later, Edward again tried to modify the orders, and this time, the court gave him sole custody. The court also ordered that a court-appointed psychiatrist evaluate Barbara, and barred her from asking for more time with her child until the psychologist had completed his evaluation. On appeal, the Court of Appeals reversed the mandatory psychiatric evaluation, but affirmed the decision to award sole custody to Edward, explaining that Barbara was "emotionally unsupportive of the child's needs," among other reasons. *Janik v. Janik* (2000) 61 Conn.App. 175, 763 A.2d 65.

Using Lawyers in Mediation

When you go to mediation, you may want the final agreement to be as close as possible to what a court would order. The problem is, most people don't know what that is. In the heat of negotiations, one parent may demand something totally outrageous, and the other parent won't even know it.

That's why—even though you go to mediation—you may need a lawyer. Your lawyer won't be in the mediation room with you, but can act as an advisor by answering questions and reviewing any agreements before you sign them.

By hiring a lawyer, you learn what is a reasonable agreement. This will help you negotiate with the other parent while still keeping your agreement close to the likely outcome in court.

If you decide to hire a lawyer, or if you already have one, be aware that many divorce lawyers do not believe in mediation. If you want the mediation to succeed and your lawyer is not supportive, replace your lawyer.

Improving Your Chances in Mediation

If you want mediation to succeed, there are things you can do.

First, consider the timing. There are moments in every dispute when settlement may be possible, and moments when settlement is unlikely. If you are considering mediation, you have to decide if this is the best time to attempt to settle.

Mediation in a Nutshell

Choosing a Divorce Mediator, Diane Neumann, Owlet, $16.95. Written by the past president of the *Academy of Family Mediators,* this book explains how mediation works, the types of disputes that are appropriate for mediation, and how to find the right mediator.

The Divorce Mediation Handbook, Paula James, Jossey-Bass, $16.00. This well-organized book explains the entire process of mediation, beginning with the decision to engage in mediation, and ending with the completed agreement. The author is a family law attorney who has mediated more than 500 divorces.

A Guide to Divorce Mediation, Gary J. Friedman, Jack Himmelstein, Workman Publishing, $12.97. Friedman, a former trial attorney, illustrates the mediation process by showing how 11 different couples fared when they chose mediation over litigation.

Using Divorce Mediation, Katherine E. Stoner, Nolo Press, $29.95. This comprehensive book from *Nolo Press* helps you understand the entire divorce mediation process— from finding the right mediator to writing your final settlement.

Second, behave yourself. It is not easy to resolve a dispute, and you will need to be patient, persistent, calm, and flexible. Resist making ultimatums, and don't be alarmed if the other parent issues ultimatums. And when you make an offer that is accepted, don't change your mind. State what you want, and then be ready to sign an agreement that gives you what you want.

Third, allow the mediator to control the process. The point of mediation is to move to a new, business-like approach to dealing with the other parent. The mediator may well have had a lot deal of experience with divorcing couples, and he or she can help you learn a new style of solving disputes.

And finally, be prepared to give on some issues. There are always issues that are more important to one parent than the other. The mediation process will highlight those areas. A good, workable agreement will give each of you the things you want the most.

Alternative Dispute Resolution

In addition to mediation, there are other forms of *Alternative Dispute Resolution (ADR)*.

ADR is a collection of techniques that help you settle your dispute. Other forms of ADR include:
- Arbitration.
- Conciliation.
- Private Courts

Arbitration

Arbitration is when you submit your dispute to a third party for a resolution. The arbitrator listens to each parent, the witnesses, reviews the evidence, and then makes a decision. In arbitration, you present your case just as if you had gone to trial, and the arbitrator makes a ruling just like a judge.

Arbitration has several advantages, chief among them that it's often less costly and much faster than a formal court proceeding. Unfortunately, arbitration still requires you to present your case, which means spending additional time and money. And for arbitration to be useful, both sides must agree beforehand not to appeal the decision—which is not always best.

Alternative Dispute Resolution

Association for Conflict Resolution (ACR)
1527 New Hampshire Ave., NW
Washington, DC 20036
(202) 667-9700
The *Association for Conflict Resolution* is a merged
organization of the *Academy of Family Mediators, Conflict
Resolution Education Network,* and *Society of Professionals
in Dispute Resolution.* This group represents almost 700
mediators in the United States, and can provide a referral
to a mediator in your area. The group also publishes
dozens of books and tapes on conflict resolution.

American Association for Marriage and Family Therapy
112 South Alfred Street
Alexandria, VA 22314
(703) 838-9808
www.aamft.org
The *American Association for Marriage and Family
Therapy (AAMFT)* is an association that represents more
than 23,000 marriage and family therapists. Clinical
Members have met the highest standards of education
and clinical experience. They can refer to you a local
therapist, and they also publish a variety of brochures,
books, pamphlets, and videotapes about marriage and
family therapy.

Association of Family and Conciliation Courts
6515 Grand Teton Plaza
Suite 210
Madison, WI 53719
(608) 664-3750
www.afccnet.org
The *Association of Family and Conciliation Courts (AFCC)*
is a group of family court judges, lawyers, mediators,
mental health professionals, court administrators, and
educators who work with families in conflict. AFCC
publishes *Family Court Review,* a quarterly newsletter
that covers family courts.

Conciliation

Another form of ADR is *conciliation*. Conciliation is very similar to mediation, and in some courts, there may not be any meaningful difference between the two.

Generally, conciliation is when you and the other parent meet separately with a conciliator, who tries to help you reach an agreement. Depending on the court, the conciliator may first meet with the attorneys, then with each parent separately. In some courts, the conciliator may also speak with the children. After talking with everyone, the conciliator will call everyone back for a summation of the problem and a review of various ways to resolve the dispute.

As with mediation, if you reach an agreement in the conciliator's office, the conciliator will write it up and ask both parties to sign it. This agreement will go to the judge, who will likely enter it into the court record—making it an official court order.

The main advantage of conciliation is that it's low-key. If an agreement is reached, you save enormous expense and the emotional strain of a full-blown trial. And if it doesn't work, you can still proceed to mediation.

Private Courts

If the other forms of ADR don't work for you, you have yet one more option—*private judging.*

You can hire a private judge, or "rent-a-judge," to do the same thing a public court judge does. The "courtroom" may be a real courtroom, or a conference room in an office building. And the judge who listens to your case may be a retired judge with plenty of experience in hearing the same kind of case you have.

If you hire a private judge, you can wait until it's time for trial, or start with the initial pleadings. Hired judges can rule on pleadings, motions, discovery, and more. And if you disagree with the decision you can even appeal to the public courts.

To move your case into a private court, both sides have to agree. Usually, the attorney for one side suggests the idea, and the other party concurs. You can agree to split the cost, or one side can cover the fees.

 "A rent-a-judge is a retired judge who sits by agreement of the parties and is given, for that case, all the powers of an active judge. Unlike an active judge, the retired judge is compensated by the parties at a rate of at least $200 per hour with no overhead attached." Judge Stewart, *California Divorce Handbook*

Advantages of Private Courts

You may choose to bypass the public court system for reasons such as the following:

To Save Stress
The legal community has a saying, "Justice delayed is justice denied." Nowhere is that more true than with child custody. If the dispute drags on for three or four years—whatever the original point—the damage to the children will far outweigh the gain. In contrast to the regular court system where it may be years before trial, in a private court the judge can hear the case quickly, make a decision, and everyone can move on in their lives.

To Save Money
This ability to decide a case quickly offers more than emotional savings—it offers real financial savings, as well. In the public courts, the parties will typically have to pay for their experts to appear on short notice—a very expensive option. Also, in the public courts, the trial may be stopped as other cases intrude on the judge's time, forcing the litigants to miss more work days to return to court. And finally, a public court trial will involve time-consuming legal procedure, slowing the case down and making the parties pay higher legal fees. None of this is true in a private court. The parties will have an early and well-anticipated trial date. The judge will give his or her full attention to the case without

interruption, and the parties can simplify the procedure, thus creating a shortened, abbreviated trial.

To Keep It Private

You may also want to take your case to a private court to do just that—keep it private. Because public court trials are normally open to the public, the decisions of the judge become part of the public record—available to anyone who wants to read it. This has certain advantages, such as protecting the public by revealing the biases of a given judge, but it also exposes the most intimate details of your personal life. By taking your dispute to a private court, you can maintain confidentiality.

To Get a Better Judge

If you've ever been in front of a judge before, you probably know there are good judges and there are bad judges. In many court systems, family law is not a sought-after assignment, and the judge who hears your case may be the most inexperienced judge around. This can lead to a legal mistake that may force one of the parents to undertake a costly and time-consuming appeal—not to mention the potential harm to the children. In a private court, the judge must be approved by both sides, so you can research his or her public record to ensure that the judge is unbiased and has plenty of experience with cases similar to yours.

 "Private judging creates a situation where the wealthy can avoid the burdens of the public courts and purchase speedy and, for them, relatively affordable justice... The unspoken message [is] that while justice is blind and available to all, it is readily accessible only at a certain monetary price."
Justice Irving R. Kaufman

Disadvantages of Private Courts

There are also plenty of disadvantages when resolving a child custody dispute, and for the following reasons, few parents opt for private courts.

Choosing a private judge can save each side thousands of dollars. For example, if each parent pays half, a three-hour hearing can cost as little as $600.

You Will Need a Lawyer

Because a private trial is still a trial, many of the rules of evidence and civil procedure remain the same. This means you will probably still need a lawyer to represent you.

You Will Lose Leverage

If your goal is to pressure the other parent—either by threatening to expose secrets, or by engaging in endless litigation—then a private court is not for you. When you take your dispute to a hired judge, you lose the ability to force the other parent into a favorable settlement. In fact, it could be argued that private courts are only useful when both parents are acting in good faith and genuinely want to resolve the dispute fairly. If your goals are anything else, a private court may not be helpful.

You Are Buying Justice

And finally, many opponents of private courts argue that they only widen the split between rich and poor, allowing the wealthy to secure justice quickly, while relegating the poor to an overburdened public court system. If you can afford a private judge, this may not seem like a disadvantage, but some insist that private courts drain quality judges from the public court system and deprive the public from the valuable precedent which helps evolve contemporary law.

 When Melvin and Jolene divorced, the district court gave Jolene residential custody of their four children. When two of the children were adults, and the other two, Clayton and Jonathan, were ages 14 and 16 respectively, Melvin filed a motion for custody of Jonathan. Jolene responded by asking for more child support. After the hearing, the district court denied Melvin's custody motion, but reduced his child support to $300 per month. *In re Marriage of Karst* (2001) Kansas No. 85,494.

Where to Find a Mediator or Judge

Judicial Arbitration and Mediation Service/Endispute
(800) 352-5267
www.jamsadr.com
JAMS is a large, well-known service that employs hundreds of mediators, arbitrators, private judges, facilitators, special masters, and referees. JAMS can send a judge to your city, or you can travel to one of their offices in more than 20 cities around the country.

For the use of a private judge, JAMS charges a professional/hearing fee, which varies depending upon the judge, and a non-refundable case management fee. Expect your fees to be $500+ per hour. JAMS reports that cases heard by them have a 90% resolution rate—whatever that means.

National Arbitration Forum
P.O. Box 50191
Minneapolis, MN 55405
(800) 474-2371
www.arbitration-forum.com
The *National Arbitration Forum* is a network of former judges, lawyers, and law professors who act as mediators, arbitrators, or private judges. NAF claims each neutral has more than 15 years experience.

To hire a mediator, you submit a form to NAF, who then assigns a mediator and sends the information to the other parent. For a case involving up to three people, NAF charges $75 for filing, $55 for administration, and $100 for scheduling a session. The hourly mediation fee is in addition to the above.

Chapter 11

Creating a Parenting Plan

✓ No court order can account for the complexity of raising children after divorce. That's why you create a parenting plan.

✓ A *parenting plan* is an agreement that describes how to handle specific issues.

✓ A parenting plan can be as simple as a few sentences, or as formal as a notarized contract. It can be a quick note, or a long novel.

✓ When you create a parenting plan, you customize the plan to include as many—or as few—issues as you want.

✓ The ideal parenting plan achieves a balance between too much and too little detail.

✓ A good parenting plan is invaluable, because the divorce may last longer than the marriage.

Parenting Apart

When parents live together, they raise their children together. When one parent is working or sick, the other can care for the children. When one parent is angry or depressed, the other can intercede to protect the children. This *parental alliance* allows the parents to complement each other's strengths and insulate each other's weaknesses.

But when you separate or divorce, this alliance is broken. The arrangement that allowed you to work together has changed. The old system is gone.

Now, you must create a new structure to raise the children. This rearrangement of responsibilities goes by many names, including *co-parenting, parenting apart, parenting agreement,* or—more simply—*parenting plan.*

Whatever it's called, it simply means that you have to identify the discrete parenting issues and decide how to handle them.

The issues generally fall into two categories:
- Decision-making issues.
- Living arrangements.

Shadow of the Law

Believe it or not, the courts actually encourage you to create your own parenting plan. Judges know that if they impose a custody decision, it's much less likely to be obeyed, but if you create your own agreement, it's much more likely to be obeyed.

That's why custody laws permit parents to create an agreement on how to raise their children. However, while you can create your own agreement, you can't make it legally binding. Only the court has the final say on what will happen to the children.

To make a parenting plan legally binding, it must be submitted to the judge, who will accept or reject it. This supervision by the judge means that—when creating a plan—

you must create an agreement that is acceptable to the judge. When you negotiate with one eye on the law, you are said to be bargaining in the *shadow of the law.*

 One month before their son Jacob was born, Michael filed for divorce from Tammie. In his divorce papers, he asked for custody of the unborn child. Tammie responded that she wanted custody. After two years of litigation, on the eve of a custody hearing, Michael and Tammie announced they had reached an agreement where Tammie would be the primary residential custodian and Michael would have visitation as described in the Circuit Court standard visitation schedule. However, Tammie decided she didn't like the agreement and refused to sign. Her lawyer quit. Michael then asked the court to enforce the agreement anyway, and the court did. *Gullett v. Gullett* (1999) 992 S. W.2d 866.

What a Parenting Plan Will Do

There are a number of advantages to making a parenting plan. By creating one, you can:

Reduce Conflict
Negotiating a parenting plan requires each parent to think through the issues that are important. This activity directs you away from blaming behavior and towards a constructive goal. By listing your priorities, you may discover you have some misconceptions about the other parent—and you may be surprised when you unexpectedly agree on some issue.

Increase Fairness
Everyone knows what's most important to them, and when you compare priorities, you may realize you don't have mutually exclusive goals. In negotiating a parenting plan, you may be able to achieve those items you regard as most important, while agreeing to the items most important to the other parent. This "win-win" result lets each of you achieve an agreement you feel is fair.

When designing your plan, consider how resilient the children are. In *Second Chances,* Judith Wallerstein reports that flexible children are much more likely to succeed with a schedule that requires a lot of exchanges. "Not all children have the flexibility to go back and forth between homes and to adjust to two different environments. Indeed, a child's basic temperament is a major contributing factor to his or her adjustment. Children who succeed... have an elusive characteristic that we are not used to considering in psychological assessments-flexibility."

Account for the Uniqueness of Your Situation

No two children are the same, and no two family situations are the same. When third parties—such as judges or mediators—make custody decisions, they necessarily revert to standard agreements and schedules. This one-size-fits-all approach happens because others don't have the time to learn about your unique family.

Since no one knows your children better than you, a parenting plan can deal with any special circumstances you choose. Parents can accommodate the psychological makeup of their children, or allow for a child's particular hobbies or interests, or even account for unpredictable work demands.

Avoid Court

A final reason to create your own parenting plan is that—by making the decisions yourself—you avoid having the judge do it. Judges make mistakes, too.

Also, when you go to court, you spend more time and money to arrive at a decision. Custody law is complex, family courts are crowded, and you will expend a lot of money to have the legal system run your life.

What a Parenting Plan Will Not Do

Of course, while a parenting plan can make your life easier, it won't do everything. Among the things a plan won't do are:

Resolve Incompatible Values or Parenting Styles
No parenting plan—no matter how detailed or inclusive—can resolve the dilemma of incompatible values and beliefs. While one parent may prefer that the children have plenty of freedom and few restrictions, the other parent may want the children to lead highly structured, organized lives.

If you were incompatible before the divorce, it's a safe bet you will be afterwards. It's unrealistic to imagine that a piece of paper will change the core values of an adult. A parenting plan can influence the behaviors of the other person, but it will not change their beliefs.

Shield the Children from the Other Parent
Practically speaking, there's not much you can do when the children are with the other parent. If that individual is unstable or dysfunctional, a parenting plan will not buffer the children from the harmful effects. A parenting plan does not give you control over them, and it won't provide a way to shield the children from a parent who is depressed, abusive, or neglectful.

Making Changes to Your Parenting Plan

As the needs and interests of your children change over the years, you'll need to update your parenting plan.

When James and Katherine divorced, they agreed James would have custody of their three children and Katherine would have plenty of visitation, including six weeks during the summer, alternate holidays, and "free, open, liberal, unrestricted [telephone] access." Katherine also could visit the children when she was in town. However, when Katherine called the children, James hung up on her, and when Katherine reserved seats on a flight for the children to visit at Christmas, James blocked the visit. Katherine returned to court, and the court gave her primary custody of the two youngest children. *Kelly v. Joseph* (2002) Alaska No. S-10116.

Here are some examples of the nearly limitless reasons why you might need to change your parenting plan:

- One parent moves away.
- One parent starts a new job with different work hours.
- One parent remarries.
- The child joins a team or other organized activity.
- The child gets a part-time job or begins dating.
- New, unexpected issues suddenly become important.

Because it's impossible to anticipate everything involved in raising children, you can establish a periodic review of the plan. The review can be scheduled for regular times, and/or triggered by certain events.

Five Big No-No's With Your Children

1. Don't give them messages to give to the other parent.

2. Don't recruit them to be your confidant.

3. Don't tell them what you really think of the other parent.

4. Don't assume they'll stay the same. The arrangement that worked fine when they were in preschool won't cut it when they're teenagers.

5. Don't compete for them with the other parent. Each parent is naturally better at certain things.

For example, because your life will be uncertain immediately following a separation or divorce, you can review the plan every few months. Then, once a new equilibrium is established, the review can occur less frequently—say once a year. Also, you can automatically review the plan when a specific event occur, such as when the children begin school, or when they become old enough to drive.

A parenting plan is a work-in-progress, and the benefit of making the plan is that it gives you a place to start.

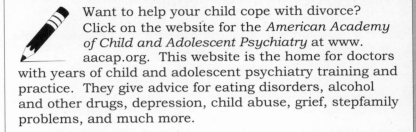

Want to help your child cope with divorce? Click on the website for the *American Academy of Child and Adolescent Psychiatry* at www. aacap.org. This website is the home for doctors with years of child and adolescent psychiatry training and practice. They give advice for eating disorders, alcohol and other drugs, depression, child abuse, grief, stepfamily problems, and much more.

Writing and Filing Your Parenting Plan

If you create a parenting plan, you can write it up and submit it to the court. Then, if the judge has no objections, it will become an official order.

It may seem unnecessary to file your plan with the court since you've already agreed, but there are good reasons to do so.

First, if the agreement is not signed by the judge, it cannot be enforced. If one parent violates the agreement, the other parent has no recourse except to file a lawsuit.

Second, if your agreement is not approved by the court, it does not change the underlying legal obligation. For example, if there is already a child support order in place, and you agree to change it, the legal requirement is not changed. That could lead to a very large over– or under-payment a few years down the road.

And third, if you include the reasons for your agreement in the court-filed document, it becomes more difficult for someone to subsequently claim he or she was coerced into making the agreement.

If you don't know your original case number and can't find your original papers, call either your attorney or the other parent's attorney. If no one had an attorney, then go to the county clerk's office and ask to see your file.

What to Put In the Agreement

Basically, you can put anything you want into the agreement.
Here are some basic items to include:

*   The original case name and case number.
*   The names, ages, and addresses of everyone.
*   A statement indicating each parent agrees to the terms of
    the agreement.
*   A statement indicating each parent knows his or her
    rights and obligations under the law.
*   A statement indicating neither parent was subject to
    coercion or duress in making the agreement.
*   That the agreement is in the best interests of the children
    and will meet their needs.

Additionally, you can add anything you want. If you want to
indicate who will take the children to school in the morning,
or who will pay the dentist, you can do so.

After Suzanne and Adrian divorced, Suzanne
took their son, Maximillian, to Italy. Before
she left, she and Adrian agreed that Adrian
would have visitation with Maximillian that
Christmas. The visitation didn't happen, and Adrian filed
a contempt complaint against Suzanne. Suzanne
responded that Adrian broke the agreement by filing a
contempt against her when they had agreed to attempt to
settle their disputes first. During the hearings, Suzanne
admitted that she wanted to remain in Italy with
Maximillian indefinitely. The probate court allowed
Suzanne to take Maximillian to Italy temporarily, but
ordered her to post a bond to ensure she would return for
the trial. Suzanne went back to Italy with Maximillian.
Convinced that Suzanne would not return, Adrian
secured a temporary custody order for Maximillian.
Suzanne ignored the order, and when the case finally
came to trial, didn't show up. The probate court found
Suzanne in contempt of court and awarded sole custody
to Adrian with supervised visits to Suzanne. The court
also froze Maximillian's passport and awarded Adrian
$35,000 in legal fees. *Hernandez v. Branciforte* (2002)
Massachusetts No. 99-P-2202.

The important thing to remember is that the agreement must spell out clearly and simply what your intentions are. That way, if either parent decides to contest it later, the agreement is more likely to withstand judicial scrutiny.

Four Tips for Writing Your Own Agreement

1. Have a lawyer draft the document in proper legal form.

2. State the specific reasons for the modification in the agreement.

3. Make sure the agreement is dated and signed by both parents.

4. File the agreement with the court.

Children's Developmental Stages

It may seem obvious, but an often overlooked fact when creating an agreement is that children grow older each year. The plan that worked fine when they were in preschool won't work when they're teenagers. So, when making your plan, consider the needs and interests of the children at their various ages and stages of development.

Here's a brief summary on the developmental stages of children and how it affects custody arrangements:

Birth to 3 Years Old
Infants and very young children are completely helpless, and must rely on their parents for everything. A parent who cares for a small child must provide food, clothing, a safe physical environment, constant attention, love, and nurturing—as well as handle the more mundane tasks such as changing diapers and toilet training.

Quality of care and consistency of care are the two most important factors when designing a parenting plan for very young children. If the parents are highly flexible and cooperative, a bird's nesting arrangement—where the children stay in one home and the parents move in and out from a separate apartment or home—is ideal. If the parents live nearby, joint physical custody may work, but the parents should buy the same crib, blanket, highchair, and so on. If the parents are not equally interested in caring for the child, one parent should be the primary caretaker, and the other parent should visit frequently—one to two hours three days a week.

 During their marriage, Justin and Melissa lived in Idaho, and had one child, Megan. When Megan was four, Melissa's mother came to Idaho, and without Justin's knowledge, picked up Megan and took her to Michigan, where Melissa joined them. The next day, Justin filed for divorce and asked for custody of Megan. The Magistrate gave Justin "physical custody eighty percent of the time and Melissa physical custody twenty percent of the time." Melissa appealed, but lost. *King v. King* (2002) Idaho No. 27271.

3 to 5 Years Old

Preschool-aged children can accomplish some tasks on their own, but still need their parents to provide a safe and supportive environment. Parents must provide the child's meals, clothes, books, and toys—as well as an unending supply of love and nurturing. Because preschoolers are very physically active, parents will need to keep up with them.

Consistency of care is the most important need for preschoolers, and parents should consider the same arrangements recommended for younger children, for the same reasons. Because preschoolers have a limited grasp of time, parents with joint custody may want to use visual aids—such as large wall calendars and color-coded lunch boxes—to remind the child when it's time to go with the other parent. If one parent becomes the primary caretaker, the other should consider taking the child for a minimum of two full weekends a month. Parents should try to maintain similar routines for bedtimes, TV-watching, meals, and so on.

Single Parent Websites

These sites have a little of everything—articles, forums, chat rooms, and even personal ads from other single parents.

Making Lemonade
www.makinglemonade.com
A fun site with good links, short articles, and active forums on a variety of subjects.

Single Mothers Online
www.singlemothers.org
The website of Andrea Engber, the founder of the *National Organization of Single Mothers (NOSM),* this site hosts an active forum and has extensive resources.

American Coalition for Fathers and Children
www.acfc.org
This organization promotes shared parenting and joint custody. The website is good starting point for single fathers.

Single Parent Central
www.singleparentcentral.com
On this website, the "Government Resources" link leads to good information, and the personals drop you into www.one-and-only.com, a dating site.

Family sites
Many general-purpose family sites have special sections for single parents, including *Parent Soup* at www. parentsoup.com and *Parents Place* at www.parentsplace. com.

Dating sites
When you look for a date on major sites, you can specify you are a single parent, or you can select other single parents. Try visiting *Match* at www.match.com, *Love@aol. com* at webcenter.match.love.aol.com, *Date* at www.date. com, or the *Yahoo!* personal ads at personals.yahoo.com.

5 to 12 Years Old

Grade-schoolers and preteens still require their parents to meet their physical needs, but now they have more complex emotional needs. On the one hand, parents must be ready to give both unstinting reassurance and guidance, while on the other, they must allow the children to start to pull away, beginning to lead lives independent of parental control. Parents must be ready to actively participate in their children's school and extracurricular activities during these years.

Consistent contact with both parents is the most important consideration for children of this age. Because children can readily understand and follow schedules, joint custody is ideal. If the parents do not want joint custody, they should each plan to spend a significant amount of time with the children.

12 to 18 Years Old

Teenagers require much less active care from their parents— but much more patience. Parents of teenage children must learn to gradually relinquish control over their children's lives, yet still provide supervision. Parents can expect that teenage children will challenge their authority in surprising and exasperating ways. At this age, children are struggling with both hormonal changes and feelings of wanting to be accepted by their peer group, so parents must allow them the limited freedom to arrange their own social lives.

Allowing teenagers to make their own decisions is the most important factor when creating a parenting plan for them. They will want to choose where they live. Because teenagers are very independent, joint custody tends to create logistical problems for them—such as having to carry clothes and schoolbooks back and forth between the two homes—so they often choose sole custody for purely practical reasons. Also, because the teenager is spending less time with both parents, the noncustodial parent can expect to see less of their child during this time.

Children's Books

At Daddy's on Saturdays, Linda Walvoord Girard, Judith Friedman (Illustrator), Albert Whitman and Co., $5.95. This gentle tale is filled with appealing watercolors that will help children cope with divorce.

The Boys and Girls Book About Divorce, Richard A. Gardner, Bantam, $5.99. At 150+ pages, this clearly-written divorce book is more suited for children who read at the "young adult" level.

Dear Mr. Henshaw, Beverly Cleary, Demco Media, $9.60. The famed children's book author has written an excellent book that describes the daily problems of a ten-year-old boy as he copes with his parents' divorce. A Newberry Medal winner.

Dinosaurs Divorce, Marc Tolon Brown, Laurence Krasny Brown, Little Brown and Co., $6.95. This classic book addresses divorce issues through the drawings of very humorous dinosaurs.

Divorce, Fred Rogers, Jim Judkis (Illustrator), Putnam, $5.99. Mr. Rogers (yes, the Mr. Rogers), gives out much-needed information for children about how divorce affects them. Recommended by *American Bookseller* and *School Library Journal.*

Mom and Dad Don't Live Together Anymore, Kathy Stinson and Nancy Lou Reynolds (Illustrator), Firefly Books, $5.95. A short picture book that helps young children cope with divorce.

Chapter 12

Creating a Custody Schedule

✓ After resolving decision-making issues, you still have to decide the living arrangements of the children.

✓ A *schedule* answers the question: where will the children live?

✓ There is no correct or incorrect schedule. Different families will create different schedules.

✓ One option, an alternate weekend schedule, allows the children to live primarily with one parent, and to visit the other parent every other weekend.

✓ Parents often use vacation time to give the noncustodial parent more time with the children.

Dividing the Child

There are only so many hours in a child's life.

When you share children, you must decide where the children will be each part of the day. Practically speaking, if the children are with one parent, they are not with the other. And, of course, when they are in school, that time is not being spent with either parent.

Creating a schedule means dividing a child's life.

Think of the child's life as a pie from which you and the other parent are each taking a slice:

Dividing the Child

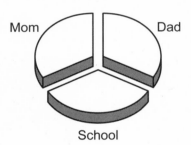

Mom   Dad

School

Because there is only so much time to divide, you will have to share. That's why some parents look at custody as a zero-sum game—a competition to acquire as much of the children's time as possible at the expense of the other parent.

Unfortunately, there is no magical solution to this dilemma. More time cannot be invented, and the child cannot be cut in two. The only thing you can do is create the best schedule possible.

 Transitions are difficult on everyone—especially the children. To make it easier, try not jumping into an activity right away, but instead, plan some quiet time, such as reading, taking a walk, or watching TV.

Creating a Schedule

When deciding how the children's hours will be divided, you will each have needs and agendas.

One parent may want a highly detailed and specific schedule, describing exactly where the children will be every moment of the day. The other parent may want a loose, unstructured schedule that lets him or her adapt to the children's needs moment-by-moment. Or both parents may want the children during a majority of the children's awake hours—something that cannot happen.

There is no one correct schedule. If a lawyer or mediator hands you a model agreement, you do not have to accept it.

Every family is unique, and the schedule that works best for you may not work for someone else. At best, your schedule is a compromise. It is a resolution of your different—and at times incompatible—desires.

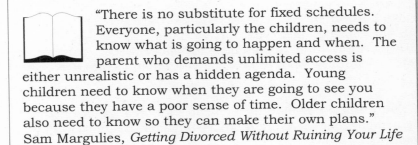

"There is no substitute for fixed schedules. Everyone, particularly the children, needs to know what is going to happen and when. The parent who demands unlimited access is either unrealistic or has a hidden agenda. Young children need to know when they are going to see you because they have a poor sense of time. Older children also need to know so they can make their own plans."
Sam Margulies, *Getting Divorced Without Ruining Your Life*

Counting the Hours

When making a schedule, you add up all of the hours each parent spends with the children. You do that because every hour has to be accounted for, and the only way you create a useful schedule is to actually add it all up and divide it.

Here are some handy amounts to remember when counting the hours and days.

Time

First of all, there are 24 hours in a day and 365 days in a year, or 8,760 hours in a year. Also, there are 168 hours in a week, and approximately 730 hours in an average month.

Time Chart

	Day	Week	Month	Year
Hours	24	168	730	8,760
Days		7	30.4	365
Weeks			4.3	52
Months				12

To use the chart, look down the left-hand column for units, then across the top row for the period. For example, there are 168 hours in one week.

The amounts in a month are an average. If you need to add up the months exactly, use the following:

Days	Month
28	February (leap year has 29 days)
30	April, June, September, November
31	January, March, May, July, August, October, December

If you want to use months as a basis for creating a schedule, remember that there are more 31-day months than 30-day months.

Two-Week Periods

Most schedules are based on a two-week period.

Basing the schedule on a two-week period allows the children to see both parents within a fairly short period of time, and allows the year to be divided up evenly. If the time periods are something else—say months—the mathematical divisions might produce a remainder—that is, part of a day.

For purposes of counting the hours, a two-week period has 336 hours. But since children obviously aren't awake that

Counting the hours may influence child support. In some states, the percentage of time spent with the child is a factor in the child support guidelines.

long, you can divide the time based on just the awake hours or on the total number of hours.

School Year

Typically, the school year is divided up into two-week periods.

Since a schedule covering the school year accounts for more than half the year, there are many different arrangements for the time, including:

Single Primary Home

Also called *home base,* a *single primary home* means the children live with one parent most of the time, and visit the other parent for specific periods.

Single primary home arrangements have several advantages. They are often best when one parent is not interested in raising the children, or when one parent has an erratic work schedule, or when the parents live too far apart to make more frequent exchanges practical. Also, if the parents simply cannot cooperate on even a basic level, a single primary home may be best because it removes the children from the middle of the conflict.

After their divorce, Daniel and Amy shared custody of their two children who lived with Daniel on weekdays and Amy on weekends. A year later, Amy wanted more time with the children, but Daniel refused. The court settled the dispute by giving Amy the children from Thursday evening until Monday morning three weeks in a row and from Thursday evening until Saturday morning of the fourth week. Daniel got the opposite. *Siekawitch v. Siekawitch* (1998) 956 P.2d 447.

The disadvantage of a single primary home is it eliminates one parent from the child's day-to-day life. This parent loses the opportunity to stay connected to his or her child, and the child loses the benefit of consistent contact with the parent. In single primary home arrangements, it's common for the visiting parent to feel a tremendous loss and to drop out of the child's life after a while.

Some variations on a single primary home include:

Alternate Weekends. The children live with one parent most of the time, and visit the other parent every other weekend. Here's how it looks:

Alternate Weekends

		Mon	Tue	Wed	Thu	Fri	Sat	Sun
Week 1	Mom	✓	✓	✓	✓	✓	✓	✓
	Dad							
Week 2	Mom	✓	✓	✓	✓	✓		
	Dad						✓	✓

Typically, the alternate weekends begin on either Friday night at 6 p.m. or on Saturday morning at 8 a.m. And they often end either on Sunday night at 6 p.m., or—if the noncustodial parent can bring the children to school—Monday morning.

Alternate Weekends and Weeknight. When parents live near each other, the noncustodial parent may see the children one weeknight as well.

Day Visits. One parent may be prevented from bringing the children to their home. This may happen when parents have supervised visitation, or when one parent lives very far away. With day visits, the visiting parent travels to see the children rather than have the children travel to him or her.

School Year/Summer. When parents live very far apart, sharing the children during the school year may be impractical. One solution is to allow the children to remain

During their ten-year marriage, Amy and Paul lived with their only child, Caleb, in Massachusetts. Amy was the principal second violinist for the Rhode Island Philharmonic Orchestra, and Paul worked in his family's business as a service manager. After they separated, Paul moved into an apartment in his parents' home, and Amy and Caleb moved into a nearby apartment. In the divorce papers, Amy was awarded sole physical custody of Caleb, and Paul had visitation "on alternating weekends from Friday at 5:30 P.M. until Sunday at 7:30 P.M., overnight every Monday and Wednesday, and on specified holidays and observances." Six months later, Amy announced she was moving to Providence, Rhode Island, and taking Caleb with her. Paul insisted the move would disrupt his relationship with Caleb, and asked for custody. The court appointed a guardian ad litem for Caleb. Before the guardian could make a recommendation, however, Amy took Caleb to Rhode Island. Paul returned to court, and the family court ordered that Caleb "reside with the father from Monday after school through Friday delivery to school," and with the mother on weekends. Amy appealed the decision, and it was reversed. *Rosenthal v. Maney* (2001) 51 Mass.App.Ct. 257, 745 N.E.2d 350.

with one parent during the school year, and then live with the other parent during the summer.

Dual-Homes

When children spend a more equal amount of time in each parent's home, the arrangement is called *dual-household*.

Dual-household arrangements may be any division of the child's time, up to and including an exact fifty-fifty split. The difference between dual-home and primary home arrangements is that the children generally spend a minimum of four overnights with each parent in a two-week period—but usually more. Dual-household indicates the parents are participating more equally in the raising of the children.

Dual-home arrangements allow the children to have a meaningful relationship with both parents, but for a dual-home schedule to work, the parents must live near each other, and they must usually cooperate on the frequent exchanges.

Some typical variations of two-home arrangements include:

Split Weeks. This can be a weekly schedule of 3 1/2 days with each parent, or 4 days with one parent and 3 days with the other, or anything similar. Often, these schedules alternate or divide the weekend days so that both parents get weekend time with the children. With this schedule, the parents must live very close, and both must be able to drop off and pick up the children from school.

Here's an example of a split-week schedule where the children live with one parent from Tuesday afternoon through Saturday afternoon and with the other from Saturday afternoon through Tuesday afternoon:

Split Week: 4/3

		Mon	Tue	Wed	Thu	Fri	Sat	Sun
Week 1	Mom	✓	1/2				1/2	✓
	Dad		1/2	✓	✓	✓	1/2	
Week 2	Mom		1/2	✓	✓	✓	1/2	
	Dad	✓	1/2				1/2	✓

Weekdays/Weekends. Parents can also share the children on a weekday/weekend schedule. In this schedule, the children stay with one parent during the school week, and go to the other parent's home every weekend.

Alternating Periods. Children can move back and forth between their parents' homes every week, every two weeks, every month, every two months, every six months, every year, and so on. If the children switch often, the parents have to live in the same school district.

Bird Nesting

This is where the children remain in one home and the parents alternate moving in-and-out. The period of time each parent stays in the home can vary. When parents choose this arrangement, each needs a separate home or apartment to stay in, or a friend or relative to live with.

Five Ways to Keep in Touch with Your Children

1. Schedule a time when you can call them.

2. Let the children call you.

3. Plan a mid-week dinner with them.

4. Send post cards, letters, or even taped greetings.

5. Go to school events, church gatherings, and team games.

Free Time

Some parents toss off the structure of a fixed-schedule and let the children stay wherever they want. This arrangement requires that both parents be extremely cooperative and involved with their children. While it gives the children the best chance of having a relationship with both parents, it also forces the parents to remain connected to each other's lives.

Holidays and Special Occasions

After deciding how to divide the school year, you also need to share the children during holidays and special occasions.

Traditional holidays and school holidays might include:
- Thanksgiving Holiday.
- Hanukkah Holiday.
- Christmas Holiday.

- New Year's Day.
- Martin Luther King Day.
- Presidents' Day.
- Memorial Day.
- Independence Day.
- Labor Day.
- Winter Vacation.
- Spring/Easter Vacation.

Special occasions include other important days, such as:
- Child's birthday.
- Parent's and sibling's birthday.
- Mother's Day and Father's Day.
- Other religious, cultural, or heritage-related days .
- Family celebrations.
- School activities.

Here are some common ways to share the holidays:

Alternate Years. Many holidays are shared by alternating the year. For example, during even-numbered years the children

While Sherry and Bradford were living in France, they had a daughter, Corrine. Then, Sherry moved with Corrine to New Mexico, and Bradford moved to Georgia. When Corrine was three years-old, Bradford filed a petition for paternity and a detailed custody plan in a New Mexico court. It was granted. When Corrine was six years-old, Bradford and Sherry agreed that Corrine would live primarily with Bradford and approximately 40% of the time with Sherry. The next year, they changed the arrangement again, this time implementing a 3-year rotating custody arrangement. During the period when Bradford had custody of Corrine, he moved to Kansas and filed a petition to make Kansas the home state for Corrine. It was granted. The next year, Bradford asked for sole custody and for Sherry and Corrine to have only supervised contact. It was denied. Bradford appealed, but lost. *Johnson v. Stephenson* (2000) 28 Kan.App.2d 275, 15 P.3d 359.

Who watches the children? School is in session about 180 weekdays a year, but a year has 260 weekdays. That means your children don't have school about 80 weekdays a year. If you get two weeks' vacation plus the standard 12 holidays, you only have 22 weekdays a year off from work. That leaves 58 weekdays a year when your children are off from school, and you can't be home to supervise them.

stay with one parent during a given holiday, and in odd-numbered years, the children stay with the other parent. Holidays and special occasions shared this way usually include Thanksgiving and the child's birthday.

Divide in Half. Some holidays, such as Christmas and Spring Vacation, are long enough for the parents to divide in half. Specifically, Christmas is often divided by giving the child to one parent from the close of school until noon on Christmas day, and then to the other parent for the rest of vacation until school starts in January. The arrangement is then reversed the following year.

Celebrate Twice. Another way to share the holidays is simply to allow each parent to schedule nonconflicting time with the children. During the time, each celebrates the holiday. For example, one parent can celebrate Christmas with the children a few days early, and the other parent can celebrate on Christmas Day.

Repeat Every Year. Finally, some days are often scheduled with the same parent every year. Examples include each parent's birthday, Mother's Day, and Father's Day.

Also, when a holiday falls on Monday or Friday, it's customary that the children remain with the parent scheduled for the weekend. For example, if a parent has the children on a weekend and the following Monday is a holiday, that parent will keep the children that extra day. Conversely, if a parent has the children on a weekend and the prior Friday is a holiday, they start the weekend a day early.

Summer Vacation

After scheduling the child's time during the rest of the year, you also need to account for summer vacations.

With the wide-open days of summer, you can let children see more of the parent they have not seen during the school year. Here are some typical ways of scheduling the summer vacation:

Block of Time. If parents share the children during the school year, then a standard summer schedule allows each parent to have the children for an uninterrupted period of time. The block of time can be any length, but thirty-day or six-week

 Calculating parenting time. Visitation scheduling software, such as *Kidmate* or *Parenting Time Calendar,* lets you enter any combination of weekday and weekend visits, holidays, etc., and print out a calendar with the exact percentage of time for each parent. You can order Kidmate at www.kidmate.com, and *Parenting Time Calendar* at www.parentingtimecalendar.com.

blocks are common. If the block is six weeks long, often the other parent is granted visitation on alternate weekends. The dates during the summer when the parents take their children can be fixed or discretionary, and if they are discretionary, each parent usually must notify the other from one to two months in advance. When parents disagree on when to take the children, one parent's wishes may have priority in even-numbered years, and the other parent's wishes may have priority in odd-numbered years.

Compensating Time. If parents do not share the children during the school year, then the summer can be used to give the noncustodial parent extra time with the children. For example, if the children see only one parent during the school year, then they may spend the entire summer with the other parent.

Chapter 13

Making Decisions

✓ Most decisions involving the children are pretty minor, but some are vital to the raising of the children.

✓ Education is the biggest issue, because the children will spend more awake time in school than anywhere else. School choice is also important because the custodial parent—or both parents if custody is shared—will have to live near the school.

✓ Routine medical care can be decided as needed, but emergency medical care must be discussed ahead of time.

✓ Where to exchange the children, how often to exchange, who will exchange, etc., will become a major decision because it may happen many times.

✓ Finally, since changes are inevitable, consider how information will be shared and how changes will occur.

Issues to Consider

When constructing a parenting plan, it's useful to consider the following items, even if you eventually decide not to include them:

Education

School may be the single most important issue simply because it accounts for most of the child's awake time. There are many topics in this category, and you may include any or all of them.

Choice of School. The child has to go to some school, but which school is a decision that must be made. Not all private schools are better than all public schools, and many large school districts have specialized—or magnet—schools with enriched programs. With so many tradeoffs, you should consult as early as possible.

School Records. Normally, the school will send home tons of paperwork, including report cards, papers, notices, and so on. Someone has to read and respond to it all, and you must decide who that someone will be.

School Conferences. Whether they call you in to tell you what a well-behaved genius your child is, or something worse, someone has to show up for the face-to-face meetings with the teachers. Meetings usually require appointments, and whichever parent has the less-demanding work day may find it easier to attend.

School Activities. School is more than academics, and you will inevitably have to attend ball games, concerts, plays, and much, much more. Also, in the early grades, some schools encourage the parents to volunteer as classroom aides.

 In many states, a divorced parent may be ordered to financially support his or her child beyond high school. In those states, as long as the child remains in college, the parent must pay support until the child turns at least 21.

When they married, Jeffrey, who is Catholic, and Barbara, who is Jewish, agreed their children would be raised in the Jewish faith. They had three children during a six-year marriage. Their faiths moved in opposite directions when Jeffrey joined the Boston Church of Christ, a fundamentalist Christian faith, and Barbara became an Orthodox Jew. Barbara tried to limit the children's exposure to Christianity, and Jeffrey objected. After hearings on the issue, the family court ordered any future disputes between the parents on religious beliefs would be arbitrated by a court-appointed guardian ad litem. *Kendall v. Kendall* (1997) Massachusetts No. SJC-07427.

School Emergencies. By definition, emergencies require fast action, so you should determine your respective authority ahead of time, and then notify the school. If you have joint legal custody, both of you should be contacted in an emergency. Otherwise, the school needs to be told exactly what the arrangement is.

Special Needs. If your child has some special educational needs, the parenting plan is an ideal place to address them. Whether it's advanced coursework or remedial assistance, it can often be accounted for in an agreement.

Paying for College. If you only have young children, this may not seem like something worth discussing for a while. However, if you take a look at tuition costs, you'll realize that someone has to start saving when the children are born.

Religion
If you both feel strongly about your faith, and you have different faiths, this is a great issue for a parenting plan.

Religious training usually boils down to one of three choices:
- Teach one religion.
- Teach both religions.
- Don't teach any religion, and let the children choose when they're older.

"Good decisions take your values and needs, and your children's values and needs, into consideration. Good decisions also stand the test of time because everyone involved gains something important. Whenever possible, the advantages of a decision should outweigh the disadvantages for everyone concerned." Mimi Lyster, *Child Custody*

In addition, if one parent wants the children to attend a parochial school, or if the other parent celebrates religious holidays that don't fall on weekends, these issues can be addressed.

Medical Care
Medical topics go beyond who takes the children in for checkups. You may also wish to consider the following issues:

Medical Providers. Choosing the child's doctor, dentist, and optometrist is critically important, and this issue must be decided before it comes up. If you use different doctors, the doctors must be told so they can exchange medical information.

Medical Decisions. If you have joint custody, this may not be an issue, because generally both parents must be consulted on medical treatments. Otherwise, you must decide who calls the shots on shots, physicals, etc.

Medical Emergencies. When a child is hurt, someone has to be in charge. If there is a reason why one parent shouldn't make emergency medical decisions, then the other parent must always be available. Alternatively, the decision-making parent can sign a medical release.

Medical Records. It's hard to imagine why, but one parent may have a reason to prevent the other from getting copies of the children's medical records. Otherwise, this issue requires coordination, since some doctors won't willingly supply duplicate records.

Insurance
With medical costs come insurance costs, and you should
assume you will have to share the burden of the premium
payments. Typically, the parent with the better medical plan
will carry the children, and other payments between the
parents will be adjusted accordingly. Insurance can include
all of the following:

- Life (for the parents).
- Major medical.
- Dental.
- Vision.
- Prescription drugs.

Child Care
With the exception of some teenage children, most children
cannot be left home alone. That means that parents who
work—or who have some other reason why they cannot care
for their children—must find appropriate child care. Child
care decisions bring up many items, including:

Child Care by a Professional. In choosing a care provider, you
must decide on the minimum qualifications. For example,
one parent may feel that paying a teenager $5 per hour to
watch the children is fine. But the other parent may not
agree to anything less than a state-licensed and bonded full-
time care provider. If you live close by, using the same care
provider can provide extra stability for the children.

Child Care by the Other Parent. If you are on good terms and
live nearby, you can use each other for child care. This has
many advantages, including continuity and consistency, and
lower child care expenses. The disadvantage is that it
requires you to cooperate. If you don't get along, the children
will be exposed to the ongoing conflict.

> **$** When establishing child support, many judges
> will order one of the parents to pay for the
> children's health insurance. Also, the
> noncustodial parent may be ordered to carry life
> insurance naming the children as irrevocable
> beneficiaries until child support is terminated.

In their study of divorced California families reported in *Dividing the Child,* Maccoby and Mnookin found that the vast majority of parents lived close enough to exchange the children by car. Initially after the divorce, the average drive time from one household to the other was 18 to 20 minutes. After three years, the parents moved slightly farther apart, and the average drive time increased to 25 to 29 minutes. Maccoby and Mnookin also found that— for the majority of families where the children lived primarily with one parent—the noncustodial parent did most of the driving.

Child Care by a New Mate. When parents remarry, the new mate may be willing to care for the children. While this sounds like an advantage, frequently the other parent will not want the new mate to meddle with the children.

Exchanges
When parents live in separate homes, the children almost always have to go back and forth between them. This means the children have to be exchanged.

Exchanging the children requires you to coordinate many items, such as where to exchange, when to exchange, who drops off, who picks up, and so on. Here are some problem areas:

Number of Exchanges. The number of exchanges clearly involves tradeoffs for everyone. The greater the number of exchanges, the less time the children wait before seeing the other parent, but the more time someone has to spend moving them back and forth. And, the fewer the exchanges, the longer the children have to wait, but the less time the parents spend moving them.

For example, if you live near each other, and share the children each week, they may be exchanged two times per week. But if you live far apart, they may be exchanged a few times per year.

Exchange Point. When deciding the exchange point, you can account for everything from the location of your homes to your respective work schedules. A very important item is whether you can cooperate enough to exchange the child at the front door of each home.

If you cannot cooperate, then the exchange point can be a neutral location, such as a:
• School.
• Day care setting.
• Relative, friend, or neighbor's house.
• Curbside (rather than the front door).
• Mall.
• Library.
• Police station lobby.

If you choose a neutral location, then you both must drive there to meet and swap the children.

 Charles and Susan divorced after seven years. In their divorce papers, the district court awarded custody of their three children to Charles and gave Susan alternate weekend visitation. Both parents were also ordered not to remove the children from Nebraska "without the court's consent unless the other party gave written consent for a temporary removal." A year later, Charles learned his contract would not be renewed as a teacher. He then married a woman in Oregon and found a teaching job in Oregon. After Susan gave Charles permission to take the children to Oregon for an extended Thanksgiving holiday, he took the children to Oregon and enrolled them in school. The next month, Charles asked the Nebraska court for permission to move the children. Susan wanted to hold Charles in contempt for taking the children from Nebraska, and she also asked for custody. The court found Charles in contempt and ordered him to bring the children back to Nebraska, then gave Susan custody. On appeal, however, the decision giving Susan custody of the children was reversed. *Tremain v. Tremain* (2002) 264 Neb. 328, 646 N.W.2d 661.

Transportation. How the children get to the other parent's house is important because it must be safe, secure, reliable, and it will happen many, many times. When the two homes are close, older children can travel back and forth by bicycle, city bus, and so on. Otherwise, someone has to move the children, and that means deciding who does it. Though one parent can assume the sole responsibility, it will clearly become a burden over time, and that parent may eventually wish to share the responsibility. Also, if one parent is responsible for transportation, and the other parent moves away, the transporting parent is forced to seek a modification of the agreement.

An alternative to the parents doing all the driving is to have a third party transfer the children. The advantage of using someone else is that you can avoid face-to-face exchanges, but then you will have to rely on yet one more person—further complicating the logistics of exchanges.

 Exchanges can add up. Imagine that you divorce when your child is exactly two years old. If you begin twice-monthly visitation, and maintain it every month thereafter, by the time your child turns 18, he or she will have been exchanged 768 times.

For those who don't want to exchange the children at all, the children can remain with the custodial parent, and the noncustodial parent may visit. In those cases, the visiting parent can rent a room in a nearby hotel or stay with a friend.

Transportation Costs. You will also have to decide who pays for the transportation of the children. As a general guideline, transportation costs are often apportioned by the relative income and ability to pay of each person.

Schedule Changes
Ironically, two people who could not get along well enough to stay together must now somehow cooperate when exchanging the children. This may be too much to ask, and for some people, last-minute schedule changes will occur frequently.

When parents are picking up the children, they may find the children are not ready on time—or not home at all. When they are waiting for the children to be picked up, they may find the other parent arrives late—or not at all. And, of course, when parents wait for a child to be returned, the other parent may show up late.

Because last-minute changes are inevitable, you must decide how the other parent will be notified, and who will pay any extra costs associated with the change.

Five Tips for Easier Exchanges of the Children

1. *Make it natural.* Time the exchanges to coincide with a drop-off or pick-up from some other activity.

2. *Make it quick.* The best exchanges are the simple ones—short and pleasant.

3. *Don't talk.* Don't use exchanges to discuss issues with the other parent.

4. *Don't worry about it.* If the child leaves an item at the other parent's house, the child is responsible for retrieving it—not you.

5. *Time to get ready.* Remind the children fifteen minutes before they will be picked up.

Travel

While travel shouldn't normally be a problem, it's possible that one parent may be planning to travel abroad with the children and then abduct them to another country. If that's a possibility, the parents can agree to restrict access to the children's passports.

Moving

Nobody stays put forever, and sooner or later someone may want to move. Moving is complicated, and involves many issues.

During the five years they lived together as an unmarried couple, Lisa Barton, a Protestant, and Alan Hirshberg, who is Jewish, had a son, Adam. When they separated, they agreed Adam would live with Lisa and Alan would have visitation. They also agreed that Adam would be exposed to both religions, but he would be raised in the Jewish faith. When Adam was five years-old, Lisa returned to court and asked for custody. Alan responded that she had broken their agreement by unilaterally removing their son from the Jewish Community Center, among other issues. Alan also asked for custody. The court appointed a psychologist to evaluate the family, who said that the boy "feels caught in the middle." The evaluator recommended that Lisa keep physical custody. The trial court agreed. *Barton v. Hirshberg* (2001) Maryland No. 2322.

For example:
- If the move will take the children away from where the other parent lives, then the visitation schedule may need adjusting.
- If the move will increase the transportation costs for visitation, then someone has to cover those extra costs. Often, the moving parent is required to pay the increased costs.
- If the parent wants to move, but the children don't, then the move may trigger a change of custody.

Sharing Information
Children's lives are very active, and when parents share children, they have to share information. The information to be shared includes school progress, school activities, illnesses, sports, friends, and so on.

The simplest way to communicate is directly with each other. A brief phone call, a short chat, a quick note—all can pass along vital information. If these approaches fail, other methods include:
- Writing a formal letter.
- Meeting with a counselor or mediator.
- Communicating through attorneys.

Because older children can talk for themselves, some parents may use them to convey information. But relying on children to carry messages poses problems, not the least of which is that the message may be distorted or incomplete. In addition, older children use leverage to get what they want, and using them may create more problems than it solves.

Making Decisions

Because you can't anticipate every possible issue that will come up, you need to decide how to decide future issues.

Generally, day-to-day issues correspond to physical custody, and include what the children eat, what they will wear, what time they go to bed, etc. Major issues generally correspond to legal custody, and include the choice of schools, elective medical attention, when to allow the child to get a driver's license, and so forth.

If you can agree on most major items, a useful division is to allow whichever parent is caring for the children to have day-to-day authority, and for both parents to jointly decide the important issues. However, if you cannot agree, the dispute will have to be resolved with the help of a third party. If one parent is not interested in making decisions about the children, the other parent may make all the decisions.

Resolving Disputes

And finally, when you cannot agree on an issue, you may be able to agree on how to resolve the disagreement. Some options include:

Custodial Parent Decides. Allowing the custodial parent to make the decisions may be best when the children live with that parent, and only occasionally visit the other parent.

When You Want a Detailed Parenting Plan

Child Custody: Building Agreements That Work, Mimi Lyster, Nolo Press, $24.95. An enormously useful book for creating a highly detailed parenting plan.

Decide With a Third Party. Many different professions help
parents resolve their disagreements. For example, the
parents may turn to a:

- Mediator.
- Counselor.
- Lawyer.
- Member of the clergy.
- Respected friend.

When parents turn to a third party for help, they can retain
the ultimate control over the decision. After that, if they still
cannot agree and must turn to litigation, the final decision-
making authority is taken away from them.

 When Theresa and Robert divorced after twelve
years, they had three children. Originally,
they shared custody with a schedule of about
50-50. Two years later, Robert asked the
Dakota County District Court for sole custody. The court
agreed, and gave Theresa liberal visitation "so long as she
continued to live within the seven-county metropolitan
area." The court also ordered that if Theresa moved
beyond the area, her parenting time would be changed to
supervised and restricted to the metropolitan area. Six
months later, Robert returned to court, alleging that
Theresa was planning to move. Theresa admitted she was
moving to Big Lake, Minnesota, which was outside the
metropolitan area. She asked that the restriction on her
visitation to supervised outside the metropolitan area be
dropped. The court suspended all contact between
Theresa and the children and gave Robert sole custody.
However, Theresa appealed, and the decision was
reversed. *Matson v. Matson* (2002) 638 N.W.2d 462.

Sample Decision-Making Checklist

	Mom	Dad
Arranging daycare	✓	
Arranging play dates	✓	
Attending PTA/PTO meetings	✓	
Attending school open houses		✓
Buying clothing		✓
Choosing schools	✓	✓
Coaching sports teams		✓
Conferencing with teachers	✓	✓
Helping choose classes	✓	✓
Helping with homework	✓	✓
Hiring babysitters		✓
Hosting play dates	✓	
Making doctor/dentist appointments	✓	
Picking up/dropping off babysitter	✓	✓
Planning holidays	✓	✓
Planning vacations	✓	✓
School volunteering	✓	
Shopping for gifts for child	✓	
Shopping for school supplies	✓	
Taking care of sick child	✓	✓
Taking to/picking up from daycare	✓	✓
Taking to/picking up from school	✓	✓
Taking to/picking up from activities	✓	✓

Hiring a Lawyer

"You know Ms. Perkins, being a divorce lawyer isn't so bad, after all."

Chapter 14

Finding a Lawyer

✓ Because child custody is so inextricably bound up in the laws, it's likely that at some point you will want to talk to a lawyer.

✓ A *lawyer* is someone who represents you in legal matters. Lawyers—or *attorneys*—are people who have passed a special test called a *bar exam*.

✓ In a few states—notably California—people can pass the bar and practice law without having completed law school. However, most lawyers have completed three years of law school and passed the bar.

✓ When you go out to find a lawyer, you'll have many choices. Some lawyers have a general practice, while others specialize. Some work by themselves, while others work in a partnership of lawyers, or *law firm*.

✓ Deciding which lawyer to hire will be the single most important decision you make.

What Your Lawyer Will Do

Generally, a lawyer has two main jobs: to uphold the law and
to protect a client's rights. More specifically, your lawyer
should do the following:

Give Legal Advice

One of the main reasons why you hire a lawyer is to tell you
what the laws are. Family law is a quagmire of exceptions,
and a knowledgeable lawyer will advise you on what you can
and cannot do. You can ask questions in advance, or simply
review decisions you've already made. And because the
lawyer is objective—and you're not—he or she can help by
telling you precisely what you don't want to hear. A lawyer's
job is to help clients adjust their expectations to the legal
realities.

Do the Legal Work

A second reason to hire a lawyer is to handle the legal work.
Legal work that lawyers do typically includes:
- Investigating the facts in the case.
- Researching prior judicial decisions.
- Reviewing new laws that may apply to the case.
- Writing and preparing legal documents.
- Delivering documents to the court and to the other party.
- Arguing in court in favor of your side.
- Questioning witnesses.
- Objecting to improper testimony, exhibits, or arguments
  made by the opposing attorney.

Not only do these tasks require unique knowledge, but the
lawyer must adhere to precise standards mandated by the
court. While you could theoretically do all of these things
yourself, it may be easier to hire someone who already knows
how to do them.

 Think the world is full of lawyers? The labor
force numbers 119 million, but only 777,000
are lawyers.[1] That's only .65% (a little over one
half of 1 percent). *The other 99.35% are
probably being sued.*

When Stanley and Shirley divorced, Shirley was represented by a lawyer, Joseph Trepel, and Stanley was represented by Pere Jarboe. After the court awarded custody of their five year-old son to Shirley, Trepel wrote a letter to Jarboe accusing Stanley of child abuse. Trepel sent a copy to Shirley, and Shirley, in turn, sent a copy to the principal of their son's school. Stanley sued Shirley and Trepel for defamation. They responded by claiming the statements made in the letter were privileged and Stanley's lawsuit should be dismissed. The circuit court agreed and dismissed the lawsuit. Stanley appealed, and the Court of Appeals reinstated the defamation lawsuit against Shirley for sending the letter to the school's principal. *Woodruff v. Trepel* (1999) 125 Md.App. 381, 725 A.2d 612, 133 Ed. Law Rep. 149.

Negotiate for You

Since most family law cases never make it to trial, a critical job of your lawyer is to negotiate for you. Deciding child custody is a contentious subject—to say the least—and long after the lawyers go home, the parents must still deal with each other. By helping you avoid dealing with the other parent, lawyers can deflect some of the blame that you and the other parent might direct toward each other. Also, if one parent is in a weak bargaining position—either because of income, knowledge, personality, or guilt feelings—hiring a lawyer can help equalize the negotiations.

Work the "System" for You

And finally, a lawyer can maneuver you through the legal system. Local family court is a small community, with the same judges and lawyers working together for many years. A good lawyer will know both the local court procedures and the personal preferences of the local judges. This knowledge may allow him or her to maneuver the case in front of the judge most likely to issue a favorable ruling. Also, by knowing the inclinations of the judge, the lawyer can give the client the most realistic advice possible about the outcome of intended litigation.

This knowledge—by the way—works both ways. While the lawyers are getting to know the judges, the judges are getting to know the lawyers. A lawyer with a good reputation imparts both credibility and believability to his or her clients.

What Your Lawyer Will Not Do

"Win" Your Case

As odd as this sounds, your lawyer doesn't win your case. You win your case. Your lawyer fights in court to get you what you want, but if what you want is not what is best for you and your children, then your lawyer "winning" will not help you in the long run.

Reduce the Cost

Lawyers are trained adversaries, and it's their job to aggressively pursue your interests. That means making unreasonable demands, filing excessive motions, and choosing litigation over settlement—all of which raises the financial and emotional cost to you. Also, because lawyers must guard against future malpractice claims, they will protect themselves by doing everything they possibly can.

 "Your lawyer is your lawyer. She is not your therapist, your plumber, your best friend, your lover, your doctor, your car mechanic, your social escort. She is a professional as a lawyer and an amateur at all those other things." Patricia Phillips and George Mair, *Divorce: A Woman's Guide to Getting a Fair Share*

Solve Your Emotional Problems

Simply put, your lawyer is not your therapist. If your problems cannot be solved by an application of the law, then your lawyer cannot solve them. Because family law has a superheated emotional component, this is one of the most common misunderstandings about lawyers.

Do Your Work for You

While lawyers can handle many tasks, it's your job to meet with the lawyer, find and prepare documents and other evidence, give depositions, attend other hearings where your presence is required, and so on. Hiring a lawyer means that you must supervise her—managing how she spends her time and your money, and deciding what needs to be decided.

Types of Lawyers

There are many different types of lawyers, and some are more suited for your needs than others. Here's a general guide:

Types of Lawyers[2]

Practice	Number	%
Solo	269,280	46%
2-10 attorneys	147,360	25%
11-99 attorneys	114,240	19%
100 or more attorneys	57,120	10%
Total	588,000	100%

Size of Practice
Of all the lawyers you can hire, about half work in a solo practice, and the rest work in firms or partnerships of different sizes.

Sole Practitioner. A sole practitioner is a lawyer who works for himself. Because he must do everything himself, a sole practitioner can get stretched pretty thin, but he can extend his capabilities by hiring other lawyers and paralegal assistants. Many excellent family lawyers are sole practitioners.

Small Firms. Two-to-ten lawyers constitutes a small law firm. Small firms—or boutiques—are where you'll find many top family lawyers. Small firms let the lawyer get involved in the entire case, but still use other lawyers as needed.

Medium-Sized Firms. Twenty-to-fifty lawyers constitutes a medium-sized firm. In these firms, only about a third of the lawyers are partners—the rest are associates. Associates are

The American Bar Association reports that "Seventeen states have specialization programs that certify lawyers as specialists in certain stated types of law. These states are: Alabama, Arizona, California, Connecticut, Florida, Georgia, Idaho, Louisiana, Minnesota, New Jersey, New Mexico, North Carolina, Ohio, Pennsylvania, South Carolina, Tennessee, and Texas."

younger, less experienced, and may do most of the work on your case.

Large Firms. Over fifty lawyers is a large firm, and over one hundred lawyers is a megafirm. Firms of this size have many highly specialized lawyers working in multiple departments. The advantage of such firms is that they are full-service— offering you legal expertise in many different areas.

Law Clinics. Law clinics handle simple, uncomplicated legal matters. They keep costs down by using standard forms and using plenty of paralegal assistants. The advantage of law clinics is that their work will often cost less overall than the alternatives. The disadvantage is that clinic lawyers are usually not exceptional family lawyers, and are often overworked.

Specialization
The law is so broad and so deep that no lawyer could possibly know it all. While a general practitioner will usually handle any type of case, practically speaking, every lawyer concentrates on some area of the law.

Some areas of lawyer specialization include:
- Domestic relations: divorce, child custody, child support.
- Estate planning: wills, probate.
- Real estate: developing, buying, and selling property.
- Criminal law: crimes.
- Personal injury: injuries, workers' compensation.
- Business law: corporations, mergers and acquisitions, taxes.
- Intellectual property law: patent, trademark, copyright.

Certified Specialist

In some states, when lawyers have pursued extra training and passed extra exams, they can call themselves certified specialists. Certified specialists in family law have not only passed a comprehensive examination, but must continue to study each year to stay current on changes in the law. They must know about child custody, child support, property division, alimony, and more. The standards for certification are set by the state bar.

How to Find a Lawyer

Finding a lawyer is easy. Finding a good lawyer isn't.

To find a good lawyer, you'll have to spend time and effort following up on leads. That's the bad news. The good news is that lawyers need you as much as you need them, so they'll make it easy for you to find them.

Here are some traditional ways to find a lawyer:

Personal Referrals

The best approach is to ask someone. "How did you like your lawyer? Did she do a good job?" There's nothing quite like the personal touch, and if you know someone who was

 After three years, Jacob and Veronica divorced. Veronica asked for custody of their child, alimony, child support, and a marital property award. After a trial but before the order was released, Veronica's lawyer met privately with the judge. Jacob was not there, nor did he have a lawyer. When the order came out, the court gave Veronica everything she wanted, including custody of their son, indefinite alimony, a marital property award, and attorney's fees. The court also entered an earnings withholding order against Jacob for child support and alimony. Jacob appealed, complaining about the secret meeting between the judge and Veronica's lawyer, and the Court of Appeals reversed every decision except for custody. *Roginsky v. Blake-Roginsky* (1999) 129 Md.App. 132, 740 A.2d 125.

satisfied with their lawyer, you may be, too. If their lawyer doesn't handle family law, or can't take your case, they may refer you to another lawyer who can.

You can ask family, friends, counselors, or even ministers for the name of a good lawyer. Here's a tip: call a local paralegal or legal typing service. They work with local lawyers every day, and may know who will be right for you. When pursuing a recommendation, remember that your case may not turn out the same. Also, because personal chemistry is so important, you may not be as comfortable with the same lawyer someone else was.

Loose lips sink ships. When asking others for a personal referral, be careful what you say. If you let slip something that could hurt you, they can be ordered to appear and testify in court. Only conversations with your lawyer are protected by attorney-client privilege.

Yellow Pages
Lawyers are almost always listed in the yellow pages. The yellow pages are a great place to find family lawyers because they usually advertise, and they train their receptionists to handle callers who saw their ad. The advantage of using ads is that they may contain useful information—such as initial consultation rates. The disadvantage is that they don't tell you how competent the lawyer is.

If you look under the heading "Attorneys" in the yellow pages, you may find that family law lawyers are listed under a subheading such as:
- Divorce.
- Family Law.
- Family Law-Board Certified.
- Marital and Family Law.

Advertising
In addition to using the yellow pages, you can also find a lawyer through advertising. Lawyers advertise in newspapers and magazines, or on billboards, radio, or TV. While an ad

What Others Think of Your Lawyer

Martindale-Hubbell Law Directory

If you want to find an attorney, try the *Martindale-Hubbell Law Directory*. This set lists almost 800,000 lawyers.

From Martindale-Hubbell you can get:
- Date of birth.
- Undergraduate and law school degree.
- Year of admission to practice.
- Bar association membership.
- Certification.
- Peer rating.

Two pieces of information are especially valuable. The year of admission to the bar says how long the lawyer has been practicing. The peer rating will tell you what other lawyers think of their colleague. These are confidential ratings, and they can be useful.

Peer rating is divided into legal ability and general recommendation. Legal ability "takes into consideration experience, nature of practice, and qualifications relevant to the profession." Legal ability ranges from "A" to "C." General recommendation evaluates, "faithful adherence to professional standards of conduct and ethics of the legal profession, professional reliability and diligence, and standards relevant to the attorney's discharge of his or her professional responsibilities." The only general recommendation rating is "V." About 30% of the lawyers score at the top: A-V.

The directory is organized by city and state, so you'll need to know the city the attorney practices in.

To view Martindale-Hubbell online, go to: www.martindale.com.

To read a bound copy, try:
- Public library.
- Courthouse law library.
- Law department in a large corporation.

When Brian and Laquetta divorced, they both wanted custody of their two children. Brian was a well-paid scientist and Laquetta was a nurse with an alcohol and narcotic abuse problem. Laquetta attended AA three times a week, and her doctor randomly tested her for drugs and alcohol. The court found that Laquetta had been more involved with the children's activities, and awarded her custody. *Smith v. Smith* (2002) Alabama No. 2001040.

will tell you the lawyer's area of practice, it probably won't tell you much about the lawyer's competence.

Publicity
Another way to find a lawyer is by reading and watching the news. News stories often contain the names of the lawyers involved in a local case, or some other useful quote by a lawyer. If the legal matter is similar to yours, you can contact the lawyer. Unfortunately, many news stories about lawyers are not really news, but are reprints of press releases put out by a public relations firm paid by the lawyer to get his or her name in the paper. This means that some of these lawyers want only high-profile cases, and if yours is not high-profile, they may pass your work on to an assistant.

Legal Plans
Sometimes you can find a lawyer by signing up for legal insurance or a legal plan. These are programs offered by employers, labor unions, credit unions, credit card companies, and so on, that allow you to pay a small membership fee in exchange for a basic amount of legal service. If you need additional legal work, you'll have to pay more. A legal plan may be a bargain if it offers the services you need. Otherwise, you must use the plan lawyers, and they may not always be as good as you want.

Support Groups
You can also find a lawyer through a support group. Some support groups help victims of domestic violence, while other groups help people deal with drug or alcohol abuse.

Examples of support groups include:
- Parents Anonymous
- Batterers Anonymous
- Parents Without Partners

To find a group, look in the phone book under community groups, crisis intervention services, or family services.

Online
If you have access to a computer, you can also find a lawyer online. There are dozens of websites that contain the name and vital information for every licensed lawyer. You can search for a lawyer based on location, expertise, and more, and then send an e-mail to the lawyer. Also, lawyers may be listed on private computer bulletin boards run by special interest groups.

Lawyer Referrals
You can also find a lawyer through a lawyer referral service. A lawyer referral service will help you find a lawyer in your area. The person who answers the phone is not a lawyer, but is a counselor trained to help determine if you need a lawyer, and if so, what kind. They'll give you the names, addresses, and phone numbers of several lawyers near you. If you go to see one, you'll usually have to pay a small fee to the referral service—say $25—that entitles you to a thirty-minute consultation.

Calling a referral service is best when you're not sure if you need a lawyer, or if you can't get a recommendation from anyone you know, or when you're new to the area. The problem with lawyer referral services is that the lawyers they refer you to are not always the most experienced or most competent. It all depends on the lawyers who participate.

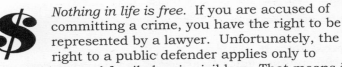

Nothing in life is free. If you are accused of committing a crime, you have the right to be represented by a lawyer. Unfortunately, the right to a public defender applies only to criminal law, and family law is civil law. That means if you need a lawyer—you have write that check.

Usually, state bar associations have referral services, as do many local bar associations. In addition, there are some private referral services.

You can find a referral by looking in the yellow pages under:
- Lawyer Referral Service.
- Lawyers.
- Legal Assistance.
- Any city, county, or state bar association listing.

Two Places for Lawyer Referrals

American Academy of Matrimonial Lawyers
150 N. Michigan Ave.
Suite 2040
Chicago, IL 60601
(312) 263-6477
www.aaml.org
If you want an experienced divorce attorney, choose a member of the *American Academy of Matrimonial Lawyers. M*embers of the AAML have been in practice for 10 years, specialize in family law, and pass an interview by the state board of examiners. There are currently more than 1,500 members in 50 states.

American Bar Association
750 N Lake Shore Drive
Chicago, IL 60611
(312) 988-5000
www.abanet.org
This national organization for lawyers lists attorneys licensed to practice. If you are looking for a recommendation, state and local bar associations will refer you to attorneys in your area. They can also tell you about mediation, lawyer discipline, and more.

---

1 *Newsweek,* July 31, 1995
2 American Bar Association Membership and Marketing Research Department, Chicago, 1993.

Chapter 15

Hiring a Lawyer

✓ Once you get the names of several lawyers, you'll have to decide which one to hire. Because each lawyer is different, the only way you'll know if you've found the right lawyer is to *interview* him or her.

✓ During the interview, be sure to ask questions about your case and about fees. Take good notes when they explain how they will charge you and what they will do for the money.

✓ When interviewing a lawyer, the important thing to remember is that you are the one doing the hiring, and the lawyer is the one being hired.

The Interview

Once you have the names of several lawyers, you'll have to decide which one to hire. You make this decision after the *interview.*

Generally, lawyers will agree to meet with you for an initial interview, or consultation, so you can evaluate them—and they can evaluate you.

Some lawyers charge you a small amount—$25 to $50—to have this meeting, while other lawyers don't charge anything. It all depends on the common practice of lawyers in your area.

Because hiring a lawyer is so important, and each lawyer is different from the next, it's desirable to interview at least three lawyers before making a hiring decision.

Interviewing three lawyers is time consuming and expensive, and may not seem worth doing. On the other hand, if you fail to perform due diligence, you can wind up with the wrong lawyer, and that may ultimately affect your life and the lives of your children.

Choose your lawyer carefully.

The interview will give you the opportunity to talk to the lawyer. You can tell him or her about your case, ask questions, and observe how well you and the lawyer communicate.

Because much happens during the interview, and hiring interviews are generally brief, it's vital that you prepare for the meeting ahead of time.

Auditions. If you think you'll spend a lot of time in court, before you actually hire a lawyer, spend a day or two in the courtroom where your case will be heard. You can learn a lot about the lawyers who appear in front of your judge. If you see someone you like, ask for a business card.

If you have little money, you may qualify for a *pro bono* or *legal aid* lawyer. Pro bono lawyers volunteer their time to help low-income litigants. Law firms use this charitable donation to train their junior lawyers. Legal aid is a social program that offers legal services to the poor. To get a pro bono lawyer, call a large law firm and ask to be included in their pro bono program. To find legal aid, look in the phone book under Legal Aid.

Preparing for the Interview

If you walk into a lawyer's office unprepared, you will use the meeting time badly—possibly not even finding out what you need to know. That's why you must prepare for the interview. Here are some ways to prepare:

Why You Want a Lawyer
The first thing to do is to identify your reasons for hiring a lawyer, and what outcome you hope to achieve. You might realize that you don't even need a lawyer, but another professional—such as a financial advisor or therapist.

If you're sure about needing a lawyer, you then must decide the level of service. Believe it or not, you don't have to dump your whole life on a lawyer and let them sort it out. You can hire a lawyer for more limited service, such as consultation, where you seek information or advice only, or negotiation, where you want the lawyer to negotiate for you.

Information for the Lawyer
The lawyer can't give you useful answers without knowing something about you. That means you must tell them about yourself. But unless you're a lawyer, you don't know what legal issues affect you, so you'll spend valuable time conveying legally irrelevant information.

The solution is to assemble the important information ahead of time. Look around and dig up valuable documents, write down vital information, and so on.

Whatever you say to a lawyer during an interview cannot be repeated. This protection—known as *attorney-client privilege*—extends to conversations you have even if you don't hire them. Interestingly enough, this also means that lawyers you interview are sometimes prevented from being hired by the other parent. As a general rule, for a lawyer to become off-limits, you must have revealed very damaging or confidential information during the interview.

Here is a list of the information and documents you may need to provide:

- Personal: names, addresses, phone numbers, ages.
- Marriage: date, place, length, date of separation or divorce.
- Children: birthdates, ages, schools.
- Work: employers, addresses, wage statements.
- Financial: tax returns, checking and savings accounts.
- Legal: prior court orders, papers you've been served with.
- Medical: insurance, illnesses, disabilities.

You won't need all of this for the initial interview, but if you're involved in a legal action, you'll eventually need to provide it.

If some information reflects badly on you, be especially sure to tell the lawyer. It's a given that the other parent will mention it, and you want your lawyer to be prepared with a response.

In addition, if you are disputing custody, you'll need to tell the lawyer why the other parent may not be fit for custody.

For example:

- Does the other parent abuse drugs or alcohol?
- Do they have a mental illness?
- Have they attempted suicide?
- Are they a spouse or child batterer?
- Are they a sexual abuser?
- Do they have a criminal record?

While this information is useful to the lawyer, if you cannot substantiate the allegations, then they remain just that—

unsubstantiated allegations. However, keep in mind that while a great deal of testimony under oath is unsubstantiated, it is assumed to be "true" if it is not refuted.

Questions to Ask the Lawyer

Besides answering questions from the lawyer, you get to ask your own questions. If you have prepared the questions ahead of time, you'll be better able to assess the lawyer's expertise.

Consider the following subjects when creating your questions:

Lawyer's Knowledge and Experience. You want to know all about the lawyer's background and expertise. Ask how long he or she has been practicing, length of time with the firm, what percentage of the practice is in family law, and what bar and professional associations they belong to. If you expect to dispute custody, ask how much experience the lawyer has had with contested cases.

Lawyer's Style. In addition to finding out about knowledge and experience, you also want to know how the lawyer works. Find out if he or she will be handling your case alone, or if it will be given to someone else—say a junior associate. Ask if paralegals and law clerks will be involved, and what they will do. Ask how the lawyer feels about settling, and if your case will go to trial if it isn't settled. And finally, find out how return phone calls are handled, and whether the lawyer will automatically send you duplicates of all correspondence.

 Nine months after Robert and Johanna married, their son was born. Five years later, on the eve of their custody trial, Robert was so depressed he attempted suicide. His lawyer, Hirschfeld, tried to cover it up, but Robert's actions were discovered, and Johanna was awarded custody. The court then sanctioned Robert's lawyer $20,000 for withholding the information about Robert, which the court called "outrageous and reprehensible." On appeal, the sanction was upheld, but the amount was reduced. *Taliaferro v. Taliaferro* (1996) 935 P.2d 911, 188 Ariz. 333, 230 Ariz. Adv. Rep. 38.

Case Questions. You'll want to know about your case, so ask plenty of legal questions. Ask the lawyer what his or her opinion of the case is, and what the likely outcome will be. Also ask how long it will take to complete. In addition, find out how the local judges have decided cases similar to yours. Also—if mediation is ordered—ask if the recommendations will be confidential, or if the judge will be given a report. Finally, if custody is in dispute, ask how evaluations are handled.

Five Mistakes Made When Hiring a Lawyer

1. Hiring the first lawyer you meet.

2. Hiring a lawyer based on price.

3. Hiring a lawyer who only practices family law part-time.

4. Hiring a litigator when you want to settle, or the other way around.

5. Hiring the same lawyer as your ex.

Client Participation and Problems. Be sure to find out what you are expected to do, and what decisions you will need to make. Also, if you have a problem, you'll need to know if the lawyer will submit to binding arbitration over the fees.

Fees. No interview is complete until you've settled fees. Most family lawyers charge by the hour, so be sure to find out the rate. Also, ask about other expenses, such as paralegal work, filing fees, and phone calls. Ask for a total estimate, even if it's only a ballpark figure. Ask about a retainer, and how—or if—it will be refunded if it's not used up. Finally, check on billing practices, and if you can pay in installments.

There are way too many questions to ask during a brief meeting, so you'll need to prioritize your questions. If you run out of time, consider making a second appointment—at the lawyer's full rates.

What the Lawyer Is Looking for During the Interview

During the interview, while you're evaluating the lawyer, he or she is evaluating you. Lawyers can—and do—turn down cases, and the lawyer will be deciding if he or she wants you as a client.

Generally, lawyers want calm, businesslike clients who are organized and rational. What lawyers don't want are clients who:
- Have a case without merit.
- Are motivated by revenge.
- Complain about the legal system.
- Have fired previous lawyers.
- Won't pay for what they need.

If you fit the above—you may have trouble hiring a good lawyer.

If you are turned down, just keep going. There is a lawyer for every case.

After the Interview

After you finish the interview, you'll have to evaluate the answers.

If you have interviewed several lawyers, you need to compare their responses and decide whom to hire. Here are some criteria to consider when evaluating the answers:

Competence. If you're not a lawyer yourself, you can't really judge competence. However, because the basis of law is what a reasonable person would do, almost every answer should make sense. If the lawyer is a specialist, you can assume he or she is current on child custody, otherwise, compare how different lawyers answered the same question. Also, make sure the lawyer can practice in the court where your case is.

Communication. Did the lawyer answer your questions—and did you understand the answers? If communication wasn't

During their eight-year marriage, Karen and Richard had a son, Timothy. When Timothy was six years-old, Karen moved in with her mother, and Timothy stayed with Richard. In their divorce papers, they agreed that Timothy would stay in the family home with Richard, and Karen would have "liberal visitation rights." The next year, Karen left New Jersey and moved to Oklahoma. Richard asked the court to order Karen not to permanently remove Timothy from New Jersey. The court agreed, and also gave him custody. A year later, Karen moved back to New Jersey and asked the court to let her take Timothy to Oklahoma. Instead of going to trial, however, the parents agreed that Karen would remain in New Jersey, and they would exchange Timothy weekly. Nevertheless, one month later, Karen decided once again to move to Oklahoma. She took Timothy with her for the summer, and when the summer was over, told Richard she was not returning Timothy. Richard immediately secured an order requiring Timothy's return, and then flew to Oklahoma and picked up the boy. Karen then came back to New Jersey and asked the court to determine whether she could take Timothy to Oklahoma. The court scheduled a hearing, and at the hearing, Karen was forced to represent herself. The family court denied Karen's request. Karen appealed the decision, arguing that her attorney had suddenly dropped her as a client only ten days before the hearing, and she had not had enough time to locate another lawyer. The appellate court reversed, deciding that her attorney acted improperly, and Karen was entitled to another hearing. *Luedtke v. Shobert* (2001) 342 N.J. Super. 202, 776 A.2d 233.

good during the interview, it may not get any better. It's not an understatement to say that communication is the most important part of the lawyer-client relationship.

Availability. Decide if the lawyer is too overloaded to handle your case, or may shunt you off to a junior associate. Keep in mind that good lawyers are busy, and lack of availability may be the price you pay for hiring a top lawyer.

Style. If you want to settle, make sure the attorney prefers negotiation. If you want to fight, make sure the lawyer is a litigator.

Honesty. You need a lawyer who is honest, even if you don't like what you hear. Try to distinguish between lawyers who agree with you, and lawyers who remain objective. If the lawyer "guaranteed" you would win, be cautious. The judge decides the case—not the lawyer.

Objectivity. If the lawyer has a gender bias, make sure that it doesn't clash with your gender bias. Hiring a lawyer of the same sex does not automatically improve your chances of winning.

Why Parents Should Not Use the Same Lawyer

If you have little disagreement over custody, it's sometimes appealing—even enticing—to save money by sharing a lawyer.

Unfortunately, now that you and the other parent are apart, you have competing interests.

If a lawyer actually agreed to represent both parents simultaneously—which they normally won't do—it represents a conflict of interest. Lawyers are bound by their ethical code to not represent both sides of a dispute or negotiation at the same time.

Of course, you can work around this restriction by waiving the conflict, but doing so may create even more problems. Often, parents without their own competent lawyer—or any lawyer—either agree to an unreasonable settlement, or

Friend or foe? Family lawyers practice against each other every day, and you should ask if your attorney has a significant relationship with the other attorney. For example, if the two attorneys are bitter enemies, that does not bode well for a peaceful settlement.

demand an unrealistic settlement. One of the advantages of involving lawyers is that they bring a businesslike demeanor to the negotiations.

Also—and for the same reasons—don't hire a lawyer recommended by the other parent. Your attorney is your attorney, and you need to hire this person on your own.

 Inadmissible evidence. In many states, it is illegal to record a telephone conversation without the other party being informed. If you make a recording without their approval, you may not be able to use it as evidence in court.

What Lawyers Cost

No doubt about it—lawyer's fees are a touchy subject. Lawyers don't work for free, and unless you earn very little or the judge awards you attorney's fees—you'll have to pay.

Hiring a lawyer really means making a cost vs. benefit decision. On the one hand, you don't want to pay more than you have to, but on the other, you want to get the best lawyer possible.

Also, since lawyers are not a standardized product—like, say a McDonald's hamburger—you can't get their prices off a big shiny board. Each lawyer is unique, and can charge whatever he or she wants. All you can do is ask the price, and then see how it compares with those of other lawyers nearby.

When you hire a lawyer, you'll have to pay fees and expenses.

Types of Legal Fees

There are some fairly standard ways lawyers charge their clients. While there are major differences between the following arrangements, the goal remains the same.

Lawyers are selling their time. The more people who want that time, the more the lawyer can charge.

Here are some common fee arrangements:

Hourly

The most common arrangement for family lawyers is to charge an *hourly fee.* Under this agreement, the lawyer charges you for each hour he or she works on your case. Rates vary depending on many factors, including how experienced the lawyer is, and whether the lawyer works in a large city—where everything seems to cost more—or a small town. Also, some lawyers charge more for time in court, and less when meeting a client in the office.

Hourly fees are typical in family law cases because so many unpredictable things happen. Custody battles, parental kidnappings, moveaways—all require a sudden and unplanned legal response. For his or her efforts, the lawyer will typically charge from a low of $75 per hour, to a high of $400 per hour. Top family lawyers in a large city can even demand as much as $500 per hour.

 Career day. Here's what your high school guidance counselor never told you. As reported in the *Los Angeles Times,* in one year California lawyers made $16.3 billion dollars in legal fees. That's more than the Gross Domestic Product of any three Third World nations. With 134,983 lawyers, it works out to approximately $120,000 annually per lawyer. New York lawyers lagged behind at $14.3 billion.[1]

Hourly rates are often divided into time units of 10 or 15 minutes. Thus, if your lawyer charges you $200 per hour in 15-minute intervals, and you talk to her on the phone for 6 minutes, your next bill will show a charge for $50 if she was rounding up to 15 minutes.

Contingency

Contingency fees are paid to the lawyer only if the client "wins" in court or is given money in a settlement. The lawyer takes a percentage of the amount awarded. Since many states forbid contingency fees in most family law cases, it's unlikely you'll find a lawyer to work for one. One exception is when a parent pursues a support delinquency. In those cases, the lawyer may take 20% to 50% of the final collected amount. More typical contingency fee cases include personal injury or medical malpractice, and workers' compensation.

Fixed

If a lawyer is willing to charge you a set amount for the legal work, that is a *fixed fee*. Fixed fees are common when the legal matter is routine, and the lawyer can use standardized forms. Because any legal matter can escalate unexpectedly, fixed-fee agreements often have loopholes that allow the lawyer to charge extra if it becomes necessary. Examples of fixed-fee arrangements include uncontested divorces, simple wills, and some personal bankruptcies. By the way, if you have children, most divorce lawyers will not work for a fixed fee because custody disputes are well-known for being volatile.

Referral

If you are referred to another lawyer, there may be a referral fee. Generally, you don't pay this, but rather, one lawyer pays the other. A referral may happen when another lawyer has the special skills or experience you need. Many states have specific rules governing how lawyers split fees, and it's prohibited when it does little more than increase your overall costs.

Statutory

If the fee for a particular type of work is set by statute, it is known as a statutory fee. These fees are approved by the court.

When Grace and Michael divorced, they agreed to joint custody of their two children and Grace was designated the domiciliary parent. Later, Grace said she wanted to move with the children from Louisiana to Ohio, but Michael objected. After a two-day hearing in district court, the judge denied Grace's request to move, stating that relocation was not in the best interests of the children. Grace appealed, and the Court of Appeals reversed. *Curole v. Curole* (2002) No. 02-CA-153.

The bottom line. Here's what one attorney had to say (in a journal for attorneys) about retainers: "The fee, which often is substantial, should neither be payable in installments nor refundable. If the client cannot afford the retainer, he or she can borrow from parents or relatives, sell a piece of jewelry or securities, refinance a car, or obtain a personal bank loan." Willard H. Da Silva, *Family Advocate*

Types of Legal Expenses

In addition to paying your lawyer's professional fee, you'll also have to pay your legal expenses.

Expenses are direct costs paid by the lawyer. Sometimes you'll have to pay the expenses up front, and sometimes you'll have to reimburse the attorney. Some expenses are fees paid to third parties, while other expenses are internal to the law firm. Because these expenses are in addition to the lawyer's professional fee, you are usually billed separately.

Examples of legal expenses include:
- Checks written to the court clerk's office for filing fees.
- Expenses incurred for the service of subpoenas.
- Wage assignments or writs of execution.
- Expenses for court reporters for depositions.
- Expenses for court reporters to prepare transcripts.
- Fees and expenses for expert witnesses.
- Copying.
- Phone calls.

Legal expenses can add up pretty quickly in family law cases. Because lawyers are always mindful that they can be sued for malpractice, they don't mind relying on many types of experts, including accountants, appraisers, actuaries, and psychiatrists. When you use experts, you'll have to pay for the time to prepare them, the time they testify, and their travel time.

Not sure which lawyer to hire? Consider this: "Those who receive the highest Martindale-Hubbell ratings and whose names appear on several family law group or association membership lists are the ones most likely to meet your expectations..." *Leonard L. Loeb,* President, American Academy of Matrimonial Lawyers, 1988-89, Chairman, American Bar Association, Family Law Section, 1978-79

Fee Agreements and Retainers

When you hire a lawyer, you sign a contract, or fee agreement. The fee agreement describes exactly how much you will be charged and for what.

The fee agreement will typically include the lawyer's hourly rate—if you are being charged that way—as well as any additional legal expenses you must pay. The fee agreement is very important, and if you do not read it carefully, there may be some unpleasant surprises awaiting you.

At the time you sign the contract, you will often have to pay a retainer fee. A *retainer fee* is the money you pay the lawyer so they will take your case. It's usually a lump-sum amount—typically between $1,000 and $15,000.

Retainer fees are generally credited against future work. That is, when the lawyer begins work, he or she first spends the money you paid them in retainer. When that money is used up, the lawyer starts billing you.

Many lawyers insist the retainer fee is nonrefundable, and that they can keep any amount you don't use. Others insist that only a portion—such as 80%—is nonrefundable. Whatever the amount, you can always negotiate this point.

Billing

Once you know what you'll pay, you have to determine how you'll pay.

While a law firm can establish any billing method it chooses, most lawyers allow clients to pay in monthly installments.

For the client, monthly billing allows payments to be spread out more evenly over time. You can also can keep better track of expenses by requesting an itemized bill.

For the lawyers, monthly billing poses problems. They realize that the legal work doesn't always keep pace with the payments, and they may have to do most of the work at the beginning of the case, only to wait a long time to be paid. This may encourage some clients to not pay at all.

Unfortunately, lawyers have little choice about monthly payments. Few clients have large sums of excess cash lying around just waiting to be spent on a lawyer.

If You Don't Pay

There's a certain irony in your relationship with your lawyer. Generally, your lawyer is your best friend until you have spent all your money, and then he or she will drop you... just like that.

If you do not pay your lawyer, he or she can stop working for you.

Read Before Hiring a Lawyer

Finding the Right Lawyer, Jay G. Foonberg, American Bar Association, $19.95. Written by a lawyer who teaches at a law school, this book not only gives advice on hiring a lawyer, it reveals how lawyers look at clients. Order directly from the ABA.

Divorce Lawyers, Emily Couric, St. Martin's Press, $14.95. This book describes 10 couples going through a divorce. Some are fighting for custody, others are battling over property distribution, one is a parental kidnapping. In all the examples, you not only meet the couples and follow their problems, but you learn a lot about divorce laws and how they influence the outcome.

There are a few exceptions that require lawyers to continue working without pay, but they only apply if your case would be prejudiced by the lawyer's discharging you. In family law, a lawyer must usually remain on your case only if a trial is imminent. Otherwise, he or she can drop you at any time.

---

1 *Los Angeles Times,* January 15, 1995

Chapter 16

Working With Your Lawyer

✓ Working with a lawyer is different from anything you've ever done.

✓ You have to furnish the lawyer with information and tell the truth—even if it embarrasses you.

✓ The lawyer must give you useful guidance on your situation, follow your directions, keep your intimate secrets truly secret, and keep you up to date on all the developments in your case.

✓ If you are unhappy with your lawyer—and most people are—you can try to work out the problem or you can fire your lawyer.

✓ You can prevent the most common problem with lawyers—money—by watching your bill and complaining before it becomes too large.

What You Must Do for Your Lawyer

It's not what your lawyer must do for you, it's what you must do for your lawyer.

You hired your lawyer to help you achieve a goal, and now you must do what it takes to make that happen. Here are some responsibilities you have to your lawyer:

Tell the Truth
You should tell your lawyer the truth for a number of reasons. First, if the other parent knows you're hiding something, they'll almost certainly mention it to their lawyer. And when it comes out—and it will come out—your lawyer won't have a good response. Second, because very few cases go to trial, your lawyer will be negotiating for you. If you tell him what your real objectives are—in your order of priority—he can fight for what you care about and give in on what you don't. And finally, because the court maintains jurisdiction over the children, if your deception is discovered later on, you can lose what you have gained.

Adjust Your Expectations
Your lawyer can only do what the law allows. If you cling to an unrealistic goal, you will probably fail, and you will make things harder for your lawyer. Child custody laws do not seek to exact revenge, but to assure the children are adequately supported and have contact with both parents. It's your job to listen to your lawyer when he or she explains that to you.

Provide Information
Your lawyer only knows what you tell him, so it's your job to walk around the house, go through your files, and look in your closets. You must pull together the pertinent papers, organize them, and hand them over.

There's no place like home. Avoid securing payment of legal fees with a lien on your home. While many lawyers will accept a lien, if you decide to change lawyers, it will create added complications.

Hidden costs. Legal actions cost more than the lawyer's hourly rate. If you work a regular weekday job, you'll probably have to miss work to talk to the lawyer, be deposed, and go to court. It's not unusual to take a day off work, wait all morning in court, and then watch as your case is continued to another day.

Listen to Advice
When you hire a lawyer, you're in charge. You're paying the bills, so the lawyer is working for you. But it's more complicated than that because you're buying professional expertise. You want guidance. So, if your lawyer tells you to do something, you might want to do it.

Give Support
Let your lawyer do what you hired him to do. If you must negotiate a side deal with the other parent, be cautious and check it out with your lawyer first. It couldn't hurt.

Ask Questions
Giving your lawyer authority doesn't mean giving him carte blanche. If you don't understand something—ask. The lawyer doesn't know what you don't know, so you must ask.

Pay Your Bill
And finally, you must pay your lawyer. This is his day job, and he has financial responsibilities just like you.

What Your Lawyer Must Do for You

Of course, your lawyer has responsibilities, too. Here are some of those obligations:

Give You Guidance
When you hire a lawyer, you're hiring a specialist to help you reach your goals. The lawyer has a responsibility to do competent work. The lawyer must analyze the legal issues, research and study the laws, and explain your rights and obligations.

After juvenile court terminated the parental rights of a father, he hired a lawyer to appeal. The lawyer submitted a brief so badly prepared and written that the Court of Appeal told her to submit another one. The lawyer ignored the court's warning and turned in yet another incompetent brief, and then said she wasn't going to argue the case orally. The Court took the highly unusual step of ordering oral argument anyway, but the lawyer showed up and told the court her client's case had no merit. "At oral argument... counsel for petitioner acknowledged that the record to which this court's review was limited did not support her client's claim for relief. Counsel for petitioner went so far as to inform this court that the case had no merit, stating that if her client had asked, she would have advised against filing the petition." Needless to say, the man lost his child. *Glen C. v. Superior Court* (2000) 78 Cal.App.4th 570.

Follow Your Directions

You—not your lawyer—have to live with the final court orders, so the final decisions must be yours. It's your lawyer's job to explain the options and then pursue your wishes.

Keep Your Secrets

You cannot be honest with your lawyer if he or she can reveal what you say. That's why attorney-client privilege prohibits lawyers from sharing your intimate secrets with the world. However, if you mention something over the phone, that privilege is lost.

Keep You Up to Date

Your lawyer must eventually return your phone calls, inform you about any settlement offers, and give you copies of everything that relates to your case.

Be Your Advocate

Your lawyer's job is to represent your best interests. He or she must handle your case quickly and carefully, and must not accept your case if there is a conflict of interest.

Charge You Fairly

Finally, your lawyer must clearly explain how you will be charged, and the amount he or she charges must be reasonable.

When You're Unhappy with Your Lawyer

Probably more than in any other area of law, attorney-client relations in family law are influenced by personal chemistry. While you can act as badly as you want, your lawyer is held to a code of professional conduct.

If the lawyer is the problem—and not you—it is usually because the lawyer is incompetent or unethical.

Incompetent Lawyer

If you're not happy with how your case is being handled, it may be because you hired an incompetent lawyer. A lawyer may be incompetent through lack of skill at being a lawyer, or through lack of knowledge about the area of law. Family law is a quickly changing field, and a lawyer who only practices part-time may not be current.

There are good lawyers and there are bad lawyers.

Examples of incompetence include missing filing deadlines, missing settlement meetings or court appearances, failing to keep you informed, and consistently forgetting the facts of your case.

School daze. Impressed with your lawyer's law school? Don't be, says attorney Jay G. Foonberg in *Finding the Right Lawyer,* "Very few law schools flunk out students, so no matter how stupid the student is, or how little the student learns in law school, chances are the student will graduate with a law degree." On the other hand, class standing is important. "I have found a very high correlation between academic achievement in law school and being a good lawyer. Good class standing is, in my opinion, indicative of excellence."

If you're not happy with the outcome of your case, don't automatically assume your lawyer is incompetent. There are two sides to every case. If you lose, it may not be because you had a bad lawyer. You may have had a bad case.

Unethical Lawyer
Lawyers can be more than just incompetent—they can be unethical or commit crimes.

Examples of unethical behavior include:
- Lying to you.
- Misusing or stealing your money.
- Abandoning you.
- Having sex with you.

Having sex with your lawyer is a particularly incendiary topic, and in some states, it is expressly forbidden by statute.

Your lawyer can also act unethically by refusing to hand over your case file after you have fired him, making a settlement offer without your permission, or colluding with the other party.

 Sex trap. "Perhaps the single most frequent ethical abuse by attorneys in the context of emotionally troubled clients involves sexual overtures toward the client. The emotional difficulties of divorcing clients render them particularly vulnerable." Lynn Feiger, *Family Advocate*

How to Solve Problems with Your Lawyer

If you feel that the problems with your lawyer are severe enough, you need to take some action. Here are some options:

Talk with Your Lawyer
If the problem is caused by a lack of communication or a misunderstanding, talking to your lawyer may solve it. If she doesn't call you back promptly, send her a letter.

Mediate or Arbitrate

If you genuinely disagree on some issue—probably fees—and you feel it's possible to reach an agreement, try mediation or arbitration. Most state bar associations have programs. Fee arbitration hearings are less formal than court hearings, you don't need to hire a lawyer to present your side, and—in some states—the lawyer must agree to participate.

 As reported in the *Los Angeles Times,* in one year the California state bar received 75,000 complaints against California lawyers.[1]

Fire Your Lawyer

You have the right to fire your lawyer for any reason. When you fire your lawyer, you must pay for the work already done, and you must notify the court of the change. In many states, your lawyer must give you your case file—even if you still owe some money. Aside from that, firing your lawyer may affect your case. The first time you fire your lawyer, the new lawyer will need time to get up to speed on your case. After that, if you continue to fire lawyers, you will alert the judge to the fact that you are an unstable litigant. And finally, after you go through a few lawyers, new lawyers won't want you as a client.

File a Complaint

Because lawyers are licensed to practice, you can also file a complaint with the state bar. Lawyers are officers of the court, and must adhere to a code of professional conduct. When you file a complaint of lawyer misconduct, the lawyer is investigated—usually by the disciplinary board of the state bar or the state supreme court. If the investigator finds evidence of unethical behavior, the lawyer can be disciplined. Typical discipline includes private warnings, probation, suspension, and—for the most egregious cases—disbarment. Lawyers take complaints very seriously, and you will undoubtedly get their attention if you file one.

To file a complaint against a lawyer, contact the state bar association.

Money talks. "In this system, you are innocent until proven broke. When you are broke, you are pretty much finished. That's the way it is, not the way it's supposed to be." *Johnnie L. Cochran, Jr.,* attorney for O.J. Simpson.

Seek Available Funds

If your lawyer has stolen your money or your property, you can contact your state's *client security fund* or *client assistance fund.* Practicing lawyers pay into those funds, and you may be reimbursed for some of your loss. For example, in California, clients are eligible for a maximum payout of $50,000. To contact the fund, call the state bar association.

Sue for Malpractice

If your lawyer has made an honest mistake that has hurt you or cost you money, you can sue for malpractice. Many lawyers carry malpractice insurance specifically for this purpose. To sue a lawyer, you'll probably need another lawyer—one who specializes in suing lawyers. Ironically, you may be able to get a referral from your state bar's lawyer referral service.

Contact the Police

If your lawyer has committed a crime, you can report it to the police. If you are not sure it's a crime, you can always talk to another lawyer.

"Most judges believe persons who go through several attorneys during one dissolution often are neurotic or unreasonable. They are considered problem clients by the bar as well as by the judges. You will understand how badly a second or third change of attorney has prejudiced your case when you hear your spouse's attorney emphasizing in all pleadings and at oral arguments before the judge that your current lawyer is your 'fourth.' Such a statement carries with it the inference that you lack stability, or your demands are unreasonable, or both." Judge Stewart, *California Divorce Handbook*

How to Save Money on Legal Fees

Finally, your problem with your lawyer might not be her performance, but that she costs too much. Here are some way to keep your costs down:

Communicate with Your Lawyer Efficiently
The first way to save money is to communicate with your lawyer efficiently. Whoever said time is money must have been looking at a lawyer's bill. Your lawyer is your lawyer—not your therapist—so if you restrict your conversation to legal matters, you can save money.

Five Mistakes Made Working With Lawyers

1. Not telling your lawyer the truth—or not wanting your lawyer to tell you the truth.

2. Having sex with your lawyer.

3. Using your lawyer as your doctor, therapist, friend-anything but your lawyer.

4. Turning your life over to your lawyer.

5. Not paying your lawyer.

Ways to communicate efficiently include:
- Write a letter instead of calling.
- If you must talk, make it brief.
- If you must meet, prepare an agenda beforehand.
- Mail the lawyer a list of important names, dates, telephone numbers, and facts.
- Deal with the secretary as much as possible.

Minimize the Role of Your Lawyer
Another way to save money is to minimize the role of the lawyer. This is simple economics. The more the lawyer does, the more she charges you. The less she does, the less you pay.

One year after Rebekah and Jackie had a child, she was convicted of misdemeanor possession of marijuana. Her sentence was suspended. The next year, she and the baby moved in with Jackie's parents, the Harrises. Then, a year later, Rebekah pleaded guilty to operating a vehicle while intoxicated (OWI). She was given another suspended sentence. Rebekah moved out, but the Harrises continued to care for the baby. The State then petitioned to revoke the suspended sentence Rebekah had received for her OWI conviction. At this point, Rebekah had no job, was being evicted from her residence, and was facing the possibility of incarceration for the OWI conviction. They all agreed to give custody of the baby to the Harrises. The Harrises initially allowed Rebekah to have unsupervised overnight visitations, but eventually limited Rebekah's visitation and required her to come to their home. Rebekah finally asked the court for custody. Before her hearing, however, she pleaded guilty to a charge of criminal mischief and was again arrested for OWI. Nevertheless, the trial court awarded custody to Rebekah. *Harris v. Smith* (2001) 752 N.E.2d 1283.

You can hire a lawyer to provide information only, to review an agreement you've already drafted, to negotiate for you, or to act as your legal coach while you represent yourself.

Watch Your Bill
A simple way to save money on legal fees is to watch your bill. Insist on regular billings that itemize your charges. If you see something unreasonable, immediately question it. Details that should appear on your bill include phone calls, messenger charges, and dates and lengths of meetings. You should also watch your bill because—once you see the costs— you can decide to more yourself or even fire your lawyer.

Hire a Specialist
Another way to save money is to hire a specialist. Hiring a certified specialist may cost you more per hour—but save you money overall. A specialist is more familiar with the law, and may be able to conclude your case more quickly.

Negotiate Your Fee

When a lawyer quotes you a fee, it's just that—a quote.
There's nothing stopping you from bargaining.

Fee Awards and Sanctions

In some cases, one parent must pay the other parent's
attorney's fees. This often happens when one parent earns a
little, and the other parent earns much more. By ordering an
award of attorney's fees, the judge seeks to remove the
advantage of the higher-earning parent. It also happens when
one parent is a litigious ex-spouse. A litigious ex-spouse is
someone who files frivolous motions intended to harass the
other parent. To discourage the litigious ex-spouse from
litigating, the judge may order that person to pay attorney's
fees. State laws usually authorize awarding attorney's fees,
but the decision is at the discretion of the judge.

Besides awarding attorney's fees, the judge can also sanction
either party. A sanction is a financial penalty for
misconduct—either yours or your attorney's. Sanctions are
commonly ordered when someone has been frustrating the
orders of the court—either by disobeying a court order, or by
intentionally delaying a court proceeding. To punish the
offending party for their behavior, the judge can order the
party to pay, or reduce the amount the party was supposed to
receive.

 Unhappy Lawyers. A poll in California Lawyer
magazine reported that "Seven out of 10
lawyers would change careers if the
opportunity arose." A RAND Corp. study found
that only half of the lawyers surveyed "would choose
again to be a lawyer."[2]

---

1 *Los Angeles Times,* October 6, 1995
2 *Los Angeles Times,* June 27, 1995

Representing Yourself

"I can't remember the names of my ex-wives.
I just call them plaintiff."

Chapter 17

Representing Yourself

✓ When you hire a lawyer, you're hiring
someone who knows the law. Your lawyer
knows which laws apply to you and has the
skills to represent you in court.

✓ But family law—like all law—is based on
common sense. If you have the time and the
desire, you can acquire enough basic
knowledge to represent yourself.

✓ Representing yourself—or being a *pro per* or
pro se litigant—allows you to save
substantially on lawyer's fees. Unfortunately,
you'll also have to learn the court rules and
procedures.

✓ If you decide to represent yourself, you can
seek out many resources for help, including
legal typing services, divorce assistance
centers, and self-help law books. You can
even hire an attorney as a legal coach.

Pro Per

If you have to interact with the legal system, either because you need to file some legal papers or because you must go to court, you're not required to have a lawyer represent you. You can also represent yourself.

If you represent yourself, you are often called a *pro per* or *pro se*. Both are Latin phrases meaning "for yourself."

Pro per litigants can do everything a lawyer can do, including:
• Write and prepare legal documents.
• Investigate prior judicial decisions.
• Conduct discovery.
• Negotiate settlements.
• Argue a case at trial.

 Many people represent themselves. One Florida judge estimates that approximately 70% of the litigants who appear before him are pro pers. A California judge estimates that half to three-quarters of the litigants he sees are pro pers. And the *Los Angeles Times* reports that as many as 84% of all child support cases involve at least one pro per parent.[1]

Representing yourself in a legal matter is a statutory right, and many people choose to do so. The right to self-represent, however, does not extend to representing others. Only licensed attorneys have the right to represent someone else.

Advantages to Representing Yourself

There are many reasons why you might want to represent yourself. These include:

To Save Money
A main reason to self-represent is to save money. In family law you are not automatically entitled to an attorney if you can't afford one. Thus, for many lower and middle-income families, access to the legal system is limited.

For example, when you're seeking a minor adjustment to child support, paying an attorney to file a modification may not be worth it. The gain in monthly support would be less than the cost of the attorney to secure the increase.

And even a parent who can afford an attorney may not want one. Some people hold the view that courts are primarily a place for lawyers to make money. For those individuals, going pro per offers psychological satisfaction.

The savings do not end with the first ruling, either. Because child custody often represents an ongoing conflict, the parent who self-represents stands to save even more over the long run.

When You Should Consider Representing Yourself

1. You have a simple matter to bring before the court.

2. You can get legal assistance.

3. You can communicate with the other parent.

4. You're dealing with a small amount of money.

5. A mistake won't hurt you in a substantial way.

To Make the Decisions
Another reason to represent yourself is to retain control over the decision making. Ultimately you—and not the attorney—have to live with the court orders. When you allow others to make the decisions for you, you lose your ability to influence the outcome.

Also, since every family is unique, you're the only one who can truly say what is best for your children. Sometimes the professionals—no matter how well-intentioned—can't understand your situation. Often, professionals will apply a *one size fits all* approach that may not be appropriate for you. In those cases, it may be best to take charge of your own affairs.

> Though Jennifer and Keith never married, they had a baby girl while living together in Keith's home with Keith's mother, aunt, and grandmother. After Jennifer and Keith's aunt argued, Jennifer moved out and took the baby with her. Keith sought custody, but Jennifer responded by seeking custody and temporary orders for support. When the court didn't rule immediately, Jennifer ran out of money and sent the baby to stay with Keith. The court awarded physical custody to Keith and ordered Jennifer to pay $50 a month in support. *Johnson v. Washington* (2000) 756 A.2d 411.

And finally, when you make your own decisions, you're more likely to have a good outcome. That is, pro pers are more likely to comply with the court orders, are less likely to relitigate, and often have less post-divorce conflict.

To Keep It from Escalating

When you hire an attorney, you're hiring an advocate to act on your behalf. It's quite likely the attorney will file accusatory motions, adopt a harsh negotiating stance, and threaten litigation at every turn. Attorneys are mercenaries in an adversary system, and those are the tools they have to work with.

If the parents are bargaining from dramatically different positions, hiring lawyers can help balance the equation. On the other hand, when it comes to family law, this confrontational approach has been criticized. When lawyers get involved, formerly pliable parents may become entrenched, hardened into extreme and polarized positions.

After the court battles are over, and the lawyers have gone home, parents still have to deal with each other.

When lawyers become involved, a simple case involving one issue can suddenly blossom into full-scale litigation. When one parent gets a lawyer, the other parent responds, and soon a case needing only a few simple forms to be filled out turns into a litigation nightmare.

By representing yourself, it's possible to lessen the adversarial nature of the proceedings, and leave yourself room to do business with your ex-spouse afterwards.

Disadvantages to Representing Yourself

There are also many reasons why you might not want to represent yourself. Here are some things you might do that could make matters worse:

Make Legal Mistakes

The fact is, a lawyer is someone who has usually completed four years of college, three years of law school, and passed a bar exam. During that time, he or she was trained to analyze complex legal problems and handle intricate legal work. You weren't. If you represent yourself, you're much more likely to make a mistake—possibly a serious one.

Also, keep in mind that many court procedures are steeped in arcane, obscure rituals initially derived from another country. While common sense usually prevails in the long run, there's no guarantee that a simple procedural error won't cost you much more than if you had hired an attorney in the first place.

And finally, realize that lawyers must stand behind their work. Not only do attorneys carry malpractice insurance, but most states have a client security fund that may reimburse you. If you represent yourself and make a mistake—you have no recourse.

Make Negotiating Mistakes

Since most cases settle, it's a pretty certain yours will, too. If you try to negotiate for yourself, you'll be hampered not only by your lack of knowledge about what you're entitled to, but also by your lack of skill at obtaining that result.

"The man who has himself for a lawyer, has a fool for a client." *Abraham Lincoln*

For some parents, this lack of knowledge leaves them vulnerable, open to being coerced into giving up their rights to a savvy or dominating ex-spouse. For others, it means just the opposite—they become outrageously unreasonable and demand an arrangement that no judge would approve. Also, a pro per is much less likely to recognize a fair settlement offer when the other party makes one.

And, of course, when you don't know how to negotiate, you don't know what's important, and you're much more likely to blurt out the wrong thing, fatally damaging your case even before you begin.

Create Problems for Court Personnel
A final reason why you may not want to represent yourself goes to the very heart of our system of justice. The adversary system assumes that each side to a dispute has roughly equal expertise. But if you represent yourself, and the other side doesn't, you may end up causing some real problems for the court personnel you deal with.

First, by representing yourself, you place the judge in a difficult position. On the one hand, he may want to help you. For the truth to come out, evidence must be presented, and the rules of evidence are tricky. On the other hand, the judge must avoid taking sides. This quandary is awkward, and some judges will respond by holding the pro per to a lesser standard than the opposing lawyer, while others will respond by constantly getting annoyed with the pro per.

The attorney involved also faces a dilemma. Professional codes require aggressive pursuit of the client's interests, yet allow only limited contact with the other party. If you represent yourself, the attorney is restrained in his or her ability to negotiate a settlement. And if you hire an attorney in some capacity as a legal coach, that attorney is still vulnerable to malpractice claims, even if he or she only provides information on part of the case.

And finally, the filing clerks and court clerks who know all the details about court procedures have neither the time—nor are they trained—to handle endless questions from pro pers.

What Happens When You Represent Yourself

If you're thinking about representing yourself, you should know how it may affect your case.

The American Bar Association conducted a study of 273 divorce cases in Maricopa County, Arizona. The results were reported in *Self-Representation in Divorce Cases.*[2]

What Happens When You Represent Yourself

	If you represent yourself...	If an attorney represents you...
Agreement	More likely	Less likely
Time	End sooner	Last longer
Cost	Spend less	Spend more
Temporary Orders	Less likely	More Likely
Litigation	Trial less likely	Trial more likely
Custody	No difference	No difference
Satisfaction	72% would do it again	79% would do it again

Type of Cases
Of all the couples who divorced during the study, almost 90% involved one side who self-represented, and 52% involved both sides self-representing. The authors examined these cases, and found that—as a general rule—when someone self-represented, the legal issues in the case were often less complex and the litigants were usually more cooperative. However, when attorneys took over, the legal issues were often more complex, and the parties were more adversarial.

Agreement
As reported in the study, when at least one side self-represented—and custody, visitation, or support was an issue—the parents were more likely to reach an agreement outside of court. The authors decided that when a parent chose to represent themselves, it may have meant the couple was able to agree before the pleadings were filed.

Expense

Also as reported, when one of the parties self-represented, the case was likely to end sooner, and the litigants were likely to spend less money. The reverse was also true—when lawyers were involved, the case usually took longer, and the litigants spent more. The authors concluded that this was to be expected, since attorneys were more likely to be involved in the more difficult cases.

Temporary Orders

As the study revealed, the attorneys were likely to request temporary orders, but none of the pro pers made such a request.

Litigation

During the study, when attorneys represented the parties, the case was more likely to result in a written agreement, or barring that—to go to trial. However, when someone self-represented, the case was more likely to be resolved through a default judgment.

Custody Decisions

Interestingly enough, when comparing child custody decisions, the study discovered there were no meaningful differences between cases involving self-representation and cases involving attorney representation. This would seem to fly in the face of common wisdom, but—at least for the litigants in the study—choosing to self-represent did not seem to influence the final custody arrangement.

Satisfaction

And finally, attorney-represented litigants said they were "significantly" more satisfied with their final result than were the self-represented litigants. To explain the result, the

"Encourage your spouse to obtain competent counsel. It is almost impossible to settle a case with someone who lacks legal advice. Cases settle when both sides conclude that a settlement gives each side about what each would obtain if the case were decided by a judge." Judge Stewart, *California Divorce Handbook*

When their daughter, Lacey, was two years-old, Jeffrey and Denise Smith divorced, and Denise was given custody of Lacey. When Lacey was five years-old, Denise married Charles Leadingham, and she took her new husband's name. Denise then asked a district court to change Lacey's surname from Smith to Smith-Leadingham. Jeffrey opposed the change, but it was granted. Jeffrey then appealed the decision, and it was reversed by the circuit court and the reversal was upheld by the Court of Appeals. *Leadingham v. Smith* (2001) 56 S.W.3d 420.

authors noted that a number of self-represented cases were one-sided, where one party went pro per but the other hired an attorney. As a group, pro pers that had to face attorneys were much less happy with the outcome.

Still, at the conclusion of their cases, 72% of the self-represented litigants said they would do it again, and 79% of the attorney-represented litigants felt the same.

How to Represent Yourself

If you decide to represent yourself, you'll be entering a brave new world with many new rules and customs.

Some of the rules may seem significant, such as the admonition to only serve legal papers on your opponent's attorney. Other rules may seem minor, such as having to use pleading paper, or having to attach a blue-back to everything. No matter what, though, you must adhere to the rules, or you'll end up spending even more time and money to correct your mistakes.

That said, there is more to going to court than simply obeying the rules. As a pro per, you'll get a chance to present your case, and when you do, you can speak in your own words. You're not a lawyer, and no one expects otherwise. Plain speaking and common-sense reasoning are fine when writing motions or talking in court.

Self-Help Law Books

If you represent yourself, you'll need to buy some self-help law books. Nolo Press carries the best-written books available.

Nolo Press
950 Parker St.
Berkeley, CA 94710
(800) 992-6656
www.nolo.com

Represent Yourself in Court: How to Prepare & Try a Winning Case, Paul Bergman & Sara J. Berman-Barrett. This excellent book should be the first book to buy if you are representing yourself. It explains court procedure in plain English—not "legalese." One valuable section is the list of objections you make to exclude improper evidence during hearings and trials.

Legal Research: How to Find & Understand the Law, Stephen R. Elias & Susan Levinkind. While you're shopping at Nolo, also buy *Legal Research.* This useful book demystifies legal research and the law library. With this book in hand, you can find the codes and cases you need. The book is so easy to understand it has been adopted as a textbook by law schools.

Nolo's Deposition Handbook, Paul Bergman & Albert Moore. If a deposition is in your future—and it's not that hard to do one if you are pro per—pick up this book. It provides instructions on how to arrange a date, prepare for the deposition, respond to questions, ask the right questions, and more. It also contains concrete suggestions and examples on how to avoid "trick" questions.

How to Do Your Own Divorce in California, Charles E. Sherman, and *How to Do Your Own Divorce in Texas,* Sherman & Simons. These two clear, helpful books contain all the necessary forms and instructions you need to do an uncontested divorce in these two states.

Getting Help

As a pro per, you can get help from many sources, including:

The Court Clerks
If you need help with legal documents, consider asking the people who handle them every day—the court clerks. Court clerks know all about the procedural details, such as which form to use and how to get copies of documents.

But before rushing to the courthouse, realize that some clerks may get annoyed by your questions. They're trying to handle everyone who needs help, and you're slowing them down. That's why—to get your questions answered—you may have to turn to other sources.

Self-Help Law Books
Some self-help law books have the correct legal forms and instructions on how to fill them out. You can use the forms to prepare pleadings and other kinds of documents. If your legal needs are simple—such as preparing a simple modification—than using a self-help book can save you money. But if your needs are more complex, or if complications arise, then you'll need to get more help.

Paralegals
If you're struggling with the legal forms, and a self-help book doesn't cut it, you can seek out a paralegal. Typically, paralegals provide help with preparing your documents so that the documents are accepted by the court. These professionals cost much less than attorneys, but—as with attorneys—there are good ones and bad ones. You'll have to check out a few to find one with acceptable credentials.

 If you decide to represent yourself, you'll need to know the mundane, prosaic details of procedure such as filing fees, service of process, and so on. You can often find this information in a desk reference. Legal secretaries, paralegals, and law librarians know where to find one. In California, try *The Paralegal's Handbook*.

"There is no doubt that a family law calendar full of pro pers is a whole lot more difficult for a judge than one in which the parties are all represented by attorneys. Pro pers frequently don't understand the law, so hearings drag on as the judge struggles to keep them on point. Necessary evidence isn't brought to court so sometimes a decision must be made without facts that might have turned the case around. The judge's attempt to lend a hand to a litigant struggling with a difficult legal point will frequently cause the other party to charge favoritism. The door in the back of the courtroom gets kicked on the way out more than it deserves." *Judge Roderic Duncan,* Alameda County Superior Court

Law Library

When you're ready to go beyond a self-help law book, you can find just about everything you need in a law library. Law libraries contain the rules of evidence and procedure, court cases, statutes, and much, much more. So much more, in fact, that you can get lost in one. If you do stop by a law library, be sure to ask the librarian for help.

Lawyers

Finally, of course, you can hire a lawyer. You don't always need to turn your whole life over to a lawyer; instead, you can choose to retain one as a *legal coach*—someone who provides you with basic information and direction—but who leaves you in charge. Having a legal coach is a practical way to handle the details of procedure so you can concentrate on the main issues in the case.

---

1 Judge Ted Coleman, Family Court Division, FL, Judge Roderic Duncan, Alameda County Superior Court, CA, *Los Angeles Times,* June 18, 2002
2 *Self-Representation in Divorce Cases,* A Report Prepared for the Standing Committee on the Delivery of Legal Services, January, 1993

Chapter 18

Preparing and Filing Court Papers

✓ If you handle your own legal paperwork, you must learn how to research the law, create the proper legal documents, and file and serve.

✓ *Rules of court* are easy to find. The court clerk can tell you, or a court website may have a copy to download.

✓ *Codes* are also easy to find. Any law library will have them, and dozens of web sites have links to the codes in every state.

✓ *Cases* are the most difficult to find because you have to search through millions of opinions to find the right one. Several websites make this job easy, including *FindLaw* and *VersusLaw*.

✓ When you create a legal document, you have to organize the facts and the law into an argument that will persuade the judge. This means you have to write clearly and coherently.

✓ Once you create your legal document, you still have to *file and serve* it. There are many rules on service, and if you make a mistake, your case can be delayed or dismissed.

How to Create Court Papers

If you've ever watched a family court judge work through his pile of cases, you'll see the judge and the clerk spend a lot of time moving around stacks of paper, opening folders, inserting documents, marking slips, and attaching notes.

Because everything in court is put on paper—and there is a lot of paper—courts have made rules about the content and form of the paperwork.

If you're going to handle your own case, you'll have to learn the rules. To create and file your own papers, you must:

- *Research the law.* This includes looking up statutes, case opinions, and rules of court.

- *Create legal documents.* If your court has forms, you will have to get copies. If you have to write a motion, you will need a sample.

- *File and serve.* You have to make plenty of copies and deliver them to everyone involved in the case.

If this sounds like a lot of work—it is. But don't be intimidated. You can always choose to do some of it yourself and hire a paralegal or lawyer to help you with the rest.

Court forms are usually easy to complete and clerks will sometimes tell you how to complete them. And with the proliferation of government web sites, many courts have their

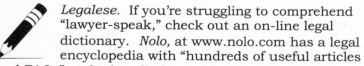
Legalese. If you're struggling to comprehend "lawyer-speak," check out an on-line legal dictionary. *Nolo,* at www.nolo.com has a legal encyclopedia with "hundreds of useful articles and FAQs" and a law dictionary that puts "legal terms in plain English." *Law.com* at dictionary.law.com, *DivorceNet,* at www.divorcenet.com, and *Divorce Source* at www.divorcesource.com also have divorce dictionaries.

forms available for free download. The hardest part for a pro per is learning the law—locating relevant case opinions and poring over the court rules.

Because this chapter relies on some knowledge of the law, if you need to learn the basics, skip ahead to *Chapter 20: Introduction to the Law,* and read that chapter first.

The Pro Per Toolbox

Like any good handyman—or handywoman—if you are going to do things yourself, you need the right tools.

Books
As a pro per litigant, you have to read everything. You have to read the relevant codes and cases, you have to read the rules of court, and you have to read every document in your case file. So, the first thing you should do is buy some good books on the law. There are plenty of excellent books in a law library, but if you actually try to buy one, you'll be stunned by the price. Yes, lawyers and law libraries get ripped off. But you don't have to spend hundreds of dollars for a legal book. You can go to a law library and for ten or fifteen dollars copy the sections you need. For a lot less money, you can buy some self-help law books. The best source for self-help books is *Nolo Press* at www.nolo.com.

Internet Law Sites
Since you are acting as your own lawyer, you need to know the laws that apply to your case. That means researching the relevant codes and cases. Here is where the internet shines. Two great sites: *FindLaw* at www.findlaw.com, and *VersusLaw* at www.versuslaw.com, are perfect for this task. Both web sites let you read all of the cases you want. You can select cases by date, subject, or case name. Reading cases will take a lot of time, but if you need to know the laws in your state, these sites are the best places to go. By the way, you can do the exact same research in a well-stocked law library, but most people can't get the time in a good law library. The law libraries available to the public are usually adequate—at best—and you could spend days walking looking for the books you need. Once you learn how, it's easy to research online.

Local Paralegal

Start looking around for a local paralegal. You'll need one. A good, local paralegal will help you with dozens of things you cannot know or do yourself. For example, generally you cannot send copies of your documents to your ex-spouse. Someone else must do it. And since everything in court can be argued about, it is likely that your ex-spouse will say you never sent the papers you were supposed to send. For that reason, as well as many others, you'll need an official person to send out papers, and then sign a document saying the papers were sent. A local paralegal will also know all of the nit-picky rules of court you may not know, such which box to check on which form. And finally, if you have a job, it's not easy to take time off work to run to court and file papers. That's another thing a paralegal can do for you.

Local Court Rules and Forms

A good paralegal can tell you this, of course, but you still need to know your local rules of court. This may include everything from the hours the filing window is open to the holidays when the court is closed. The rules may also tell you the specific forms to use. Some courts will have a blank set of forms you can buy for a few dollars and then copy as needed, while other courts may have them available on a web site where they can be downloaded for free. You'll need them, and you'll need to know how to fill them out.

Samples of Legal Documents

In addition to the court forms, you'll also need samples of other documents you must prepare. Depending on what the document is, to find a good sample you may need to get creative. Consider making friends with a secretary in a divorce lawyer's office. Or plan on spending time in the courthouse reading other case files. Or camp out in a law library and read the examples in the law books. The examples are usually good, but you have to adapt them to your specific needs.

Office Supplies

If you think your case will take a while, buy a copier with an automatic document feed. Yes, they are expensive, but you have to make numerous copies of every piece of paper that passes through your fingers, and running to the local copy

Where to Find the Law

If you want to read statutes, all of these sites can link you to the state and federal laws. But if you want to research case law, start with *Cornell, FindLaw,* and *Versuslaw.* The first two are free, and *Versuslaw* charges a small fee.

Cornell Law School Legal Information Institute
www.law.cornell.edu
This major free legal website has plenty of information. Start with "Constitutions & codes" and "Court opinions," then use the search box to locate more information.

FindLaw
www.findlaw.com
Don't be overwhelmed by this highly-visited, free legal web site. For research, click on "Laws: Cases & Codes."

VersusLaw
www.versuslaw.com
This paid site has an easy-to-use search box for case law. The standard plan for $8.95 per month works well.

Law Guru
www.lawguru.com
A meta-legal search site that can help you find something if you don't know where to start.

Nolo Press
www.nolo.com
The legal publisher has links to federal and state statutes.

AllLaw.com
www.alllaw.com
A general website with links to federal and state statutes.

The Law Engine
www.thelawengine.com
This site has links to federal and state laws, and jumps to VersusLaw for case opinions.

shop can get really old. Beyond this major expense, you'll need two- and three-hole punches, a heavy-duty stapler, labels, envelopes, paper, etc. You can buy these things as you figure out what you need.

Researching the Law

Before you plunge into legal research, you must first decide what you need to know. For many routine issues in family court, you don't need to know the law at all.

For example, if you are asking for child support, you don't have to spend time reading the cases on child support. The court will have a form to fill out that contains everything the judge needs. And since the judge must use a mathematical table or formula anyway, you may not need to do anything else. So, for simple issues, you can usually skip the research.

However, if you have a difficult problem and you need to educate the judge on some part of custody law, or you need to convince the judge you know what you're doing, then you have to research the law.

 After their divorce, Kim and Robert were awarded joint custody of their two daughters. Robert then remarried, and soon problems occurred between Robert's new wife, Kim, and the children. A court eventually granted Kim sole custody and ordered Robert to keep his daughters 100 yards away from his new wife at all times. The Colorado Court of Appeals disagreed and reversed. *In re Marriage of Martin* (2002) 42 P.3d 75.

Codes, Cases, and Rules

If you already understand law in general terms, you know law is divided into criminal and civil, substance and procedure. Thinking about the law this way is okay, but for non-lawyers, there is a better way. When you research the law, you are reading *codes, cases,* and *rules.*

Codes are named after the subjects they address, such as the *Motor Vehicle Code,* the *Internal Revenue Code,* and the *Code of Civil Procedure.* You can find the codes by looking them up in a law library or on the internet. When you do, you will find that codes are sometimes very precise, and sometimes very vague.

Where am I? If you are in a law library, you are surrounded by legal encyclopedias, code books, case reporters, form books, practice manuals, law school journals, and much more. The easiest way to find what you need? *Ask the librarian.*

That's why there is case law. Case law is the collected body of legal opinions published by the review courts in your state. Case law is created when a decision by a trial court is reviewed by a higher court, and the higher court publishes an opinion on how the law should apply to that set of facts. This opinion becomes a new law, and all of the judges in the state must follow it when they have a similar case. You find case law by looking up the cases.

The other laws you need to locate are the court rules. Rules are made when court officials—usually the state's highest judges—meet and agree to make a new rule. Court rules describe the forms you use, the amount of time you have to file something, and so on. Court rules address problems that come up in the day-to-day running of the court system.

Finding Rules

Because finding court rules is pretty easy, let's start there.

The easiest way to find the rules is to go to court and ask the clerk. The clerk should tell you where to get a copy of the rules. It's also possible the rules are on a website—if your court has one. To find out if your court has a website, look through the state court links at *Nolo* at www.nolo.com, *AllLaw.com* at www.alllaw.com, or the *National Center for State Courts* at www.ncsconline.org. If you still haven't found your court rules, you can ask a local paralegal, walk into a law library and ask the librarian, or consult with a local lawyer.

Here's a court rule from California:

TITLE ONE. Appellate Rules

DIVISION I. Rules Relating to the Supreme Court and Courts of Appeal

CHAPTER 1. Rules on Appeal

PART I. Taking Civil Appeals

Rule 2. Time to appeal

(a) Normal time

Unless a statute or rule 3 provides otherwise, a notice of appeal must be filed on or before the earliest of:

(1) 60 days after the superior court clerk mails the party filing the notice of appeal a document entitled "Notice of Entry" of judgment or a file-stamped copy of the judgment, showing the date either was mailed;

(2) 60 days after the party filing the notice of appeal serves or is served by a party with a document entitled "Notice of Entry" of judgment or a file-stamped copy of the judgment, accompanied by proof of service; or

(3) 180 days after entry of judgment.

In this example, the rule says that you have at least 60 days— but not more than 180 days—to file a Notice of Appeal. What is implied is that if you wait more than 180 days to file a Notice of Appeal, your appeal will be dismissed.

Notice that this rule is about procedure. Like all court rules, it addresses the kinds of papers you file and how much time you have to file them.

If you want to know what the law says about where children live, or how much a parent pays in support, you have to read codes.

Finding Codes

Codes are also easy to find. You can find the codes in any adequate law library. But if you can't drop into a law library, go online. There are dozens of web sites with links to the codes in every state.

You can find the codes by entering a search in any major search engine, or at a major legal site, such as *Cornell Law School Legal Information Institute* at www.law.cornell.edu or *Findlaw* at www.findlaw.com, or go to a major divorce site, such as *Divorce Net* at www.divorcenet.com. You'll find links right to the codes.

For example, here is part of the code from Texas:

CHAPTER 154. CHILD SUPPORT

SUBCHAPTER A. COURT-ORDERED CHILD SUPPORT

§ 154.002. Child Support Through High School Graduation

(a) If the child is fully enrolled in an accredited secondary school in a program leading toward a high school diploma or enrolled in courses for joint high school and junior college credit pursuant to Section 130.008, Education Code, the court may render an original support order or modify an existing order providing child support past the 18th birthday of the child.

(b) The request for a support order through high school graduation may be filed before or after the child's 18th birthday.

(c) The order for periodic support may provide that payments continue through the end of the month in which the child graduates.

In Texas, the law allows child support to continue after a child has reached age 18. The law also says that the child has to be a full-time student in high school, and the support will end the month that he or she graduates.

Sometimes codes spell out the law clearly, and sometimes they don't. For that reason, you also have to read cases.

Finding Cases

Unlike codes and rules, cases are not always easy to find.

Yes, there are legal websites that have millions of case opinions, and yes, there are law libraries filled with large books that cumulatively contain millions of case opinions.

But that's the problem. There are *millions.* So, finding the right case can take a lot of time. That's why if you are in a law library, you look in an index journal, and if you are online, you enter a search.

Law Library

When you are in a law library, start your search by looking in *American Jurisprudence* or *Corpus Juris.* These two legal encyclopedias have table of contents organized by subject. Or, you can look in *American Law Reports.* You look up child custody or child support, and then narrow your search among the dozens of subentries under these main topics. If you already have a case name and you want to follow that case to other relevant cases, use *Shepard's Citations for Cases* or the *West* digest system.

As you follow the trail of references, eventually you will end up at *case reporters.* These are large, bound books that contain case opinions. The reporters are organized by category and region. For example, there is an *Atlantic Reporter,* a *Pacific Reporter,* a *Federal Reporter,* and so on. Then there are specific state reporters, such as *California Reporter.*

If you have access to a good law library and plenty of time on your hands, researching cases in a law library is fine. But with the abundance of websites that contain much of the same information—plus search tools to help you find what you want—it makes more sense to do your research online.

Websites

Legal websites give you the ability to search through millions of cases in seconds. After signing up at a website such as *Findlaw* at www.findlaw.com or *Versuslaw* at www.versuslaw. com, you enter your search arguments in a search box. The website then looks for the cases that meet your search criteria.

Here's an example from Versuslaw:

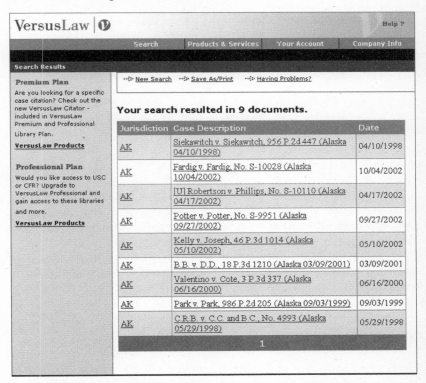

This list of Alaska cases was the result of a search for "Siekawitch." Siekawitch is the name of the parents in the case, so that case came first in the list. Following that case are other cases that contain the same name somewhere in the opinion.

When Karen and Wade divorced in South Dakota, Karen was given custody of their two children. Then, Karen and the children moved to Minnesota, and Wade moved to Missouri. Six years later, Wade asked the South Dakota circuit court to modify his child support. The court agreed, and modified the support amount. Five years after that, Karen registered the South Dakota support order in Minnesota. Wade then asked the Minnesota district court to vacate the registration of the South Dakota order. Karen then asked the Minnesota court to assume jurisdiction over custody and support. The Minnesota district agreed with Wade, and vacated the registration of the South Dakota child support order. *Stone v. Stone* (2001) 636 N.W.2d 594.

If you have searched on a common name, then the other cases might not always be relevant. But if the name is pretty unique, then you will have a list of other cases that refer to your case. The date is also important, because you want to read every case that refers to it and came afterwards.

You don't have to know the name of a case to search. You can also enter "child custody" or "child support." If you do, you will probably get a long list of cases. If you're not sure where to start, try entering a vague or broad search topic, then start reading. Eventually you can do more searches, each time making the search criteria more specific until you eliminate the cases that are not helpful, and include the cases that are.

Reading Cases

However you arrive at a case, you then read it to see if the case is useful. You have to see if the specific facts and the law in the case will help you convince the judge to do what you want.

Here's the first page from an Alaska case:

Filed 4/10/98

IN THE SUPREME COURT OF ALASKA

DANIEL S. SIEKAWITCH,	)	
	)	
Plaintiff and Respondent,	)	S-8233
	)	
v.	)	
	)	Super. Ct.
AMY SIEKAWITCH,	)	No. 3AN-95-4803 CI
	)	
Defendant and Appellant.	)	
	)	

This appeal arises out of a dispute between Daniel and Amy Siekawitch over the custody of their two children. The parties filed a petition for dissolution of marriage in which they agreed that Daniel would have physical custody and that they would amicably arrange for visitation. Their subsequent efforts to agree upon a visitation schedule failed, and Amy moved for a "Specific Physical Custody Schedule." Following a hearing, the superior court ordered the parties to share physical custody equally. Daniel appeals on three grounds. First, he argues that the superior court violated his due process rights by failing to provide him with notice of its intention to modify physical custody. Second, he argues that the superior court erred by failing to find a change in circumstances sufficient to modify custody. Finally, he argues that the superior court erred by failing to consider the proper statutory criteria in determining the best interests of the children. We affirm.

1

In this case, the father, Daniel, was given physical custody of the two children. After the mother, Amy, had problems visiting the children, she asked the trial court to change the custody order to joint physical custody. The trial court agreed. Daniel appealed the decision, but lost.

Because this opinion was written by the highest court in Alaska, it is the law in Alaska. So, if another case came into an Alaska trial court with the exact same or very similar set of facts, the trial judge would have to decide the case the same way the Alaska Supreme Court did.

Notice how specific case law is. Unlike code law which is general, case law describes specific people and what happened to them. That's why there are millions of cases.

When you research cases, you have to read a lot to find the ones that are similar to you. Sifting through this mountain of writing is what makes legal research so time-consuming.

Creating Documents

Once you find the codes, cases, and rules, you then have to create the documents you need.

Creating legal documents means nothing more than assembling the facts and the law into the proper format. If you are filling out a court form, that's easy. But if you have to create a motion from scratch, that can be difficult.

Forms

Just about every court uses pre-printed forms for routine family law matters—petition for divorce, request for child support, request for temporary restraining orders, etc.

To get the forms, it's likely that if your court has a website you can download the forms you need. Or, you can buy the forms from the court clerk, or ask a local paralegal who can get you the forms.

To fill out the form, you have several choices. You can pore over the instructions and then try it yourself, or you can buy a self-help law book, or you can go to a local paralegal and pay him or her to complete the form.

Here's an example of a typical court form:

STATE OF NORTH CAROLINA

_____ County

File No.

In The General Court Of Justice
☐ District ☐ Superior Court Division

Name Of Plaintiff

Address

City, State, Zip

CIVIL SUMMONS

☐ **ALIAS AND PLURIES SUMMONS**

G.S. 1A-1, Rules 3, 4

VERSUS

Name Of Defendant(s)

Date Original Summons Issued

Date(s) Subsequent Summons(es) Issued

To Each Of The Defendant(s) Named Below:

Name And Address Of Defendant 1

Name And Address Of Defendant 2

A Civil Action Has Been Commenced Against You!

You are notified to appear and answer the complaint of the plaintiff as follows:

1. Serve a copy of your written answer to the complaint upon the plaintiff or plaintiff's attorney within thirty (30) days after you have been served. You may serve your answer by delivering a copy to the plaintiff or by mailing it to the plaintiff's last known address, and

2. File the original of the written answer with the Clerk of Superior Court of the county named above.

If you fail to answer the complaint, the plaintiff will apply to the Court for the relief demanded in the complaint.

Name And Address Of Plaintiff's Attorney (If None, Address Of Plaintiff)

Date Issued

Time ☐ AM ☐ PM

Signature

☐ Deputy CSC ☐ Assistant CSC ☐ Clerk Of Superior Court

☐ ENDORSEMENT
This Summons was originally issued on the date indicated above and returned not served. At the request of the plaintiff, the time within which this Summons must be served is extended sixty (60) days.

Date Of Endorsement

Time ☐ AM ☐ PM

Signature

☐ Deputy CSC ☐ Assistant CSC ☐ Clerk Of Superior Court

NOTE TO PARTIES: Many counties have **MANDATORY ARBITRATION** programs in which most cases where the amount in controversy is $15,000 or less are heard by an arbitrator before a trial. The parties will be notified if this case is assigned for mandatory arbitration, and, if so, what procedure is to be followed.

AOC-CV-100, Rev. 10/01
© 2001 Administrative Office of the Courts

(Over)

This is a summons from North Carolina. You send this form to your former spouse to tell him or her to show up in court on a certain day. To complete the form, you write or type your name and address, the date of the hearing, and so on.

Courts use forms for simple, routine matters. So, if your court business is routine, you can usually fill-out a form. However, many issues are not routine, and then you have to create a legal document.

 Thomas and Debra had two children during their seven-year marriage. After they moved from Michigan to Kentucky, Thomas was convicted of cocaine possession and spent ninety days in jail. Debra took the children back to Michigan. Debra then divorced Thomas, and she was awarded sole custody of the children. The next year, Debra married Darren, and they had a son. A few months later, however Debra died. Darren was appointed permanent guardian of the children. At this point, both Thomas and Darren both asked for custody of the children. A circuit court awarded Darren physical custody. A year later, Thomas tried again, and this time, the circuit court found that "a presumption in favor of a natural parent exist[s]" and awarded custody to Thomas. *Greer v. Alexander* (2001) 248 Mich.App. 259, 639 N.W.2d 39.

Legal Documents

Legal documents, such as motions, declarations, etc., take time to create because you're starting from a blank piece of paper.

Unlike a form with boxes to fill in, in a legal document, you have to explain what you want the court to know. And you have to do that in a coherent and understandable way. That means you have to express yourself in a written narrative that is complete.

Here's a sample of a legal document:

1   Martha Caulfield
       16 Bancroft Rd.
2   Madison, NJ 07940
       745-9254
3

4   Attorney for Plaintiff, MARY KINSELLA

5
         SUPERIOR COURT OF THE STATE OF NEW JERSEY
6
              IN AND FOR THE COUNTY OF MORRIS
7

8
   MARY KINSELLA,   )   Case No. 503461
9   )
       Plaintiff,   )
10   )   MOTION FOR
       v.   )   EVIDENTIARY HEARING
11   )
12   JOHN KINSELLA,   )
)
13   Defendant.   )
)
14

15   TO DEFENDANT AND HIS ATTORNEY OF RECORD:

16   PLEASE TAKE NOTICE THAT on March 4, in Department 7 of

17   above-entitled court, Plaintiff hereby moves for an evidentiary hearing.

18   This motion is based upon well-established case authority that requires an

19   evidentiary hearing when there are facts in dispute. If "...relief hinges on the

20   resolution of factual disputes, then the court should order an evidentiary

21   hearing [citations]." *People v. Babbage* (1997) 150 N.J. 726, 696 A.2d 655.

22   Defendant has possession of videotapes that allegedly contains

23   evidence supporting defendant's position regarding plaintiff's conduct while

24   exchanging the two minor children, Maggie and John, Jr. Defendant has not

25   provided a copy of this tape to plaintiff, nor has defendant attempted to

26   introduce this tape as evidence. Nevertheless, defendant has shown this tape

27   to numerous individuals, including the babysitter, Barbara White, the teacher

28   for John, Jr., Sasha Sokolov, and several other unnamed individuals.

This motion asks the court to hold a hearing to make fact findings. The moving party, Mary, is complaining about videotapes made by her former spouse, John, during the exchange of the children. She is asking the trial court to set a date for another hearing. If John opposed this motion, he would create his own document stating his reasons why the evidentiary hearing should not occur.

There are a number of required elements to this document. While it varies from state-to-state, it's likely that the legal documents in your state will look pretty similar.

 If your local court has a website, you can often find plenty of useful information, such as court hours, court holidays, official forms you can download, and more. To find your local court, try entering the court name in any major search engine, or check *Nolo* at www.nolo.com, *AllLaw.com* at www. alllaw.com, the *National Center for State Courts* at www. ncsconline.org, *Court.Net* at www.courts.net, or the *American Bar Association Network* at www.lawtechnology. org/lawlink. They all have links to state court websites.

Writing Legal Documents

The elements to include in a legal document include:

Caption
The top half of the first page contains the case information— or *caption*. The caption identifies everyone involved, the courthouse, the case name, the title of the document, etc. On page two, you omit the caption, and continue the narrative at the top of the page.

Line Numbers
Down the left-hand side of the page are line numbers. This is pretty standard, though the particular style used by your court might be slightly different. Line numbers are used to refer to specific portions of text, such as "page 3, lines 5-8."

To find out what style your court uses, you have to get a sample. You can always find one by going to the courthouse and reading a few case files. These files are public documents, and if you find a particularly active case, you will see many samples. You can also ask a local paralegal (see why finding a paralegal is so important?) or go to a law library and ask the librarian where the form books are. Believe it or not, lawyers need samples, too, and the law books they use have plenty of sample documents.

Narrative

Below the caption, and continuing until the signature lines at the end, is the narrative. This is where you write what you want the court to know and what you want the court to do.

Usually, there is no rigid format to the narrative, but there are several standard phrases you must include. For example, you may have to include the phrase "I am the Plaintiff (or Defendant) in this action, and I swear the following is true" or something like that. The specific wording will be unique to your local court. The best way to find out is to locate a sample and copy the phrases.

Once you write down the stock phrases, the rest of the narrative is free-flowing. To get through this part, it helps to create an outline. The elements of the outline should include:

1. *Facts:* Facts the court needs to know.
2. *Law:* The law that applies to those facts.
3. *Argument:* Why the court should agree with you.
4. *Remedy:* What you want the court to do.

Facts

If you are unsure how to start, it's a good idea to start with the facts. This is as simple as it sounds. Just write down what happened.

For example, in the Alaska case cited earlier in the chapter, Amy would have written down a list of things Daniel did to frustrate her visitation. Then, Amy would have added an explanation of the current custody order.

Law

After writing down the facts, you then say what the law is. In the Alaska case, Amy would have described the Alaska codes and any cases relating to physical custody and frustrating visitation.

Argument

After including the law, you then say how it applies to the facts in your case, and why the judge should agree with you. Because Amy was asking the court to change the custody order, she would also include the codes and cases that support her position that she should be given joint physical custody. She would point out that parents frustrating visitation has happened before, and when it has, the higher courts have ruled that the trial court should modify the custody order.

Remedy

Finally, if you have not said it earlier, you have to tell the judge what you want. Here is where Amy would have said she wanted the custody order changed to give her joint physical custody. If you have organized your narrative clearly, your remedy will be well-supported by the facts and the law. You goal is to make a thorough, persuasive argument and convince the judge you are right.

Citing the Law

When you refer to case opinions or other documents in court papers, you have to correctly "cite" the material. There is a specific, formal way to label your information. At first glance, citations appear strange and cryptic. But once you learn how to read a cite, they are pretty simple.

In legal papers, there are many different kinds of documents you can refer to. The most common are published case opinions. Other documents include statutes, regulations, rules, pending bills, law review articles, books, newspapers, journals, briefs, and so on.

Because you will probably rely on published cases in your court papers, the following summarizes how to handle those citations.

Case Citations

When you refer to a specific case opinion, you have to cite the case. A case citation indicates the people involved, the date when the opinion was published, and where the case can be found in the official legal journals.

Here's an example from a New Mexico case:

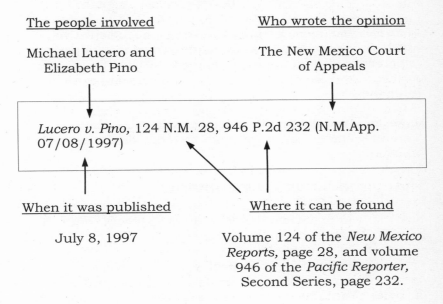

The people involved

Michael Lucero and
Elizabeth Pino

Who wrote the opinion

The New Mexico Court
of Appeals

Lucero v. Pino, 124 N.M. 28, 946 P.2d 232 (N.M.App. 07/08/1997)

When it was published

July 8, 1997

Where it can be found

Volume 124 of the *New Mexico Reports,* page 28, and volume 946 of the *Pacific Reporter,* Second Series, page 232.

You could refer to the case in a sentence such as:

"When custody is awarded to a third-party and the parent does not appeal, that parent cannot re-open the case at a later date claiming a violation of constitutional rights. *Lucero v. Pino,* 124 N.M. 28, 946 P.2d 232 (N.M.App. 07/08/1997)"

If you refer to the same case without citing to something else first, you can abbreviate the cite as:

Id. at 32.

In this example, *Id*—a Latin phrase—tells the reader to look backward, and 32 is the case page number.

If you refer to the same case later after you have cited to something else, you can abbreviate the cite as:

Lucero v. Pino, 124 N.M. at 32.

Please note that this book uses a slightly different style. The cite in this book is *Lucero v. Pino* (1997) 124 N.M. 28, 946 P.2d 232. This alternative cite style is also acceptable.

Whenever you quote the law in your legal documents, you must say where the law can be found. Of course, in day-to-day practice, divorce lawyers rarely cite cases. That's because most custody cases settle, making it unnecessary to quote law to the judge.

However, if you are representing yourself, you must accurately cite the law if you want to persuade the judge that you are correct.

Filing and Serving Documents

Now that you've created the necessary paperwork, you still have to file and serve the documents.

This is where buying a good stack-feed copier comes in handy. Before you go anywhere or do anything, make plenty of copies. You'll need the original plus one or more copies for the court, one copy for each person in the case, and a file copy for yourself. If your former spouse has a lawyer, you only have to send one copy to the lawyer. If your case involves child support, you may need a copy for the District Attorney. If there a lawyer or an advocate representing your child, you will need a copy for this person, too.

Now that you've got plenty of copies, take your papers and your checkbook and head down to your local courthouse.

Filing

To file your papers, you have to go to the courthouse and hand them to the clerk. In many courts, lawyers and paralegals can file papers by fax or mail. However, this professional courtesy is usually reserved for legal professionals, and pro pers typically have to bring their own papers to the courthouse.

When you go to the courthouse, bring the originals, several copies, and a checkbook or some cash. You will need to file the original plus one or more copies. You will also often have to pay a fee. The fee could be as little as $5 or $10, or as high as $200 or $300. It all depends on what the court charges.

Once you enter the courthouse, ask the guard to tell you where you should file your papers. You will usually be directed to stand in line for the court clerk. If there are several lines, be sure to stand in the right one!

The clerk will review your papers to ensure that they are complete and that you have not made any errors. If you have made an error, the clerk may be helpful and correct the error, or hand them back and tell you to fix them and return.

 When Peter and Sandra divorced, they agreed on joint custody of their two children with equal parenting time. Four years later, Peter filed an emergency motion asking for sole custody. The court granted his motion and suspended Sandra's contact with the children until she obtained counseling. The court also said the guardian ad litem could change the custody schedule at any time. On appeal, the decision to award Peter custody was upheld, but the order granting the guardian ad litem authority to change the custody schedule was reversed. *In re Marriage of McNamara* (1998) 962 P.2d 330.

If your papers are accepted for filing by the clerk, and you need a hearing date, the clerk will select the date and tell you what it is. Typically, you'll have to pay a fee for a hearing date, though again, it all depends on the nature of the hearing and the court rules.

In some instances, such as filing an answer to moving papers already filed by your ex-spouse, you may be told to bring the documents directly to the courtroom and give them to the clerk in the courtroom. If that happens, you may not be allowed to go directly to the clerk, but instead, will have to hand the papers to the bailiff, who will give them to the clerk.

With certain papers, you will have to write the hearing date on the document—or the clerk will do it for you—and then send a copy to everyone involved. When you send copies of your documents to everyone, it is called service.

Service

Filing your documents with the court is only half the job. You still have to give everyone a copy.

Service is important. If you make a mistake, the judge can dismiss or delay your case, or ignore what you wrote. So it's a good idea to serve your documents correctly.

There are many rules about service. If you are the first person to go to court and you are starting the case, it is likely you will have to serve a copy of your papers by personal service. If you are responding to something from your ex-spouse, or if your case is on-going, you can probably mail your papers. Typically, however, you cannot serve your papers yourself, but rather, another adult has to do it for you.

Personal Service
When you personally serve somebody, you have another adult hand that person the papers. There are rules about who can personally serve legal papers. In some courts, you have to use the sheriff or a process server. If you do, you usually have to pay a fee. In other courts, you can use any adult not connected to the case.

If the papers have to be personally served—and the court clerk can tell you if they do—the server will have to locate the person and personally deliver the documents.

As you can imagine, not everyone likes a stranger coming up to them and sticking papers in their face. In fact, personal service can become very confrontational. Most states allow servers to drop the papers at the feet of the person being served if he or she refuses to accept the papers. Or, the server can nail the papers to the door if the person refuses to answer.

Once service is complete, the server needs to fill out a form stating where and when service occurred.

Here's an example of a form for service:

Service forms are usually not complicated, You have to include case information, the name of the person who did the service, and when it happened. The main reason for the form is that the server swears under oath that they really did deliver the documents.

Service by Publication
If you don't know where your former spouse is, you can often serve the documents by paying for a box in a local newspaper.

This kind of service is more time-consuming and difficult, because before you go to the newspaper, you first have to make a reasonable effort to locate your ex-spouse. Generally, you have to ask family and friends, check telephone books, check voter registration information, and so on. You have to do enough to convince the judge you have really tried to locate your ex-spouse, and he or she has simply vanished.

When you serve by publication, you usually have to prepare and file an additional document with the court listing all of the things you did to find your ex-spouse. If you convince the judge, you will be allowed to proceed with your case by placing a notice in a newspaper that runs for several weeks. Once the newspaper has finished running the notice, you can ask the court to rule on your case without your former spouse being there.

Chapter 19

Arguing in Court

- ✓ In family court, most issues are decided in *hearings* that last from five minutes to an hour. Full-day hearings are rare.

- ✓ Hearings are informal and let the judge manage the hearing as he or she sees fit. When you argue at a hearing, bring to the judge's attention the facts he should know and what you want him to do.

- ✓ If you are having a *trial,* you must prepare ahead of time. You have to subpoena your *witnesses* and arrange your *exhibits.*

- ✓ Trials are formal presentations where you question witnesses and introduce evidence.

- ✓ Depending on the witness, you ask *open, closed,* and *leading* questions. You usually ask friendly witnesses open-ended questions, and hostile witnesses closed or leading questions.

- ✓ When you want to prevent something from becoming evidence, you *object.* There are many forms of objections, including *irrelevant, hearsay,* and so on.

- ✓ To introduce physical evidence, you have to prove that the evidence is both relevant and authentic. You do that by *laying foundation.*

Your Day in Court

When you arrive in court, you will have either a hearing or a trial. Hearings are common in family law, and most issues are decided during a hearing. Trials are unusual, and if you are scheduled for trial, you will know ahead of time.

The main difference between the two is the formality. Hearings are informal and allow the judge to manage the hearing as he or she sees fit. Trials follow a formal, predictable pattern of questioning, objecting, and arguing.

Always plan on arriving at the courthouse before your case is scheduled to be called. If your courthouse has metal detectors—and many do—you will spend time just getting into the building. On a busy day, you may not be able to park near the building, and will have to drive around looking for a spot.

Hearings

Before your case is called, you usually have to check-in with the clerk or bailiff. This means quietly stating that you are present. Sometimes you don't have to check in, but instead, the judge or clerk will read the names of the scheduled cases. If your case is announced, you have to answer that you are present.

By *calling the calendar,* the judge is going through the cases and figuring out which ones are going to be heard and how long each one will take. With this information, the judge can plan the day. If you or your opponent are not present when your case is called, the judge can delay it to later in the day, delay it to another day, or take it off the court calendar completely.

While waiting for your case to be called, if you are representing yourself, you can talk to the lawyer representing your former spouse. However, most lawyers don't want to have a private conversation with an opposing party who is in pro per. To do so might appear as if the lawyer is making a secret deal.

When Megan gave birth to her daughter, Chantel, she was not married to the father, Larry. However, at the hospital, Larry signed a Certificate of Parentage legally establishing his paternity. After leaving the hospital, Megan and Chantel moved in with Megan's mother and stepfather, Beverly and Kevin Nelson. Twelve days later, Megan died in a car accident. At Megan's funeral, Larry told Beverly he wanted custody of his daughter, but Beverly refused to give Chantel to him. The Nelsons then asked to be appointed guardians for Chantel, arguing that "[d]oubt exists with respect to the infant's paternity." Larry complained that the Nelson's were depriving him of contact with his daughter. A probate judge granted temporary guardianship to the Nelsons, then transferred the case to the family division. After a full hearing, the family court decided the Nelsons could do a better job raising Chantel, and named them as guardians. Larry appealed the decision, and the Court of Appeal agreed with the family court. Larry appealed again, and the New Jersey Supreme Court reversed, ordering that Chantel be immediately transferred to Larry. The New Jersey Supreme Court decided that "Upon the death of the custodial parent, in an action for guardianship of a child... a presumption exists in favor of the surviving biological parent. That presumption can be rebutted by proof of gross misconduct, abandonment, unfitness, or the existence of 'exceptional circumstances,' but never by a simple application of the best interests test." *Watkins v. Nelson* (2000) 163 N.J. 235, 748 A.2d 558.

Sooner or later, the judge or clerk will announce your case. You are expected to stand up and walk over to the *counsel tables*. Once there, you and your opponent will *state your appearance*. This means saying that you are present.

At this point, the formalities are over and the hearing is underway. Now, the judge will consider the pleadings and any other issues brought to his attention. Depending on the judge, you may begin to speak, or wait until the judge tells you to. When you do speak, you will be arguing your case.

Argument

When you argue your case, you bring to the judge's attention the facts he should know and what you want him to do. Time is very short in hearings, and judges usually know the law, so you need to concentrate on the facts.

There are no magic words to say, just clearly explain the facts. Here is an example of argument during a hearing:

Argument During a Hearing

Advocate: Your honor, the facts are that when Ms. Romano went to pick up her children, she was angry and out of control. When her daughter didn't want to go with her, she then slapped the girl so violently that the child needed emergency treatment at the hospital. Ms. Romano then tried to cover up her violent abuse by lying that the child fell off a swing. However, the photographs of the injury, and the sworn testimony of the doctor who treated the child, reveal that the girl was violently abused.

If you and your former spouse are both representing yourselves, expect the judge to take control. Judges believe that pro pers cannot boil down the issues to the key points, and thus, feel they have to do the work.

If your ex-spouse has an attorney, the judge will probably ask the attorney to explain the issues. You will be allowed to speak, but the judge will be more interested in what the lawyer says. Yes, this is bias, but it's how the legal system really works.

Here are some general rules about argument:
- Do not interrupt your opponent, and do not allow your opponent to interrupt you.
- When you refer to the judge, call the judge "Your Honor."
- When you refer to law, be prepared to give the full citation.
- Keep your points relevant to the issues.
- Stay cool and professional.

The main purpose of the hearing is for the judge to figure out which issues have been settled and which are still contested. If you and your former spouse have agreed on any issue, inform the judge. The judge will then only address the issues still in dispute. Normally, each side can argue why the judge should rule in his or her favor.

Oral argument is not easy, and skilled lawyers know how to think fast on their feet, throw out surprises to keep the other side off balance, and take control of the hearing by talking non-stop.

Unless you have had a lot of court experience, you will not impress the judge with your brilliant oration. Just stick to the facts and demand that the judge pay attention.

After the Hearing

Depending on the judge and the local rules of court, the hearing will not last long. Twenty minutes is common, though some courts may allow a hearing to stretch out for an hour or more. In family law, an all-day hearing is unusual.

You know the hearing is over when the judge tells you. At that point the judge may make a *ruling*, or take it *under submission*, which means the judge will make a ruling later. If the issues have not been fully addressed, the judge can continue the case to another day. This is normal, and it could take several—or even several dozen—hearings for the judge to make a ruling.

Trials

A trial begins just like a hearing. You check-in with the clerk or bailiff, wait for your case to be called, and then walk over to the counsel table and state your appearance.

After that, however, a trial is different. Even in a family courtroom—which is run more loosely than other courtrooms—trials require more formality. For an explanation of the basic steps of a trial, please see *Chapter 23: Trials and Appeals.*

John Hill and Soheyla Matin occasionally lived together during a ten year period. During one of their breakups, Soheyla was awarded custody of their child by a California court. They both moved to Florida and lived together for a few more years, then Soheyla moved out with the child. Two years later, John filed an ex parte motion in circuit court asking for temporary custody. His motion contained allegations about Soheyla's drinking and poor parenting skills. The court granted the emergency order and gave custody to John, but the Court of Appeals reversed. *Matin v. Hill* (2001) 801 So.2d 1003.

Depending on your judge, you may have to give an *opening statement.* You don't have to worry about addressing the jury or even selecting jurors, since family law trials are *bench trials.* But you do have to worry about the judge, since he or she is the person who is making the decision in your case.

If there are any potential witnesses in the courtroom, you or your opponent should ask the judge to *exclude all witnesses.* This means the witnesses must wait outside the courtroom and cannot come in until they are called.

Questioning Witnesses

After the opening statement, the moving party calls witnesses and introduces evidence. To call a witness, you state the name of the person and then the bailiff or clerk will tell the witness to take the stand.

When a witness takes the stand, he or she must sit near the judge and be sworn in. The clerk will ask the witness "Do you solemnly swear to tell the truth, the whole truth and nothing but the truth, so help you God?" By requiring the witness to tell the truth, if the witness lies, he or she can be charged with the crime of perjury. In reality, however, many people lie in family court, and very few are charged with perjury. After the witness agrees, whoever called the witness asks questions.

The witness can be an ordinary witness, an expert witness, or a hostile witness, and the phase of the trial can be direct-examination, cross-examination, redirect, or re-cross. Depending on the type of witness and the phase of the trial, you ask open, closed, and leading questions.

Open Questions

If you are questioning someone supportive to your position, you generally ask *open questions.* These questions allow the witness to answer in his or her own words.

For example, suppose you are questioning a family member. This witness has first-hand knowledge of a fact you want to prove. To bring out this knowledge, you ask the witness simple, open-ended questions, such as:

Open Questions

Advocate: Ms. Baker, please tell us what happened last year on June 21, at approximately 5pm.

Ms. Baker: I have a daycare business in my home, and on that day I was watching the two children, Max and Amy. At 5pm, Amanda, the mother, arrived to pick up the children. We were in the backyard when she rang the bell. I went to the front door to let her in. She asked where the children were, and I told her they were in the back. She went to the backyard, and I went into the kitchen. A few moments later, I heard Amy crying. I looked through the kitchen window and from where I stood, I could see Amanda strike Amy.

The main point to remember is that you not only have to ask the witness about the facts you want to prove, but you must prove the witness has first-hand knowledge of the facts.

For example, if the witness saw your ex-spouse harming the children, you first have to ask the witness about the day, time, hour, etc., to establish the witness has first-hand knowledge of what he or she will say.

Closed Questions

A *closed question* elicits a short, specific answer that brings out a specific detail. You can use this questioning at any time with any kind of witness.

For example, suppose you are questioning a babysitter. Because a babysitter is probably not experienced in testifying, you may need to ask specific questions to draw out the facts. Here's an example:

Closed Questions

Advocate: Ms. Baker, how long have you been running a daycare business?

Ms. Baker: Three years.

Advocate: How many children do you watch on an average day?

Ms. Baker: Five to six.

Advocate: On June 21 of last year, were you watching any children in your professional capacity as a babysitter?

Ms. Baker: Yes.

Advocate: How many children and what were their names?

Ms. Baker: I was watching two children on that day, Max and Amy.

Advocate: Are these the two children of Tony and Amanda Romano, the plaintiff and defendant in this case?

Ms. Baker: Yes.

Closed questioning helps bring out information from a witness. If you only rely on narrative or open-ended questions for friendly witnesses, the witness may forget a crucial fact.

Leading Questions

Leading questions are usually used on uncooperative—or *hostile*—witnesses. If you are questioning a witness who does not want to reveal a specific fact, or if you are trying to *impeach* a witness by proving that he or she lied, you may need to ask leading questions.

Here's how you might question a difficult witness:

Leading Questions

Advocate: Mrs. Romano, isn't it true that you went to Ms. Baker's home last year on June 21st at approximately 5pm?

Ms. Romano: I don't recall what time it was.

Advocate: Did you go to Ms. Baker's home last year on June 21st?

Ms. Romano: Yes.

Advocate: And when you arrived at her house that day, was it after noon and before 6pm?

Ms. Romano: Probably.

Advocate: Is that yes or no?

Ms. Romano: Yes.

Advocate: And when you arrived at Ms. Baker's home in the afternoon, isn't it true that you knocked on the front door and Ms. Baker let you in?

Ms. Romano: I always knock on the front door.

Advocate: You didn't answer my question. Did you knock on the front door and did Ms. Baker let you in on the day in question?

Ms. Romano: Yes.

Cold feet. It's a good idea to always subpoena your witnesses. Court can be an intimidating place, and even family or friends may suddenly change their mind about testifying.

Leading questions are the opposite of open-ended questions. You do not ask the witness to explain something, but rather, you ask the witness a specific question that calls for a "yes" or "no" answer. Leading questions require very precise, persistent questioning because the witness may not want to reveal what you want revealed, and you have to force the witness answer the questions.

Types of Witnesses

You question different witnesses differently during a trial. Here's an overview.

Ordinary Witnesses

If you call yourself, a family member, or a friend in a child custody case, you are calling an ordinarywitness. This witness does not have any special training, but has first-hand knowledge of a fact you want to prove. To bring out this knowledge, ask the witness simple, open-ended questions.

Expert Witnesses

Expert witnesses do not have first-hand knowledge, but they have special skills and knowledge that allows them to testify. To question an expert witness, you begin by asking questions that demonstrate the expert's professional credentials so that he or she can be accepted as an expert on a particular

I'm mad as hell! If you're fed up with the lawyers, judges, and psychologists in divorce court, go online and share your complaints. One site, www.familylawcourt.com, gets more than 600 hits a day, according to *California Lawyer* magazine. Another site, www.nationalcoalition.net forced changes to the local family court.

subject. In child custody matters, a typical expert witness is a mental health professional who has evaluated the family. After asking the expert questions about his or her training and experience, you then ask the court to accept the witness as an expert on the area of expertise. If the court agrees, you then ask the expert to explain his or her opinion.

Hostile Witnesses

In a child custody battle, you will probably question the other parent, a family member, or a friend of the other parent. Since this person is unlikely to be candid, you can ask to declare this witness a hostile witness. If the judge agrees with you, you then can ask leading questions.

Objections

When you object, you tell the judge a statement or other piece of evidence may be improper. You must object the moment you become aware of the problem, and then the judge decides if your objection is correct. The decision to admit or exclude evidence is complex, but generally, the judge decides if the evidence is relevant and has been correctly introduced.

To object, state in a loud voice, "Objection, Your Honor," and then state your reason for the objection. Here is a short list of common objections.

Irrelevant

You can object when something is not relevant to the case. For example, suppose you are disputing child custody and your ex-spouse testifies that you and your new mate engage in bizarre sex acts. This fact might not be relevant unless your former spouse also shows that the alleged sex acts are witnessed by the children.

Hearsay

Hearsay is anything attributed to someone who is not in court. Because the statement is not being repeated by the person who allegedly said it, there is potential to lie, and that is why the statement is excluded. However, there are many exceptions that allow hearsay to be admitted, including excited utterances and present sense impressions.

Argumentative

If the statement is argumentative—that is, the question or answer does not reveal evidence, but instead is an argument in the form of a question—you can object. For example, if you were on the witness stand, and the opposing lawyer asked you, "You don't expect the court to believe you, do you?" That would be an improper question.

Lack of Foundation

If a piece of evidence has not been properly introduced, you should object on this ground. For example, if your former spouse is testifying about something else, and then suddenly blurts out that you don't care about the children, you could object on several grounds, including lack of foundation.

Physical Evidence

In addition to evidence from witness testimony, you may have documents or other physical evidence in your case. To introduce physical evidence, you usually have to follow some specific steps.

 When Jessica and Marvin divorced, Jessica was designated the primary residential custodian of their two children, Gavin and Danielle, and Marvin was given visitation. Three years later, Jessica told Marvin she was remarrying and moving to Lewistown. Marvin asked the court to give him custody, but his request was denied. Six months later, Jessica took Gavin to a doctor, who diagnosed Gavin with Attention Deficit/Hyperactivity Disorder (AD/HD). Marvin also brought the children to a psychologist, who diagnosed Danielle with adjustment disorder with anxiety and underlying emotional distress and Gavin with adjustment disorder with mixed anxiety and depressed mood. Armed with this new information, Marvin again asked for custody, this time complaining that the children were not "adjusting well" to Jessica's new husband. The district court gave him custody of the children. *In re Marriage of Drake* (2002) 310 Mont. 114, 49 P.3d 38, 2002 MT 127.

"Our litigation system is too costly, too painful, too destructive, too inefficient for a truly civilized people." *Warren Burger,* Supreme Court Chief Justice

Marking Exhibits

Depending on your judge's preference, you may have to arrive in court early and ask the clerk to mark your exhibits. This is easy to do. Usually, you just put a label on the exhibit, and the clerk enters the number or letter into the exhibit list. You can also do this during the trial if the judge allows. You also identify your exhibits and show them—or give a copy—to the other side.

Laying Foundation

Before the judge can accept physical evidence, you have to lay foundation. This means proving through testimony that the exhibit is relevant and authentic. Laying foundation is easy if everyone agrees, but if the other side objects, you have to thoroughly demonstrate why the judge must admit the evidence. For example, if you are introducing a document, you may have to subpoena the keeper of the document just to testify that the document is authentic and has not been forged or tampered with.

Receiving Evidence

Once you are finished laying foundation, but before you can use it, you have to ask the judge to admit the evidence. This is easy. For example, if you are the plaintiff, and this is your first exhibit, you would say, "Your Honor, I request that this document be received as Petitioner's Exhibit 1." If the judge agrees, the document is now part of the evidence and you can refer to it.

Do It Yourself

Plenty of sites sell divorce forms, but most forms you need are probably free on your court website. If you need help doing the paperwork, you can check out one of the many fee websites.

Law Info
www.lawinfo.com
Click on "Legal Resource Center," select "Family Law" and your state, and you will see links to free official legal forms you can download.

Find Forms
www.findforms.com
This site sells "Premium" forms, but before you buy, click on "Free Court Forms" and search to see if the forms you need are already available for download.

Divorce Direct
www.divorcedirect.com
A divorce forms website supported by National eForms. They prepare your divorce forms for a fee: "$200.00 for a divorce or legal separation package which does not involve children and $250.00 if children are involved."

Complete Case
www.completecase.com
If you have an uncontested divorce, this site charges $249.00 to produce the filled-in forms you print, sign, and file with the court. Filing instructions are included.

Our Divorce Agreement
www.ourdivorceagreement.com
For $149.00, this site will prepare a "Memorandum of Understanding," a spreadsheet for dividing your assets and liabilities, and financial disclosure forms for you and your spouse.

How Courts Work

"I wish to continue the case, your Honor.
My client still has $500 left."

Chapter 20

Introduction to the Law

- ✓ Because your life will be affected by many laws and rules, it helps to have an understanding of basic law.

- ✓ Federal and state laws are organized in groups called *substance* and *procedure, civil* and *criminal.* Child custody and child support are civil substantive law, though other laws also apply.

- ✓ *Uniform laws* are model laws passed individually by each state. Two important uniform laws are the *Uniform Child Custody Jurisdiction Act,* which addresses interstate custody disputes, and the *Uniform Interstate Family Support Act,* which addresses interstate support problems.

- ✓ *Case law* is a written opinion from a higher review court, such as an appellate court, that clarifies federal and state laws.

- ✓ *Court rules* are made by state or local judges, and address common procedural issues such as time limits, etc.

- ✓ *Policies* are informal preferences of an individual judge. In child custody, the particular bias of a particular judge is very important.

Where Laws Come From

When you get divorced, you will be controlled by many laws. Lawyers, judges, paralegals, the District Attorney, even police officers and social workers—will all know the laws and tell you what you can and cannot do. That's why it helps to know basic legal concepts and terms.

As you navigate the maze of laws, keep in mind that child custody is composed of laws—formal, written-down rules that tell you what you can and cannot do—and policies—informal, subjective rules that spring from the personality of the judge who hears your case.

Here's a diagram:

Where Laws Come From

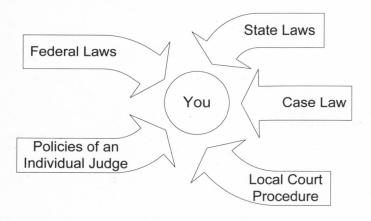

When it comes to custody, some of the rules, such as *federal statutes,* may never apply to you, while others, such as *local court procedure,* may only affect you if you actually go to court. Nevertheless, as a separated or divorced parent, you must learn the new rules.

Since there are many sources of rules and laws, it can be confusing to decide what's important and what's not. The best place to start—and the source of most rules—are *federal and state laws.*

Federal and State Laws

When thinking about the laws in the United States, it's useful to remember that the United States is just that—a group of states. That is, America is really a collection of individual states banded together by a common constitution, called the *United States Constitution.*

This means there is one unifying federal government and 50 individual state governments. In each government, a body of lawmakers—called a *legislature*—creates laws. The U.S. Congress creates *federal statutes,* and *state legislatures* create *state* statutes.

You need to know this because wherever you go, there are two sets of laws that apply to you—the laws of the state you are in, and the laws of the federal government. The laws of the state only apply to people who live or work in that state, while federal laws apply to everyone in the entire country.

There are many other types of law—such as *ordinances, regulations,* and *administrative codes*—but they normally don't affect you just because you're a separated or divorced parent.

Federal Statutes
Federal statutes cover many issues, but are usually limited to topics specifically mentioned in the U.S. Constitution—crimes, bankruptcy, immigration, interstate commerce, and so on.

When child custody is involved, there are some federal laws you need to know, such as the *Parental Kidnapping Prevention Act.* However, most of the laws that influence your case are state laws.

State Statutes
State statutes are where you'll find many of the laws that affect you. State laws, or codes, cover many issues, such as: contracts, corporations, landlord-tenant relationships, personal injuries, real estate, worker's compensation, and much more.

State law also includes family law, which includes divorce, child custody and child support.

Federal and state statutes are organized by subject and published in books. Federal laws can be found in a series of books called the *United States Code,* and state laws can be found in state code books. You can find both types of books in a law library.

As you begin to understand the laws that affect you, you'll discover that child custody and child support are always determined by the state. Because each state can—and does—create its own laws, this creates endless complications.

For example, on a simple level, the very words used to decide the issues may change. In New York, money paid to an ex-spouse for their benefit is called *alimony.* In California, that same payment is called *spousal support.*

On a more substantial level, when custody is set by a court in one state, and a parent moves to a different state and tries to have it changed, this creates problems. The courts in both states must decide who has authority to make the decision.

How Law Is Organized

To create some order out of a diverse collection of laws, lawmakers have devised a system. This system groups together laws that are similar.

The type of law can be criminal or civil, substantive or procedural.

Criminal Law
Criminal law concerns offenses against society. When a person commits a crime, the state charges them. In order to prove the defendant guilty, the prosecution must convince a jury beyond a reasonable doubt. If the accused person is convicted, the punishment is usually imprisonment.

Criminal defendants have many rights, including the right to a jury trial if the crime carries a punishment of six months or more in jail or prison. Also, the jury must reach a unanimous verdict for the person to be found guilty. Additionally, a criminal defendant has the right to have an attorney appointed if he or she cannot afford one.

Civil Law

Civil law, on the other hand, concerns private disputes between two individuals or businesses. When someone violates a civil law, they are sued by another person—the plaintiff. To prove the defendant is liable, the plaintiff must convince a judge or jury by a preponderance of the evidence. If found liable, usually that person has to pay.

Civil defendants don't automatically have the right to a jury trial, and if they do, only three-fourths of the jurors must agree. Also, civil defendants do not automatically have the right to have an attorney appointed if he or she cannot afford one.

The laws of child custody and child support are civil law.

Substantive Law

Substantive law governs the behavior of people. Substantive laws describe the rights we enjoy and the responsibilities we have to each other.

Substance is specific to the issue you're involved in. For example, substantive criminal law includes assault and battery, burglary, drunk driving, murder, rape, etc.

 Before their daughter was born, Kelly and Stephen decided to place their child up for adoption with Jan and Michael Rosman. The Rosmans took the child home from the hospital after her birth. However, less than 30 days later, Stephen changed his mind and decided he wanted custody. Even though the Rosmans and Kelly opposed him, Stephen persevered, and after a five-day trial, he was given sole custody. The court also ordered Kelly to pay child support and the Rosmans to pay Stephen's attorney fees. On appeal, the decision to make the Rosmans pay Stephen's fees was reversed, but the custody decision was upheld and Kelly still had to pay child support. *Mize v. Kendall* (2001) 621 N.W.2d 804.

When Kristine and Thomas divorced, they had two boys, ages 11 months and 3 years. Both parents were on active duty in the United States Army when they divorced, and by agreement, they shared joint custody with Thomas having primary residential custody. Kristine was given "reasonable visitation privileges at times mutually agreed upon." Four years later, when Thomas was about to be sent to Korea for a year, Kristine filed a motion asking for temporary custody of the children during the year Thomas was gone. Thomas stated the children would live with his present wife, Leisha, and his grandparents while he was gone. The court denied Kristine's request, and Thomas kept custody. *In re Marriage of Rayman* (2002) Kansas No. 88,051.

Substantive civil law includes bankruptcy, civil rights law, contracts, employment law, etc. As you can imagine, there are all kinds of substantive laws that you already know, such as the *Motor Vehicle* and *Internal Revenue* laws.

Procedural Law
Procedure is how you do things in the legal system.

For example, if you want your ex-spouse to produce a copy of his bank statements prior to a hearing, you are using a procedural law—called *discovery*—which forces the other party to divulge information. The laws of procedure do not distinguish whether you're involved in a divorce trial or a criminal trial—the procedure is pretty much the same.

Examples of criminal procedure law include arrests and arraignments, extradition, indictments, jury selection, plea bargains, and probation. Examples of civil procedure law include depositions, interrogatories, pleadings, production of documents, and summary judgments.

While federal courts must follow the *Federal Rules of Civil Procedure*, state courts are free to make up their own procedures, and there are differences in procedural laws from one state to the next.

When you deal with the legal system, you will constantly run into laws. It helps to remember that many laws you encounter are procedural. If you're told you have a certain number of days to file a court document—that is a procedural law. You must obey procedural laws to have your issues presented in court. If you do not obey the procedural laws, the judge cannot—or will not—do what you want.

Once you have followed the procedural laws to bring your issues to court, you then have to argue how the substantive laws apply to convince the judge to rule in your favor.

Uniform Laws

One of the problems created when each state makes its own custody laws is that some people try to shop around, looking for a court in a state that will give them a favorable decision.

That's why the *National Conference of Commissioners on Uniform State Laws (NCCUSL)*—a group of judges, lawyers, and law professors—has created a set of model laws. These uniform laws are drafts of laws that each state may adopt in whole, in part, or not at all.

By adopting uniform laws, states remove some of the inconsistencies inherent in interstate custody and support orders. Unfortunately, not all states have adopted the laws, and when they have, they may have changed them. This, of course, makes uniform laws no longer uniform.

While many uniform laws have not been adopted by all states, two laws, the *Uniform Child Custody Jurisdiction Act* and the *Uniform Interstate Family Support Act,* have been adopted by all states.

 If you want to read about a uniform law that was adopted by your state, look in a law library for the *Uniform Laws Annotated (U.L.A.)* series. These books contain the laws, states that adopted the laws, and summaries of cases that interpreted the laws.

Uniform Child Custody Jurisdiction Act (UCCJA)

This uniform law addresses the problems of interstate child custody disputes. When a parent asks a court to make a custody ruling, the court must decide if it has authority to make a custody order. This law designates which state is the "home state" of the child and gives that court authority to make a custody order.

Generally, the law makes the home state wherever the child had lived for the past six months. But there are exceptions. If the court decides that it is an "inconvenient forum" to hear the case—which could be based on something as vague as another state having a closer "emotional connection" to the child—the court can decline the case. Or if the child is involved in a case in another state—known as a "simultaneous proceeding"—then under the UCCJA, the court must refuse the case.

Every year, tens of thousands of parents ask a judge to establish or modify child custody, and the cases involve problems that invoke the UCCJA.

Uniform Interstate Family Support Act (UIFSA)

By 1998, all states adopted this uniform law to replace the two prior interstate child support laws, the *Uniform Reciprocal Enforcement of Support Act (URESA)* and its revised version *RURESA*. This uniform law addresses the problems of creating and enforcing child support orders across state lines.

Among other elements, UIFSA eliminates the problem of two states making different support orders. It does this by giving the first state "continuing, exclusive jurisdiction" over child support. UIFSA also addresses the problem of a support order made in one state that must be enforced in a second state. This law limits the role of the court in the second state to enforcing the order. UIFSA reduces the authority of the court in the second state to enforcing the support order and doing little else—with only limited exceptions.

Interstate support problems are as common as interstate custody problems, and courts throughout the U.S. turn to these two uniform laws for guidance.

The *Uniform Child Custody Jurisdiction Act* specifically prevents two states from deciding custody of the same child at the same time. The law states, in part: "A court of this State shall not exercise its jurisdiction under this Act if at the time of filing the petition a proceeding concerning the custody of the child was pending in a court of another state exercising jurisdiction substantially in conformity with this Act, unless the proceeding is stayed by the court of the other state because this State is a more appropriate forum or for other reasons." *Uniform Child Custody Jurisdiction Act, Section 6(a).*

Case Law

Another source of rules that affect you are *case laws*.

When a court decides a case, the decision may influence future cases with similar circumstances. That's because each judge tries to be consistent and decide similar cases in similar ways. This history is called case law.

A judge may follow previous decisions for three reasons:

Persuasive Authority
Sometimes a previous case has no formal authority over cases that follow it, but the decision by the court was so clearly written, thorough, and well-reasoned, that other judges voluntarily choose to follow it. This is called *persuasive authority.*

Interpreted Statute
When lawmakers write laws, they frequently create text that is difficult to understand or full of words that have specialized meaning. Eventually, a judge has to apply the law, and he or she must interpret what those words mean. When a judge decides a case by *interpreting* a statute, he or she guides the decisions of future judges.

Established Precedent

When someone doesn't agree with the decision of a trial judge, they can appeal that decision to a higher court—called an appellate court. When the justices in the appellate court reach a decision, their decision creates a precedent. A *precedent* is a decision that judges must follow when deciding future similar cases.

Because the court system is organized in a hierarchy, decisions made by higher courts are formally binding on lower courts—but not the other way around. Also, decisions made by courts in one state are only binding on lower courts in that same state. Only the very top court in the nation—the U.S. Supreme Court—makes decisions that every other court must follow.

You can find a complete description of how to cite many different kinds of source material in *The Bluebook: A Uniform System of Citation.* This compact book, published by the Columbia, Harvard, University of Pennsylvania, and Yale Law Reviews, is an excellent authority for writing citations.

Precedent is an important part of the law, and judges strive to make decisions consistent with earlier cases. However, when a judge decides a case, he or she is only resolving a given set of facts and a specific legal issue. Because—like snowflakes— virtually no two cases are exactly the same, judges in future cases can deviate from the decision by differentiating the case based on some inconsequential point. Also, a judge can decide a case differently by reasoning that the times have changed, and the precedent no longer holds.

Local Court Procedure

The next set of rules that affect you are known as local court *rules.* These are the rules specific to each of the thousands of family courts across the nation.

Courts make local rules to manage caseflow. For example, on a typical day, many dozens of people may be ordered to appear, a sizable number of attorneys may represent them, all the proper forms must have been filled out, copies of the forms will have to have been given to both the judge and the other party, and so on. Ensuring that all this gets done is a complex logistical undertaking, and it must occur every day the court is open.

Court rules are designed to process people and paperwork through the system. The rules help move people through the court, yet give everyone a chance to tell their story.

 This international custody dispute began when Devra and Nicholas, who were married in Colorado and Greece and had two children in Greece, came to Colorado for medical treatment for one child. Nicholas returned to Greece, but Devra stayed in Colorado with the children. Nicholas repeatedly asked her to return to Greece with the children, but Devra refused. Nicholas finally filed for divorce in Greece and was granted custody by a Greece court. Devra filed for divorce in Colorado, but a magistrate decided Colorado had no authority over Nicholas. Relying on the Hague Convention and the UCCJA, Nicholas then asked the Colorado court to order Devra to turn over the children to be delivered to Greece. She did so and then appealed, but the Court of Appeals agreed the Greece court was the proper place to decide custody. *In re Marriage of Jeffers and Makropoulos* (1999) 992 P.2d 686.

Court rules come from two places:

State Rules of Court

State rules usually apply to all courts within the state. A typical example is when a statute requires that certain information be given to the court—the state rule will specify the exact document that is to be used. State rules often come from the state's supreme court. They may be tailored for different counties or for different types of courts, such as municipal courts, superior courts, appellate courts, and so on.

Local Rules of Court

Local rules apply only to a particular courthouse. These rules can be quite detailed, and may include everything from the size of the paper used, to how many holes must be punched and on what edge. Local rules are created by the personnel in the local court.

When you have a dispute, you must not only understand the laws that apply, but also the rules that dictate how the dispute will be resolved. You may have a good case, but if you don't follow the rules, it will not proceed.

If you hire a local attorney, you can assume that he or she will know the local court rules. If you represent yourself, you'll need to learn the rules.

Policies of an Individual Judge

The final rules that affect you are the *policies* of the individual judge.

This one person will be making the major decisions in your life. The trial judge will decide who gets custody of the children and who pays support.

Judges play such a significant role due to two reasons: the laws allow for individual discretion by the trial judge, and each judge will interpret a situation differently.

Judge's Discretion

Though the laws in each state specify how to decide a dispute, they are—by necessity—somewhat vague. If the laws were written with exacting precision, there would be times when a strict application of those laws would be unfair. Thus, judges are given the authority to tailor the broad intent of the law to the special circumstances of your case.

This makes the individual trial judge very important. In family law, the judge must listen to all the evidence, decide what is relevant, and then apply the correct laws to reach a decision. And he or she must decide based on a preponderance of the evidence.

Judge's Interpretation

When evaluating evidence, a judge must interpret the facts to arrive at a solution. How the judge interprets those facts reflects his or her opinions and prejudices.

A judge is not a computer, and he or she will have a certain outlook, belief, and attitude. When a judge evaluates a set of facts, he or she will attempt to categorize those facts and make a decision. Over time, the accumulated history of those decisions reveals the individual thinking of the judge.

The policies of an individual judge may include whether to:
- Favor mothers or fathers in awarding custody of the children.
- Accept or decline the recommendation made by a custody evaluator.
- Encourage or discourage joint custody awards.
- Consider or dismiss the child's custody preference.
- Accept or deviate from the guideline amount of child support.
- Award attorney's fees to one parent.

Lawyers know how important the personality of the judge is, and that's why they have a saying:

"Don't tell me the law, tell me who the judge is."

 How important is the judge? Here's what Lynne Gold-Bikin, former head of the American Bar Association's family law section, had to say, "Judges have enormous discretion. You can take the same set of facts and put them in front of five different judges and get five different results."

Chapter 21

Courts, Calendars, and Judges

✓ Our legal system is based on two people fighting. The person who "wins" the fight is deemed right.

✓ To fight—or *litigate*—you go to court. There are many kinds of courts, and in each state, the same type of court can have a different name. Generally, though, you will go to a family court or divorce court.

✓ In court, your case will be scheduled on the calendar, which is a list of all cases before the court.

✓ On the day your case is scheduled, it will be heard by a judge. Judges appear to have unlimited authority, but in reality, they are constantly being monitored and evaluated.

✓ In order for the court to hear your case, it must have *subject-matter jurisdiction*. In order for the court to make orders on a person, the court must also have *personal jurisdiction*.

✓ Because judges have well-known prejudices when it comes to child custody, lawyer try to find a judge more willing to rule in their favor. The tactic of changing venue is known as *forum shopping*.

The Adversarial System

To understand what courts do, you first have to understand what our system of justice is based on. To settle disputes, we use the *adversarial system.*

The adversarial system assumes that when two people fight, the truth will emerge. Each side rigorously advances its version of the facts to a third party who listens to the evidence and then decides.

The adversarial system developed many hundreds of years ago when people engaged in trial by combat to settle their disputes. Whoever survived the battle was deemed right.

Today, people hire lawyers to fight for them. Each person is an adversary, and the lawyers are their combatants. And when they fight—or litigate—they follow certain rules to ensure the fight proceeds in a fair and orderly manner.

The adversarial system resolves many kinds of disputes, but critics say it works poorly when it comes to family law. They point out that parents become enemies, fighting to beat their opponent. This is the opposite of what is needed, because after divorce parents must cooperate to raise the children.

Regardless of the merits of the adversarial system, it is the basis of our system of justice.

What Courts Do

If you fight over custody of your children, you must go to court. A court is where disputes are resolved.

The courthouse is the building where you go to resolve a dispute, and the courtrooms are where the court conducts its business.

Courts do many things. For example, they:
- Provide a forum for people to air their disputes.
- Punish criminals by separating them from society.
- Protect individuals from abuse of government power.
- Make a formal record of legal status.

You're being watched. Family disputes are so confrontational that some parents smuggle in concealed weapons in order to hurt someone— the other parent, the judge, or maybe the opposing lawyer. Courts have responded by installing pervasive video surveillance and metal detectors at the door. Some judges even wear a bulletproof vest. You should assume that when you enter a courthouse, your behavior is being monitored.

When you go to court to decide custody, the court will decide whatever issue you cannot agree on. The court may decide who has legal custody and who has physical custody, who has visitation, and who pays child support and how much is paid.

By the way, notice that the words *court* and *judge* are interchangeable. This is common parlance. A lawyer may say, "the court ordered something" when she really means the judge ordered it.

Court System

Because there are many different kinds of cases, there are many different kinds of courts.

The largest division of courts is *federal* and *state*. Federal courts hear cases involving federal law, and state courts hear issues involving state law.

Federal Courts
Since family law is state law, you probably won't find yourself in a federal court. A case can only be filed in federal court if it involves federal laws or the U. S. Constitution.

If you do somehow land in a federal trial court, you will first be heard in one of the 94 U.S. District Courts around the country. If you appeal, you will go to one of the 13 Federal Courts of Appeals. Then, if you decide to appeal again and your case is chosen to be heard, you go to the highest court in the land—the United States Supreme Court.

State Courts

More likely, however, when you dispute child custody, you will do so in a state court.

Each state has created a state court system to resolve legal disputes not covered by the federal courts. Because federal courts only address a narrow range of legal issues, state courts handle the vast majority of legal problems.

The state court systems handle almost every kind of case imaginable, including cases involving criminal behavior, personal injuries, real estate transactions—and child custody.

 State courts are where the action is. As reported by the *American Bar Association,* of about 20 million civil cases a year, 19,700,000 were filed in state courts, and only 227,000 were filed in federal courts.[1]

Court Structure

Within each state, the courts are further subdivided. Dividing courts allows states to handle many different types of legal problems more efficiently. Unfortunately, it also makes the court system more difficult to understand.

Since each state is free to create its own court structure— within the limits of the state constitution and the U.S. Constitution—every state has its own system.

There are as many different state court systems as there are states.

When you go to court for child custody, the court you go to is determined by how your state has organized its courts. While there is no single model of state court systems, there are many similarities.

Generally, states organize their courts into layers, with the lowest layer being trial courts that hear small problems—such as traffic offenses and small claims—and the highest being the supreme courts that only listen to cases on appeal. This hierarchical organization allows judges in the upper courts to review the decisions made by judges in the lower courts.

Here's an example of a typical state court system:

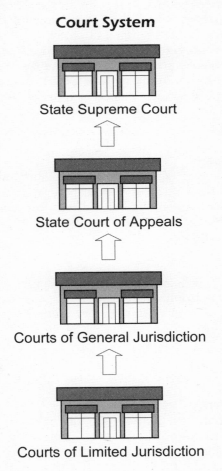

Court System

State Supreme Court

State Court of Appeals

Courts of General Jurisdiction

Courts of Limited Jurisdiction

Supreme Court
The highest court is usually called the *Supreme Court*. These courts do not conduct trials, but rather, review the decisions made by the appellate courts below them. They are often called the court of last resort because—if you appeal your case—this is as far as you can go.

When Sonya and Louis divorced, Sonya was given physical custody of their three children, and Louis was given visitation from Tuesday evening until Thursday evening each week, plus time over the summer. Four years later, Sonya asked the circuit court to reduce Louis' visitation. Louis asked for custody. After the judge spoke to the children in private, the judge changed custody to Louis, claiming that Sonya was "verbally abusive" with a "volatile temper." Sonya appealed, noting that there was no record of the interview with the children. The Court of Appeals agreed with her, and reversed. *Foskett v. Fosket* (2001) 247 Mich.App. 1, 634 N.W.2d 363.

Court of Appeals

Below supreme courts are intermediate appellate courts, usually called the *Courts of Appeal.* These courts review the decisions of the trial courts below them. Appeals courts do not retry cases, but rather, review the case to see if the law was correctly applied.

Trial Courts

The lowest two levels of courts are *trial courts.* Trial courts are where you actually file a lawsuit. It is in the trial court that you present your evidence, give testimony on the witness stand, and so on.

States divide up their trial courts in many different ways. Here are the two most common groupings:

Courts of General Jurisdiction

Courts of general jurisdiction typically hear cases involving serious criminal and civil offenses. These courts may be called Circuit Court, District Court, or Superior Court. They can usually hear all types of cases, without limits on the type of criminal behavior or the amount of money involved.

Courts of Limited Jurisdiction

The lowest courts are also trial courts, but they are limited to hearing specific types of cases. They are usually called County Court, Municipal Court, or Magistrate Court. They typically hear civil cases involving small dollar amounts, and also involving minor criminal offenses. Traffic offenses and small claims are examples of cases heard in courts of limited jurisdiction.

Family Court

If you dispute child custody, you may well end up in a family court. Depending upon your state, these trial courts can have either limited or general jurisdiction. The proceedings in each family court are different, but generally mediation is encouraged over litigation.

Courthouse

Once you find the right court, you'll have to go inside. While each courthouse is different, they almost all have the same rooms—or departments—that are necessary for the court to function.

When you walk through the courthouse, be sure to look for the clerk's office. This is where you go to file your court papers, retrieve copies of your case record, and pick up a copy of the court rules. The office is only open during posted hours, and there may be long lines.

Many courthouses also have law libraries open to the public. Here you can do research or browse through the legal newspapers.

And finally, you'll need to find the courtroom where your case will be heard. A courtroom is where the judge works. Judges typically have their own courtrooms, and the judge's name may be posted outside the door. In some places, the courtroom may be called a department, but it is still a courtroom.

What's in a name? Courts are known by different names in different states. For example, in many states the highest court is called the *Supreme Court*. However, in New York, the highest court is called the *Court of Appeals* and the *Supreme Court* is a trial court.

Courtroom

Like courthouses, courtrooms are also laid out in different ways, but they usually have the same elements.

When you first walk in, you enter the spectator area—the place in the back of the courtroom where you wait your turn. This part is usually separated by a bar or partition.

While you're waiting, the judge works at the bench—a desk or raised platform in front of the courtroom. No one can walk in the area near the bench—called the *well*—without his or her permission.

When it's your turn, you sit at the counsel table—the table where you and your lawyer face the judge. There are usually two tables—one for you and one for the opposing party.

When you testify, you sit in the witness stand—a boxed-in area usually next to the judge.

And finally, when it's appropriate to have a conversation "off the record," the judge may have a whispered conversation at the bench, or may adjourn to his or her *chambers*—a private office near the courtroom.

Court Rules

When you enter a court, you'll have to obey the rules of the court. Some rules are issued by the state, and are called *state rules of court*. Other rules are issued by the court, and are called *local rules of court*.

Court rules can be quite specific, and may include how much time you have to respond to a motion, the size and type of paper you must use, etc. Copies of the court rules are usually available in the clerk's office or the courthouse law library.

A knowledgeable local attorney is supposed to know the court rules, and if you have hired such an attorney, you may not have to learn the rules yourself. However, if you choose to represent yourself, you will have to learn the rules.

Court People

Everyone in court has a special name, including you.
Here are some:

Parties

You and the other parent are known as *parties* or
litigants. The person who started the lawsuit is the
moving party, plaintiff, or *petitioner.* The other person is
the *responding party, defendant,* or *respondent.* If you are
representing yourself, you are a *pro per* or *pro se.* If you
are appealing, you are an *appellant* and the other person
is an *appellee.*

Judge

The *judge* is the man or woman who supervises the
courtroom. Other words for judge include *court* or *bench.*
If the judge is temporary—such as a lawyer filling in—he
or she is a *judge pro tem.* A *commissioner, magistrate,
master,* or *referee* is a court-appointed official who
handles routine matters.

Lawyer

A *lawyer, attorney,* or *counsel* represents you.

Clerk

A person who keeps track of court documents and
physical evidence is called a *court clerk, county clerk, civil
clerk,* or *judge's clerk.*

Bailiff

A *bailiff* is a peace officer who keeps order in the
courtroom. Bailiffs are usually armed and in uniform.

Court Reporter

A *court reporter* records every word said during the official
court proceedings.

Witnesses

Witnesses are people who testify under oath about
information they possess. *Ordinary witnesses* testify to
what they have seen or heard, and *expert witnesses*
testify to their opinions.

Calendar

When someone files a lawsuit, the court must schedule a time when that suit will be heard. The schedule of cases with their dates and times for hearing or trial is called the *calendar*.

The calendar is prepared each day by the court clerk, who usually posts it near the front door of every courtroom. When you arrive at the courthouse, you must check the court calendar to make sure your case is indeed scheduled for that day.

There are several different ways to schedule—or calendar— cases, but typically courts apportion caseloads in one of two ways:

Master Calendar

When courts follow the master calendar format, they divide up the cases among the available judges. Generally, the master calendar judge calls out each case and asks for a time estimate from the attorneys, then assigns the case to an available judge. This method almost guarantees that different phases of your case will be heard by different judges. For example, pretrial motions may be heard by one judge, but if you go to trial, it may be heard by a different judge.

 After six years of marriage, Kim and Scott divorced. Kim was given physical custody of their two children, Devin and Dustin, and Scott was given liberal visitation. Three years later, however, after constant litigation, Kim suddenly moved to Guam, taking the children with her. Scott discovered she had moved when he went to pick up the children and Kim's house was empty. The court immediately gave Scott temporary custody of the children, suspended his child support, and found Kim in contempt and ordered her to return the children at once. Kim ignored the court order. Scott then traveled to Guam with the order and picked up the children. Scott was given full custody of the children. *Sanford v. Arinder* (2001) 800 So.2d 1267.

I'll take my case to the Supreme Court! If you get an unfavorable judgment in a lower trial court, you can always appeal the decision. But there are limits to how far you can go. Certain high courts—including the U.S. Supreme Court—turn down the vast majority of cases that are submitted to them. This means the decision of the last appellate court stands.

Direct Calendar

The opposite approach is the direct calendar system, where the case is assigned to one judge who hears it from start to finish. Usually the judge is assigned by the court clerk in an automatic rotation. Under this format, the same judge will:

- Hear all motions.
- Preside at the settlement conference.
- Conduct the trial.
- Render a decision.

The court calendar determines not just the day you have to go to court, but which judge will hear your case.

Judges

Judges are people who have been given the authority to resolve disputes. They are the public officials who remain neutral while the two opposing parties advance their version of the facts.

Because custody cases are decided by a judge, his or her most important role may appear to be that of an umpire or a referee. But trial judges have many roles, including:

- Presiding over pretrial and settlement conferences.
- Ruling on pretrial motions and discovery disputes.
- Presiding over trials.
- Ruling on trial procedure, such as allowing or excluding evidence.
- In bench trials, deciding who wins, who loses, and how much someone pays.
- Managing the caseflow.

A Las Vegas attorney filed a complaint against Judge Frances-Ann Fine with the Nevada Commission on Judicial Discipline. The lawyer complained Judge Fine had violated numerous rules of the Nevada Code of Judicial Conduct and provisions of the Administrative and Procedural Rules for the Nevada Commission on Judicial Discipline. Specifically, the judge had secretly talked with a therapist about her evaluation in a child custody dispute by calling the therapist at her home to discuss the child. In another custody dispute, the judge appointed her first cousin as a mediator, and then did not reveal the relationship to the parties. And in a different custody dispute, the judge told the evaluator to meet secretly with her in chambers to discuss the child. The Commission ruled Judge Fine had violated various rules, and removed her from office. *Fine v. Nevada Commission on Judicial Discipline* (2000) 116 Nev. 1001, 13 P.3d 400.

In particular, judges are acutely aware they must manage the flow of cases through their courtroom. This is a response to the belief that most lawsuits drag on and cost too much. Judges can move cases through the system by setting time limits for parts of the case, and then monitoring the progress to ensure compliance.

Because judges do so much, it's impossible to underestimate their importance. When you present your dispute to a judge, he or she will be the sole fact finder. The judge will listen to the evidence, decide what that evidence establishes, draw inferences from those facts, and then apply the law to reach a decision.

This makes the individual preferences—or bias—of the judge very, very important in determining the outcome of your case.

Selecting Judges

Since judges play such an important role, it stands to reason they don't become judges by simply walking in and applying for the job. In fact, judges become judges by appointment or election.

Appointment. In the federal court system, all of the judges are appointed for life by the President. This includes the 649 district court judgeships, the 179 appeals court seats, and the nine seats on the Supreme Court. But in the state court system, only about two-thirds of the states appoint their judges, with the rest requiring the judges to run for election.

When states appoint a judge, typically a panel of lawyers and nonlawyers recruits and evaluates applicants. The panel then recommends the names of the most qualified to the governor, who makes the final selection, subject to the approval of the legislature.

Election. When judges are required to run for election, a judge must win a seat by a majority of the popular vote in a general election. In these states, judges must regularly run for retention, and if they do not get enough votes, the seat may be vacated.

Finally, a few states follow a mixed system, where judges are appointed initially but must run for election thereafter.

Evaluating Judges
Once a judge becomes a judge, all states monitor and evaluate his or her performance. This not only ensures that people get a fair trial, but that the judge improves over time. Typically, the evaluation program is run either by the highest court or

Real judges don't do family law. Don't be surprised if your judge doesn't want to be there. Some family court judges don't have the personality to handle social problems, while other judges want to do more prestigious assignments—such as death penalty cases. Still other judges may feel overwhelmed by the workload. That's why, "If you find that your judge appears tired, a bit testy, and willing to approve any settlement terms so long as you settle, keep in mind you are seeing the results of a society that talks a lot about the importance of family and children but has seldom put its money behind either." Judge Stewart, *California Divorce Handbook*

some state association. Judge evaluations are usually composed of anonymous feedback by the same people who appear before them—lawyers, jurors, litigants, and so on.

Disciplining Judges

And finally, all states have procedures for disciplining judges. Discipline procedures vary from state to state, but every state has a commission that investigates complaints about a judge and recommends possible sanctions—including removal from office.

Sanctioning. If a judge's behavior or performance is problematical, the disciplining body can apply various sanctions, including reprimands, censure, or suspension.

Firing. A judge whose problematical behavior or performance is more serious can be involuntarily retired or fired. In addition, judges who are elected may be subject to recall, where the voters vote in a special election to decide if the judge should be removed from office. Because federal judges are appointed for life, they can only be removed by impeachment, but they are subject to lesser sanctions, including removal of their work.

Because they work in a public setting, judges are constantly being watched and evaluated.

Jurisdiction

When you file a lawsuit, you must also decide which court to file it in. Not every court can hear every case. Generally, you must file your case in the court that has jurisdiction. *Jurisdiction* is the authority of the court to decide a particular case.

Justice delayed is justice denied. Don't be surprised if you wait all morning in court, only to have your case continued to another day. In some cities, cases are routinely delayed three or four years before finally coming to trial.

Non-Judges

Faced with an overwhelming number of cases and a limited supply of full-time judges, many courts solve the problem by assigning cases to other court officials, such as a:

Judge Pro Tem

A *judge pro tempore* is a temporary judge. He or she is often a practicing attorney, and may know the law as well as a regular judge. A judge pro tem has all the powers of a regular judge, but typically serves only with the consent of the parties—which means you can insist on having a permanent judge.

Master or Referee

A *master* or *referee* is generally a court-appointed official who handles routine, uncontested matters. In some courts, masters hear pretrial motions, rule on discovery issues, and more.

Commissioner or Magistrate

A *commissioner* or *magistrate* is often someone who helps the judge determine the facts in a case. Depending on the court system, this individual may also conduct trials.

Deciding where to file your case is one of most important decisions you will make.

Jurisdiction can be very simple or very complex—it all depends on your circumstances. For example, if both you and the other parent have never been involved in custody proceedings before, there is no custody proceeding going on somewhere else, and you have both lived in the same state for the last six months, then jurisdiction may be straightforward. But if someone has moved, or if there are prior orders from a different court, or if custody is currently in dispute in a different court, then determining which court has jurisdiction can get complicated.

Carol and John separated two years after marrying, and finally divorced two years after that. When they first divorced, they shared equal custody of their son. But within the next few years, they both returned to family court repeatedly for custody. Finally, the judge had enough. He observed that "every proceeding with [Carol] has been difficult. She interrupts the Court and appears to be unable to control her outbursts." The judge decided that Carol "may endanger the child's physical health and/or his emotional development." John was awarded custody of his son. *Gonzalez v. Devlin* (2002) Deleware No. 160, 2001.

For the court to have jurisdiction over your case, it must have authority over both the legal issues raised and the people involved. This is called subject-matter jurisdiction and personal jurisdiction.

Subject-Matter Jurisdiction

Subject-matter jurisdiction simply means the court can hear that type of case. For example, family courts can hear child custody and child support cases, but not bankruptcy cases. Subject-matter jurisdiction is usually determined by state statutes. For a court to have subject-matter jurisdiction, a party to the suit must generally have lived in the state six months, though some states allow as little as 90 days, while other states require a full year.

Personal Jurisdiction

The court must also have the authority to make orders involving the people named in the lawsuit. This personal jurisdiction is usually established when the respondent is either personally served with an order from the court within the state, or it is demonstrated that they have had minimum contacts in the state. If the court does not have personal jurisdiction over someone, it cannot make enforceable orders against that person.

Because we live in a highly mobile society, jurisdiction can easily become a problem. For example, when some parents disagree with a custody decision, they simply move to a new state and file for a modification there. Other parents take the law into their own hands and kidnap the children to a different state, where they seek a change in orders.

Jurisdiction can become a nightmare if two states each enter separate—and different—custody orders. Because federal courts do not have the authority to decide custody or settle a custody dispute caught between different states, the case could conceivably bounce back-and-forth indefinitely between the two states.

Because state borders have become such huge obstacles to deciding and enforcing child custody, uniform laws have been adopted to resolve the problem.

Venue

Aside from jurisdiction, you may also have to decide venue. Venue is the city, county, or district where you file your lawsuit.

Venue is established by state law, and—unlike jurisdiction— can easily be changed. Parents can file a motion for a change of venue simply for the convenience of going to a more accessible courthouse, or even for the convenience of their witnesses.

Venue is typically changed in high-profile criminal trials so that the defendant can find a less biased jury, but there is no reason why it cannot be changed in family court.

In California, lawyers can use a peremptory challenge to challenge the judge—but that doesn't mean they will. Judges don't like being challenged, and lawyers know that if they succeed, someday they'll appear before that judge again... and he'll remember. That's why "there is a saying among lawyers that once you challenge a judge, you must do so whenever assigned to that judge for the rest of your career." Judge Stewart, *California Divorce Handbook*

Uniform Child Custody Jurisdiction Act (UCCJA)

The *Uniform Child Custody Jurisdiction Act (UCCJA)* is a uniform law that has been adopted by every state. This law provides a set of guidelines for deciding child custody. It lists four factors a court must consider when deciding whether to accept a child custody case or defer to another court.

Under the UCCJA, a court can decide custody only if it meets one of the following tests:

1. *Home State.* The court is in the child's home state. Home state means the child has lived there for the past six months, of if the child is absent "because of his removal or retention by a person claiming his custody or for other reasons, and a parent or person acting as parent continues to live in this State."

2. *Best Interest.* The court can decide custody if it is in the best interest of the child to do so. This usually means the child has significant connections to other people in the state, or that it will harm the child's "future care, protection, training, and personal relationships" if the case is heard elsewhere.

3. *Abandonment.* The court can also assume jurisdiction if the child has been abandoned, or if there is reason to believe that the child will be abused or neglected if returned home.

4. *No Other State.* Finally, if no other state meets the above tests—or if another state meets the tests but chooses not to decide custody—the court has jurisdiction.

The purpose of this act is to reduce the problems created when courts in different states make conflicting custody orders. Under the UCCJA, jurisdiction is clearly spelled out, discouraging parents from "shopping around" for a court in another state that will give them a better custody order.

Forum Shopping

When judges make custody decisions each day, they acquire a reputation among the lawyers who appear before them. This preference—or judicial bias—of the judge will influence the outcome just as assuredly as any statute or precedent. That's why some lawyers try to maneuver the case so that it will be heard by a judge who is more likely to decide in their favor. This is called forum shopping.

A forum is the court where the hearing or trial takes place. Forum shopping is the effort to move the case to another courtroom, and hence, another judge.

Many lawyers consider forum shopping a legitimate tool to aggressively represent their client. Most judges, however, object to forum shopping because it implies they won't make an impartial decision.

 After a nine year-marriage, Bradley and Kimberly divorced. Kimberly was given custody of their two children and Bradley was given reasonable visitation. Three years later, Kimberly married a master sergeant in the U.S. Air Force who was stationed in Washington, D.C. Kimberly asked the district court to allow her to take the children from Nebraska to Virginia to be with her new husband. Bradley opposed and asked for custody. The judge allowed Kimberly to move, but made numerous conditions. First, the judge himself assumed custody of the children. Then, the judge specified Kimberly could not take the children to live in any other state other than Virginia or Nebraska without his permission. And finally, the judge specified that if Kimberly's new husband ever was transferred outside the United States and Kimberly chose to join him with the children, physical custody of the children would revert to a one-year with Bradley and one-year with Kimberly arrangement. Kimberly appealed, and custody of the children was returned to her and the long list of conditional orders was reversed. *Vogel v. Vogel* (2002) 262 Neb. 1030, 637 N.W.2d 611.

How the court assigns cases dramatically influences your chances to forum shop:

Master Calendar

When cases are assigned under the master calendar system, attorneys have many ways to forum shop. For example, when the master calendar judge calls out for a time estimate, the lawyer can estimate less time to get assigned to the judge who is hearing short motions, and more time to get assigned to the judge who is hearing long motions. Also, since the judges under this system routinely rotate assignments, the lawyer can delay filing a motion, or get "sick" for a short time, thus waiting for a new judge to be assigned. Or, the lawyer can wait for the judge to go on vacation, knowing another judge will be assigned.

Direct Calendar

When courts assign cases under the direct calendar format, there is much less opportunity to forum shop. Under this format, judges are usually assigned in automatic rotation, and then remain with the case until it completes. To choose a particular judge, an attorney would have to stand in the clerk's office watching the order of judges being assigned, and then suddenly leap into line at the appropriate point. This may happen, but it's probably unusual.

View from the Bench

California Divorce Handbook: How to Dissolve Your Marriage Without Financial Disaster, James W. Stewart, Prima Publishing, $18.95. Judge Stewart offers fascinating glimpses into the daily life of a family court judge.

---

1 *Law and the Courts: A Handbook of Courtroom Procedures,* American Bar Association, 1995. If you're wondering where the other 73,000 cases were filed—the ABA didn't say.

Chapter 22

Motions, Hearings, Decisions, and Orders

✓ When you go to court, you have to follow the rules of procedure.

✓ After you start your case, but before you start a trial, you are in the pretrial phase.

✓ During pretrial you conduct *discovery*, where you find out what evidence the other side has. Common forms of discovery include *depositions*, *interrogatories*, and *subpoenas*.

✓ If you want the court to do something, you file a motion. Typical motions include a *Motion for a Protective Order*, a *Motion for Examination by a Mental Health Expert*, and a *Motion for a Paternity Test*.

✓ After you file a motion, the court schedules a hearing to decide the motion, and at the end of the hearing, makes a decision.

✓ During pretrial, It is normal for numerous motions and hearings to be held, and for the case to be continued many times. Cases that last for three or four years are not unusual.

✓ At some point, you may have to attend a *settlement conference*, where you try to resolve the dispute before a trial.

Civil Procedure

When you take a dispute to court, you must follow a specific set of rules that govern how the dispute is handled. These are the rules of *civil procedure.*

To some people, procedure can seem like red tape or technicalities. Certainly, procedure can be complex, and at times may appear to fly in the face of common sense.

However, procedure is critical in helping the judge reach a fair decision. With a few exceptions, following procedure means the judge must wait until both sides have had a chance to tell their story before making a decision. This protects your rights as well the rights of the other parent, and it is the essence of our legal system.

Because custody and support disagreements are private disputes between two individuals, they are governed by civil law, and are controlled by the rules of civil procedure.

These rules come from laws passed by the state legislature or from rules issued by the State Supreme Court. They include:
- Who can sue whom, and for what.
- What documents you need to file, and when.
- How much time you have to bring a lawsuit.
- What kind of trial you can have.
- What kind of remedy you can ask for.
- What you can do if you lose.
- How you can enforce a judgment.

No matter how good a case you have, you must follow the rules.

 Generally, the rules of civil procedure for state courts are modeled after the *Federal Rules of Civil Procedure,* but each state can have its own version. To find out the rules for your state, look in the state statutes for a section called *civil procedure.*

How a Civil Case Proceeds to Trial

Unless you're in court regularly, you may not know how a civil case proceeds to trial. Here's a diagram:

Pretrial

```
┌─────────────────────┐
│     Complaint       │
└─────────────────────┘
          ↓
┌─────────────────────┐
│      Answer         │
└─────────────────────┘
          ↓
┌─────────────────────┐
│     Discovery       │
└─────────────────────┘
          ↓
┌─────────────────────┐
│      Motions        │
└─────────────────────┘
          ↓
┌─────────────────────┐
│     Hearings        │
└─────────────────────┘
          ↓
┌─────────────────────┐
│     Settlement      │
│    Conference       │
└─────────────────────┘
```

Generally, the *pretrial* phase encompasses everything that happens from when the case begins until the trial, and the *post-trial* phase encompasses everything that happens after the trial.

Pleadings

You begin a lawsuit by filing a legal document with the court. Each side submits one or more documents that state a version of the facts and what needs to be done. These initial documents are called *pleadings*.

Complaint

The first paper filed in a lawsuit is a *complaint* or *petition*. You complete a form and give it to the clerk of the court, along with a filing fee. The person who makes the complaint is the *petitioner* or *plaintiff*, and the other side is the *respondent* or *defendant*.

The complaint contains several important pieces of information. First, it has the plaintiff's version of the facts. The plaintiff describes what happened and what wrongs were committed. The specific offenses are listed in a series of counts. Second, the complaint states the legal basis for the lawsuit, including the laws that apply, and shows that the court has jurisdiction to hear the case. And finally, the complaint ends with the prayer for relief. This is what the plaintiff wants the court to do—either make a monetary award or a court order. In a custody suit, the remedy sought might be for sole custody or increased visitation.

Summons and Service

After the complaint is filed, the other person must be told about the lawsuit. In federal and state courts, the clerk of the court issues a *summons,* which contains the name of the plaintiff, the name and address of the plaintiff's lawyer (if there is one), the case number, and how much time the defendant has to respond.

 After their divorce in Delaware, Thomas and Karen agreed that Karen would be the primary residential parent of their child and Thomas would have visitation. Two years later, Karen remarried and wanted to move to Connecticut. She sought sole custody. The court kept the joint custody arrangement but allowed Karen to move away. A year later, Karen walked into a Connecticut court and asked that the case to be transferred from Delaware to Connecticut because Connecticut was now the home state of the child. Connecticut took jurisdiction and informed Delaware, but the Delaware court refused to relinquish jurisdiction. The case remained in Delaware. *Butler v. Grant* (1998) 714 A.2d 747.

A *plaintiff* or *defendant* in a lawsuit generally can't serve his or her own pleadings or motions on the other party. At the very least, another adult must do it. Some states allow any adult not connected to the suit to serve legal papers.

Because our system of justice is based on a struggle between two combatants, it's only fair that the person being sued knows about it. That's why there are very strict rules about how the summons and complaint are given to the defendant. The lawsuit will not proceed unless the court is convinced the other party has been given proper notice.

The summons and complaint can be served on the defendant by:

- A sheriff, marshal, or constable.
- A process server.
- Certified or registered mail.
- An adult who is not a party to the action.

Answer

If you receive a complaint, you have an opportunity to file your response—called an *answer.* While the amount of time varies, you'll typically have between two and four weeks.

In your answer you respond to the allegations made against you. You can admit some charges, deny others, and say you can't respond to the rest because you don't have enough information. If you do not respond to something, that can be interpreted as an admission that it's true. Also, you can add facts which may prove that you're not at fault, or offer a reason which may justify your actions.

If you don't respond to a complaint, and you don't show up for the hearing, the plaintiff can get a default judgment. This means the plaintiff wins the suit without having to prove anything. If that happens, you can try to get the judgment set aside by offering valid excuses for your oversight, such as being in the hospital or that your attorney failed to act in a timely manner.

Instead of filing an answer, you can challenge the complaint with various kinds of motions, such as a *motion to dismiss,* a *motion to strike,* or a *motion for a summary judgment.* You argue that the court does not have jurisdiction, or the complaint does not state a legally valid claim. You can also file a *motion to quash service* by insisting that you were not served properly.

Counterclaim and Reply

If the defendant answers the complaint by making his or her own claims against the plaintiff, those complaints are contained in the *counterclaim.* Sometimes the counterclaim is part of the answer, sometimes it is filed separately.

When one side raises new allegations, the other side can file a reply to the new allegations raised, which means the plaintiff can reply to the counterclaim.

Discovery

After the pleadings have been filed, each side tries to learn more about the facts in the case. You do this through *discovery.*

Discovery is a set of legal procedures that each side uses to force their opponent to reveal information. Through discovery, you can learn what the other person is claiming, what potential witnesses have to say, and whether any physical evidence exists. Discovery lets you find out what evidence the other side will present, thus ensuring you won't face any surprises at trial.

Because you don't know what the other side knows, the rules limiting discovery are quite broad and generally allow one side to seek any information that is "reasonably calculated to lead to the discovery of admissible evidence." Thus, you can ask for information that is not admissible itself, but may lead to something that is.

Discovery is a necessary part of trial preparation because most people are reluctant to reveal information. By letting each side force the other to answer questions, the judge can see everything important and—hopefully—reach the correct decision.

Unfortunately, discovery can also be used as a weapon to harass the other side. Aggressive attorneys wage discovery wars where they seek reams of information about everything possibly related to the case. This inundates the other side and creates huge legal fees.

To combat such abuses, many courts require discovery to be completed within a short period of time. Each side must quickly disclose everything relevant to the case. If the lawyers disagree over what needs to be revealed, those disputes can be brought to the judge's attention in a short discovery motion hearing, or can even be discussed over the telephone. If the judge finds that one side has failed to cooperate (for example, by giving evasive or argumentative answers), that side can be fined.

Here are the most common forms of discovery:
- Depositions.
- Interrogatories.
- Request for admission of facts.
- Request for production of documents.
- Subpoenas.

Depositions

A widely used form of discovery is a *deposition*. A deposition is when someone is asked questions by an attorney. That person is placed under oath, and a court reporter records all answers.

 Discovery can easily cost more than $10,000 in lawyer's fees, and you'll pay extra for expert witnesses and a court reporter. Also, don't forget to include the time you lose from work to appear for a deposition.

The main difference between a deposition and live testimony is that the deposition occurs outside court—usually in a lawyer's office. However, the person answering the questions is still under oath, so the answers must be as truthful as if that person was actually testifying in court.

Who Can Be Deposed
Both the plaintiff and the defendant can be deposed. In addition, anyone else not named in the lawsuit—but who might be a potential witness or who might possess useful information—can be ordered to answer questions. If an important witness cannot testify at trial, a deposition can be taken and read in court.

The Purpose of a Deposition
The main reason for "taking a deposition" is to prepare for trial. Depositions allow each side to know what a witness will say in court, thus helping to prepare the case.

But depositions are also used to undermine the opposing party. The questions asked are designed not only to elicit helpful information, but to find information damaging to the other side.

Lawyers try to get the person being deposed to make an inconsistent statement or an admission against interest.

Because every answer in a deposition is being recorded, one of the goals of the opposing lawyer is to trap the person into making an inconsistent statement. Anything said in a deposition can be read back at trial, so if the person changes an answer, the opposing lawyer can argue that—at the very least—everything this person says is unreliable, and at worst—this individual is a bald-faced liar. Lawyers actually practice how to successfully impeach a witness during trial.

How a Deposition Is Taken
Typically, a deposition is taken at one of the lawyer's offices, but it can also be done in a hotel room or even your home. A court reporter is present to record the questioning, and whoever is being deposed can have a lawyer there. In addition, the other party has the right to attend.

Court Papers

Everything in court has a name. Here are some terms:

Affidavit
An *affidavit* is a written statement wherein the author swears under penalty of perjury that the facts stated are the truth. The affidavit must be notarized.

Brief
A *brief* is a written legal argument submitted to the court.

Case
A *case* is a dispute taken to court.

Case File
A *case file* is the folder that contains all the legal documents relating to a case.

Case Number
A *case number* is the unique number assigned by the court clerk when the case is filed.

Case Record
The *case record* includes all papers filed with the court, including transcripts of hearings and trials.

Declaration
A *declaration* is the same as an affidavit, except that it does not have to be notarized. Affidavits and declarations are used in place of live testimony.

Docket Sheet
A *docket sheet* is a court paper that lists everything that happens in a case. Case files and docket sheets are usually public records.

Petition
A *petition* or *complaint* is a legal document filed with the court that requests some action.

Most depositions only last a few hours, but conceivably they could stretch to a few days, or even a few weeks. After the questioning is finished, the court reporter types up the transcript, and the witness signs a copy in front of a notary. This makes the answers as important as if they were said in a courtroom.

If you are being deposed, you will first receive a subpoena and a notice, and you will generally have at least ten days' warning.

What Can Be Asked at a Deposition

When you are questioned during a deposition, you can be asked about any aspect of the case. The scope of questions allowed is quite broad, even if the questions themselves would not be allowed at trial. You may also be required to bring copies of any documents relevant to the case. These can include financial records or other documents in your possession. If you must bring something, it will be specified in the subpoena or notice.

 When Sharon married Kenneth, Sharon was Assistant Solicitor for the National Labor Relations Board, and Kenneth was the Executive Director of the National Education Association Staff Organization. Eventually, Sharon became the Chief Counsel for the Senate Judiciary Committee, and Kenneth became the Assistant Executive Director of the American Federation of Television and Radio Artists and Screen Actors Guild. During these busy Washington, D.C., careers, they had two children. Then Sharon filed for divorce and secured a protection order against Kenneth, who was ordered to move out of the house. At the trial one year later, the court concluded that Kenneth "has been very involved in the children's activities and has made them a priority in his life," while Sharon "is simply more devoted to and absorbed by her work and her career than anything else in her life, including her health, her children and her family." The court awarded sole custody to Kenneth. *Prost v. Greene* (1995) 652 A.2d 621.

Paper trail. If you are representing yourself, keep good records of all requests and agreements. When the other side promises to do something, send them a letter confirming what they said.

While you generally must answer what you are asked, your attorney can object to improper questions. For example, if you are asked to reveal privileged information—such as conversations protected by attorney-client privilege—you don't have to answer. Or if a question is totally irrelevant, you can refuse to answer. Also, your attorney can object to questions that are confusing, vague, or ambiguous.

If the attorneys disagree over whether a question can be asked, they may have to resolve the dispute in front of a judge.

In addition to questions about your home, work, and income, you may be asked about raising the children.

For example, you could be asked:
- Who takes the children to and from school?
- Who is the primary contact with the teachers?
- Who makes the children their meals, washes their clothes, and helps them with their homework?
- Who takes the children to their after-school activities?
- Have you ever hit, confined, or physically disciplined your children?
- Have you ever kissed, caressed, or fondled your children in a sexual manner?
- Have you ever been arrested, convicted of a felony, or served time in prison?
- Have you ever used alcohol, drugs, or illegal substances?

How to Answer Questions at a Deposition
There are some specific strategies that you can pursue when you are deposed. As a general rule, the more information you give the opposing lawyer, the more it can hurt you—so you want to answer honestly but briefly.

First, plan on practicing ahead of time with your lawyer. If he or she grills you like crazy in private, you'll be better equipped for the opposing attorney.

Second, when asked a question, listen carefully. Many questions are trick questions designed to trap you. The classic trick question is, "Do you still beat your wife?" By answering with a simple "No," you've agreed with the questioner's implied assumption that you beat your wife at one time.

Three Steps to Formulating an Answer

Step 1. Do you understand the question?

"I don't understand the question. Please explain."

Step 2. Do you understand the question but don't know the answer?

"I don't know."

Step 3. Do you understand the question and know the answer?

Answer it.

Third, before answering, pause a moment. This gives your lawyer time to object to an improper question, and keeps you from tossing out an off-the-cuff response.

Fourth, when answering a question, stay calm. The other lawyer will be watching you for signs of stress. Don't give any clues as to what's important. Try to answer with the same inflection and timing in your voice, and try to keep your body language consistent.

Fifth, when you answer a question, don't volunteer anything. Answer what is asked, and nothing more. Try to answer "Yes," "No," or "That's not correct" as much as possible. If you decide to explain something, you will give the other side more material, and they will also know this is an area that concerns you. That can only lead to more questions you may not want to answer.

And finally, avoid admissions against interest. In a deposition, frankness is deadly. You have to tell the truth, but don't bring up anything that can hurt you. And when you do reveal something negative, try to make it sound as positive as possible.

 Fast track. Many courts have rules designed to move a case through the court system as quickly as possible. These include: deadlines on when each phase of the case must be completed, limits on how much information can be requested from the opposing party, and mini-trials or neutral evaluations that encourage the parties to settle.

Interrogatories

Another way to pry information loose from the opposing party is through *interrogatories.* Interrogatories are written questions that you send to the other side. The other party must answer all of your questions in writing, and—as with depositions—the person is under oath to answer truthfully when answering.

The rules governing interrogatories vary from state to state, and include how many questions you can ask and how much time the party has to answer. You can use this discovery method along with a deposition, or instead of one. Generally, however, you can only direct interrogatories to the other party named in the lawsuit, and not at third parties.

Interrogatories are a much less expensive way to gather information than depositions, but they have their drawbacks. Because you're not present when the other side responds, you may get vague or incomplete answers. The solution is to phrase very specific questions asking for factual information.

What You Can Ask in an Interrogatory
Generally, you can ask the same questions as in a deposition, but you may not want to. Interrogatories are best suited for nailing down factual information or establishing the validity of documents for trial.

The type of subjects you might want to cover in an interrogatory include the person's vital statistics, employment history and income, financial information, and any arrests or convictions.

If you receive an interrogatory, it's a good idea to review it with your lawyer before answering. You may be able to answer many questions "N/A" for not applicable. For example, if some questions ask about a criminal past, and you have no criminal past, you can mark the answers "N/A."

Military delay. The *Soldiers' and Sailors' Civil Relief Act of 1940 (SSCRA)* 50 U.S.C. App. Section 501 and following, protects active duty members of the military—including the activated National Guard—from worrying about court problems at home. This federal law delays all civil court actions—including divorce, child custody, and child support—until the soldier can appear in court.

Request for Admission of Facts

You can also get information by asking the other side to agree to certain facts. When one party to a lawsuit asks the other side to agree that some statements are true, it's called a *request for admission of facts.*

Typically, the other side either admits or denies the statements you make. You can use whatever facts they admit as evidence in the trial without having to prove it. This discovery tool has some usefulness because you can save time and money. If the other side refuses to acknowledge any facts, you have to prove each fact you need in your case, and the legal effort involved could be considerable.

Request for Production of Documents

When you need copies of certain documents, you can make a *request to produce documents.* This is a written request you make for the other party to hand over copies of relevant papers.

When child support is an issue—which it almost always is— the income of the other parent is extremely relevant, and you can request copies of bank statements, pay stubs, and so on.

What You Can't Do with Discovery

1. *Ask for privileged information.* You can't ask the other side to reveal confidential conversations, such as between lawyers and clients.

2. *Overwhelm the other side.* You can't inundate the other party with discovery requests beyond their resources to comply.

3. *Be abusive.* You can't seek information solely designed to embarrass or harass the other party.

4. *Request irrelevant information.* You can't ask for facts unrelated to the case.

Subpoenas

A final way you can secure information is with a *subpoena.* A subpoena is a court order that requires someone to do something. You issue a subpoena when you want a witness to give testimony—either at a deposition or in court.

You can also issue a type of subpoena called a *subpoena duces tecum.* This allows you to get copies of documents that are in the control of someone else. That might be school records, police records, bank records, etc. If you use these records at trial, you also may have to subpoena the official who maintains the records to vouch for their authenticity.

You must serve a *witness subpoena* or a *subpoena duces tecum* far enough in advance for the other person to have time to respond. Court rules will specify the number of days ahead of time you must serve the subpoena.

To subpoena someone, have your lawyer prepare the subpoena, then arrange for it to be served on the witness. Generally, you don't need the court's permission to issue a subpoena unless you're trying to get copies of government documents. If the other party ignores the subpoena, they can be held in contempt, and a sheriff can be ordered to bring them to court.

Motions

Once the pleadings have been filed, you can ask the court to do certain things. These include stopping the other parent from doing something—such as moving away with the children—or forcing the other parent to do something—such as answering discovery questions. You file a *motion* to ask the court to issue orders.

Typically, you make pretrial motions when you want to:
- Ask that the lawsuit be dismissed.
- Enforce discovery by requiring the other side to answer certain questions or to produce certain documents.
- Limit discovery by protecting yourself from having to answer certain questions or having to produce certain documents.
- Maintain the status quo by ordering the other side to refrain from doing something.

How to File a Motion
Either party can file a motion before, during, or after the trial. Depending on what you want, you usually submit your motion to the court in writing, and the other side responds. If the other side objects to what you're asking for, the judge holds a hearing where each side makes a short oral argument. Finally, the judge either grants or denies the motion.

If you have an urgent need, you can make an emergency motion, such as a request for a *temporary restraining order (TRO)* or a *preliminary injunction.* If the court approves these motions, they stop the other party from taking certain actions prior to the trial.

You don't always have to file a motion to get what you want. If you can reach an informal agreement with the other party, you can notify the court by filing a stipulation. A *stipulation* is an agreement between the parties that certain facts are true or that a certain procedure will be followed. Typically, both parties sign the stipulation and file it with the clerk.

Here are some common pretrial motions:

Motion for a Summary Judgment

If there is no disagreement over the facts in the case, either party can file a *motion for a summary judgment.* This tells the judge that everyone agrees on the facts, and the only thing left is to decide how the law should be applied. If the motion is granted, the judge reads all of the written arguments and evidence, and then makes a ruling—without having a trial. If the motion is denied, the parties proceed to trial.

 Tommy and Cynthia were married in Florida, then moved to Georgia, North Carolina, then back to Florida. During this time they had two children. When they separated, Cynthia took the children to Georgia and sought custody. Tommy stayed in Florida and sought custody. The Georgia court decided it had jurisdiction, awarded sole custody to Cynthia and supervised visitation to Tommy. A year later, a Florida circuit court decided it had jurisdiction, awarded Cynthia temporary custody, and gave Tommy "supervised followed by unsupervised visitation." Cynthia refused to comply with the Florida order and was held in contempt. Florida then gave Tommy custody. The Georgia trial court then decided that Florida had jurisdiction, but Cynthia appealed, and the Georgia Court of Appeals reversed. *Thompson v. Thompson* (1999) 241 Ga.App. 616, 526 S.E.2d 576.

Lawyers' Law Books

If you want to read what lawyers read, contact the *American Bar Association*. Be prepared—some books are low-priced, but others will wipe out your wallet.

American Bar Association
750 North Lake Shore Drive
Chicago, Illinois 606111
(312) 988-5603
www.abanet.org

The American Bar Association Family Legal Guide. A BIG, thick, practical guide to family law. Very readable.

Law and the Courts: Volume One — The Role of Courts and *Law and the Courts: Volume Two — Court Procedures.* These two booklets concisely explain the court system. Volume two covers pretrial motions, hearings, settlement conferences, trials, and appeals.

The Complete Guide to Mediation: The Cutting-Edge Approach to Family Law Practice. Gives an overview of the mediation process, including how to enforce an agreement. Explains how a lawyer should represent a client who chooses mediation.

The Child's Attorney: A Guide to Representing Children in Custody, Adoption, and Protection Cases. Written by an expert on child abuse, this book addresses the ethical issues involved in representing children. Includes sample forms and a table of over 250 cases.

Child Abuse: A Police Guide. This pocket-size booklet describes the role of police in child abuse cases, including investigation, arrest, and protective custody.

Sexual Abuse Allegations in Custody and Visitation Cases. Contains the latest findings on false allegations and an extensive focus on expert evaluation and child witness testimony.

The advantage of a summary judgment is that it saves everyone a tremendous amount of money. Also, because most of the legal activities are skipped, the litigants get a much quicker court decision. On the other hand, because summary judgments are just as final as if you had actually gone to trial, if you get a decision you don't like, you can't change your mind and opt for a trial.

If you file a summary judgment motion, you attach supporting documents, such as affidavits or declarations—sworn statements under oath—and other written evidence. If the other party has filed a summary judgment motion, and you want a trial instead, you respond by arguing that some facts in the case are in dispute.

Motion to Quash Service
If you want to dismiss the lawsuit without having to answer, you can file a *motion to quash service.* This motion argues that the defendant was not served properly, or that the case is outside the jurisdiction of the court. If this motion is granted, the lawsuit may be thrown out, and the moving party has to start all over again. If the motion is denied, the lawsuit continues.

Motion to Dismiss
Another motion filed before the answer is a *motion to dismiss* for failure to state a claim. This is where the defendant asks the judge to dismiss the lawsuit because the complaint states a legally meaningless claim. In other words, the motion argues that even if the allegations were true, it doesn't matter—the plaintiff isn't entitled to anything.

If a motion to dismiss, or *demurrer,* is granted, the lawsuit may be thrown out, or the plaintiff may be given the chance to amend the complaint and file it again. If the motion is denied, the defendant will usually get some time—such as 30 days—to answer.

Motion to Strike
You file this motion when some parts of the complaint are flawed, such as when the allegations have already been decided by another lawsuit. If the motion is granted, the deficient parts of the complaint are removed.

Motion for Preliminary Orders

When parents first separate and can't agree on custody of their children, either one can file a *motion for preliminary orders* that asks the court to create temporary orders. These orders can include child custody, child support, or any other issue that needs a temporary resolution until trial.

 Jennifer was not married to Richard when their child was born in El Paso, but Richard established paternity one year later. The Texas district court then gave Jennifer permanent custody, Richard visitation rights, and ordered Richard to pay child support. Two years later, Jennifer and the baby moved to Las Cruces, New Mexico, and Richard moved to California. Nine months after that, Richard returned to El Paso. When he tried to resume his visitation, he was unsuccessful, so he asked a New Mexico district court to recognize and enforce the visitation portion of the Texas judgment. Jennifer responded by asking the New Mexico court to increase Richard's child support. Richard countered that Texas had continuing, exclusive jurisdiction over child support, and thus, New Mexico was not allowed to modify or even enforce the Texas order. The New Mexico court agreed, and dismissed Jennifer's requests. However, Jennifer appealed the decision, and the New Mexico Court of Appeals reversed part of the decision. The appellate court decided that Jennifer could ask the New Mexico court to enforce the child support order from the Texas court. *Harbison v. Johnston* (2001) 130 N.M. 595, 28 P.3d 1136, 2001-NMCA-051.

Motion for a Protective Order

A parent who is feeling threatened or harassed by the other parent can file a *motion for a protective order.* This motion asks the court to protect the victimized parent. If the parent is alleging domestic violence or other physical harm, the court can issue a temporary restraining order. If the parent seeks protection from unreasonable discovery requests, the court can limit the scope of discovery.

Motion to Compel Discovery

When there is a dispute about discovery, the opposite of a protective order is a *motion to compel discovery.* This motion asks the court to force the other side to answer certain questions or to produce certain documents. For example, if you send an interrogatory, and the other side refuses to complete it, you can file a motion to compel. If the judge grants the motion, the party will be ordered to answer the questions. A person who refuses can be fined or held in contempt of court, which can mean a jail sentence.

 If you file a *motion to compel,* be sure to include a request for sanctions. This request asks the court to punish the other side by giving you something—such as attorney's fees.

Motion for Examination by a Mental Health Expert

In custody disputes, it's normal for one side to file a motion requiring all parties to submit to a psychological examination. These examinations are usually performed by a mental health expert, who may rely on interviews and psychological tests to reach a conclusion. The recommendations made by the custody evaluator are evidence, and may be adopted or rejected by the judge.

Motion for a Paternity Test

When paternity is in doubt, either parent can make a motion for a paternity test. This motion asks the court to order the man to undergo a paternity test. Paternity tests have an extraordinary degree of accuracy, and are often the only evidence relied on to prove or disprove paternity. Mothers may file this motion to establish a father's responsibility, or fathers may file to either disprove paternity, or to secure rights to a child when the mother denies his fatherhood.

Motion for a Continuance

This motion asks the court to delay the impending hearing, conference, deposition, and so on, because the party needs additional time. Either side can file for a *continuance,* and if it is granted, the case will be delayed a certain length of time.

Motion for Sanctions

A final motion is a *motion for sanctions.* This asks the court to punish the other side because they have misused the legal process. Typical examples include if one side files frivolous motions—that is, motions without a valid legal basis—or if one side files for repeated continuances seemingly to delay the proceedings. If the motion is granted, the penalized party may have to pay a fine, may be limited in their discovery, or may be found in contempt.

Hearings

Both before and after the trial, you may have to attend one or more *hearings.* A hearing is any appearance you make before a judge or other court official where you present your case.

Pretrial hearings are usually limited to deciding specific issues prior to the trial, while post-trial hearings often involve enforcing or modifying the court judgment. An example of a pretrial hearing might be to establish child support, while a post-trial hearing might be to adjust the support amount.

Court hearings are serious, and you must appear when scheduled. If you don't go, the judge can issue a bench warrant authorizing the police to arrest you and bring you to court. If you don't have a good reason for missing the hearing, the judge can hold you in contempt.

In addition to attending hearings to decide various motions, you may also have to attend several other kinds of hearings:

Pendente Lite Hearing

A *pendente lite hearing,* or temporary hearing, is when the judge first makes temporary custody and support decisions. At this pretrial hearing, the judge seeks to create orders that maintain the status quo in the children's lives.

Et tu Brute? Practically speaking, it's a bad idea to force a reluctant witness to testify. He or she can hurt you more than help you.

When Charles and Crystal divorced after a two-year marriage, Crystal and their daughter moved in with her parents, the Yonkers. Charles and Crystal initially agreed that physical custody of the baby would be with the Yonkers, but that when Crystal notified the court she was ready to assume custody, "physical custody of the minor child shall revert back to [Crystal] and said child will remain with [Crystal] until she reaches the age of eighteen (18) years or graduates from high school." Two years later, however, after Crystal remarried and had another child, she returned to court, complaining that her parents had thwarted her visitation with her daughter. She asked for custody. Her parents objected, stating that her new husband, Oscar, was "a known child molester." After an investigation, the circuit court discovered that during his divorce from his previous wife, Oscar had been charged with two counts of child molestation and one count of battery involving a child. He had pleaded guilty to the battery, but the molestation charges were dismissed. After reviewing this evidence, the referee gave the Yonkers physical custody. However, Crystal appealed, and the decision was reversed. *Heltzel v. Heltzel* (2001) 248 Mich. App. 1, 638 N.W.2d 123.

Judges know that when parents first separate, everyone's life is blown apart. The parents have to set up two households where there formerly was one, and the children have to go back-and-forth. It's hard on everyone, and it takes time to adjust. The last thing the judge wants to do is change the home of the children—or their school. Thus, in a pendente lite hearing, the judge seeks to stabilize the children's lives. If the children were living primarily with one parent before the hearing, the judge may want that to continue.

Temporary orders have a lasting impact on future decisions.

Because most custody decisions seek to avoid disrupting the children's lives, the temporary hearing may be the single most important hearing you have. All future custody decisions will take into account the existing arrangements of the children.

Don't rush back to court. "Judges do not want the court system overburdened by litigants who request multiple pre-trial hearings. Judges are happy to help in fine-tuning previous orders, but are loathe to revisit problems that have been adequately assessed at previous court hearings." *Michael Brennan*, Attorney-at-Law

Order to Show Cause Hearing

Another type of hearing is called an *order to show cause hearing.*

In family law, an order to show cause hearing usually involves enforcement of the current orders, or it occurs when someone wants to change the current orders. The responding party must show why the motion should not be granted.

Ex Parte Hearing

The essence of our judicial system is fairness, which means both sides get a chance to talk to the judge. However, there are times when one side alone can talk to the judge. A hearing where only one side is present is an *ex parte hearing.*

Ex parte hearings occur under very specific circumstances. Generally, they are used to address crisis situations where someone will be harmed—such as when there is a threat of domestic violence. An ex parte hearing is considered an emergency proceeding, and can happen with little or no notice to the other side.

If an order is issued at an ex parte hearing, it will generally last only until both sides attend a full hearing. This may be a few weeks or even longer, depending on how busy the court is.

By the way, if one side doesn't show up, and the other side wins by default, that's also considered an ex parte hearing.

In Camera Hearing

A final type of hearing is an *in camera hearing.* This is when the judge has a private meeting in his office. Often, lawyers meet with the judge to resolve issues, or the judge may speak with the children. This hearing is not open to the public, giving everyone involved privacy.

Conferences

In addition to hearings, you may also have to attend *conferences.* A conference is less formal than a hearing, and may occur without the judge. Conferences are a useful part of the process because they create opportunities for the parties to settle, or—at the very least—simplify the issues involved.

Pretrial Conference
Depending on the local court terminology, a *pretrial conference, status conference,* or *issue conference* is when the parties meet to decide the issues that remain to be resolved. The goal of the conference is simply to narrow down the dispute to the core issues. The more that can be agreed on ahead of time, the less that needs to be decided at trial.

If this conference occurs just before the trial, you may have to prepare a pretrial memorandum that lists the issues still in dispute and the evidence you plan to introduce.

Settlement Conference
A *settlement conference* is a final chance to settle and avoid a trial. The goal of the conference is to bring the parties together to see if there isn't some way to resolve the lawsuit. Settlement conferences can be voluntary or mandatory.

Settlement conferences are a very useful way to resolve disputes, and—in some courts—the judge can exert considerable pressure on the parties to settle. While the judge

"Judges in family law deal with large volumes of cases and only remember the difficult ones that appear repeatedly in court. A judge hearing a case from beginning to end will make a determination early on as to which parent is being difficult. So, do not lose your temper and act irrational in court with a judge who you will be seeing again and again." *Custody for Fathers*

has no official power to force an agreement, he or she may be able to comment on the reasonableness of each parent's position. This view of how the judge might rule can dislodge an intransigent parent from a hardened position and cause the parties to move towards an agreeable middle ground.

In some courts, the settlement conference has evolved into a mini-trial, where each side actually presents their evidence and the judge makes an intended ruling. While this is not a complete trial, when the likely ruling is indicated by the judge, the parents are further encouraged to settle.

Race to the courthouse steps. The moving party has a distinct advantage in the legal process. By striking first, the moving party puts the responding party on the defensive, and makes that party answer the allegations within 30 days. This can lead to an early, favorable ruling. Then, the moving party delays trial as long as possible, and when it finally does come, argues that there is no change of circumstances.

Orders

The purpose of all this activity is to create *orders.* An order is an instruction from a judge. The judge can tell you to do something or order you not to do something, and if you ignore what the judge says, you can be held in contempt of court.

Depending on when they're made, orders may be called something else. Orders made before a trial can be called *temporary orders,* while orders made at the end of a trial are called *judgments,* and orders made thereafter are called *post-judgment orders.*

Here are some typical orders:

Pendente Lite Orders

Pendente lite means pending the litigation, which is another way of saying these are temporary orders. Temporary orders are intended to stabilize the situation, and will generally last until you reach an agreement or complete a more extended hearing or trial. Pendente lite orders may include custody arrangements, support amounts, expert witness fees, and more.

Ex Parte Orders

Ex parte orders often arise from emergency situations. Generally, they occur when someone is in danger or something is at risk. The emergency may involve violence, such as one parent hitting the other, or other danger, such as a parent threatening to kidnap the children.

 The *Violence Against Women Act,* 42 U.S.C. § 13981, protects victims of gender-motivated violence. This federal law states that gender-based violence is a violation of the victim's civil rights. The law says, in part: "A person (including a person who acts under color of any statute, ordinance, regulation, custom, or usage of any State) who commits a crime of violence motivated by gender and thus deprives another of the right declared in subsection (b) of this section shall be liable to the party injured, in an action for the recovery of compensatory and punitive damages, injunctive and declaratory relief, and such other relief as a court may deem appropriate."

Ex parte means "by one side," and ex parte orders arise when only one side has had a chance to tell their story. That's designed to prevent the other side from doing something by not giving them advance warning. Because ex parte orders are based on the story told by one side, they last only until a hearing when both sides can be present. At the hearing, the judge can decide to vacate the orders, or make them permanent.

Like all court orders, ex parte orders are not enforceable until they have been properly served. If the other parent cannot be served, you may have difficulty enforcing the orders. However, once the orders have been served, and the other parent violates them, the judge can hold that parent in contempt of court.

Restraining Orders

Restraining orders are orders that stop someone from doing something. If the orders are temporary, they are called *temporary restraining orders,* or TROs. Restraining orders can apply to both parents equally, or to either parent individually.

In some states, certain types of mutual restraining orders automatically take effect when the parents file for divorce or a paternity action. These stop the parents from:

- Removing the children from the state without prior written permission from the court or the other parent.
- Disposing of any marital property.
- Altering insurance policies held for the parent or the children.

Other restraining orders occur after a hearing—ex parte or not. And still other restraining orders originate when the court is not in session, and the judge verbally issues the orders over the phone to a law enforcement officer. These truly emergency orders may not last long, but they give the parent time to get into court to file for more permanent orders.

Restraining orders can cover a variety of situations, but they are commonly used to protect one parent from the other. Typically, the allegations include that one parent has beaten the other parent, beaten the children, threatens to kidnap the children, or harasses the parent at work or on the phone. To prevent further assaults, the judge issues an order restraining

Resist mutual restraining orders. "Some judges prefer to issue temporary restraining orders against both parties when one party files papers with the court requesting protection against domestic violence. You should protest this practice (which equates your conduct with the abuser's) and remind the judge that the law allows mutual restraining orders only if both parties appear and show evidence justifying the mutual orders." Patricia Phillips and George Mair, *Divorce: A Woman's Guide to Getting a Fair Share*

A *protection order* doesn't guarantee your protection. If the other parent decides to ignore the order, you are still at risk until the police arrive. In addition to obtaining the order, use common sense to safeguard yourself and your children.

the conduct of the dangerous parent. The order may even require this parent to leave the family home and not return— it's otherwise known as a *kick-out order.*

If you have been issued a restraining order, be sure to give a copy to the police department. If there is a disturbance and you call them, they will need to see a certified copy of the order before they can act.

Contempt Orders

A judge who feels that someone is challenging the court's authority can declare that party to be in *contempt of court.* Contempt of court is serious, and the person charged with contempt must convince the judge to withdraw the order or be punished. Possible punishments range from a stern lecture by the judge, to a substantial fine, to several months—or longer—in jail. The punishment is intended to pressure the defiant parent into obeying the judge's orders.

Depending on the nature of the misbehavior, contempt can be criminal or civil. *Criminal contempt* typically occurs right in front of the judge—such as when someone "loses it" and starts yelling at the judge. *Civil contempt* often occurs away from court—such as when a parent fails to pay child support. With this indirect contempt, the judge must see evidence before finding the person in contempt. Also, while someone who is found guilty of criminal contempt may be jailed on the spot, someone found guilty of civil contempt may get a limited amount of time to comply.

In family law, contempt actions typically occur when a judge needs to enforce a child custody or child support order. Typically, if one parent fails to pay support, or the other parent fails to comply with visitation orders, a contempt action is brought by the other side.

When Sheri and Jeffrey divorced, they had no children but Sheri was pregnant. Several weeks after their daughter was born, the divorce papers were amended to give Sheri sole legal and physical custody. Six years later, Jeffrey discovered that Sheri was using her maiden name for their daughter's last name at school, and he asked the court to order her to use their combined last name. His request was denied. Jeffrey then asked that their daughter's last name be legally changed to their combined last names. That request was denied, as well. *In re Marriage of Charnogorsky* (1998) 302 Ill.App.3d 649, 707 N.E.2d 79, 236 Ill.Dec. 234.

How to Save Money During Pretrial

The simplest way to save money during pretrial is to settle. As a general rule, the longer the dispute drags on, the more it will cost you, but the quicker you reach an agreement, the more you'll have left in your pocket.

Of course, for you and the other parent to reach an agreement, the other person must be reasonable, and that may not always happen. In the real world, people engage in litigation for all sorts of reasons. Maybe someone has an ax to grind or is out for revenge.

So, if you can't settle, here are some other ways to save money.

Mediate First

Even before you hire a lawyer, you may be able to work out a solution with a mediator. In some courts, you'll be ordered to see the court-appointed mediator anyway, and the mediator may be empowered to make a recommendation to the judge that will likely be adopted. For this approach to work, both parents must take it seriously. A parent who has already decided to litigate "no matter what" will see this as just a momentary diversion.

Make a Cost vs. Benefit Decision

If mediation fails and litigation is in your future, you need to make a cost vs. benefit decision. Admittedly, this is immensely difficult when caught up in the heat of the moment. Child custody being what it is, money may seem to be of secondary importance at the time. It's not.

You don't help yourself or your children if you wipe out financially just to gain an advantage. Custody orders can be reversed on appeal, or they may be modified a few years down the road. That satisfying victory you gain today may be very fleeting indeed.

To make a good decision, you first need to decide on your goals. Do you want sole custody, or can you live with joint? Is the other parent truly unfit, or are they just different from you? Do you need to control the children all the time, or can you let them go with the other parent and not worry?

Once you have decided—or at least thought through—your goals, you need to test those goals against reality. For example, you may want sole custody—but is it likely to be granted? Or you may want to cut off the other parent from having access to the children—but is it possible? The answers to these questions will probably come from an experienced family attorney, and you may have to interview several.

Litigation blues. "Part of the problem is the American legal system. Majestic in many respects, it provides lawyers with procedural options that can make the client's pretrial experience far more time-consuming, expensive, and vexing than the trial itself. Everything from a motion to dismiss to a five-day deposition can put every other aspect of your life on hold: forget about getting any work done, forget about spending time with your family, forget about your vacation plans." *You Don't Always Need A Lawyer*

When you test your goals, keep in mind that courts only deal in financial and practical solutions. The judge decides a schedule for the children, orders someone to pay support, and that's about it. If you want something more, you may want the court to do something it can't do.

Also, when you talk to a lawyer, ask about costs. The real costs. For example, it's not uncommon for certain kinds of motions to run as much as twelve hours of attorney time. At $250 per hour, that's $3,000. Depositions, expert witnesses, attorney preparation—all are costs someone will have to pay.

Once you have set your goals and tested those goals, you have to make a decision. Is what you hope to gain worth what you will have to spend?

Only you can answer that question. If you decide that it makes sense—that is, it's cost-effective—to engage in full-scale litigation, then do it. However, if you can achieve most of what you want at lesser cost, consider that. You can save money during pretrial by simply being rational and not engaging in needless legal battles.

Limit Discovery
If you still must continue with a lawsuit, there are other ways to save money. One way is to limit discovery.

You can limit discovery by agreeing to exchange information quickly and inexpensively. This may not work if you have substantial disagreements with the other party, or if the other party is not being forthcoming. But you can save on your attorney's fees if you provide your attorney with all the information he or she needs, and the other side with all the information to which they're entitled.

You can also limit discovery by using a single expert. It's amazingly expensive to use three different experts—yours, the other parent's, and the judge's. By using one impartial expert to resolve issues, you eliminate duplication of effort and cut costs by two-thirds. For this to work, the other parent has to agree, and you both have to be prepared to live with an opinion you may not like.

Shortly after Barry and Patricia divorced, Patricia announced she was moving out-of-state to "start life over again." Both parents sought custody of their four-year-old son, Jeffrey. Patricia had been married four times and had three children from her previous relationships, and Barry had been married twice. A custody investigator noted that Patricia's oldest daughter was actually the primary caretaker of Jeffrey, and recommended that Patricia be given physical custody. The court agreed. *McQuade v. McQuade* (1995) 901 P.2d 421.

Make Regular, Reasonable Settlement Offers

Throughout pretrial, you can continue to make regular settlement offers to the other side. If you make offers by mail, the opposing lawyer cannot ignore the letters, even if the other parent wants to. Also, if you try to schedule a private conference and the other side refuses to attend, you can document that effort.

Key moments when conferences are useful:
- When you first hire your lawyer—to settle as many issues as possible.
- When a minimum amount of discovery is finished—to stop the litigation before the bills really go through the roof.
- When discovery is completed—to save whatever money you have left.

When you make a series of offers, don't become entrenched and continue to make substantially the same offer each time, but rather, use the process to look for an alternative that satisfies both sides. It's possible that each parent has a different agenda, and there may be a creative solution that will give you both what you want.

Avoid Sanctions, Seek Sanctions

If you fail to settle and actually go to trial, it's a safe bet that someone is being unreasonable. The judge knows this, and he or she will try to figure out who it is.

In most states, the judge can order one party to pay the other's attorney's fees and court costs. This sanction is intended to punish the paying party for misconduct. The misconduct can include engaging in bad-faith efforts to defeat discovery, or refusing to make genuine efforts to settle. If you make genuine attempts to settle and don't engage in misconduct yourself, you avoid being sanctioned, and increase the chances of the other side getting sanctioned.

Sanctions are serious. Despite your ambivalence towards your ex, most judges will not impose sanctions unless someone's behavior is truly outrageous. A certain amount of antagonism is inherent in adversarial situations, and sanctions are only imposed in the most extreme cases. If you ask for sanctions, be sure of your facts.

Chapter 23

Trials and Appeals

✓ If you anticipate a custody trial, you should
   know basic trial procedure.

✓ Custody trials are always held in front of a
   judge—there is no jury. The moving party
   begins by calling *witnesses* and introducing
   evidence. Then the responding party calls
   witnesses and introduces evidence.

✓ To testify in court, you sit near the judge and
   answer questions. When the other side wants
   to exclude something you said, they *object*.

✓ To introduce physical evidence into court—
   such as a document or photograph—you must
   establish the authenticity of the evidence by
   laying foundation.

✓ To win the case, you must present enough
   evidence to convince the judge that you are
   right.

✓ After the trial, if you do not like what the
   judge decided you can *appeal*. An appeal
   means to ask a higher court to reverse the
   trial court because the lower court made
   reversible errors.

Types of Trials

There are two types of trials—judge trials and jury trials.

In a *judge trial,* or *bench trial,* the judge listens to the evidence, decides what's relevant, and then reaches a decision. In a *jury trial,* the jury listens to the evidence and reaches a verdict. In family law, all trials are bench trials.

The lack of a jury in a family law trial reduces some of the legal complexities—such as jury instructions—but it also requires the judge to decide what is to be believed and how much weight to give to each facet of the testimony.

Trial Procedure

A trial is conducted in a series of steps, or stages. The order of these steps is designed to give both sides an equal chance to tell their story.

While the order of battle is fairly strict, judges often have the flexibility to combine or eliminate certain steps in order to shorten the trial. For example, in some courts, the lawyers make dramatic opening statements, but in others, the judge simply reads the pleadings, and the opening statements are skipped. Conversely, some courts expect closing arguments, while in others, the arguments are bypassed because it's presumed the judge already understands the issues.

However your court handles the trial, there is a standard order to how evidence is presented, and in most cases it is followed. This order is called *trial procedure.*

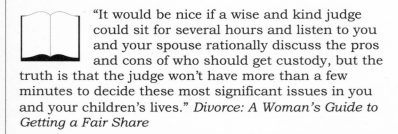

"It would be nice if a wise and kind judge could sit for several hours and listen to you and your spouse rationally discuss the pros and cons of who should get custody, but the truth is that the judge won't have more than a few minutes to decide these most significant issues in you and your children's lives." *Divorce: A Woman's Guide to Getting a Fair Share*

The Stages of a Trial

A trial consists of the following stages:

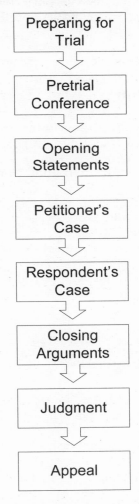

Strictly speaking, preparing for trial and a pretrial conference occur before the trial, and thus, are in the pretrial phase, but because these occur right before a trial, they are included here. Once everyone has assembled in court with the evidence, documents, exhibits, and witnesses—the trial begins.

The formal trial begins with the opening statements, continues through the presentation of the evidence, and ends with the judgment. Sometimes, instead of issuing a judgment, the judge takes the matter under submission. If that happens, the formal trial ends, and the decision comes a short time later.

Here is what you can expect when will have a trial.

Preparing for Trial

If settlement fails and trial is inevitable, there are some simple, basic things you can do to prepare.

As you read this section, keep in mind that it's still possible you won't have a trial. Any number of people arrive at the courthouse on the day of trial, only to suddenly strike a deal. If that seems wasteful and expensive—given the expense of pretrial activities—it is. But some people simply refuse to believe they're going to court until they actually get there.

However, you can't rely on this, and you must prepare for trial. Here are ways to get ready for your court appearance:

Prepare Evidence

Judges are persuaded by evidence, so you'll need yours ready-to-go. Evidence includes witnesses, documents, exhibits, and anything else you plan to present in court.

Witnesses. Witnesses who can testify on your behalf are crucial to making a strong case. Experts are probably experienced at testifying, but teachers, friends, and family members may not be, so your lawyer will need to prepare them. By asking potential witnesses to practice in your lawyer's office, you help them be more effective when testifying, and you get a chance to assess their performance. Because some witnesses can be easily tricked or confused, the opposing attorney could turn their testimony against you, and you may want to drop them. In addition, your lawyer can plan the order for calling the witnesses. Experienced trial attorneys know that witnesses should not just be called in any order, but should be scheduled to testify in a way that builds your case effectively.

When Liam and Christina divorced, Christina was given primary physical custody of their son. The divorce decree also ordered both parents to not allow their son to be in the presence of any person "under the influence or . . . in possession of an illegal or controlled substance." A year later, Christina was convicted of possessing marijuana. Liam asked the court to award him custody, but the trial court refused. Liam appealed, and the higher court reversed the decision. *In re Marriage of Diezsi* (2002) 201 Ariz. 524, 38 P.3d 1189.

Documents. If you have any tangible evidence, such as documents, photographs, audiotapes, or videotapes, you'll need to pull them together. Be aware that you'll need the originals in court—copies are usually not acceptable. For that matter, any evidence you bring may not be admissible until your attorney establishes its foundation. Documents you could bring include bank statements, school records, receipts, tax returns, diaries, etc. If you need to play an audio- or videotape, the courtroom may not be properly equipped, and you'll need the necessary equipment.

Exhibits. If you have a reason to use an exhibit, you'll need to create the exhibit ahead of time. Charts, graphs, diagrams— all are useful ways to convey an idea. But keep in mind that anything you glue together will have to be lugged into the courtroom. Charts tall enough for everyone to see across the room get bulky and are a pain to carry for long distances.

A Trial Notebook. You'll want to put all your evidence into a convenient form. Trial attorneys use trial notebooks. A trial notebook can be a notebook, a folder, or anything else you find at the stationery store. Even if you have an attorney, there's no reason why you can't create your own trial notebook to hold the papers you'll need for the trial.

Prepare Mentally
In addition to pulling the evidence together, you'll need to pull yourself together. That means doing what athletes do before a game—prepare yourself mentally.

Practice with Your Lawyer. If you have to take the witness stand, you'll want to be as confident and knowledgeable as you can. The best way to do that is to practice. You want to practice your own testimony, so you won't forget the points you need to make, and practice answering questions, so you won't be flustered when the opposing attorney interrogates you. An absolute must is to practice how to answer questions. You'll probably be surprised at how little you can say. Both lawyers can cut you off, and when they do, you'll have to stop.

Visit a Courtroom. Surprisingly, trials in real life look just like trials on TV, except there are no commercials. Still, don't rely on reruns of "Matlock" or "LA Law" to prepare for your day in court. Take a trip. Go down to the courthouse. Sit in a courtroom. Watch how the attorneys talk to the judge, and how witnesses testify. Be aware, though, that judges notice people who come into the courtroom, and if you're sitting in the same court as the judge who will be trying your case, he or she may remember you.

Prepare Physically

You also need to prepare physically. A trial is a stressful situation, and you need to be rested, refreshed, and alert. Getting into that condition means following some basic, common sense advice on how to handle stress.

The night before, put out your clothes, arrange your papers, have a good dinner, and then go to bed early. Even if you lie in bed awake, at least you're in bed, and not up and out. Also, write down the courthouse address, the name of the judge, and your lawyer's phone number. Getting lost on the way to court is no fun at all. In the morning, pack a light lunch. Who knows if you'll like what they're serving in the courthouse cafeteria? And finally, leave early. Accidents always happen at inconvenient times, and arriving late to your own trial would be very inconvenient indeed.

Prepare the Children

Finally, in addition to preparing yourself, you need to prepare the children. While the judge may not make a judgment that same day, he might, and the lives of the children could suddenly change. So you'll need to say something.

What you say, of course, depends on their age. If they're old enough to be testifying, then they already know what's going on, and you may not need to add anything. On the other hand, if they're younger, they may not necessarily grasp the significance of a trial, so you may be limited to giving a short, simple explanation and reassurance that you will say more later. In either case, since you can't predict what the judge will do, you can't make any guarantees to the children.

Pretrial Conference

Before the actual trial begins, the judge and lawyers may meet in a pretrial conference. This meeting is to identify all the issues still in dispute, so the judge can limit the evidence to those issues before the court and exclude everything else.

At this meeting, the judge may also set a time limit for the trial. The time limit is important because the lawyers must complete the trial within the time allotted or the judge can declare a *mistrial*.

Trial Brief

In some courts, the lawyers must create a *trial brief* to bring to the pretrial conference. A trial brief is a document that summarizes the issues still in dispute and where you stand on those issues.

Sticker shock. "Litigation can be a black hole right here on Earth, absorbing most of one's time and tens of thousands of one's dollars... As of this writing, in large American cities, simple cases that go to trial consume $10,000 to $20,000 in legal fees and expenses, including travel, witness fees and expenses, phone calls, overnight delivery services, local messenger services, transcripts, and photocopying—lawyers like to charge 20 to 50 cents a page. Some firms even charge for word processing. Not uncommon are cases that take $50,000 to $100,000 in fees and expenses and five or more days of trial." *You Don't Always Need a Lawyer*

The trial brief can include:
- Your present arrangement and present orders.
- The problems you've had since temporary orders were issued.
- The orders you are requesting to solve those problems.

The purpose of the trial brief is to help the judge understand the case, so any documents you attach—such as school reports, charts, or photographs—are useful.

Opening Statements

After the pretrial conference, the formal trial begins. In some courts, this is when the lawyers make their *opening statements.*

The opening statement is a verbal outline about what to prove during the trial. It should identify the issues involved, outline the evidence to be presented, and describe the orders being sought.

Don't be surprised if the opening statements are skipped in bench trials. The judge has already read the pleadings and trial briefs, and opening statements are not always needed.

Petitioner's Case

After the opening statements are finished, the *petitioner's case-in-chief* begins. This is when the petitioner presents evidence that supports whatever allegations are being made.

The petitioner made the complaint, and must now meet the burden of proof. That is, because the petitioner made the initial allegations, he or she must persuade the judge.

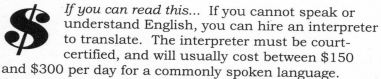

If you can read this... If you cannot speak or understand English, you can hire an interpreter to translate. The interpreter must be court-certified, and will usually cost between $150 and $300 per day for a commonly spoken language. Contact the court clerk to make arrangements.

Though Debbie and Mark were never married, six months after their son, Sawyer, was born, the court gave Debbie temporary custody and Mark visitation rights. But over the next six years, they waged "a protracted battle over custody and visitation rights." At one point, the district court ordered the sheriff to supervise the exchange of Sawyer between the two parents, and at another time, Mark was held in contempt for violating an order that prevented Debbie and Mark from speaking to each other. Finally, Debbie asked the court to terminate all contact between Mark and Sawyer, complaining about Mark's verbal outbursts. The court limited Mark's contact with Sawyer to phone calls, email and mail. *Arneson-Pengra v. Nelson* (2001) 307 Mont. 60, 36 P.3d 874, 2001 MT 242.

In family law, the burden of proof is by a preponderance of the evidence. Thus, to win the case, the petitioner must present enough evidence to demonstrate that his or her version of the facts is more believable than the respondent's version of the facts.

When organizing the evidence, lawyers know there is a tactical advantage to when facts are revealed. Experienced lawyers will present the evidence to build to a convincing conclusion.

Evidence

Any information you present to prove your case is called *evidence*. To win the case, you must present enough evidence to convince the judge that you are right.

Physical Evidence
Physical evidence includes anything tangible, such as calendars, diaries, school records, medical records, and so on. For example, physical evidence might include the following:

Diary. You can use a diary to keep track of specific events, such as school activities, other activities, and any contacts you have with the other parent. Often, you can refer to a diary to refresh your memory when testifying.

Trial notebook. Do what the lawyers do, and organize your written evidence into a trial notebook. This is an 8 1/2" x 11" binder with tabbed sections for each area. By using a trial notebook, you might convince the judge that your information is both reliable and accurate.

Portfolio. You might impress the judge by assembling a short portfolio of your positive attributes. Include anything significant, such as awards, diplomas, certificates, etc.

Police Reports. Anyone can walk into a police station and file a report, so the courts recognize a police report for what it is— a one-sided description. Unless the officer was an eyewitness, a police report may have limited value. Even worse, someone who routinely files police reports may appear to be abusing the system.

Photographs, Videotapes, and Audiotapes. In court, photographs are much easier to present than videotapes or audiotapes, but all may impress the judge if used appropriately.

Charts and Graphs. A simple graph can make your point, but you'll need to make it large enough to read across the room. Also, expect the opposing attorney to challenge the data it represents.

Witnesses
You can also introduce evidence through the testimony of *witnesses.* A witness testifies under oath about what they have seen or heard, or gives an opinion about some aspect of the case.

Ordinary Witnesses. An ordinary witness testifies to his or her personal knowledge. In legal terms, the witness must have firsthand knowledge of an event by having experienced it through one or more of the five senses (sight, hearing, taste, smell, and sound). Normally, except for reimbursement of costs, you can't pay an ordinary witness to testify.

Expert Witnesses. Expert witnesses are people qualified to offer a professional opinion. An expert witness may be asked for a custody recommendation, and the expert's opinion will matter to the judge. Psychologists and other mental health professionals are considered expert witnesses. Experts are usually paid for their time.

Character Witnesses. Character witnesses are used to demonstrate a parent's skill and involvement with the children. Friends, relatives, clergy—all can testify on your behalf. Because character witnesses are obviously biased, they may have limited value with the judge.

Impeachment Witnesses. An impeachment witness is called to demonstrate that the other parent or one of the witnesses lied. Because credibility is crucial in child custody, an effective impeachment witness can make the judge question the entire testimony of a person shown to be a liar.

Rules of Evidence
Because evidence is so important, there are rules governing what you can introduce and how you can introduce it. These are called the *rules of evidence.*

The rules of evidence help distinguish between information that is important and believable, and information that is unimportant and unbelievable. For some testimony to be admitted into evidence, it must be both relevant and material. That is, it must relate to the issues involved, and it must be significant enough to matter.

Evidence rules also protect the judge from easily falsified evidence. For example, under the right circumstances, a written document can be very convincing, but it can also be counterfeit. That's why you have to show that it is both genuine and accurate. To authenticate a written document,

Your state's rules of evidence can usually be found in the *Evidence Code* in the *Rules of Civil Procedure.* To find these statutes, check with a law librarian.

you may have to call the author to testify, and for a photograph, you may have to call the photographer.

In family law, judges hear everything and then decide what is admissible. In theory, they're supposed to ignore inadmissible evidence. In reality, it's hard to *unring a bell*. Highly damaging inadmissible testimony will influence the judge.

During the trial, many arguments will occur over whether some piece of evidence is relevant and material. Even if the evidence qualifies on other grounds, it still may not be admitted because it's deemed to be hearsay.

Hearsay

Hearsay is repeating what someone else said. For example, if Beth were testifying, and she said, "Steve told me that..." what Steve said—or didn't say—is hearsay. Hearsay is "a statement, other than one made by the declarant while testifying at the trial or hearing, offered in evidence to prove the truth of the matter asserted." Thus, if Beth were trying to prove something by what Steve said—that's hearsay.

Black's Law Dictionary says, "Hearsay does not derive its value solely from the credit of the witnesses, but rests mainly on the veracity and competency of other persons. The very nature of the evidence shows its weakness, and it is admitted only in specified cases from necessity."

Hearsay testimony is particularly liable to outright lying—or at least gross misrepresentation—because the person who made the statement is not being directly asked and is not on the witness stand where he or she can be cross-examined.

Hearsay can get complicated, and there are some exceptions that allow hearsay to be admissible—such as excited utterances and statements made against interest—but generally, hearsay cannot be offered as evidence.

When called to testify, witnesses can be subjected to several rounds of questioning.

The order of questioning is:
- Direct examination.
- Cross-examination.
- Redirect examination.
- Recross-examination.
- Direct Examination.

A witness called to testify for the first time must take the stand and be sworn in. This means he or she must walk over to the witness stand and answer "Yes" when asked to swear to tell the truth. After that, the witness can be questioned.

Once sworn in, the witness must then tell the truth. If a statement is shown to be a lie, the witness can be charged with perjury. In reality, however, people are rarely punished.

The attorney who calls the witness asks questions first. This initial round of questioning is called *direct examination.*

 If your best friend testifies, he or she may be declared an *incompetent witness.* That's a witness considered too biased to be objective.

Direct Examination

In direct examination, the attorney asks questions in a very specific way. Generally, these are broad, open-ended questions that lead to short, narrative answers.

Direct testimony lets the witness explain the situation in his or her own words. The witness may testify to matters of fact—such as the authenticity of a document—or recall events personally witnessed. And an expert witness can state a professional opinion. For example, a psychologist may give an opinion as to which parent should be awarded custody.

A witness called during the case-in-chief must appear credible. If the testimony seems unbelievable, or if the witness criticizes the side who called him, the testimony can be very damaging.

At times, the attorney may ask an inappropriate question, or the witness may say something improper. When that happens, the opposing attorney can object. An *objection* is how the opposing attorney indicates a possible violation of the rules of evidence.

When an objection is raised, the attorneys may briefly argue their position to the judge, who then makes a ruling. If the judge sustains an objection to a question, the witness does not have to answer. If the judge denies or overrules an objection, the witness has to answer.

If the judge decides that some testimony is inadmissible, the opposing attorney may make a *motion to strike,* which is a request that the judge delete the testimony from the record.

Cross-Examination

After direct examination is finished, the opposing attorney is allowed to cross-examine the witness.

Cross-examination is used to test the truthfulness of the statements made by the witness during direct examination. In this round of questioning, the opposing attorney tries to undermine the credibility of the witness's testimony.

After living together for several years in Canada, Sharif and Naima had a child. Three years later, Naima took the baby and secretly moved to Minnesota. Sharif asked a Canadian court for custody, insisting they had been married in Kenya, among other facts. His request was granted, and he then secured an emergency order through a Minnesota court to have the child returned under the *Hague Convention on the Civil Aspects of International Child Abduction.* Naima responded by insisting they were never married and Sharif had abused her. The Minnesota court awarded custody to her. However, the Minnesota court did not state any factual reason why it had reached its decision, and when Sharif appealed, the decision was reversed. *Salah v. Awes* (2001) 629 N.W.2d 99.

Think court is crowded? In one family court, 5,206 domestic cases were filed in a single year.[1] If the judge actually listened to each case, he would have to decide more than 20 cases a day.

Because cross-examination is adversarial in nature, the style of the questioning is different. Instead of asking open-ended questions, the attorney asks leading questions that call for a simple "Yes" or "No" answer.

Cross-examination questions are generally limited to matters that were brought up during direct testimony. However, if the witness is ruled a hostile witness, the opposing attorney may be able to broaden the scope of the questioning.

Cross-examination provides much of the drama in a trial. Generally, the opposing attorney asks questions loaded with a distorted interpretation of the facts. The witness must answer, even if it means admitting to something damaging.

To impeach the witness, the opposing attorney will try to get the witness to make a statement that is inconsistent with previous testimony, or shows a bias, or shows the witness stands to gain financially or in some other way from a particular outcome in the case.

Cross-examination not only reveals dishonest statements made by the witness, but also helps acquire evidence for the other side.

Redirect Examination

After the opposing attorney has finished questioning the witness, the first attorney can ask more questions. This *redirect examination* lets the witness add detail to the cross-examination answers. During redirect, the witness can clarify responses and try to recover from any damaging admissions. Because redirect is limited to matters raised in cross, some attorneys may skip it and move on to new evidence.

When Hope filed for divorce from Jeffrey after a ten-year marriage, the district court gave her temporary physical custody of their three children. However, Jeffrey stayed in their four-bedroom home, while Hope moved four times, finally staying in a mobile home with her boyfriend. The court decided "the children's best interests would be served by placing them in their familiar family home," and awarded Jeffrey physical care of the children. *In re Marriage of Harrelson* (2002) Iowa No. 2-112 / 01-1206.

Recross-Examination

After redirect comes *recross-examination,* where the opposing attorney again questions the witness. This back-and-forth continues until the witness is fully questioned.

Respondent's Case

When the petitioner's case-in-chief is over, the moving party rests, and the *respondent's case-in-chief* begins. This is when the respondent argues his or her version of the facts.

The respondent presents a case just as the petitioner did—by introducing evidence and calling witnesses. As before, the witnesses undergo the same rounds of questioning: direct, cross, redirect, and recross-examination. This time, however, the respondent's attorney conducts the direct examination, and the petitioner's attorney does the cross-examination.

In this phase, the respondent not only wants to contradict allegations made by the petitioner, but also support any counterclaims she made.

When the respondent's case-in-chief is finished, the petitioner is allowed to rebut any evidence the respondent introduced. This phase of the trial is called *sur-rebuttal.* And after the sur-rebuttal is done, there can follow a *sur-sur-rebuttal.* This back-and-forth continues until time runs out.

How to Appear in Court

Your day in court will be one of the most important days of your life. To win your case, you must appear physically, mentally, and emotionally sound. In fact, your appearance is so crucial that it may persuade the judge even more than the evidence you present.

Here are some practical tips about appearing in court:

First, you want to dress properly. In the world of courts, this means dress for business. A good rule of thumb is to imagine that you're going on a job interview. Conservative business attire—coupled with good grooming—conveys the image of a stable role model for your children. Ripped jeans, tank tops, and excessive jewelry conveys the opposite.

Second, you want to behave properly. Courtrooms have their own etiquette, and you'll need to conduct yourself accordingly. For example, if the other parent is on the witness stand, and is lying—stay calm. Don't get angry or agitated. It will only make you look like an overwrought, emotional person. If you sit quietly and wait your turn, you'll appear to be both stable and in control. If you need to tell your attorney something, write a short note and slide it across the table.

Third, you want to be ready. After arriving at the courthouse early, look on the court calendar or docket to find your courtroom or department. Then, check in with the clerk. If court is in session, wait until the judge takes a break. Tell the clerk you're present, and while you wait for your case to be called—stay close. If things move faster than anticipated, you could be called very quickly.

 Your fifteen minutes. All cases decided in the court system are a matter of public record, but if you want to keep your private matters private, you can ask for a gag order. When considering a request to seal the court record, the judge decides if the likely publicity will harm the children.

And fourth, treat everyone with courtesy. If you address the judge, call him or her "Your Honor." Call the opposing attorney "Mr." or "Mrs." And remember, you can't talk to the judge or the other attorney privately. Obey the rules that restrict when you can talk.

How to Testify in Court

Since child custody involves your fitness as a parent, it's a safe bet that sooner or later you'll have to testify. There's no trick to being an effective witness; all you have to do is answer questions. Family court judges hear conflicting stories every day, and they routinely decide who is telling the truth and who's not.

 Politeness pays. The court clerk knows everything about how to move your case along. The clerk can't give you legal advice, but can explain the court rules and procedures. Whatever else you do—be nice. The clerk will tell the judge if you've been rude.

Here are some tips to help you convey your story in court:

During direct examination you want to show the judge what an honest, credible person you are. You can't tell the story of your life, but you can indicate what you're doing right and what the other parent is doing wrong. You'll only have a little time to talk, so plan to speak in short, comprehensive sentences. Also, consider owning up to whatever you've done wrong. Better to reveal a negative up front than to let the opposing attorney do it on cross-examination. And finally, expect to stick to current events—don't dwell on long-ago slights. What seems important to you may not be to the judge.

During cross-examination you want to avoid being provoked into an angry outburst by the opposing attorney. No matter how insulting the questions are—and they will be insulting— they're only questions, so stay calm and answer honestly. If you can slip in a criticism of the other parent, so much the better. Remember, you're on the defensive during cross, so the less said the better. The opposing attorney is determined to find something wrong with you, so resign yourself to being abused on the witness stand.

Five Reasons Why You Won't Like Your Day in Court

1. *Flaws.* Your weaknesses and weird fetishes will be revealed to everyone.

2. *Backstabbing.* Your best friend may testify against you.

3. *Humiliation.* The opposing attorney will make you look an evil, dysfunctional psychopath.

4. *Surprise.* If your children testify, their answers may shock you.

5. *Karma.* Your past misdeeds may come back to haunt you.

If You Settle

Don't be surprised if you never finish trial. Amazingly, many parents arrive in court and even begin a trial, only to suddenly—miraculously—find some middle ground.

Or the judge may read the pleadings, listen to some of the evidence, and then suggest a reasonable outcome. This suggestion, of course, is blatant coercion—but it's very effective. Only the most recalcitrant parent ignores a judge's comments in a bench trial.

If you do reach an agreement, the judge may enter a consent order. This order has the same legal effect as a judgment, except that because you agreed to it—you can't appeal.

What was that? If your agreement is read into the court record—pay attention. Once the agreement is entered, it's as good as law. If the words are changed—even slightly—and you don't object, you will be bound by the new orders.

Closing Arguments

After all the evidence has been presented, and both sides have rested, the attorneys may then make *closing arguments*. This is a summation of the main points in each side's case.

When attorneys make closing arguments, they must stick to the issues and evidence presented. Each attorney reviews the evidence favorable to their side and the evidence damaging to the other side, and asks the court to rule in their favor. If custody is disputed, each attorney may state the living arrangements being sought.

As they did at the start of the trial, the moving party goes first and the responding party follows. After the initial go-round, the arguments can go back-and-forth as each attorney rebuts the other. In some courts, closing arguments are deemed unnecessary in bench trials and are skipped altogether.

Post-Trial Memorandum

If the trial was long and complex, each attorney may have to submit a written *memorandum* to the judge. A post-trial memorandum includes a description of the evidence presented, relevant statutes and case law, and the remedy being sought.

Judgment

Finally, it's over. After all the pleadings, depositions, witnesses, testimony, and arguments—it's over. The trial is finished. You have had you day in court, and now the judge must make a decision.

Sometimes the judge will render an immediate judgment—
called a *ruling from the bench.* If the judge issues new orders
while you are still in court, you are expected to obey the new
orders immediately.

More commonly, though, the judge will delay making a
decision. If the judge takes the matter *under submission,* he
may want to review the trial transcript, review his notes on
the witnesses, examine the physical evidence, or consult
relevant statutes and case law. When this happens, the judge
will send a written decision to the attorneys two weeks to two
months later.

Along with the decision, you may receive a document called a
Findings of Facts and Conclusions of Law. This explains the
facts the judge determined were true and the application of
law based on those facts. This is a very important paper, and
you will need to review it if you are considering an appeal.

 When Michelle's daughter, Catherine, was
born, Michelle was not married. Two months
later, the father established paternity and
asked the court for visitation. Family court
granted visitation with the baby girl, and also appointed
Elizabeth O'Connor as a law guardian for Catherine.
Over the next year, the parents fought over visitation and
both filed complaints. Before the hearing in family court,
Michelle wrote a letter to the court complaining that
O'Connor was ignoring her concerns and not bringing
them to court. After the hearing, the court decided that
Michelle "has been bordering on a pathological obsession
with this child. Her appearance, her demeanor, [and] her
testimony, [display] that she is rigid and unrealistic [and]
that she clings to some inappropriate judgments."
Michelle then sued O'Connor, the law guardian,
complaining that she had "breached her duties as a
fiduciary and an attorney for the child" by failing to
advocate and protect the child. Michelle's lawsuit was
dismissed. *Bluntt v. O'Conner* (2002) New York No. CA
01-01062.

If you actually go to trial, don't expect it to last long. One judge estimates that average family law trial lasts between 3 and 4 hours.
California Divorce Handbook

You will also receive an order specifying the remedy to be applied. In civil law, the two types of remedies are for money—such as when a judge orders one parent to pay the other—and equitable—which concerns a person's behavior.

Depending on the case, the judge can order whatever remedy is necessary. For example, in a case of domestic violence, the judge may also order compensatory damages, which are payments for loss due to injury, and punitive damages, which are payments designed to punish the wrongdoer.

In addition, the judge may seek to stop future violence by issuing an injunction, which prevents someone from doing something. If one parent already had a temporary restraining order, the judge may make it a permanent injunction.

Post-Judgment Litigation

When Yogi Berra said, "It ain't over till it's over" he could just as easily have been talking about the legal system instead of baseball. With the trial over and the judgment rendered, you might think the case is over. But it's not. Instead, you begin post-trial.

When custody is involved, just as much can happen after the trial as before it. For example, you may have to file various post-trial motions. These can involve enforcement, to order a parent to comply with the existing orders, or a modification, to change the orders to fit a changed set of circumstances.

Also, post-trial is when you file an appeal. To *appeal* a case means to ask another court to review the judge's decision. You appeal when you disagree with the trial judge and want another court to overturn the judgment. Either side has the right to appeal, but usually only the "losing" party wants to.

Appellate Courts

If you file an appeal, you move your case to a higher court called an *appellate court.* Most states have several layers of appellate courts, starting with the *court of appeal,* and ending with the highest court, often called the *state supreme court.* When you first appeal, you begin in the court of appeal.

Perhaps the most surprising thing about appellate courts is that they don't retry the case. When you appeal, you don't get a second chance to call your witnesses and make your arguments. Instead, appellate courts exist solely to review the law. The appellate court will not review the facts that lead to the ruling, but rather, decide only if the correct law was applied and the correct procedures were followed.

Appellate Decisions

Because appellate courts are strictly concerned with the law, they limit their decisions to the following:

Affirm the Judgment
If the appellate court agrees with the lower court's judgment, it *affirms the judgment.* If you are the appellant—the party who filed the appeal—you must then appeal to a higher court or end the case.

Reverse the Judgment
If the appellate court rules that the trial court's decision was wrong, it can *reverse the judgment.* This means the trial court's decision is erased. The court will then either send the case back for retrial, or modify or correct the judgment in some other way.

 An *appeal* is different from a *modification.* An appeal is made in a different, higher court, and seeks to alter the original judge's ruling. A modification is made in the same trial court, and seeks only to change part of the original order because there are new facts.

Remand the Case

The appellate court can also send the case back to the lower court for some other action, such as to correct an error made by the judge. If the case is *remanded,* the trial judge must follow the instructions from the higher court.

Dismiss the Appeal

The appellate court can also *dismiss the appeal* if it has no merit or if the court does not have jurisdiction.

Vacate the Judgment

When the appellate court completely wipes out the judgment of a lower court, it is said to *vacate the judgment.* This can occur when a higher appellate court—such as a state supreme court—reviews the opinion of a lower appellate court and completely replaces the court's opinion. Vacated judgments cannot be used as precedent.

Grounds for an Appeal

If you get a judgment you don't like, your first reaction may be to rush back into court and appeal. But wait. Before you do, you'll need to determine if you have grounds for an appeal.

When Heather and Robert divorced, they agreed Robert would have physical custody of their only child, Bailey, and Heather would have reasonable visitation. They also agreed Heather would pay Robert $201 per month in child support. Thereafter, "the parties litigated the custody issue often." Three years later, they agreed that Heather would have physical custody, Robert would have reasonable visitation, and Robert would pay Heather $313 per month in child support. They also agreed Heather could move with Bailey to Arkansas. The following year, Robert returned to court, complaining that Heather was not letting him visit or communicate with Bailey. Specifically, Heather had moved with Bailey from Arkansas to Alabama without notifying Robert or the court. The court gave Robert custody. *Paulsen v. Paulsen* (2001) 10 Neb.App. 269, 634 N.W.2d 12.

Put the cart before the horse. Believe it or not, you should begin preparing your appeal before the start of your trial. As odd as that sounds, it's based on the fact that your attorney must object to all improper evidence and procedures as they occur. These potential judicial errors are the sole basis for your appeal, and you must get your objections into the record to raise the issues.

To successfully appeal your case, you must show that the trial judge either made a mistake in interpreting the law, or made a mistake in the trial procedure. And this mistake must have been so significant that it affected the outcome of your case.

That is why you review the *Findings of Facts and Conclusions of Law.* This document explains the judge's legal reasoning and helps you determine whether you have the basis for an appeal.

When You Cannot Appeal
Like everyone else, judges make mistakes, and some judicial errors are allowed. If the judge made a harmless error—one that did not affect the outcome of the trial—the judgment may stand.

Likewise, because the trial court is the finder of fact, if the judge chose to believe one parent and not the other, that's usually within a judge's discretion, and is also not the basis for a reversal.

When You Can Appeal
On the other hand, if the mistake was significant enough to harm you, you may have a reversible error. Here are some errors you can use:

Error in interpreting the law. If the judge didn't apply the correct law, or misinterpreted the law that was applied, you might have the basis for an appeal. Because legislatures routinely write confusing statutes, this happens more than you think.

Error in determining the facts. If the judge made a mistake with the evidence, either by admitting irrelevant facts, or by excluding relevant ones, you might successfully appeal. Generally, you'll need clear and convincing proof of this.

Abuse of discretion. In family law, the judge has plenty of discretion to decide who is telling the truth and who is not, and what is best for the situation. However, the judge must remain within the standards of law, and if he doesn't, you may be able to appeal.

Prejudice. If the judge displays a bias towards you because of your race, gender, age, and so on, you may have grounds for an appeal. To prove this error, you must show that the judge ignored the law and decided the case solely due to prejudice.

Follow the rules. If you appeal, obey the original court ruling while the appeal is pending. A parent who ignores orders from a lower court can be sanctioned. Even worse, noncompliance can invalidate the appeal altogether. If you cannot obey the trial court's orders, seek an immediate, temporary stay of execution.

Miscalculation. Sometimes the judge adds up the numbers wrong. For example, when computing child support, the judge may do the math incorrectly. If an unintentional error happens, you may be able to file for a modification with the trial court, rather than make an appeal.

How to Appeal

If you believe you have grounds for an appeal, you'll have to file some documents with the court. Once you do, you become the appellant, and the other party becomes the appellee. Here are the general steps to appeal your case:

Check the Deadline

The date when your judgment was entered in the court record—called the *entry of judgment*—is critical, because all

states have a deadline for how long you have to appeal.
Generally, it's 30 to 120 days. If you miss the deadline, you
lose the right to appeal.

File Notice of Appeal

To appeal your case, you must file a *notice of appeal*. This
starts the period when you must complete the paperwork.
During this time your attorney must serve notice that you are
appealing, and the other party will be able to respond.

If you are appealing an appeal, such as taking a decision from
a court of appeals to a supreme court, you may have to file a
Petition for Writ of Certiorari. This document requests the
court to consider your appeal. Higher appellate courts can
deny your petition, effectively ending your ability to appeal
any further.

Trial Tips

The Divorce Handbook: Your Basic Guide to Divorce, James
T. Friedman, Random House, $13.00. This excellent book
written by a family law specialist offers concise answers to
many questions.

Assemble Record

After filing your notice, you have to *assemble the record* for
the review court. This involves telling the court reporter to
transcribe the court proceedings, and then telling the court
clerk to copy and bind together all of the paperwork—the
transcripts, the pleadings, etc. As the moving party, you will
have to pay for the preparation of the record, and if it was a
long trial, it can cost several thousand dollars or more.

Prepare Briefs

Then, you must write and file a *brief* explaining your reasons
for the appeal. The brief must show that the judge made
errors that resulted in a miscarriage of justice. In your
arguments, you must cite the facts in the case and quote
relevant law so persuasively that the review court has no
choice but to agree with you that the judge was wrong and the
ruling must be reversed or vacated.

Make Oral Arguments

You may also have to make *oral arguments* in front of the appellate court. These arguments are usually optional, and if they are made, usually last between 15 and 30 minutes. The justices will have read the briefs, so the time is used for asking questions.

Decision and Opinion

After the oral arguments—if they were made—the justices discuss the case and vote on whether to affirm or reverse the trial court's decision. Usually, one justice is assigned to write the opinion that explains the decision. Other justices are free to author their own concurring or dissenting opinions. These opinions are published, and become the basis for future legal decisions.

---

1 Cases filed during the fiscal year 1991-1992. Source: Richard A. Curtis, Commissioner, Los Angeles County Superior Court (Pomona, California)

Difficult Problems

"Behind in your child support? We can help!"

Chapter 24

Mistreatment of Children: Abuse, Neglect, and False Accusations

- ✓ If a parent—or any adult—hurts a child, it is called *child abuse*.

- ✓ *Physical* child abuse involves beating, burning, and spanking. *Sexual* child abuse involves molestation. *Emotional* child abuse involves severe humiliation. Other forms of child abuse include *neglect, endangerment,* and *abandonment*.

- ✓ In custody battles, allegations of child abuse are common, with the vast majority turning out to be false.

- ✓ Every state must investigate a credible child abuse complaint. Social workers, child care workers or the police will respond.

- ✓ When a complaint is investigated, the investigator looks for evidence, such as injuries not caused by normal childhood playing or statements from the child which indicate abuse.

- ✓ If there is reason to believe a child has been abused, the child will be taken from the parent.

Child Abuse

When an adult hurts a child, it is called *child abuse.* Child abuse and child neglect cover many forms of injury and cruelty to children, including physical harm, emotional harm, and neglect.

Parents have a responsibility to protect their children. Not only are parents prohibited from hurting their children, but they must ensure that other adults don't hurt them, either. This includes being responsible for the behavior of other family members, baby-sitters, and anyone else with access to the children.

Types of Child Abuse

There are many types of child abuse and neglect. They include:

Physical Abuse
Physical abuse is physically hurting a child. Beating, burning, bruising, or kicking a child are all examples of physical abuse. When a parent punishes a child by spanking, it may be considered physical abuse if the child is injured, even if the injury is only temporary.

Sexual Abuse
Sexual abuse is when an adult molests or otherwise uses a child for sexual pleasure. Examples of sexual mistreatment include fondling, anal or oral intercourse, and vaginal or anal penetrations. Sexual abuse can also include placing the child in inappropriate situations, such as exploiting the child in prostitution or pornography.

 "Many states, faced with civil lawsuits, criminal prosecutions, and mounting public outrage over abuse cases... have in the past decade regularly toughened their codes. They've also squeezed out caseworker discretion by sharpening definitions of abuse and standardizing the decision-making process." *Los Angeles Times*

During their marriage, Heidi-Lynn and Wallace had a son and a daughter. Six years later, Heidi-Lynn filed for divorce and asked for sole custody. At trial, several witnesses testified that Heidi-Lynn had struck her daughter, and when Wallace had stepped in, Heidi-Lynn struck him. Nevertheless, the fifth circuit family court awarded sole custody to Heidi-Lynn, stating that she "did not commit family violence as asserted by [Wallace], but administered physical discipline to the parties' children permitted by [law]." *Rezentes v. Rezentes* (1998) 965 P.2d 133.

Emotional Abuse

Emotional abuse is subjecting a child to extreme humiliation that deprives the child of dignity and self-esteem. Examples of emotional abuse include humiliating the child in front of family and friends, isolating the child for long periods of time, and using language that causes the child emotional harm.

Neglect

Child neglect occurs when an adult fails to meet the basic needs of the child. Physical neglect involves failing to provide the minimum food, clothing, and shelter needed by the child. Medical neglect involves failing to provide the basic medical, dental, and psychiatric care needed by the child. Educational neglect concerns the failure to educate the child according to the state's educational laws. And developmental neglect concerns the failure to provide the basic nurturing and cognitive stimulation needed by the child.

Endangerment

Endangerment involves reckless behavior by an adult that causes—or could cause—harm to the child. An example of physical endangerment includes leaving a young child alone in an area where dangerous items are within reach.

Abandonment

Abandonment is leaving a child alone or with someone else in such a way as to indicate that you are abdicating parental responsibility. For example, leaving a child in a dumpster and walking away would qualify as abandonment.

Child abuse and neglect are defined by both federal and state laws. The *Child Abuse Prevention and Treatment Act (CAPTA)* is the federal law that provides minimum guidelines states must incorporate in their definitions of child abuse. Based on these guidelines, each state then provides its own definition of child abuse. Though the standard varies, most states define abuse in terms of "harm or threatened harm" to a child's health or welfare.

The Reality of Child Abuse

Identifying the exact number of children abused each year is difficult because many reports turn out to be false.

For example, in Los Angeles, an estimated 25,000 families—or about 50,000 children—are reported each month to the *Department of Children's Services* as possible abuse cases.[1] About one-third of those cases are closed within ten days because the allegations are unfounded or cannot be proven, and only 3% actually go to court.

Nationally, one survey estimated that approximately 3,000,000 abuse and neglect reports are made each year, but only one-third are substantiated after an investigation.[2]

Also, abuse allegations are common with custody disputes. As one researcher found, when custody is in dispute, over 83% of abuse and neglect allegations turn out to be false.[3]

Still, despite the high number of false reports, many children are abused or neglected each year. And the number of reports is climbing. From 1976 to 1993, the number of child abuse accusations rose an astonishing 333%, and the number of sexual abuse accusations increased by over 1,400%![4]

Reporting Child Abuse

All states have laws that require suspected child abuse to be reported. Usually, these reports are made to an agency called the *Department of Children and Family Services (DCFS)*, or *Child Protective Services (CPS)*, or something similar. If the police are notified, they may investigate, or contact the agency.

Who Has to Report
Depending on your state, virtually everyone who works with children may be required to report suspected abuse. This includes:
- Doctors.
- Nurses.
- Teachers.
- Day Care Workers.
- Health Care Workers.
- Social Workers.
- Police.
- Sheriff.

These *mandated reporters* are usually protected from being sued by the family, and in some states, the reporter's identity is kept secret. In addition, many states have abuse hotlines so that neighbors and family members can make anonymous reports.

What to Report
Generally, you do not need absolute proof of child maltreatment to make a report. Usually, you only need reasonable suspicion or a reasonable cause to believe that abuse has occurred.

This suspicion may be based on direct evidence or circumstantial evidence. Direct evidence includes your own observations of a parent's abusive behavior or the child relating some harmful behavior by an adult. Circumstantial evidence includes suspicious injuries to the child, or signs of

 "Nationwide, police make about 12% of all reports received by child protective agencies. This percentage is about the same as that for such other professional groups such as medical (11%), education (12%), and social services (12%)."[5]

"Everyone's on the defensive. They're afraid that if they don't make a report, they'll be deemed criminals if they inadvertently put a child back in the hands of a real abuser." *Dr. Richard A. Gardner,* Professor of Child Psychiatry, Columbia University

mistreatment by looking at the condition of the child. While you don't need incontrovertible proof, you can't simply make accusations based on some vague "gut feeling" either. Generally, you must have evidence to support your claim.

Failure to Report

To encourage reports, many states sanction mandated reporters for failure to report. In some states, failure to report is a misdemeanor with a possible fine and imprisonment, but in others, the penalties are virtually nonexistent. In addition, failing to report can often lead to a civil lawsuit, and indeed, many police officers, doctors, teachers, and even family members have been sued for not protecting the child.

Child Abuse Database

In some states, when a report is made, it is logged into a *child abuse database.* The database, or registry, keeps track of everyone suspected of child abuse, even if it turns out to be false.

Child abuse reports. Federal law requires every state to report child abuse. 42 U.S.C. § 5119, states, in part: "In each State, an authorized criminal justice agency of the State shall report child abuse crime information to, or index child abuse crime information in, the national criminal history background check system. A criminal justice agency may satisfy the requirement of this subsection by reporting or indexing all felony and serious misdemeanor arrests and dispositions."

This list of suspected abusers helps authorities know who has been accused before. The database may also be used by certain employers when making a background check—for example, in screening an applicant for a child care position.

Unfortunately, once you are logged into the database, it's not easy to get out. A parent who has been the target of an unfounded accusation may be listed for a few months, a few years, or even for life.

Investigating Child Abuse Accusations

It's not easy to investigate child abuse. The officials who do it complain that the process is confusing and frustrating. On the one hand, they must gather enough evidence to determine if the charge has a factual foundation—that is, if it's true—but on the other, they must avoid traumatizing the child even more.

"The fact is, we have some nice, good, well-meaning people on the central registry. Nice, good people don't always do what's right. For most of them, it's never going to happen again. But we do find some people repeat. That's why we have a registry. So we can know of the second or third incident." *Eric Sage,* Iowa Department of Human Services

As well as anybody, these officials know that "a child's world revolves around the family, and no matter how dysfunctional that family may be, it is usually the only one the child has ever known." That's why the case is often handled by social workers, rather than law enforcement personnel.

Child Protective Service Agencies

In many states, caseworkers are responsible for investigating child abuse. These workers interview the family, inspect the home, and may make "suggestions" on how to correct the problem. If the parents do not accept their suggestions, the caseworkers often have the authority to force them. For example, they caseworkers may be able to require the parents to undergo counseling. If more serious measures are required, the caseworkers can compel the parents to submit to a lie detector test, or they may even be able to deny access to the children.

The Police

While child protective agencies often call the police for help, usually the police only get involved in more serious cases, such as those involving injuries or sexual abuse. Typically, police intercede when:

- A parent is uncooperative, or is threatening a caseworker.
- The problem is serious enough to arrest the parent.
- The child is in immediate danger and must be placed in custody.
- An emergency occurs after hours, and an immediate response is needed.

Because the police have the legal authority to protect citizens (including children), they are best equipped to deal with a dangerous parent. Absent a court order, only the police can forcibly enter a home, remove a child, and place the child in protective custody.

 "About 1 million cases [a year] are substantiated, most with a finding of some credible evidence. In about 40% of those million cases, sexual and physical abuse can be shown by such means as x-rays, radiology reports, or rape tests."[6]

Physical Evidence

When abuse has occurred, physical evidence often exists. Police and caseworkers will search for this evidence and carefully document it. They may take pictures, have the child x-rayed, or make written descriptions.

Suspicious Injuries

Suspicious injuries are injuries suggesting physical abuse. These are not injuries from normal childhood playing—such as bumping or falling down. Rather, they are injuries with the

distinctive characteristics of abuse. Investigators look for
these indicators:

Type of injury. Some injuries are almost impossible for
children to do to themselves, such as a fracture to the upper
thigh in a toddler, while other injuries are almost always
caused by others, such as abdominal injuries.

Shape of injury. Many assaults on a child leave telltale
marks. For example, there may be choke marks around the
neck, or injury from a belt buckle or coat hanger, which leave
distinctive signs of abuse.

 When O. J. Simpson was arrested on the
charge of murdering his ex-wife, Nicole Brown
Simpson, he voluntarily placed his two
children in a guardianship with their maternal
grandparents, Louis and Juditha Brown. After he was
acquitted in the criminal trial, Simpson requested
termination of the guardianship. The Browns opposed
him. A long trial was held in Orange County Superior
Court, and Judge Nancy Wieben Stock granted Simpson's
motion to terminate guardianship. On appeal, the
decision was reversed, but the Browns dropped the
matter and O.J. kept his children. *Simpson v. Brown*
(1998) 67 Cal.App.4th 914.

Location of injury. Children often bang into things and injure
their hands, elbows, knees, and shins. But they rarely hurt
their thighs, upper arms, buttocks, and genital and rectal
areas.

Number of injuries. A child who has many injuries, some new
and some old, is unlikely to be merely an accident-prone
child. Multiple injuries often indicate abuse.

Corporal Punishment
Parents are allowed to punish their children, and some
injuries may result from corporal punishment. For example,
a parent is usually allowed to spank a child's bottom with an
open hand. Some states allow the use of a hairbrush or belt.

But if the punishment is excessive, it may be abuse. To distinguish between reasonable and excessive, the official must consider the child's age and misconduct, the parent's purpose, and the degree of harm. It is not abuse if the injury is a true accident where the parent could not have foreseen the consequences.

Other Physical Evidence

Besides injuries to the child, other physical evidence may exist. For example, if a child was beaten or burned, the instrument that was apparently used—such as a belt, stick, iron, or cigarette lighter—may be considered evidence. In sexual abuse cases, the child's clothes may be ripped or stained, and may contain blood, semen, or pubic hair. In child neglect cases, the home may contain drugs, firearms, or poisons accessible to the child.

Hotlines

Child Abuse... (800) 422-4453

Child Care .... (800) 424-2246

Domestic Violence .... (800) 799-7233

Missing and Exploited Children .... (800) 843-5678

Runaway Youth .... (800) 621-4000

Interviewing the Children

When a child abuse accusation is made, the child will almost always be interviewed.

Generally, the investigating official will attempt to interview the child in private, away from the parents. The interviewer will ask vague, open-ended questions, such as "Can you tell me what happened?" or "I can see you're upset, and I'd like to know about it." The child is allowed to answer in his or her own words, and the interviewer is trained not to react with shock or disapproval. The interviewer is also taught not to suggest answers to the child.

If you feel pressure building to the point where you want to lash out at your child, try these tips from *Parents Anonymous:* take 10 deep breaths, phone a friend, take a hot bath, or put on some music.

The purpose of the interview is to gather information. Even very young children are considered reliable enough to explain what happened. In fact, children are often considered the best source of information regarding possible mistreatment.

If the child gives information that requires some action to be taken, and the child is old enough, the interviewer may explain the situation. The child may also be assured that he or she is not to blame for what has happened, or for what may happen to the parents.

Child Describes Abuse
When a child makes a statement that indicates abuse, the investigator must decide if the child is telling the truth. Some hold that children never lie, and unless there is a reason to discount the child's statement, it must be believed. Others point out that—like adults—children lie, exaggerate, and fantasize. For example, an older child may claim abuse to escape an intolerable home situation. To evaluate the statement, the investigator will look for indicators, such as convincing details and descriptions.

Child Denies Abuse
Similarly, when a child denies abuse, but there is reason to believe it has occurred, the investigator must determine if the child is telling the truth. To some people, this a catch-22 situation—denial of abuse indicates abuse. But others know that children may be threatened or bribed by their parents, or may fear retaliation if they reveal the abuse. To discover what happened, the investigator will compare the child's injuries with the explanation. For example, if the child claims he got into a fight with a playmate, or fell down some stairs, the injuries should fit the accident.

"Only half of children with physical findings of sexual abuse reveal abuse when questioned. Children falsely deny abuse for many reasons: embarrassment, mixed feelings for the offender, not wanting to get a parent in trouble." *Los Angeles Times*

When court-appointed mental health professionals interview a child, they frequently qualify their conclusions because they can't say for sure what really happened. Often, they conclude their reports with phrases such as "I can't say for certain that a molestation occurred, but some event happened to put the child in turmoil."

Interviewing the Parents

In addition, the investigator may interview the parents. They will be asked to provide an explanation for the injury, and if they cannot give a satisfactory answer, they may be suspected of child abuse.

When listening to a parent, the investigator will consider if the explanation is consistent with the injury, such as when a parent says a child suffered terrible burns when she stepped into a tub of hot water. They will also decide if excessive or inappropriate force was used, such as when a parent disciplines a child, but claims it was necessary to punch the child in the head.

While many injuries do not automatically establish abuse, investigators may err on the side of caution. And even if a parent is believed, there are times when an investigator may feel that the child needs protection, such as when a parent is indifferent to the injury.

Protective Custody

All forms of abuse and neglect hurt children, but some types do not pose an immediate threat. Rather, they harm the children through long-term exposure. In those cases, the child is often left in the home, and the family is given time to correct the problem.

But in extreme cases, the police have authority to remove the child from the home and place them in protective custody. The police may remove a child when:

- The child has been beaten, poisoned, or burned.
- The child has been tortured or viciously punished.
- The child has been sexually abused.
- The parents cannot provide for the child's basic needs.
- The parents may flee with the child.
- The child is in immediate danger due to conditions in the home.

Depending on the laws of the state, there are three ways a child may be placed in protective custody:

Parental Consent
In many states, the consent of the parents is often sought before removing the child from the home. Caseworkers know that forcing some parents to cooperate may only hinder their long-term efforts to correct the situation. Some parents respond to an intrusion into the family by becoming defensive and combative. Other parents, however, might agree to relinquish the child as a welcome relief from the ever-present burden of child-raising.

Prior Court Order
If the parents do not cooperate, the child can also be taken into protective custody through a court order. These cases may represent parents who have had time to correct the situation, but have been unwilling to do so. Having a court review a potential removal helps ensure it is the correct decision.

 If you have a problem with Child Protective Services, check out *CPSWatch* at www. cpswatch.com. This organization "educates the public about CPS assaults against the traditional family." They publish technical bulletins to help parents regain and keep custody of their children.

Emergency Removal

And finally, if the parents do not cooperate, and if the child is in such immediate danger that there is no time to get a court order, the police may make an emergency removal.

Emergency removals are literally life-and-death decisions, and generally happen only when the child will be harmed during the short amount of time it takes for the caseworker to respond. If a child is removed in this way, all states require a hearing within a short time—usually 48-72 hours.

Arrests

Although child protective agencies focus on maintaining the family, when abuse has occurred, the police may arrest the abuser.

Before they arrest someone, the police must have probable cause. This means the officer must have a reasonable belief that a crime was committed and the suspect did it. Since all forms of abuse are crimes, once abuse is substantiated, arresting a parent becomes a possibility.

However, a parent is normally arrested only when the officer believes that doing so is the only way to protect the child, or if the parent interferes when the officer tries to take the child into protective custody.

Hearings

Once it's established that child abuse has occurred, a court hearing will be held to resolve the issue.

The purpose of the hearing—and any subsequent trial—is to either correct the problem that led to the abuse so the family successfully reunited, or to terminate all parental rights.

 Better safe than sorry. When an officer or caseworker places a child in protective custody, they are given immunity from civil liability. But if they don't remove the child, they may be liable and possibly sued by family members.

Michael and Elizabeth were unmarried teenagers when they had a daughter. A few weeks after the baby was born, Elizabeth went to pick her up from Michael's mothers house. There was a physical fight. Ten months later, Michael filed a petition in district court describing the domestic violence, and asked for temporary custody of the child. The court awarded physical custody to Michael's mother, and gave Elizabeth visitation. Elizabeth was unable to appeal the decision because, a few months later, she was sent to the Girls' School for two years for a juvenile offense. Afterwards, she attempted to re-open the custody order, but her motions were denied. The baby stayed with Michael's mother. *Lucero v. Pino* (1997) 124 N.M. 28, 946 P.2d 232.

If a voluntary plan can be worked out, the family will be supervised by the agency, and may be subject to future oversight. If the parents lose their rights, the legal bonds are cut, and the child is free to be adopted. Or, the child may be placed in the home of a relative or in a foster home.

False Accusations

When child custody is in dispute, it's not unusual for false accusations to be made. Specifically, sexual abuse allegations are such a common weapon that they have their own name— sexual allegations in divorce.

Accusations are often made without substantiating evidence, and against parents who have no history of suspicious behavior. They may be pure fabrications—such as stories that are completely concocted—or they may be based on recovered memory—such as when an older child "remembers" an event from her past.

While the timing of such an accusation make it suspect, some argue that it is natural time for repressed examples of dysfunction to come out when the family splits apart. Others insist the accusations are a ploy to gain an advantage.

Sue me. You can sue the other parent for accusing you falsely, but don't expect to win. As Kim Hart, director of the *National Child Abuse Defense and Resource Center* says, "You have to prove malice, and that's almost impossible."

Why Parents Make False Accusations

Parents have many reasons to make false accusations, including:

Getting Revenge
Clearly, some people are motivated by revenge. An angry parent looking to "get even," or a jealous parent seeking to sabotage the child's relationship with the other parent need look no further than a false allegation. Abuse accusations—whether true or not—effectively destroy the reputation of the accused. The charges often bring a stigma that can alienate parents from friends, coworkers, and family. And because the accused is generally assumed to be guilty until proven innocent, the damage is done when the charges are made—whether or not they turn out to be true.

Gaining a Tactical Advantage
Another reason to make a false accusation is that it automatically gives the accuser a tactical advantage. Under some circumstances, the accusation itself may be enough to cut off the other parent's contact with the children until the

Why do parents make false accusations? "It's simple, fast, and guaranteed to achieve the desired result. In one fell swoop, she can get her husband completely out of her and her children's lives and assure herself complete custodial control. And in one fell swoop, she can completely destroy the man's life, and any semblance of a normal relationship between him and his children." *Anne P. Mitchell,* attorney, San Jose, CA

investigation is finished. And that could be months—or even a year. This gives the accuser a powerful weapon to use—one that can bring attention, sympathy, and maybe even victory—all without even having to prove that he or she is telling the truth.

Starting a Criminal Investigation
And finally, an abuse accusation forces the other parent to endure a criminal investigation. This probably means spending money on a lawyer to defend against the charges. Because prosecutors often have much greater resources than parents, a hard-working, middle-class parent may be financially devastated by the legal defense needed to defend against such a charge.

When You Are Accused

Guilty Until Proven Innocent, Kimberly A. Hart, National Child Abuse Defense and Resource Center, $25.00. This excellent book has very specific, very detailed information for those accused of child abuse. Written by the director of *The National Child Abuse Defense and Resource Center,* it provides useful, day-to-day information that is required reading for anyone fighting a false accusation.

What to Do If You Are Accused

If you are accused of abusing your children, the first time you hear about it may be after your children are interviewed by caseworkers. That means there is already a case building against you.

As attorney Melvin Belli says, "First, get yourself one hell of a good child-custody lawyer." You'll need immediate expert legal advice on how to protect yourself during the investigation. And if the attorney you hire recommends that you plead guilty—but you are innocent—get another lawyer.

Second, ask the judge to appoint an attorney for your child. This attorney can help move the case to a conclusion so you won't be left dangling for months with the charge hanging over your head.

Third, cooperate fully with the police and caseworkers. Show up for appointments, answer all questions honestly, and admit to any contact you've had with your children. If you get defensive or argumentative, you don't help your case.

Answering False Accusations

National Child Abuse Defense and Resource Center
Kimberly Hart, Executive Director
P.O. Box 638
Holland, OH 43528
(419) 865-0513
www.falseallegation.org
The volunteers at NCADRC assist parents who have been falsely accused. They are not attorneys, and cannot read case files, motions, or reports. They can, however, offer "lay person" advice and refer you to an attorney, mental health professional, or physician in your area who is knowledgeable about false accusations. They also sell some excellent books, including *Guilty Until Proven Innocent.*

Abuse-Excuse
www.abuse-excuse.com
This is the website of Dean Tong, a father who was accused of child abuse during his own custody battle. The website provides resource information for handling abuse, neglect, and sexual child abuse accusations. You can consult with Dean, or order his engaging book, *ASHES to ASHES... Families to Dust.*

Fourth, demand a polygraph test. While the results are not admissible in court, if you pass, it will convince some people you are innocent. If the police won't schedule a polygraph for you, you can arrange your own, but be sure the examiner has a reputation for competence and neutrality. Also, consider demanding that the other parent submit to a polygraph. If the other parent refuses or fails it, that will help your case.

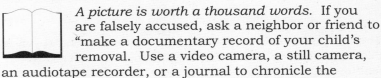

A picture is worth a thousand words. If you are falsely accused, ask a neighbor or friend to "make a documentary record of your child's removal. Use a video camera, a still camera, an audiotape recorder, or a journal to chronicle the events. In court a judge will find the conduct of police or social workers, and your child's reaction to being removed, useful in rendering a decision." *Parents Magazine*

Fifth, consider hiring a mental health professional. When caseworkers evaluate an abuse accusation, they rely on "indicators" such as nightmares, bed-wetting, and thumb-sucking. The problem is, these behaviors are common, and there's a good chance that a perfectly normal child could be seen as an abuse victim. While it can be difficult, you may be able to find a psychologist willing to refute the charges.

And finally, insist on a hearing. If you've been cut-off for more than 90 days, ask for a hearing to resolve the issue and to reestablish your access to the child. In some states, however, if the police or child protective agency is still investigating, the judge must defer until their work is complete.

Richard and Rebecca had one child during their nine-year marriage. When they divorced, they agreed to share in parenting decisions. However, one year later, Richard filed a petition seeking sole custody. Richard complained that Rebecca was interfering with his visitation and that she had filed a false complaint with the Department of Children and Family Services (DCFS), for which he was investigated and arrested, though Rebecca's complaint was deemed unfounded and Richard was subsequently found not guilty. The court decided Rebecca had engaged in "substantial parental alienation," and increased Richard's residential custody from the first Saturday after the close of the school year until the first Saturday in November. *In re the Marriage of Divelbiss* (1999) 308 Ill. App.3d 198, 719 N.E.2d 375, 241 Ill.Dec. 514.

Family Abuse

These heart-wrenching books were written by the survivor of what has been called "the worst child abuse case in California."

A Child Called "It": An Abused Child's Journey from Victim to Victor, David J. Pelzer, Health Communications, $9.95.

The Lost Boy: A Foster Child's Search for the Love of a Family, David J. Pelzer, Health Communications, $10.95.

---

1 *Los Angeles Times,* August 16, 1995
2 The National Committee for the Prevention of Child Abuse, 1993.
3 Dr. Melvin Greyer, Family Law Project of the University of Michigan
4 The National Committee for the Prevention of Child Abuse, 1993
5 *Child Abuse: A Police Guide,* Douglas J. Besharov, Police Foundation and the American Bar Association, 1987
6 The National Committee for the Prevention of Child Abuse, 1993

Chapter 25

Access to Children: Kidnapping, Custodial Interference, and Moveaways

✓ If you've ever seen pictures of children on milk cartons, you've seen children who are missing or who have been kidnapped.

✓ A kidnapped child is often caught in a custody tug-of-war. Some parents take the child as a prelude to an interstate custody fight. Other parents remove the child from the country.

✓ If your child has been kidnapped, and he or she is in the U.S., many organizations can help you, including the *National Center for Missing and Exploited Children*.

✓ If your child has been taken outside of the United States, you must use the *Hague Convention on the Civil Aspects of International Child Abduction* to locate and recover your child.

✓ If your child is not kidnapped, but the other parent won't let you see him, you have to bring your complaint of custodial interference to the judge.

Parental Kidnapping

Parental kidnapping is when one parent takes the children and refuses to return them. This is also called *child-snatching.*

While either parent could kidnap the children, typically the noncustodial parent abducts the children in order to thwart a custody order. The kidnapping parent then moves with the children in order to block access by the other parent.

The Reality of Parental Kidnapping

No one really knows how many family abductions occur each year. Statistics quoted by different sources vary widely and often favor a particular view.

One study, released by the *United States Department of Justice,* estimates that there were more than 350,000 abductions in one year. Here's what the study found:

The Reality of Parental Kidnapping[1]

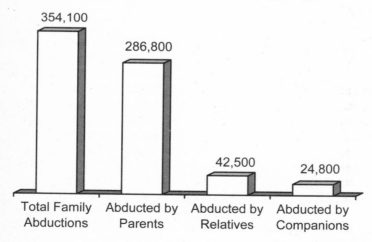

These figures were based on cases that required active intervention by police and social agencies, and did not distinguish between true parental kidnapping and other problems, such as custodial interference.

Statistics can also be misleading when trying to determine how many children are recovered. The *Justice Department* found that many of the children were returned within seven days, with only 10% still missing a month later. But one national organization, *Child Find of America*, estimates that only "one in three missing children who are abducted by a parent are eventually found or returned."

And according to the *State Department*, the vast majority of family abductions result in the child staying within the United States. As reported in the *Los Angeles Times*, in one year, "there were [only] 1,200 active custody cases involving an American child abroad."[2]

"If the petitioner for an initial decree has wrongfully taken the child from another state or has engaged in similar reprehensible conduct the court may decline to exercise jurisdiction." *Uniform Child Custody Jurisdiction Act, Section 8(a).*

Why Parents Kidnap

While parents have many justifications for kidnapping their children, their reasons often fall into three categories:

Disagreement with the Custody Order
Sometimes a parent who loses custody may feel they didn't get a reasonable or fair hearing in court. This parent may feel like a second-class citizen in their children's lives, and is convinced he or she has a "natural right" to the children that supersedes what any court says. This parent may decide to "overrule" a custody order by kidnapping the children to enforce the "correct" custody decision.

Fear of Harm to the Children
Some parents may kidnap their children to protect them from the other parent. They may believe that the other parent is a bad parent with an erratic or unacceptable lifestyle, or that the other parent is abusing or endangering the children.

Physical, sexual, and even psychological abuse are all reasons that have been used to justify a kidnapping, even when there the court has investigated the accusations and is unconvinced.

Revenge Against the Other Parent

To paraphrase a common quote, child custody involves "good people acting their worst." Some parents may kidnap the children simply to get even. Of course, revenge has nothing to do with what is best for the children, and everything to do with how the parent feels.

Anticipating a Kidnapping

As the famed attorney Melvin Belli said, "The best way to deal with child-snatching is to prevent it from ever happening at all." This means anticipating the possibility that your former mate will kidnap the children and taking steps to prevent it.

First, consider the time when a kidnapping is most likely to occur. Because of the stress and uncertainty of custody proceedings, many abductions occur right before or right after a custody decision.

Second, take a good look at the other parent. Has he or she threatened to snatch the children? If so, take it seriously. Or if the other parent has the profile of a probable kidnapper—be cautious.

Keeping Children Safe

Raising Safe Kids in an Unsafe World, Jan Wagner, Avon Books, $11.00. 30 simple lessons in a bright and readable book.

When Parents Kidnap, Geoffrey L. Greif, Rebecca L. Hegar (Contributor), Free Press, $27.95. Contains detailed case histories of parental kidnappings, including the effect on the "left behind" parent and the long-term impact on the children.

William and Christine were not married when they had their daughter, Dana. For the first ten months, Dana lived with Christine in Washington, D.C., and William lived nearby. Then, William kidnapped Dana and took her to North Carolina. Christine immediately filed for custody in the District of Columbia and it was granted, but while she was trying to enforce her order, William asked a North Carolina court for custody without mentioning the D.C. order. It was granted. Christine then brought the earlier D.C. order to the attention of the North Carolina court, and William's custody order was vacated. A year after he kidnapped Dana, William returned Dana to Christine. *Mitchell v. Hughes* (2000) 755 A.2d 456.

Here are the traits to look for in the other parent:
- History of violence or child abuse.
- No stable community ties.
- Poor employment history.
- Poor finances or trying to escape creditors.
- Has job skills useful in other states or knows someone who will provide financial support.

Third, before the other parent disappears, assemble all the identifying information you can, including driver's license number, social security number, and bank account and credit card numbers.

Fourth, if you think it can happen—tell somebody. You can ask teachers, school bus drivers, and other people to be alert for suspicious people. Your lawyer can request an order barring the other parent from taking the children out of state, and the Passport Office can withhold issuing passports for the children unless a valid custody order is included.

Fifth, prepare your children by making sure they've memorized your phone number, including the area code. They will also need to know how to call you collect, or you can give them a telephone credit card.

And finally, eliminate the reason for a parental kidnapping by allowing the other parent to remain connected to the children. An involved parent has less reason to snatch the children.

Five Warning Signs of a Kidnapping

1. The other parent threatens to kidnap the children.

2. The other parent just lost custody.

3. The other parent is paranoid or unstable.

4. The other parent has easily transferable job skills that allow him or her to work in another state or country.

5. The children are between the ages of three and nine—the most likely age for an abduction.

What to Do If Your Children Are Kidnapped

If your children are kidnapped, the first few hours are critical.

First, call the police. They will need to see a notarized or certified copy of your current custody orders. If the children are still in the state, the district attorney or state attorney general can get involved. If the children are in another state, the FBI can be notified.

Then, call your lawyer, who can obtain a felony warrant against the kidnapper and initiate a contempt proceeding, which lets you recover your costs and fees. Also, your lawyer can request that the *Federal Parent Locator Service* be used to track down the missing parent.

After that, call everyone else, including your ex-spouse's family members, friends, neighbors, and employer. Some may say nothing, but others might give you a lead to the whereabouts of your children.

If you still haven't located your children, call the media. You can notify newspapers, television stations, and radio stations about your plight. You can also print up posters with your children's names, photos, and description. If you call a missing children's organization, such as *Child Find of America,* they can register you in their database.

And finally, consider hiring a private investigator. This can cost you tens of thousands of dollars—or more—but may be your only hope of finding your children. An investigator can track a kidnapper through mail, bank records, and even the transfer of school records.

Kidnapping Laws

Once you find the children, your problems may not be over. If the other parent has taken them to another state and initiated a custody proceeding in that state, you must then deal with jurisdiction.

The fact is, child custody is determined by state laws, and each state may decide it differently. That means a parent can lose custody of the children in one state, kidnap them to a different state, and seek a modification there.

 After six years of marriage, Kim and Scott divorced. Kim was given physical custody of their two children, Devin and Dustin, and Scott was given liberal visitation. Three years later, however, after constant litigation, Kim suddenly moved to Guam, taking the children with her. Scott discovered she had moved when he went to pick up the children and Kim's house was empty. The court immediately gave Scott temporary custody of the children, suspended his child support, and found Kim in contempt and ordered her to return the children at once. Kim ignored the court order. Scott then traveled to Guam with the order. Scott was given full custody of the children. *Sanford v. Arinder* (2001) 800 So.2d 1267.

To avoid this kind of interstate legal dispute, all states have adopted a uniform law known as the *Uniform Child Custody Jurisdiction Act.*

Uniform Child Custody Jurisdiction Act

The *Uniform Child Custody Jurisdiction Act* is a uniform law that has been adopted by all states. This uniform law establishes the standards a court must apply in order to establish jurisdiction.

The UCCJA makes one court—and one court only—responsible for the child. Under the law, the case can only be heard by the court where the child has the closest connection. Specifically, for the case to be heard in a given jurisdiction, it has to meet one of the following tests, in order of priority:

1. *Home State.* If the child has lived in the state for the past six months, or was in the state for six months but was recently removed, that state is considered the home state and the court can hear the case.

2. *Best Interests.* If the child has significant connections to others in the state, or it is in the best interests of the child to remain in the state, the court can hear the case.

3. *Abandonment.* If the child has been abandoned, or was mistreated or abused elsewhere, the court may hear the case.

4. *No Other State.* Finally, if no other state meets one of the tests or if another state does but chooses not to hear the case, the court can hear the case.

When the UCCJA is followed, interstate conflicts are avoided. Before hearing a case, the judge must look to see if another state already has made a decision, or if there is a case pending, or if another state has higher authority. Only if the court has the highest claim to the child can the case be heard.

 Fighting fire with fire. If your children have been kidnapped and you know where they are, consider the consequences before kidnapping them back. For one thing, retaliation can keep the chain of abductions going. For another, a kidnapping involves physical dangers to the children. And finally, kidnapping is against the law.

When Brenda began her divorce from Peter in Colorado, she said they had no children and she was not pregnant. She moved to Arizona, and a few months later, discovered she was pregnant with twins. She amended her divorce papers in Colorado to request custody of the unborn children. The Colorado court awarded Brenda "custody of the infants upon their birth." Nine months later, Brenda filed a complaint in an Arizona court seeking under the UCCJA, in both Arizona and Colorado, to establish jurisdiction in Arizona. The Colorado and Arizona judges spoke by telephone, and agreed that Arizona should assume jurisdiction. *In re Marriage of Tonnessen* (1997) 941 P.2d 237, 240 Ariz. Adv. Rep. 18.

Thus, if a parent kidnaps the children and goes to another state, and then in the new state seeks custody, the court in the second state will decline to accept the case and the court in the first state will keep the case.

Parental Kidnapping Prevention Act
In addition to the UCCJA, the federal government enacted the *Parental Kidnapping Prevention Act (PKPA)*. This federal law specifically requires states to recognize and enforce custody decisions made in other states.

The name of the act is slightly misleading, because it applies to all cases where a court in one state is asked to enforce or modify a custody order from another state.

While the UCCJA sets guidelines for deciding initial jurisdiction, the PKPA sets guidelines for deciding continuing jurisdiction. As with the UCCJA, a court must look to the four factors—home state, best interests, abandonment, and no other state—to determine if has jurisdiction to decide child custody.

In addition, this law prevents a court from assuming jurisdiction is there is an active case involving the child occurring in another state.

Federal and State Parent Locator Service
Another legal tool available to parents seeking to recover
children are *Federal and State Parent Locator Services.*

Federal law originally created the parent locator service to find
parents to enforce child support orders. However, federal law
extends the use of the service to finding parents who may be
guilty of "unlawful taking or restraint of a child."

The locator service searches a number of government
databases, including Social Security records, Veterans
Administration, etc.

 If your child is taken by the other parent,
federal law allows you to use the *Federal
Parent Locator Service* to search. 42 U.S.C. §
663, states, in part: "The services of the
Federal Parent Locator Service... shall be made available
to each State for the purpose of determining the
whereabouts of any parent or child when such
information is to be used to locate such parent or child
for the purpose of (1) enforcing any State or Federal law
with respect to the unlawful taking or restraint of a child;
or (2) making or enforcing a child custody or visitation
determination."

International Kidnappings

An even more disturbing problem occurs if children are
kidnapped to another country. A parent who takes children
to a foreign country bypasses American kidnapping laws.

To address some of the enormous difficulties in international
child abductions, many countries—including the U.S—passed
laws adopting the *Hague Convention on the Civil Aspects of
International Child Abduction.*

The Hague Convention
The Hague treaty is an international agreement among
countries to coordinate the return of kidnapped children. It
ensures that custody rights in one country are respected in
another country.

Besides the United States, other countries that have adopted the treaty include: Argentina, Belgium, Canada, China, Denmark, France, Germany, Hungary, Israel, Italy, Luxembourg, Mexico, Netherlands, Norway, Panama, Romania, South Africa, Spain, Turkey, United Kingdom, and Yugoslavia.

Unfortunately, not all countries have adopted the treaty. Countries that have not include: Colombia, Costa Rica, Ecuador, El Salvador, Fiji, Guatemala, Honduras, Iceland, Mauritius, Moldova, Nicaragua, Paraguay, Thailand, Turkmenistan, Uzbekistan, and Zimbabwe.

> "A parent who communicates an intention to re-abduct a child may encounter a lack of support from the State Department or U.S. embassies abroad. Just as parental abduction is a crime in the United States, it is a crime in almost every country. In that view, United States embassies abroad and the State Department will not do anything to facilitate a re-abduction." Maureen Dabbagh, *The Recovery of Internationally Abducted Children.*

The Hague treaty is a document composed of 45 articles that explain the rights and responsibilities of "contracting states"— that is, countries who have adopted this international treaty.

Article 1 explains the scope of the treaty: "a) to secure the prompt return of children wrongfully removed to or retained in any Contracting State; and b) to ensure that rights of custody and of access under the law of one Contracting State are effectively respected in the other Contracting States."

Signatory countries must establish a "central authority" that acts as an advocate for returning children under the treaty. The central authority must:
- Discover the whereabouts of a child who has been wrongfully removed or retained.
- Prevent further harm to the child or prejudice to interested parties by taking or causing to be taken provisional measures.

The *International Child Abductions Remedies Act,* 42 U.S.C. § 11601, states, in part: "The Convention on the Civil Aspects of International Child Abduction, done at The Hague on October 25, 1980, establishes legal rights and procedures for the prompt return of children who have been wrongfully removed or retained, as well as for securing the exercise of visitation rights. Children who are wrongfully removed or retained within the meaning of the Convention are to be promptly returned unless one of the narrow exceptions set forth in the Convention applies... The Convention and this chapter empower courts in the United States to determine only rights under the Convention and not the merits of any underlying child custody claims."

- Secure the voluntary return of the child or to bring about an amicable resolution of the issues.
- Exchange, where desirable, information relating to the social background of the child.
- Provide information about the laws in connection with the application of the Convention.
- Initiate or facilitate the institution of judicial or administrative proceedings with a view to obtaining the return of the child and to make arrangements for organizing or securing the effective exercise of rights of access.
- Where the circumstances so require, to provide or facilitate the provision of legal aid and advice, including the participation of legal counsel and advisers.
- Provide such administrative arrangements as may be necessary and appropriate to secure the safe return of the child.
- Keep other countries informed with respect to the operation of the Convention.

After a parent submits an application to the central authority, and officials conclude the child was wrongfully taken, "the authority concerned shall order the return of the child forthwith."

However, under the treaty, the foreign government can still refuse to return the child for a number of reasons, including that "there is a grave risk that his or her return would expose the child to physical or psychological harm or otherwise place the child in an intolerable situation" or "the child objects to being returned and has attained an age and degree of maturity at which it is appropriate to take account of its views."

While it is difficult for a parent to recover a child in a country that has adopted the treaty, it becomes much more difficult to recover a child from a country that has not adopted the treaty. That's because in a non-signatory country, a U.S. custody order has no legal relevance. The parent who seeks to recover his or her child must travel to the foreign country and gain custody there.

In practical terms, it is very difficult for an American citizen to travel to a foreign country, locate his or her children, hire a local advocate, and convince a local court to award them custody so they can take the children to the U.S. The enormous cost, time, language differences and cultural differences all impede a parent seeking to do that.

And if the country has not adopted the Hague convention, the United States government can do little to help. But the reverse is not true. When children from other countries are kidnapped to America, U.S. courts must recognize and enforce a custody decree made in another country, unless it is shown that the child is in danger.

 Federal kidnapping law. In addition to the Hague Convention, there is a specific federal law that addresses taking children out of the country. 8 U.S.C. § 1204, states, in part: "Whoever removes a child from the United States or retains a child (who has been in the United States) outside the United States with intent to obstruct the lawful exercise of parental rights shall be fined under this title or imprisoned not more than 3 years, or both."

When Parents Kidnap

National Center for Missing & Exploited Children
Charles B. Wang International Children's Building
699 Prince Street
Alexandria, VA 22314
(703) 274-3900
(800) THE-LOST
www.missingkids.org
The NCMEC helps parents and law enforcement officers find missing children. Call the toll-free hotline for sightings. Publishes: *Parental Kidnapping: How to Prevent an Abduction* and *What to Do if Your Child is Abducted.*

Child Find of America
P.O. Box 277
New Paltz, NY 12561
(800) I-AM-LOST
www.childfindofamerica.org
Child Find helps parents search for abducted and runaway children. *Child Find* assists with the initial report to police, referrals to State Clearinghouses and the NCMEC, and to local and national organizations that will assist with posters and investigations.

Child Search Ministries
P.O. Box 73725
Houston, Texas 77273
(281) 350-KIDS
www.childsearch.org
Child Search provides investigators that help locate your child and counselors that help manage the crisis. *Child Search* also distributes photos to TV programs, magazines, newspapers, and fax-networks.

American Parental Abductions Resource & Support
La Mesa, CA 91943
www.parentalabductions.org
Provides resources and support for victims of abducted children. Includes state by state legal information, instructions on handling an abduction, links to missing children databases, and more.

Custodial Interference

Custodial interference is when one parent interferes with the other parent's access to the children.

Custodial interference differs from parental kidnapping in that the children are usually not abducted. Instead, it often involves a more minor dispute over access—one parent wants to see the children, and the other parent won't allow it.

Custodial interference isn't always a case of "You can't see the kids!" It may also occur when one parent impedes communication by ripping up letters or cutting off phone calls. Or it may occur when one parent delays the exchange by telling the other parent to wait outside until the children are ready, and then taking an hour to get them ready.

Whatever form the obstruction takes, if a parent's custody is interfered with, it is considered custodial interference.

Reasons for Denying Contact

Parents have many reasons for blocking access. Some may be acceptable to a judge, and some may not. Here are some:

Anger at the Other Parent
Children make easy pawns in a custody war, and some parents may use them as weapons. One obvious example is when the noncustodial parent stops paying child support, and the custodial parent retaliates by denying visitation. Another motivation is jealousy, such as when one parent has remarried, and the other parent is jealous of the new mate.

Children Are Endangered
Another reason to block access is when a parent endangers the children. For example, if one parent arrives to pick up the children and has been drinking heavily or using drugs, the other parent may refuse to turn over the children. Threats to the children include the possibility that the parent may kidnap them, or is likely to abuse or molest them. Protecting the children is often considered a good-cause defense for custodial interference.

Children Won't Go

If the children are old enough—that is, usually teenagers—
another reason for custodial interference is that the children
don't want to go. If the children are not old enough to decide
for themselves, a parent must make a good faith effort to
comply with the court orders, even if the children object.

How to Enforce Your Custodial Rights

If the other parent won't let you see your children, you must
enforce your custodial rights. While there is no single way to
do that, you'll probably have to hire a lawyer and go to court.

Realize, however, that while the other parent must cooperate
by allowing you to see your children, if your custody order
only specifies "reasonable" visitation, and you are the
noncustodial parent, it may be difficult to prove your access
was impeded. The lack of specific visitation times in vague
custody orders works against noncustodial parents.

Nevertheless, if your access to the children has been
hindered, and a valid court order is in place, the simplest
solution is to ask the judge to find the other parent in
contempt of court. If he or she is found guilty of civil
contempt, the judge can impose a fine, or even a jail sentence.

 Ava, a U.S. citizen, married Onno, a Dutch
citizen, in Connecticut, and they had one
child. They lived in the U.S. for nine years,
then moved to Holland. Three years later, Ava
sought a divorce in Holland claiming that Onno was
abusing their child, and asked to take the child to the
United States. The court denied her request and gave
custody to Onno. Ava took the child to the U.S. anyway.
Once in the U.S., Ava filed for divorce and sought
custody, but Onno demanded the child be returned to
Holland, citing the *International Child Abduction Remedies
Act*. However, the Connecticut court decided Onno "has
sexually abused this child" and refused to send the child
back because it "would cause grave risk of physical and
psychological harm to him." *Turner v. Frowein* (2000)
Connecticut No. Sc 16165.

For assistance when a child is abducted to another country, or when a child from another country is abducted to the U.S., contact the *United States State Department Office of Citizen and Consular Services.*

In some extreme cases, custodial interference may also be a reason for switching custody. In theory, this response isn't designed just to "punish" the recalcitrant parent, but rather, to solve the access problem by awarding custody to the more cooperative parent.

And finally, if visitation has been consistently sabotaged, the judge can suspend child support. This is a highly individual decision, with some judges using it when necessary, while others would never even consider it. In general, the interference must have been both deliberate and persistent enough to warrant the punishment.

Failing to Visit

There is, of course, another side to all this, and that's when the noncustodial parent fails to visit the children.

As a legal matter, failing to visit may be a violation of a court order and could be considered contempt of court. As a practical matter, failing to visit rarely is as important to the judge as, say, paying child support. Parents who pay their bills but don't see their children are often safe from legal repercussions.

However, if one parent fails to visit, and that action costs the other parent money—the judge may order that the injured party be compensated.

Moveaways

A final problem that involves access to the children occurs when the custodial parent wants to *move away*.

In one year, the *Federal Parent Locator Service* received 2,307,274 requests for locating a parent.[3]

Moveaways are common after parents have separated or divorced. The custodial parent may want to move to start a new job, or to follow a new mate, or to be closer to family.

But when the custodial parent wants to move far away, and the noncustodial parent has substantial visitation, the result is that much of the visitation time with the children is lost. The increased distance effectively shuts out the noncustodial parent from being involved in the children's day-to-day lives.

This makes moveaways a difficult issue to resolve. A moveaway pits the right of the custodial parent to move against the right of the noncustodial parent to see the children.

Moveaway Laws

To prevent parents from simply picking up and moving with their children, many courts routinely include a notice requirement in the court orders.

For example, some courts require the custodial parent to give 30 or 45 days' written notice before making a move. Other courts include restraining orders preventing the custodial parent from moving unless the court gives permission. And still other courts require that the noncustodial parent agree before a custodial parent can move.

 Daily journal. If your access to the children has been blocked, be sure to keep a daily log of events. This written evidence will come in handy in court.

If you agree about the move, you need only file the agreement with the court. But if there is a dispute, the court has to make the decision.

Because there are no firm guidelines for moveaways, courts must evaluate each case individually. Typically they consider if the move is in the child's best interests, or if there are pragmatic reasons for the move, or how the move will affect the child's relationship with the noncustodial parent.

 This is the well-known case that established the right of the custodial parent to move away. Paul and Wendy divorced when their two children, Paul and Jessica, were four and three years old. After Wendy moved with the children to a local apartment in Tehachapi, the trial court awarded the parents joint legal custody and gave Wendy sole physical custody. Paul saw the children weekly. A year later, Wendy accepted a job in Lancaster, about 40 minutes away, and sought to move with the children. Paul tried to block the relocation of the children, but the trial court allowed her to move. Paul appealed, and the Court of Appeal reversed. However, the California Supreme Court reversed the appellate court, deciding that "a parent seeking to relocate does not bear a burden of establishing that the move is necessary as a condition of custody... Instead, he or she has the right to change the residence of the child, subject to the power of the court to restrain a removal that would prejudice the rights or welfare of the child." *In re Marriage of Burgess* (1996) 13 Cal.4th 25.

Allow Move
Generally, a court is more likely to allow a move if it is shown to be in the child's best interests. The judge will decide if the move is being made in good faith and will lead to enhanced job opportunities for the custodial parent or to an improved family relationship.

If the move is allowed, the judge may divide the increased costs for visiting between the parents, or—more likely— require the custodial parent to pay the entire amount. In

Rebecca and Tommy were married in Indiana and their child was born in Indiana. Three months later, they moved to Louisiana. Six months after that, Tommy filed for divorce in Louisiana, claiming that Rebecca had "abandoned the matrimonial domicile" and taken the child with her. Rebecca filed for divorce back in Indiana. After talking to the Indiana judge on the telephone, the Louisiana judge transferred custody and visitation issues to Indiana, but kept jurisdiction over other issues in the divorce. *Henry v. Henry* (2002) Louisiana No. 02-CA-147.

addition, the judge may revise the schedule to give the noncustodial parent more time with the children during holidays and summer.

Prohibit Move

However, if the judge believes the custodial parent is acting in bad faith and is trying to sabotage the noncustodial parent's time with the children, the move may be prevented. Since adults have a right to travel, the court cannot stop the parent from moving, but can switch custody if that happens. The reasoning is that a change of residence is grounds for the change in custody.

---

1 *Survey of Missing, Abducted, Runaway, and Thrownaway Children in America,* First Report, Executive Summary (U.S. Justice Department, Office of Juvenile Justice, May 1990)
2 *Los Angeles Times,* November 13, 1994
3 *Child Support Enforcement Fifteenth Annual Report to Congress,* 1986-1990.

Chapter 26

Support for Children: Establishing Paternity and Collecting Child Support

- ✓ Child support generates endless complaints, but in fact, it is a flawed and imperfect mechanism for transferring money between separated or divorced parents.

- ✓ In order to collect child support, the receiving parent must locate the paying parent, establish paternity—if necessary, establish a support order, and then enforce the order.

- ✓ Once a support order is in place, many tools are available to enforce the order, including wage assignments, diversion of government benefits, property liens, and more.

- ✓ If the paying parent has moved to another state, the *Uniform Interstate Family Support Act* requires a court in the second state to honor and enforce an existing support order.

The Reality of Child Support Collections

While statistics can be misleading, there is one circumstance that virtually everyone agrees on—many parents with custody don't receive child support.

Though a great deal has been written about *deadbeat parents*—parents ordered to pay but who fail to comply— astonishingly, this is not the biggest reason why many custodial parents don't receive support.

According to the *Census Bureau,* in one year there were 11.5 million single parent families, but only 6.2 million—or 54%— had a support award.[1] This means that almost half the custodial parents didn't collect child support because no one was ordered to pay them.

When the *Office of Child Support Enforcement* investigated the problem, here's what they found:

Why Parents Don't Have a Child Support Order[2]

Reason	%
Did not want an award	21.9%
Did not pursue an award	19.3%
Paternity could not be established	16.5%
Parent unable to pay	14.5%
Parent could not be located	13.6%
Other settlement	8.6%
Final agreement pending	5.6%
	100%

Didn't Want Child Support
As it turns out, 41% of the parents didn't have an order because they didn't want or pursue one. When asked why, some said they were afraid of the other parent and wanted to minimize his or her involvement with the children. Others said they didn't know where the noncustodial parent was, and didn't want to look.

The ties that bind. Once child support is ordered, it remains a debt until it is paid. It cannot be erased by a bankruptcy or subsequent modification. And the court can tack on all reasonable costs incurred in collecting the support as well as penalties on top of that!

Couldn't Get a Child Support Order

But when parents did seek an award, many found it difficult to get. In some families, the noncustodial parent disappeared and couldn't be located. And many never-married single mothers, had to establish paternity—but couldn't do so.

Couldn't Enforce a Child Support Order

And of course, even when custodial parents did establish an award, there was no guarantee they would get paid. The *Census Bureau* found that only 51% of the parents received full payments, 24% received partial payments, and 25% received no payments at all.[3]

To explain the gap, some have suggested that the support is too high, and the paying parents don't earn enough. Others have suggested that the gap is due to more personal reasons, such as a desire for revenge or retaliation. Whatever the cause, it's clear that a custodial parent faces many obstacles to collecting child support.

The times are a' changing. As reported in *Time Magazine,* "Fourteen percent of 'deadbeat dads' are actually moms."[4]

How to Collect Child Support

Collecting child support is not automatic. Just because you have custody of the children, don't expect the payments to automatically flow in. There are many obstacles to collecting child support, and you may have to overcome some—or all—of them to get that check.

Scarlett and Christopher married one month after Scarlett gave birth to a child. At the time, Scarlett was 19 and Christopher was 17. They first lived with Scarlett's mother, but within a year, Scarlett moved out to live with another man, Brian. A few months later, Scarlett and Christopher reconciled, but by then, Scarlett was pregnant again. Three years later, Scarlett and Christopher broke up for good. The court made a temporary order of joint custody, but a subsequent paternity test revealed that Christopher was not the father of either child. The court, however, decided the children had an established relationship with Christopher and ordered joint custody, with Christopher as the primary custodian. Scarlett appealed, and it was the Court of Appeals reversed. *Consalvi v. Cawood* (2001) 63 S.W.3d 195.

To collect child support, you must:
- Locate the other parent.
- Establish paternity (if necessary).
- Establish the support order.
- Enforce the support order.

Finding a Parent

For many custodial parents, the first obstacle to collecting child support is simply to locate the noncustodial parent. In order to establish paternity, obtain a support order, and enforce that order, the receiving parent must find the paying parent. In addition, the paying parent's income and assets must be identified.

Parent Locator Services
In every state there is a child support enforcement agency. These agencies access federal and state parent locator services to track down missing parents.

The parent locator services find missing parents by doing computer searches through the records of a variety of government agencies, including the following:

- Social Security Administration
- Department of Motor Vehicles
- Department of Corrections
- Bureau of Employment
- Internal Revenue Service
- Veterans Administration

In addition, state parent locator services can look for missing parents by examining voter registration rolls, tax and property rolls, records of utility connections, and so on.

Because it's pretty difficult to exist without leaving some kind of paper trail, parent locator services are very successful. The *Office of Child Support Enforcement* reports that parent locator services successfully find a missing parent 70-80% of the time.

Using the Parent Locator Service

To access the parent locator service, you'll need to submit a request to the child support enforcement agency. You can either have your attorney do it, or you can complete the application yourself. In some states, you can request that the District Attorney do it. Depending on your situation, it may cost as little as $25.

When you submit the request, you'll need to supply the agency with information about the missing parent. At the minimum, they will need the parent's name and social security number. If you don't know the social security number, it can often be found on tax returns, bank account statements, credit applications, hospital records, police records, and so on.

"If the noncustodial parent works, drives a car, pays taxes, receives any kind of government compensation or benefits or has engaged in any one of a number of activities from registering for the draft to going to jail, there's an excellent chance of [the parent locator service] finding him." Marianne Takas, *Child Support: A Complete, Up-to-Date Guide to Collecting Child Support*

In addition, any other information you provide the agency can only help. If you know the missing parent's birthdate, current employer, or even creditors, that will improve your chances.

While there may be some differences in time limits, by law, every child support agency must conduct the search shortly after you file the application, usually within 30 days. Because many parents remain in the same state after splitting up, the first search will be through the state parent locator. If the state search is unsuccessful, another state may be searched, or the federal parent locator may be accessed.

Other Ways to Find a Parent
Of course, there is another way to find a missing parent—look for that person yourself. As a practical matter, there is nothing stopping you from doing your own investigation, and indeed, it's possible you may be successful where others are not. Here are some standard investigative techniques:

Documentation. You maybe able to find the other parent simply by poring over every scrap of paper you can find. Look carefully at tax returns, medical records, loan applications, licenses, etc. Unless you waited years before starting to look, something is bound to be current.

Networking. You can talk to past employers and business associates, as well as parents, relatives, friends, and even former neighbors for clues to the whereabouts of the missing parent. Also, check clubs, organizations, or unions he or she belonged to.

 During the five years Angela and Wayne lived together, they had a daughter, Chelsea. When they separated, Angela filed a paternity suit in order to get child support from Wayne. Once the DNA tests proved Wayne was the father, he asked for custody. A Chancery Court awarded him custody, explaining that Angela "had written several hot checks... she had lived with a convicted felon with a violent past and... [she had] lied to the court about pulling a knife and threatening to commit suicide." *Hickman v. Culberson* (2002) Arkansas No. CA 01-581.

Public Records. You're allowed to search the following public records: records of the state for titles to property, voter registration rolls, and even the Department of Motor Vehicles. In addition, you can do an address verification through the post office.

 In one year, California spent more than $30 million to establish paternity for 90,000 California children born to unmarried women."[5]

Establishing Paternity

If you were not married when the child was born, another obstacle to collecting child support may be to establish paternity. Establishing paternity is when a court decides who the father is.

Paternity disputes typically arise when a mother seeks child support or some other benefits, and the man denies that he is the father. These disputes can also arise when a man wants certain legal rights with the child, and the mother denies that he is the father.

Once paternity is established, the man is formally deemed to be the father, and the child gains many of the rights and benefits that he or she would have had if the parents had been married.

Why You Should Establish Paternity

Perhaps the single biggest reason to establish paternity is that it's necessary to get a child support order. Even if the father can't afford to support the child now, once the obligation is in place, the child becomes entitled to receive support until adulthood.

Also, once paternity is established, the child is eligible to receive the father's medical and life insurance. Medical coverage is expensive, and the father may be ordered to carry

Approximately 90% of fathers attend the birth of their children, regardless of whether the parents are married or ever intend to get married.[6]

the child under his policy. In addition, the child will have access to the father's medical records, and can learn any relevant medical history.

Establishing paternity also gives the child the right of inheritance. If the father dies, the child will be able to make claims against his estate, and possibly become eligible to receive social security, veterans benefits, retirement benefits, and so on.

From a father's point of view, establishing paternity is necessary if the mother denies that he is the father, and he wants to pursue his right to custody and visitation. Once paternity is established, he can pursue custody as if he had been married when the child was born.

And finally, establishing paternity allows the child to know who the father is. Paternity is crucially important for the child, whose very identity is uncertain when the biological parents are unknown. Knowing both the father and mother allows the child to learn about his or her heritage, and offers the chance to have a connection to both "sides" of the family.

How to Establish Paternity

There are several approaches to establishing paternity. The easiest—and by far the simplest—is for the father to *voluntarily acknowledge* that he is the father. A father can sign a written admission of paternity, under oath, which is filed with the court. This makes him the acknowledged father of the child.

In many states, fathers are asked to sign paternity acknowledgment forms while the mother is still in the hospital. Depending on the state, these forms may or may not be legally binding, but they do provide critical information about the potential father if he subsequently disappears.

If either the man or the woman denies that the man is the father, either one may start a *paternity suit*. A paternity suit is a lawsuit that decides who the child's father is. While some states impose a time limit, many allow a paternity suit to begin any time before the child reaches adulthood.
In a paternity suit, the court attempts to determine if the man is the father of the child. Science being what it is, that usually boils down to *blood* and *genetic tests*. If either side to the suit requests it, all parties must submit to testing.

Genetic Testing

Every cell in your body has *DNA,* or *Deoxyribonucleic acid.* Half of your DNA comes from your biological mother, and the other half comes from your biological father.

Because the DNA in your body is so unique, it is considered legally and scientifically reliable to establish paternity (or eliminate the possibility of paternity) by examining the DNA in the children and parents.

That's why there are many laboratories that perform paternity tests using DNA samples. The DNA samples can come from almost anything—blood, hair, small swabs of skin, even semen. And DNA testing can even be done on an unborn child when the mother is only in the tenth week of pregnancy!

 Pamela gave birth to a child while married to Donald. When they divorced three years later, they shared custody. However, two months after the divorce was final, Pamela insisted Donald was not the child's father, and blood tests established with 99% probability that the father was Chris, the man Pamela married after Donald. Pamela sought to terminate Donald's relationship with the child. The Superior Court agreed, but the Arizona Court of Appeals reversed. *In re Marriage of Worcester* (1997) 245 Ariz.Adv.Rep. 15.

To conduct the tests, you have to send a small group of cells—say from inside your cheek—to the lab. Then, for several hundred dollars or more, the laboratory will compare the *DNA markers* from the parents and the child, and state with a degree of certainty whether the man is the father or not.

Like all tests, DNA testing can be done simply and cheaply, or with great complexity and cost. It all depends on how many markers you want the laboratory to compare.

If the DNA between the mother and father and child match, the man is said to be the father with as much as a 99.9% degree of certainty. But if the DNA between the father and the child does not match, the man is said to be excluded from being the father with a 100% degree of certainty.

While genetic testing cannot absolutely prove that a man is the father, it can absolutely prove that he is not the father. That is one reason why a wrongly accused man will demand a test—to clear his name. Also, if the mother had sex with several men around the baby's conception, she might ask all candidates to submit to testing.

Because paternity tests are not absolute perfect, there is room for other evidence in a paternity suit. Generally, the court will listen to any evidence that establishes a link between the father and child, such as:

- *Physical evidence:* Pictures, gifts, and letters the father sent to the child.
- *Testimony:* The dates and times the father and mother had sex; if the father ever described the child as "his" to other people.
- *Documentation:* The father's signature on the birth certificate; the father adding the child's name to his insurance policies.

Interestingly enough, in many states, if the parents were married when the child was conceived, there is a presumption that the husband is the father unless proven otherwise. And in a few states, the husband is presumed to be the father no matter what the tests prove!

Paternity Testing

There are labs all over the country that will perform a paternity test for you. To find one, try entering "paternity test" in any major search engine. Generally, for the evidence to be admissible in court, the labs require that a cotton swab is collected by a professional. Here are some typical companies:

DNA Diagnostics Center
205 Corporate Court
Fairfield, OH 45014
(800) 613-5768
www.dnacenter.com
Standard testing for one child and one alleged father—with or without the mother—is $420. The lab requires a small blood sample or a swab from inside the cheek to collect cells. Testing takes five business days to complete.

Genetest Corporation
2316 Delaware Ave
Buffalo, NY 14216
(877) 404-4363
www.genetestlabs.com
Standard three person testing is $495. The lab wants the parties to visit a hospital or clinic for collection of blood or "buccal" swabs—swabs taken inside the cheek. Results are promised in five to seven days.

Genelex Corporation
12277 134th Ct. NE
Suite 130
Redmond, WA 98052
(800) 523-3080
www.genelex.com
Genelex tests 16 genetic markers "instead of the 8 to 10 tested in most labs." The lab requires authorized professionals to collect the buccal swabs. A test admissible in court costs $475, and the lab promises five to seven day turnaround.

Enforcing a Child Support Order

Finally. You've found the noncustodial parent, you've established paternity (if necessary), and you've successfully secured a court order requiring child support be paid to you. Your problems are over. Not!

If you are the receiving parent, not only are your problems not over, but you may find that it's more difficult to enforce the support order than it was to get it in the first place.

Five Reasons Why Parents Don't Pay Child Support

1. Want to "get even" because visitation was frustrated or denied.

2. Believe the other parent should support the children.

3. Want the other parent to get a job.

4. Convinced the children don't need the money.

5. Don't like to be ordered to do anything.

That's because a paying parent who is self-employed, unemployed, works in another state, works for cash, or moves around a lot can throw up all sorts of roadblocks between you and your support check.

Fortunately, there are many resources available to help you enforce a court order. Some resources, such as the IV-D agency, won't cost you a thing. Others, such as work done by a private collection agency, will cost you a percentage of the funds collected.

No matter what, though, the ultimate responsibility for enforcing the court order is yours. If you are not receiving your child support and you don't do anything about it, no one else will, either.

Enforcement Methods

Here are some tools to help enforce a child support order:

Wage Assignments

A paying parent who is steadily employed or has some source of regular income will be subject to a *wage assignment.* A wage assignment, or *wage withholding,* is when the monthly child support is automatically withheld from the paying parent's paycheck by the employer. The employer then sends the money to the receiving parent, or forwards it to the court clerk or IV-D agency, who then sends it to the receiving parent. Depending on the state, a wage assignment will either be automatically ordered or must be requested.

 Approximately 33% of all child-support cases involve delinquent parents who have moved across state lines.[7]

A wage assignment works best when the paying parent is employed by someone else and doesn't change jobs frequently, or when the parent receives regular income from sources such as a pension, retirement fund, trust, social security, disability, or annuity payout. If a paying parent is self-employed, unemployed, or changes jobs frequently, a wage assignment may not be effective. In all states, the maximum amount that can be withheld is set by the *Consumer Credit Act*—55% to 65% of the person's income.

Diversion of Government Benefits

If the paying parent is unemployed, you can attach his or her *benefits.* This allows you to deduct the child support payment from unemployment compensation, worker's compensation, or other benefits, and have it sent directly to you.

Delinquency Notices

If the paying parent is self-employed or works irregularly, you could send monthly billing statements. That way, if the parent falls behind, you can send *delinquency notices.* With some self-employed parents, this may be all that is needed.

Juanita was not married when she gave birth to a baby girl. One year later, she named Lawrence as the father and asked family court for sole custody, legal determination that Lawrence was the father, child support, pregnancy and confinement expenses, and attorney fees. Lawrence denied that he was the father and asked for a blood test. Juanita then presented a declaration of paternity signed by Lawrence and the child's birth certificate with Lawrence named as the father. Family court decided that Lawrence was the father, and awarded Juanita $1,140.75 for child support arrearages, $2,612.50 for lost leave benefits and $520.00 for medical expenses. *Elery v. Martin* (1999) 4 S.W.3d 550.

Posting Bonds or Depositing Funds

Another way to collect from self-employed parents is to require that the paying parent *post a bond or deposit funds* into a security account. This money is used to guarantee that the child support payments will be made. If the paying parent falls behind, the receiving parent can withdraw from the fund, and the paying parent has to replenish it. Or, the judge can order the entire bond forfeited if payments are missed. The amount that can be posted varies, but it may be up to two years of support.

Credit Checks

If the paying parent is earning income under the table, such as receiving payments in cash, or placed assets in someone else's name, you can request the IV-D agency perform a *credit check*. To find hidden assets and income, look for:

- Commissions and bonuses.
- Excessive deductions.
- Bank accounts, stocks, or bonds.
- Elaborate real estate, cars, boats, or motorcycles.
- Extravagant jewelry, art, or coin collections.

Also, self-employed, under the table earners may list fraudulent loans to the business or maintain inordinately high retained earnings.

Wage Garnishments

If the paying parent owes back support, you have a whole host of methods to collect the money. One choice, a *wage garnishment,* works just like a wage assignment. That is, the amount is deducted from the paying parent's paycheck and is then sent to the receiving parent. For this method to work, the paying parent must have a steady source of income. Garnishments are available for any money-based legal judgment.

Property Liens

If the paying parent owes back support, you can also place a *lien* on personal property. A lien is a claim that gives you the right to be paid first when the property is sold. The lien is not actual cash, but rather, it's an order preventing the owner from selling, transferring, or borrowing against the property until the debt is paid or the lien is removed. Liens can be made against homes, land, jewelry, coin and art collections, boats, motorcycles, and much more. However, in many states, you cannot place a lien on a primary residence.

If the paying parent has funds in a bank account, you can impound the money or seek an order to withhold and deliver, which places the assets with the court. If the paying parent owns a company, the company can be placed in receivership, with the trustee ensuring that the child support is paid.

Federal Support Enforcement. Enforcing a child support order is usually a state problem, but failing to pay child support can escalate to a federal offense if it meets the criteria of the *Deadbeat Parents Punishment Act,* 18 U.S.C. § 228. This federal law requires that the arrearage "has remained unpaid for longer than two years or is greater than $10,000" and the child lives in a different state from the debtor parent, or the arrearage "has remained unpaid for a period longer than 1 year, or is greater than $5,000" and the debtor "travels in interstate or foreign commerce with the intent to evade a support obligation." If the qualifications are met, the debtor can be punished by a fine and imprisonment up to two years.

Tax Refund Diversion

Another approach to collecting back child support is to divert the income *tax refund* of the paying parent. The state agency or Internal Revenue Service can attach the parent's refund and send it to the IV-D agency, who then forwards it to the receiving parent. If this happens, the paying parent will be notified and given a chance to contest it. If the paying parent has filed a joint return and part of the money belongs to a new spouse, the new mate can seek some money under the injured spouse provisions. If the claim is honored, and you have already received the money, you will have to give it back.

Receiving parents can also request the *IRS Full Collection Service* to satisfy back support. This invokes the full power of the IRS to seize property, attach assets, and close businesses. This tactic may be best when the paying parent is self-employed, lives in another state, and owes at least $5,000.

Civil Contempt

When a parent owes back support, you can request a *contempt of court* hearing. At the hearing, the parent will be ordered to explain why the support is past due. If he or she could not pay due to a loss of work or lack of money, that person cannot be found in contempt. But if the parent was able to pay but chose not to, the judge can declare him or her in contempt.

Civil contempt is serious, and a parent found guilty of contempt can be punished in many ways. The judge can order extra child support payments to make up the difference, require that a bond be posted, or even send the parent to jail until back payments are made. If the delinquent parent doesn't show up for the hearing at all, the judge can issue an arrest warrant.

 Civil vs. criminal. If the contempt is *civil*, the person is being punished for not doing what the court wants. Generally, he will have a chance to comply with the court orders to avoid punishment. But if the contempt is *criminal*, the person is being punished to prevent a repetition of certain behavior, and he may be jailed on the spot.

Deadbeat profiteers. If you are thinking about hiring a private child support collection agency, be prepared to pay a large portion of the money collected. One company, *Allegiance Child Support Enforcement,* charges a one-time administrative fee of $150.00 plus 33% of all money recovered. Other private collection agencies, such as *Child Support Network* and *Supportkids,* charge similarly. You can find these companies by searching on the internet under "child support enforcement."

Criminal Nonsupport

An even more serious tactic is to file *criminal nonsupport* charges against the paying parent. Criminal prosecution for nonsupport means the paying parent is accused of criminally neglecting the child by failing to pay support. Depending upon the state, it may be a misdemeanor or a felony.

When a district attorney files charges of criminal nonsupport, a warrant is issued, and the parent is arrested and arraigned. The parent has the right to a jury trial, where the evidence can be refuted. If the parent is found guilty or pleads guilty or no contest, he or she may be offered probation, or may be put in jail for a year or more.

Criminal nonsupport works against debtor parents who are self-employed and who flee across state lines. Many states will extradite a parent if the laws of the state make non-payment of court-ordered child support a felony.

License Blocking

Other methods include *license blocking,* which revokes or prevents the renewal of the driver's license, business license, or professional license of the paying parent. This method succeeds when the paying parent has a profession that requires a license, such as a doctor, dentist, hairdresser, etc.

Report to Credit Bureaus

Child support delinquencies are now reported to *credit bureaus,* which harms the paying parent's credit rating. The IV-D agency must report any delinquency over $1,000.

Child Support Agencies (IV-D)

Beginning in 1974, Congress passed a series of federal laws to help parents establish paternity and collect child support. These laws created a national child support enforcement agency called the *Office of Child Support Enforcement (OCSE),* and required each state to create a local child support enforcement agency. Because the federal law is found under Title 42, Chapter 7, Subchapter IV, Part D, the state child support agencies are usually referred to as "IV-D agencies."

The intent of the original law was to reduce the number of parents on welfare, but subsequent amendments have expanded the role of the IV-D agencies. The state agencies can help you to:

- Establish paternity through such tools as voluntary acknowledgement, blood testing, or genetic testing.
- Locate parents using the *State* and *Federal Parent Locator Service (FPLS),* which searches a variety of government databases, including DMV records, Veterans Administration, etc.
- Review support orders for compliance with state guidelines.
- Initiate changes to current support orders, such as adding payments for needed medical insurance, child care expenses, etc.
- Initiate enforcement of support orders through such methods as wage withholding, contempt of court proceedings, diversion of federal and state tax refunds, diversion of public benefit payments, etc.
- Initiate enforcement of support orders from members of the military.
- Coordinate support enforcement across state lines under the *Uniform Interstate Family Support Act (UIFSA).*

Each state gives their IV-D agency a different name, but you can find the phone number and address for your state agency in the appendix.

Report to "Most Wanted" Lists
In some states, a receiving parent who reports the
delinquency to the IV-D agency can anticipate a publicly
announced *"most wanted" list* mentioning the delinquent
parent. These lists are an attempt to shame delinquent
parents into paying up.

Private Collection Agency
And finally, if all else fails, a receiving parent can hire a
private collection agency. These private services use the same
procedures as any other collection service, such as dunning
letters, phone calls, etc. Often, they work for a percentage of
the amount collected, which may range from 20% to 40%.

Collecting Across State Lines

Paying parents who move across state lines create special
problems. That's because the responsibility for enforcing a
support order rests with the state, and each state has its own
court system, rules, and laws.

However, federal and uniform laws have been passed that
require states to cooperate when it comes to child support
enforcement.

Uniform Interstate Family Support Act (UIFSA)
This uniform law is the tool used to enforce a child support
order between states. Because this law has been enacted in
all states, there is a consistent approach to enforcement
across the nation.

The law sets up a procedure for different courts in different
states to coordinate with each other. The law makes it easier
for a receiving parent in one state to collect support from a
paying parent in a different state.

In short, UIFSA gives one court *continuing and exclusive
jurisdiction* to create or modify child support. The law allows
one court in one state to make a support order, but then
prevents a second court in another state from making another
support order or modifying the first order.

The Uniform Interstate Family Support Act eliminates multi-state support problems by requiring that once a child support order is made, a court in another state can do little more than enforce it.

This uniform law also allows for wage-withholding across state lines by letting the receiving parent send the child support order directly to the paying parent's employer.

Full Faith and Credit for Child Support Orders Act (FFCCSOA)
This federal law also requires one state to enforce a support order made by another state.

Like the UIFSA, the FFCCSOA also grants *continuing and exclusive jurisdiction* to the first court to make a support order.

The Full Faith and Credit for Child Support Orders Act assigns jurisdiction to the court in the state where the child lives or where either parent lives. It then requires any subsequent court to enforce the order—and not modify it—unless certain requirements are met.

How to Improve Your Chances of Collecting Child Support

When it comes to child support, there are other ways to increase your odds of getting that check. Here are some suggestions.

 A cold day in hell. If you do not receive your child support, you will be standing in a long line waiting for that check. In one year, the *Census Bureau* estimated that 10 million parents owed approximately $39 billion in support. In Los Angeles County alone, the *Bureau of Family Operations* opens approximately 9,000 cases per month and has a current caseload exceeding 615,000.

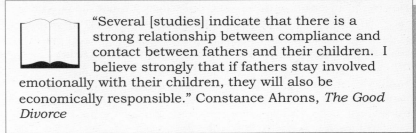

"Several [studies] indicate that there is a strong relationship between compliance and contact between fathers and their children. I believe strongly that if fathers stay involved emotionally with their children, they will also be economically responsible." Constance Ahrons, *The Good Divorce*

Have a Joint Custody Agreement

Simply stated, the single best way to collecting child support is to have a joint custody agreement. Here's why:

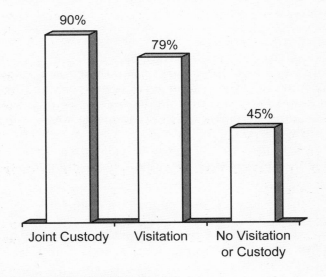

Fathers Who Pay Child Support

Notice that fathers with joint custody were much more likely to pay than other fathers—especially fathers with no visitation at all.

It's not hard to imagine why. When parents have joint custody, each maintains a separate relationship with the children, and both parents are encouraged to act responsibly. But if custody is restricted and visitation reduced, the parent who is cut off—the father or mother—is discouraged from accepting responsibility.

However, if joint custody won't work for you, consider some other strategies to improve your chances of collecting support.

Obtain and Keep Current a Wage Assignment Order

When the paying parent earns regular wages, a wage assignment makes the payments as painless as possible. Virtually every other alternative increases the potential for noncompliance. If the paying parent changes jobs, you must send the order to the new employer.

Be Your Own Detective

You know the other parent best, so it's your job to keep track of the details, such as where he or she works, vehicles that are purchased or sold, an increase in wages, any changes in residence, etc.

Work within the System

The IV-D offices are staffed by civil servants, and when you work with them, you must work within their rules. No matter how frustrated you get, yelling at a caseworker won't help. Also, writing letters to your Congressman or Senator will only get you a standard reply letter. Try focusing your complaint on key state officials, such as the governor, director of the IV-D agency, and members of the state legislature. Send a brief, factual letter to these people, and you may get help.

The big picture. "Remember what the big picture is to you. You want to create a situation in which the path of least resistance for the IV-D program to take is to treat you fairly and decently. Do not get sidetracked into a tirade about how horrible the IV-D program is in general. If you want to form a crusade to reform the IV-D program, do it. But do it after it no longer matters whether key persons think you are reasonable or not. People who were patient, reasonable and fair and who got the sympathetic attention of key people in state government got justice." Bruce Walker, *The Single Parent*

Collecting Child Support

U.S. Department of Health and Human Services
Administration for Children and Families
Office of Child Support Enforcement
370 L'Enfant Promenade SW
Washington, DC 20447
(202) 401-9373
www.acf.dhhs.gov/programs/cse

Every state has a Child Support Enforcement Agency.
Also called a IV-D office, these agencies help parents
establish paternity and enforce child support orders. The
federal office issues policies while the state offices actually
run the program. The state offices can:

- *Find an Absent Parent.* The agency has many
  resources to find absent parents, such as the Parent
  Locator Service that looks through IRS records, DMV
  records, etc.
- *Establish Paternity.* The agency can help a mother
  legally identify the father by establishing paternity. If
  the father doesn't acknowledge paternity, the office
  can arrange for blood tests.
- *Establish the Support Obligation.* If a parent needs to
  secure or modify a child support order, the agency
  attorneys can represent the parent in court.
- *Enforce a Child Support Order.* Once a valid order is in
  place, the caseworkers can help parents enforce the
  order by arranging for wage attachments, diversion of
  income tax refunds, posting of cash bonds, etc.

**Association for Children for Enforcement of Support
(ACES)**
2260 Upton Avenue
Toledo, OH 43606
(800) 738-ACES
www.childsupport-aces.org
An organization that provides information about child
support enforcement and how to collect current and back
support. Publishes *How to Collect Child Support* and
Child Support Reference Book.

1 U.S. Bureau of the Census, *Current Population Reports*
2 Office of Child Support Enforcement, U.S. Department of Health and Human Services, June 1993
3 U.S. Bureau of the Census, *Current Population Reports*
4 *Time Magazine,* June 19, 1995
5 *Los Angeles Times,* August 6, 1996
6 U.S. Department of Health and Human Services, Administration for Children and Families
7 *Los Angeles Times,* May 14, 1995

Appendix

Now that you've read about the laws of custody and support, you may need answers to specific questions. Because child custody laws are different in each state, you'll need to do further research—such as talking to a lawyer or spending time in a law library.

This appendix contains information to help you get started. Keep in mind, though, that the laws are constantly changing, so you will need to verify the current laws in your state.

Child Custody

What is the age of majority? This is important because when your child reaches this age, he or she is *no longer a child.* That usually means the court no longer has authority to make custody and support orders. Your adult children can live where they want and the support order will end. However, many states extend the age of majority for specific various reasons.

How is custody divided? In some states, a court can make different awards for legal and physical custody. In others, a custody award combines both legal and physical custody.

Is mediation authorized? Many states authorize or require mediation. If the parents cannot reach an agreement in mediation, the court will hear the case.

Will mediation be confidential? When parents use a mediator, generally the mediation session is confidential, and the mediator cannot testify in court about anything said during the session. This can only change if both parents expressly waive their right to confidentiality and let the mediator testify.

Is joint custody allowed? Some states allow joint custody only if both parents agree. Other states allow joint custody even if one parent objects. A few states require joint custody unless there is demonstrable harm to the parents, or the arrangement is not in the best interests of the children.

Will a custody evaluation be required? A court can order a custody investigation or evaluation to help it make a decision.

Are the child's preferences considered? Almost all states include the preferences of the child when deciding custody or visitation. However, it is likely that only the preferences of older children—usually teenagers—will be considered.

Can the court appoint someone to represent my child? In many states, the court can appoint an attorney, a *Court Appointed Special Advocate (CASA),* or a guardian ad litem to represent your child in court.

Paternity

Does marriage create a presumption of paternity? Often, when a woman was married when she conceived a child, her husband is assumed to be the father. If the child is not his, it must be demonstrated (through genetic testing or other means) that he is not the father.

Does the father's name on the birth certificate establish paternity? If a woman is not married when she has a child, another way to establish paternity is for the father to put his name on the birth certificate. Some states assume a man who signs a birth certificate is the father.

Is genetic testing used to establish paternity? When parents dispute paternity of a child, judges will order genetic testing. Even though these tests (blood type, DNA) are highly accurate, the laws do not rely on the results 100%, but instead, assign a *probability* that the tests are accurate. It is still possible that a man can be excluded as the father through genetic testing, but the court can conclude that he is the father anyway!

Child Abuse

Who must report child abuse besides professionals? In every state certain professionals are legally required to report signs of child abuse. These mandated reporters include: health care workers, school personnel, day-care providers, social workers, law enforcement officers, and mental health professionals. In addition, most states require other adults to report signs of child abuse, including: animal control officers, veterinarians, commercial film or photograph processors, etc. Approximately 18 states require any adult to report suspected child abuse.

Are there legally recognized exceptions to child abuse? Many states recognize that there are reasonable exceptions to behavior that might otherwise be classified as child abuse. The most common exception is a religious exemption for parents who choose not to seek medical care for the child due to religious beliefs. Other exceptions include corporal punishment, cultural practices, and poverty.

How long are child abuse complaints kept? Once a child abuse report is made, it is often stored in a central registry or database. Many states have laws that limit how long the record will be kept in the database.

Child Support

What model is used? Different states have different ways to calculate child support. The most common—called the *Shared Income* model—assumes that the support amount should reflect the combined income of both parents. The *Percent of Income* model assumes that the noncustodial parent's income should be the basis for support, because the custodial parent is already supporting the child. The Melson model uses a more complicated formula that factors in the estimated cost of raising the child while prorating the support obligation between the parents.

Whose income is used? Depending on the guideline model, the income used to calculate support—or the income base— may be the noncustodial parent or both parents.

What methods are used to enforce a support order? When child support is not paid, the parent who is owed the money has many tools to collect the money. Many states allow income tax refunds to be diverted, while others can withhold state benefits (such as unemployment). In addition, most courts will hold a parent in contempt for failing to pay child support, which gives the court to use additional methods to enforce the support order.

What types of income cannot be withheld? Certain income is automatically excluded from child support calculations and from enforcement methods. Typically, this includes social security, military disability, etc.

What are the limits on income withholding? A parent ordered to past-due pay child support cannot have his or her entire paycheck taken. Not only are there limits imposed by federal law—the *Consumer Credit Protection Act (CCPA)*—but some states impose their own limits. For example, in Alabama, if the noncustodial parent is supporting a new family, that factor is taken into account and reduces the upper limit of what he or she can be ordered to pay.

When does support end? Child support usually ends when the child reaches the age of majority—but not always. Some states extend child support while the child is in high school and still living with the custodial parent, and a few states allow support to continue if the child is unable to function as an independent adult.

Does support end if the child leaves home early? If the child moves away from the custodial parent before reaching the age of majority, depending on the state, support may not end automatically.

Can support be ordered beyond the age of majority? In some states, even though the child has reached adulthood, the court can order support to continue. This often occurs when the child—now an adult—is a full-time student and is not living independently. Usually the court will order support to continue until graduation.

What is the time-limit for collecting past-due support? If a parent is owed child support, he or she can often take steps to collect the support long after the child has reached adulthood. However, many states place a time limit on collecting the debt, forcing the parent who is owed support to act or forfeit the debt.

Is interest charged on past-due support? Almost all states
allow the court to tack on interest and fees to an unpaid child
support bill. Some states allow the interest to compound with
each passing year, while others keep the interest simple.

Alabama

Child Custody

What is the age of majority?
19.

How is custody divided?
Legal and physical combined.

Is mediation authorized?
Yes.

Will mediation be confidential?
Yes.

Is joint custody allowed?
Available if both parents agree.

Will a custody evaluation be required?
Not specified.

Are the child's preferences considered?
Yes.

Can the court appoint someone to represent my child?
Yes.

Paternity

Does marriage create a presumption of paternity?
Yes.

Does the father's name on the birth certificate establish paternity?
Yes.

Is genetic testing used to establish paternity?
Yes, 97% probability.

Child Abuse

Who must report child abuse besides professionals?
Anyone giving aid or assistance to children.

Are there legally recognized exceptions to child abuse?
Yes, religious exemption.

How long are child abuse complaints kept?
Expunged 5 years from completion of investigation.

Child Support

What model is used?
Shared Income.

Whose income is used?
Both parents.

What methods are used to enforce a support order?
State income tax refund intercept, license revocation/ suspension, property seizure and sale, withholding of state funds or benefits, consumer credit (credit bureau) reporting, passport, contempt.

What types of income cannot be withheld?
Military disability, SSI, TANF.

What are the limits on income withholding?
The maximum amount that can be deducted from the non-custodial parent's disposable

income for child support is: (a) 50% percent if the noncustodial parent supports a second family and is behind 12 weeks or less in his/her child support obligation; (b) 55% percent if the noncustodial parent supports a second family and is more than 12 weeks behind in his/her child support obligation; (c) 60% percent if the noncustodial parent does not support a second family and is behind 12 weeks or less in his/her child support obligation; or (d) 65% percent if the noncustodial parent does not support a second family and is more than 12 weeks behind in his/her child support obligation.

When does support end?
19, unless the child is emancipated prior to that time.

Does support end if the child leaves home early?
No.

Can support be ordered beyond the age of majority?
No.

What is the time-limit for collecting past-due support?
20 years from date of judgment for purpose of obtaining an order of support.

Is interest charged on past-due support?
Yes, 12% per year.

Addresses

Alabama Bar Association
415 Dexter Ave.
Montgomery, AL 36104
(334) 269-1515
www.alabar.org

Department of Human Resources
Division of Child Support
50 Ripley Street
Montgomery, AL 36130
(334) 242-9300

Office of Child Support
Enforcement Region IV
61 Forsyth Street, S.W.
Suite 4M60
Atlanta, GA 30303
(404) 562-2900

Alabama Head Start
Alabama Department of
Children's Affairs
RSA Tower, Suite 1670
201 Monroe Street
Montgomery, AL 36130
(334) 223-0502

Admin. for Children and Families
Child Day Care Partnership
50 Ripley Street
Montgomery, AL 36130
(334) 242-1425

Alaska

Child Custody

What is the age of majority?
18. 19 if unmarried and pursuing a high school diploma or equivalent level of technical or vocational training and residing with custodial parent, guardian or designee of the parent or guardian.

How is custody divided?
Legal and physical combined.

Is mediation authorized?
Yes.

Will mediation be confidential?
Yes.

Is joint custody allowed?
Permitted despite one parent objecting.

Will a custody evaluation be required?
Not specified.

Are the child's preferences considered?
Yes.

Can the court appoint someone to represent my child?
Yes.

Paternity

Does marriage create a presumption of paternity?
Yes.

Does the father's name on the birth certificate establish paternity?
No.

Is genetic testing used to establish paternity?
Yes, 95% probability.

Child Abuse

Who must report child abuse besides professionals?
Employees of violence, assault, or drug and alcohol treatment programs, film and photographic processors.

Are there legally recognized exceptions to child abuse?
Yes, religious exemption.

How long are child abuse complaints kept?
Indefinite.

Child Support

What support model is used?
Percent of Income.

Whose income is used?
The income of the noncustodial parent is used in primary custody cases. Both parents' income is used in shared or divided custody cases.

What methods are used to enforce a support order?
License revocation/suspension, property seizure and sale, withholding of state funds or

benefits, consumer credit (credit bureau) reporting, withhold and deliver orders for commercial fisherman turning in their catch to the processor, criminal non-support prosecution.

What types of income cannot be withheld?
Exempt funds such as TANF, SSI, VA disability and Native Dividends without an Alaskan court order specifically authorizing the garnishment of the Native Dividend.

What are the limits on income withholding?
40% of disposable income after mandatory deductions, but may go to 65% under certain circumstances.

When does support end?
When the child reaches the age of majority.

Does support end if the child leaves home early?
No.

Can support be ordered beyond the age of majority?
Yes.

What is the time-limit for collecting past-due support?
No statute of limitations on the collection of child support arrears.

Is interest charged on past-due support?
Yes, 6% for past due support, from the date the order was issued, 12% if order was issued prior to 10/1/1996.

Addresses

Alaska Bar Association
P.O. Box 100279
Anchorage, AK 99510
(907) 272-7469
www.alaskabar.org

Child Support Enforcement Division
550 West 7th Avenue
Suite 310
Anchorage, AK 99501
(907) 269-6900

Office of Child Support Enforcement Region X
2201 Sixth Avenue
Blanchard Plaza
Suite 600
Seattle, WA 98121
(206) 615-2547

Alaska Head Start
Department of Education & Early Development
333 West 4th Ave.
Suite 320
Anchorage, AK 99501
(907) 269-4518

Admin. for Children and Families
Division of Family and Youth Services
P.O. Box 110630
Juneau, AK 99811
(907) 465-3207

Arizona

Child Custody

What is the age of majority?
18.

How is custody divided?
Legal and physical separate.

Is mediation authorized?
Yes.

Will mediation be confidential?
Yes.

Is joint custody allowed?
Permitted despite one parent
objecting.

**Will a custody evaluation be
required?**
Not specified.

**Are the child's preferences
considered?**
Yes.

**Can the court appoint someone
to represent my child?**
Yes.

Paternity

**Does marriage create a
presumption of paternity?**
Yes.

**Does the father's name on the
birth certificate establish
paternity?**
No.

**Is genetic testing used to
establish paternity?**
Yes, 95% probability.

Child Abuse

**Who must report child abuse
besides professionals?**
Parents, anyone responsible for
children, clergy.

**Are there legally recognized
exceptions to child abuse?**
Yes, Christian Science treatment,
unavailability of reasonable
services.

**How long are child abuse
complaints kept?**
Expunged when child turns 18-
25 years after the date of the
report.

Child Support

What model is used?
Shared Income.

Whose income is used?
Both parents.

**What methods are used to
enforce a support order?**
State income tax refund
intercept, license revocation/
suspension, property seizure and
sale, withholding of state funds
or benefits, consumer credit
(credit bureau) reporting.

What types of income cannot be withheld?

One-half of a debtor's disposable earnings is exempt. In the case of a prisoner, the mandatory deduction is 25% of the prisoner's gross wages until the prisoner's account exceeds a $50 balance.

What are the limits on income withholding?

One-half of disposable earnings for any pay period is exempt.

When does support end?

If child turns 18 while in school or high school equivalency program, support will continue while attending high school equivalency program, but not past 19 with certain limited exceptions.

Does support end if the child leaves home early?

No.

Can support be ordered beyond the age of majority?

Yes.

What is the time-limit for collecting past-due support?

The right to collect unpaid child support expires at end of the 3 year period from emancipation of last child who was subject to court order unless reduced to written money judgment. If reduced to written judgment, the right to collect lasts until paid in full.

Is interest charged on past-due support?

Yes, 10% per year from the date of the court order.

Addresses

Arizona Bar Association
111 West Monroe
Suite 1800
Phoenix, AZ 85003
(602) 252.4804
www.azbar.org

Division of Child Support
Enforcement
P.O. Box 40458
Phoenix, AZ 85067
(602) 252-4045

Office of Child Support
Enforcement Region IX
50 United Nations Plaza
Room 450
San Francisco, CA 94102
(415) 437-8400

Arizona Head Start
Governor's Division for Children
1700 West Washington
Suite 101-B
Phoenix, AZ 85007
(602) 542-3483

Admin. for Children and Families
Department of Health Services
1647 East Morten
Suite 230
Phoenix, AZ 85020
(602) 674-4220

Arkansas

Child Custody

What is the age of majority?
18 or when child has graduated from High School, whichever occurs later.

How is custody divided?
Legal and physical combined.

Is mediation authorized?
No.

Will mediation be confidential?
Not specified.

Is joint custody allowed?
No statutes.

Will a custody evaluation be required?
Not specified.

Are the child's preferences considered?
No.

Can the court appoint someone to represent my child?
No.

Paternity

Does marriage create a presumption of paternity?
Yes.

Does the father's name on the birth certificate establish paternity?
Yes.

Is genetic testing used to establish paternity?
Yes, 95% probability.

Child Abuse

Who must report child abuse besides professionals?
Prosecutors, judges, Youth Services employees, domestic violence shelter employees.

Are there legally recognized exceptions to child abuse?
Yes, corporal punishment, poverty.

How long are child abuse complaints kept?
Expunged promptly.

Child Support

What model is used?
Percent of Income.

Whose income is used?
Noncustodial parent.

What methods are used to enforce a support order?
State income tax refund intercept, license revocation/suspension, property seizure and sale, withholding of state funds or benefits, consumer credit (credit bureau) reporting.

What types of income cannot be withheld?
None.

What are the limits on income withholding?
None, other than the limits in the Consumer Credit Protection Act (CCPA).

When does support end?
18 or when child has graduated from High School, whichever occurs later.

Does support end if the child leaves home early?
No.

Can support be ordered beyond the age of majority?
Yes.

What is the time-limit for collecting past-due support?
Five years past age 18 for arrears that have not been adjudicated. Adjudications are good for ten years and can be revived every ten years thereafter.

Is interest charged on past-due support?
No.

Addresses

Arkansas Bar Association
400 West Markham
Little Rock, AR 72201
(501) 375-4606
(800) 609-5668
www.arkbar.com

Office of Child Support
Enforcement
P.O. Box 8133
Little Rock, AR 72203
(501) 682-8398

Office of Child Support
Enforcement Region VI
1301 Young Street
Suite 914
Dallas, TX 75202
(214) 767-9648

Arkansas Head Start
523 South Louisiana
Suite 301
Little Rock, AR 72201
(501) 371-0740

Admin. for Children and Families
Division of Child Care and Early
Childhood Education
P.O. Box 1437
Slot F150
Little Rock, AR 72203
(501) 682-8590

California

Child Custody

What is the age of majority?
18, except an unmarried child who has attained the age of 18 years, is a full-time high school student, and who is not self-supporting, is considered a minor until the child completes the 12th grade or reaches 19, whichever occurs first.

How is custody divided?
Legal and physical separate.

Is mediation authorized?
Yes.

Will mediation be confidential?
Yes.

Is joint custody allowed?
Permitted despite one parent objecting.

Will a custody evaluation be required?
Court ordered.

Are the child's preferences considered?
Yes.

Can the court appoint someone to represent my child?
Yes.

Paternity

Does marriage create a presumption of paternity?
Yes.

Does the father's name on the birth certificate establish paternity?
No.

Is genetic testing used to establish paternity?
California law requires a paternity index of 100 and does not specify a percentage to create a presumption of paternity.

Child Abuse

Who must report child abuse besides professionals?
Firefighters, animal control officers, film and photographic processors, clergy.

Are there legally recognized exceptions to child abuse?
Yes, informed medical decision, reasonable force, religious exemption.

How long are child abuse complaints kept?
Expunged 10 years after most recent report.

Child Support

What model is used?
Shared Income adjusted according to the percentage of time each parent has primary physical responsibility for child.

Whose income is used?
Net monthly disposable income of both parents.

What methods are used to enforce a support order?

State income tax refund intercept, license revocation/ suspension, property seizure and sale, withholding of state funds or benefits, consumer credit (credit bureau) reporting, application for collection by the Secretary of the Treasury, civil or criminal contempt proceedings.

What types of income cannot be withheld?

Needs based income sources, such as TANF, CalWORKs, SSI, and General Assistance are not subject to wage withholding.

What are the limits on income withholding?

A maximum of 50% of net disposable income.

When does support end?

When the child reaches the age of majority.

Does support end if the child leaves home early?

No.

Can support be ordered beyond the age of majority?

Yes.

What is the time-limit for collecting past-due support?

There is no statute of limitations in California. Child support is enforceable until paid in full.

Is interest charged on past-due support?

Yes, 10% per year. Interest accrues from the date of entry of judgment.

Addresses

California Bar Association
180 Howard Street
San Francisco, CA 94105
(415) 538-2000
www.calbar.ca.gov

California Department of Child
Support Services
Customer and Community
Services Branch
P.O. Box 419064, MS-30
Rancho Cordova, CA 95741
(866) 249-0773

Office of Child Support
Enforcement Region IX
50 United Nations Plaza
Room 450
San Francisco, CA 94102
(415) 437-8400

California Head Start
California Department of
Education
Child Development Division
560 J Street
Suite 220
Sacramento, CA 95814
(916) 324-8296

Admin. for Children and Families
Central Operations Branch
Department of Social Services
744 P Street
Mail Stop 19-50
Sacramento, CA 95814
(916) 324-4031

Colorado

Child Custody

What is the age of majority?
19.

How is custody divided?
Legal and physical separate.

Is mediation authorized?
Yes.

Will mediation be confidential?
Yes.

Is joint custody allowed?
Permitted despite one parent
objecting.

**Will a custody evaluation be
required?**
Not specified.

**Are the child's preferences
considered?**
Yes.

**Can the court appoint someone
to represent my child?**
Yes.

Paternity

**Does marriage create a
presumption of paternity?**
Yes

**Does the father's name on the
birth certificate establish
paternity?**
No.

**Is genetic testing used to
establish paternity?**
Yes, 97% probability.

Child Abuse

**Who must report child abuse
besides professionals?**
Christian Science practitioners,
veterinarians, firefighters, film
and photographic processors.

**Are there legally recognized
exceptions to child abuse?**
Yes, corporal punishment,
cultural practices, reasonable
force, religious exemption.

**How long are child abuse
complaints kept?**
Sealed no later than 10 years
after child turns 18; amended,
sealed, or expunged at any time
by the director upon good cause
shown.

Child Support

What model is used?
Shared Income.

Whose income is used?
Both parents.

**What methods are used to
enforce a support order?**
State income tax refund
intercept, license revocation/
suspension, property seizure and
sale, withholding of state funds
or benefits, consumer credit
(credit bureau) reporting,
contempt of court, Rule 69

Procedure (judicial hearing held to solicit testimony regarding employment /assets).

What types of income cannot be withheld?
All income types can be withheld.

What are the limits on income withholding?
None, other than the limits in the Consumer Credit Protection Act (CCPA).

When does support end?
Colorado's age of emancipation was lowered from 21 to 19 years of age. There are still orders that state child support will continue until 21 years of age and are enforceable unless review and adjustment is completed.

Does support end if the child leaves home early?
No.

Can support be ordered beyond the age of majority?
Yes.

What is the time-limit for collecting past-due support?
No limitations. Although if the arrears are reduced to Judgment there is a 20 year statute of limitations on the Judgment.

Is interest charged on past-due support?
Yes. Prior to 6/30/75, 6% simple interest; 7/1/75 to 6/30/79, 8% simple interest; 7/1/79 to 6/30/86, 8% compounded interest; 7/1/86 to present, 12% compounded interest.

Addresses

Colorado Bar Association
1900 Grant St.
Suite 900
Denver, CO 80203
(303) 860-1115
www.cobar.org

Division of Child Support Enforcement
Division of Human Services
303 E. 17th Avenue
Suite 200
Denver, CO 80203
(720) 947-5000

Office of Child Support Enforcement Region VIII
1961 Stout Street
Room 924
Denver, CO 80294
(303) 844-2622

Colorado Head Start
Office of Bill Owens
136 State Capitol
Denver, CO 80203
(303) 866-4609

Admin. for Children and Families
Department of Human Services
Division of Child Care
1575 Sherman Street, First Floor
Denver, CO 80203
(303) 866-5958
(800) 799-5876

Connecticut

Child Custody

What is the age of majority?
18.

How is custody divided?
Legal and physical separate.

Is mediation authorized?
Yes.

Will mediation be confidential?
Yes.

Is joint custody allowed?
Available if both parents agree.

Will a custody evaluation be required?
Not specified.

Are the child's preferences considered?
Yes.

Can the court appoint someone to represent my child?
Yes.

Paternity

Does marriage create a presumption of paternity?
Yes.

Does the father's name on the birth certificate establish paternity?
Yes.

Is genetic testing used to establish paternity?
Yes, 99% probability.

Child Abuse

Who must report child abuse besides professionals?
Substance abuse and sexual assault counselors, clergy.

Are there legally recognized exceptions to child abuse?
Yes, Christian Science treatment.

How long are child abuse complaints kept?
Indefinite.

Child Support

What model is used?
Shared Income.

Whose income is used?
Both parents.

What methods are used to enforce a support order?
State income tax refund intercept, license revocation/suspension, property seizure and sale, withholding of state funds or benefits, consumer credit (credit bureau) reporting, withholding of lottery winnings, contempt, criminal prosecution.

What types of income cannot be withheld?
None.

What are the limits on income withholding?
85% of the first $145 of disposable income per week is exempt from withholding.

When does support end?
18, except in cases where decree of dissolution of marriage, legal separation or annulment is entered on or after July 1, 1994, support continues for unmarried children residing with a parent until completion of twelfth grade or the age of nineteen, whichever occurs first.

Does support end if the child leaves home early?
No.

Can support be ordered beyond the age of majority?
Yes.

What is the time-limit for collecting past-due support?
None.

Is interest charged on past-due support?
No.

Addresses

Connecticut Bar Association
30 Bank Street
New Britain, CT 06050
(860) 223-4400
www.ctbar.org

Department of Social Services
Bureau of Child Support
Enforcement
25 Sigourney Street
Hartford, CT 06105
(860) 424-5251

Office of Child Support
Enforcement Region I
John F. Kennedy Federal Bldg.
Room 2000
Boston, MA 02203
(617) 565-10205

Connecticut Head Start
Department of Social Services
25 Sigourney Street
Hartford, CT 06106
(860) 424-5066

Admin. for Children and Families
Department of Public Health
410 Capitol Avenue
Mail Station 12
DAC, P.O. Box 340308
Hartford, CT 06134
(860) 509-8045

Delaware

Child Custody

What is the age of majority?
18.

How is custody divided?
Legal and physical combined.

Is mediation authorized?
Yes.

Will mediation be confidential?
Yes.

Is joint custody allowed?
Available if both parents agree.

Will a custody evaluation be required?
Court ordered.

Are the child's preferences considered?
Yes.

Can the court appoint someone to represent my child?
Yes.

Paternity

Does marriage create a presumption of paternity?
Yes.

Does the father's name on the birth certificate establish paternity?
No.

Is genetic testing used to establish paternity?
Yes, 99% probability.

Child Abuse

Who must report child abuse besides professionals?
None.

Are there legally recognized exceptions to child abuse?
Yes, religious exemption.

How long are child abuse complaints kept?
Retained at the discretion of the Division.

Child Support

What model is used?
Melson.

Whose income is used?
Both parents.

What methods are used to enforce a support order?
State income tax refund intercept, license revocation/ suspension, property seizure and sale, withholding of state funds or benefits, consumer credit (credit bureau) reporting, wage withholdings to employers, incarceration, lump sum payments, wage withholdings to employers.

What types of income cannot be withheld?
Supplemental Social Security Benefits.

What are the limits on income withholding?

None, other than the limits in the Consumer Credit Protection Act (CCPA).

When does support end?

18 and the child is no longer in high school.

Does support end if the child leaves home early?

No.

Can support be ordered beyond the age of majority?

Yes.

What is the time-limit for collecting past-due support?

No statute of limitations on collection of past due support.

Is interest charged on past-due support?

No.

Addresses

Delaware Bar Association
301 North Market Street
Wilmington, DE 19801
(302) 658-5279
www.dsba.org

Division of Child Support
Enforcement
Delaware Health and Social
Services
1901 North Dupont Hwy
P.O. Box 904
New Castle, DE 19720
(302) 577-4863

Office of Child Support
Enforcement Region II
26 Federal Plaza
Room 4114
New York, NY 10278
(212) 264-2890

Delaware Head Start
State of Delaware Department of
Education
Improvement and Assistance
Branch
Townsend Building
P.O. Box 1402
Dover, DE 19903
(302) 739-4667

Admin. for Children and Families
Department of Services for
Children, Youth and Families
1825 Faulkland Road
Wilmington, DE 19805
(302) 892-5800

District of Columbia

Child Custody

What is the age of majority?
21, or at the point the minor is self supporting through marriage, employment or military service.

How is custody divided?
Legal and physical combined.

Is mediation authorized?
No.

Will mediation be confidential?
Not specified.

Is joint custody allowed?
Available if both parents agree.

Will a custody evaluation be required?
Not specified.

Are the child's preferences considered?
Yes.

Can the court appoint someone to represent my child?
Yes.

Paternity

Does marriage create a presumption of paternity?
Yes.

Does the father's name on the birth certificate establish paternity?
No.

Is genetic testing used to establish paternity?
Yes, 99% probability.

Child Abuse

Who must report child abuse besides professionals?
None.

Are there legally recognized exceptions to child abuse?
Yes, religious exemption, poverty.

How long are child abuse complaints kept?
Expunged upon successful challenge by subject or the 18th birthday of the child, or 5 years after termination of social rehabilitation services, whichever occurs first.

Child Support

What model is used?
Shared Income.

Whose income is used?
Noncustodial parent.

What methods are used to enforce a support order?
State income tax refund intercept, license revocation/suspension, property seizure and sale, withholding of state funds or benefits, consumer credit (credit bureau) reporting, lottery winnings.

What types of income cannot be withheld?
Disability, SSI.

What are the limits on income withholding?
None, other than the limits in the Consumer Credit Protection Act (CCPA).

When does support end?
21.

Does support end if the child leaves home early?
No.

Can support be ordered beyond the age of majority?
Yes.

What is the time-limit for collecting past-due support?
None.

Is interest charged on past-due support?
No.

Addresses

District of Columbia Bar
Association
1250 H Street NW, Sixth Floor
Washington, DC 20005
(202) 737-4700
www.dcbar.org

Office of Paternity and Child
Support Enforcement
Department of Human Services
800 9th Street, S.W., 2nd Floor
Washington, DC 20024
(202) 724-1444

Office of Child Support
Enforcement Region III
150 S. Independence Mall West
Suite 864
Philadelphia, PA 19106
(215) 861-4000

District of Columbia Head Start
717 Fourteenth Street, NW
Suite 450
Washington, DC 20005
(202) 727-8113

Admin. for Children and Families
Human Services Facility Division
614 H Street, NW
Suite 1003
Washington, DC 20001
(202) 727-7226

Florida

Child Custody

What is the age of majority?
18.

How is custody divided?
Legal and physical combined.

Is mediation authorized?
Yes.

Will mediation be confidential?
Yes.

Is joint custody allowed?
Permitted despite one parent objecting.

Will a custody evaluation be required?
Not specified.

Are the child's preferences considered?
Yes.

Can the court appoint someone to represent my child?
Yes.

Paternity

Does marriage create a presumption of paternity?
Yes.

Does the father's name on the birth certificate establish paternity?
No.

Is genetic testing used to establish paternity?
Yes, 95% probability.

Child Abuse

Who must report child abuse besides professionals?
Judges, religious healers.

Are there legally recognized exceptions to child abuse?
Yes, religious exemption, corporal punishment, poverty.

How long are child abuse complaints kept?
Expunged 7 years after last entry, or when child is 18, whichever date is first.

Child Support

What model is used?
Shared Income.

Whose income is used?
Both parents, and in specified circumstances, income of the child(ren) or new spouse may be considered.

What methods are used to enforce a support order?
License revocation/suspension, property seizure and sale, withholding of state funds or benefits, consumer credit (credit bureau) reporting, judgment by operation of law (clerk of court), contempt of court, order of commitment or writ of bodily

attachment, and remedies as available for enforcement actions.

What types of income cannot be withheld?

US Dept. of Veterans Affairs disability benefits, except as remuneration for employment defined in 42 USC, Section 659 (a) and (h), and Unemployment Compensation are excluded from the definition of income for withholding purposes. However, the Title IV-D program can intercept unemployment compensation benefits.

What are the limits on income withholding?

None, other than the limits in the Consumer Credit Protection Act (CCPA).

When does support end?

18.

Does support end if the child leaves home early?

No.

Can support be ordered beyond the age of majority?

Yes.

What is the time-limit for collecting past-due support?

None.

Is interest charged on past-due support?

No.

Addresses

Florida Bar Association
650 Apalachee Parkway
Tallahassee, FL 32399
(850) 561-5839
www.flabar.org

Child Support Enforcement
Program
Department of Revenue
P.O. Box 8030
Tallahassee, FL 32314
(850) 922-9590

Office of Child Support
Enforcement Region IV
61 Forsyth Street, S.W.
Suite 4M60
Atlanta, GA 30303
(404) 562-2900

Florida Head Start
Florida's Collaboration for Young
Children and Their Families
The Holland Building
Suite 146
600 South Calhoun Street
Tallahassee, FL 32399
(850) 414-7757

Admin. for Children and Families
Department of Children &
Families
Child Care Services
1317 Winewood Blvd.
Building 6 Room 389A
Tallahassee, FL 32399
(850) 488-4900

Georgia

Child Custody

What is the age of majority?
18.

How is custody divided?
Legal and physical separate.

Is mediation authorized?
No.

Will mediation be confidential?
Not specified.

Is joint custody allowed?
Available if both parents agree.

Will a custody evaluation be required?
Court ordered.

Are the child's preferences considered?
Yes (age 14).

Can the court appoint someone to represent my child?
Yes.

Paternity

Does marriage create a presumption of paternity?
Yes.

Does the father's name on the birth certificate establish paternity?
No.

Is genetic testing used to establish paternity?
Yes, 97% probability.

Child Abuse

Who must report child abuse besides professionals?
People who produce visual or printed matter.

Are there legally recognized exceptions to child abuse?
Yes, religious exemption, corporal punishment.

How long are child abuse complaints kept?
Expunged 2 years after classification.

Child Support

What model is used?
Percent of Income.

Whose income is used?
Noncustodial parent

What methods are used to enforce a support order?
State income tax refund intercept, license revocation/suspension, property seizure and sale, withholding of state funds or benefits, consumer credit (credit bureau) reporting, lottery intercept, contempt.

What types of income cannot be withheld?
TANF, SSI, VA Disability.

What are the limits on income withholding?

None, other than the limits in the Consumer Credit Protection Act (CCPA).

When does support end?

18, however, a support order entered after 7/1/92 may provide for the extension of child support to age 20 if the child is still in high school.

Does support end if the child leaves home early?

Yes.

Can support be ordered beyond the age of majority?

No.

What is the time-limit for collecting past-due support?

None for child support orders issued on or after July 1, 1997.

Is interest charged on past-due support?

No.

Office of Child Support Enforcement Region IV
61 Forsyth Street, S.W.
Suite 4M60
Atlanta, GA 30303
(404) 562-2900

Georgia Head Start
Georgia Office of School Readiness
10 Park Place South
Atlanta, GA 30303
(404) 656-5957

Admin. for Children and Families
Department of Human Resources
Office of Regulatory Services
2 Peachtree Street, NW
32nd Floor, Room 458
Atlanta, GA 30303
(404) 657-5562

Addresses

Georgia Bar Association
104 Marietta St. NW
Suite 100
Atlanta, GA 30303
(800) 334-6865
(404) 527-8700

Child Support Enforcement
P.O. Box 38450
Atlanta, GA 30334
(404) 657-3851

Hawaii

Child Custody

What is the age of majority?
18.

How is custody divided?
Legal and physical combined.

Is mediation authorized?
No.

Will mediation be confidential?
Not specified.

Is joint custody allowed?
Available if both parents agree.

Will a custody evaluation be required?
Court ordered.

Are the child's preferences considered?
Yes.

Can the court appoint someone to represent my child?
Yes.

Paternity

Does marriage create a presumption of paternity?
Yes.

Does the father's name on 'the birth certificate establish paternity?
Yes.

Is genetic testing used to establish paternity?
There is no percentage of paternity that creates a presumption. However, if genetic test results do not exclude the possibility of paternity and there is a minimum combined paternity index of five hundred to one, a presumption is created.

Child Abuse

Who must report child abuse besides professionals?
Employees of recreational or sports activities.

Are there legally recognized exceptions to child abuse?
No.

How long are child abuse complaints kept?
Expunged promptly where the report is found to be unsubstantiated or dismissed on the merits after adjudicatory hearing.

Child Support

What model is used?
Melson.

Whose income is used?
Custodial parent. The child's income may be considered if the child is over 18 age or if there is an exceptional circumstance which warrants the consideration of such income.

What methods are used to enforce a support order?

State income tax refund intercept, license revocation/suspension, property seizure and sale, withholding of state funds or benefits, consumer credit (credit bureau) reporting, garnishment, statutory liens.

What types of income cannot be withheld?

Income that federal law precludes from withholding.

What are the limits on income withholding?

None, other than the limits in the Consumer Credit Protection Act (CCPA).

When does support end?

If not addressed in the order, child support is not automatically terminated. An order terminating child support is entered if the child is not entitled to continue to receive child support.

Does support end if the child leaves home early?

Yes.

Can support be ordered beyond the age of majority?

Yes.

What is the time-limit for collecting past-due support?

The 33rd birthday of the child or 10 years after the judgement was entered, whichever is later.

Is interest charged on past-due support?

No.

Addresses

Hawaii Bar Association
1132 Bishop St.
Suite 906
Honolulu, HI 96813
(808) 537-1868
www.hsba.org

Child Support Enforcement Agency
Department of Attorney General
Kakuhihewa State Office Building
601 Kamokila Boulevard, Suite 251
Kapolei, HI 96707
(808) 587-3695

Office of Child Support Enforcement Region IX
50 United Nations Plaza
Room 450
San Francisco, CA 94102
(415) 437-8400

Hawaii Head Start
Hawaii Department of Human Services Benefit, Employment, and Support Services Division
820 Mililani Street
Suite 606, Haseko Center
Honolulu, HI 96813
(808) 586-5240

Admin. for Children and Families
Department of Human Services
Benefit, Employment & Support Services Division
820 Mililani Street
Suite 606, Haseko Center
Honolulu, HI 96813
(808) 586-7050

Idaho

Child Custody

What is the age of majority?
18.

How is custody divided?
Legal and physical separate.

Is mediation authorized?
Yes.

Will mediation be confidential?
Yes.

Is joint custody allowed?
Required unless health or safety compromised.

Will a custody evaluation be required?
Not specified.

Are the child's preferences considered?
Yes.

Can the court appoint someone to represent my child?
No.

Paternity

Does marriage create a presumption of paternity?
Yes.

Does the father's name on the birth certificate establish paternity?
No.

Is genetic testing used to establish paternity?
Yes, 98% probability.

Child Abuse

Who must report child abuse besides professionals?
None.

Are there legally recognized exceptions to child abuse?
Yes, religious exemption.

How long are child abuse complaints kept?
Indefinite.

Child Support

What model is used?
Shared Income.

Whose income is used?
Both parents.

What methods are used to enforce a support order?
State income tax refund intercept, license revocation/ suspension, property seizure and sale, withholding of state funds or benefits, consumer credit (credit bureau) reporting.

What types of income cannot be withheld?
Unearned income: i.e. Social Security Supplement (SSI).

What are the limits on income withholding?
The Consumer Credit Protection Act (CCPA) limits withholding to 50-65%. Idaho policy limits withholding to 50% of disposable income.

When does support end?
18.

Does support end if the child leaves home early?
No.

Can support be ordered beyond the age of majority?
Yes.

What is the time-limit for collecting past-due support?
Any enforcement action must be commenced prior to the youngest child's 23rd birthday.

Is interest charged on past-due support?
No.

Addresses

Idaho Bar Association
P.O. Box 895
Boise, ID 83701
(208) 334-4500
www2.state.id.us/isb

Bureau of Child Support Services
Department of Health and Welfare
P.O. Box 83720
Boise, ID 83720
(208) 334-6535

Office of Child Support Enforcement Region X
2201 Sixth Avenue
Blanchard Plaza
Suite 600
Seattle, WA 98121
(206) 615-2547

Idaho Head Start
Idaho Head Start Association, Inc.
200 North 4th Street
Suite 20
Boise, ID 83702
(208) 345-1182

Admin. for Children and Families
Department of Health & Welfare
Bureau of Family & Children's Services
450 W. State Street
P.O. Box 83720
Boise, ID 83720
(208) 334-5691

Illinois

Child Custody

What is the age of majority?
18.

How is custody divided?
Legal and physical combined.

Is mediation authorized?
Yes.

Will mediation be confidential?
Yes.

Is joint custody allowed?
Permitted despite one parent objecting.

Will a custody evaluation be required?
Court ordered.

Are the child's preferences considered?
Yes.

Can the court appoint someone to represent my child?
Yes.

Paternity

Does marriage create a presumption of paternity?
Yes.

Does the father's name on the birth certificate establish paternity?
Yes.

Is genetic testing used to establish paternity?
Yes, 500 to 1 C.P.I.

Child Abuse

Who must report child abuse besides professionals?
Homemakers, substance abuse treatment personnel, Christian Science practitioners, Funeral home directors, film and photographic processors.

Are there legally recognized exceptions to child abuse?
Yes, plan of care, religious exemption, school attendance.

How long are child abuse complaints kept?
Expunged no later than 5 years after determination. Reports of sexual abuse, serious physical injury, or death of a child may be retained longer than 5 years, but are expunged or amended upon good cause shown.

Child Support

What model is used?
Percent of Income.

Whose income is used?
Noncustodial parent, but deviations from the guideline can be based on consideration of the income of the child or the custodial parent.

What methods are used to enforce a support order?
State income tax refund intercept, license revocation/suspension, property seizure and sale, withholding of state funds or benefits, consumer credit (credit bureau) reporting, suspension of driver's license.

What types of income cannot be withheld?
Income excludes any amount required by law to be withheld, other than creditor claims, including, but not limited to Federal, State and local taxes, Social Security and other retirement and disability contributions, union dues, any amounts exempted by the Federal Consumer Credit Protection Act, public assistance payments, unemployment insurance benefits except as provided by law.

What are the limits on income withholding?
None, other than the limits in the Consumer Credit Protection Act (CCPA).

When does support end?
18 unless the order provides otherwise.

Does support end if the child leaves home early?
No.

Can support be ordered beyond the age of majority?
Yes.

What is the time-limit for collecting past-due support?
None.

Is interest charged on past-due support?
Yes, 9% per year.

Addresses

Illinois Bar Association
Illinois Bar Center
Springfield, IL 62701
(217) 525-1760
www.illinoisbar.org

Illinois Department of Public Aid
Division of Child Support
Enforcement
Marriott Building
509 South Sixth Street
Springfield, IL 62701
(217) 524-4602

Office of Child Support
Enforcement Region V
233 N. Michigan Avenue
Suite 400
Chicago, IL 60601
(312) 353-4237

Illinois Head Start
Illinois Department of Human
Services
10 Collinsville Avenue
Suite 203
East St. Louis, IL 62201
(618) 583-2083
(618) 583-2088

Admin. for Children and Families
Department of Children & Family
Services
406 East Monroe Street
Station 60
Springfield, IL 62701
(217) 785-2688

Indiana

Child Custody

What is the age of majority?
21.

How is custody divided?
Legal and physical separate.

Is mediation authorized?
Yes.

Will mediation be confidential?
Yes.

Is joint custody allowed?
Permitted despite one parent objecting.

Will a custody evaluation be required?
Not specified.

Are the child's preferences considered?
Yes (age 14).

Can the court appoint someone to represent my child?
Yes.

Paternity

Does marriage create a presumption of paternity?
Yes.

Does the father's name on the birth certificate establish paternity?
No.

Is genetic testing used to establish paternity?
Yes, 99% probability.

Child Abuse

Who must report child abuse besides professionals?
Staff member of any public or private institution, school, facility, or agency.

Are there legally recognized exceptions to child abuse?
Yes, corporal punishment, prescription drugs, religious exemption.

How long are child abuse complaints kept?
Expunged not later than 10 working days after any of the following occur: court determination that abuse or neglect has not occurred; administrative officer finds that report is unsubstantiated; or criminal court dismisses charges or enters a not guilty verdict. Otherwise, expunged not later than when child reaches 24.

Child Support

What model is used?
Shared Income.

Whose income is used?
Custodial parent.

What methods are used to enforce a support order?
State income tax refund

intercept, license revocation/ suspension, property seizure and sale, withholding of state funds or benefits, consumer credit (credit bureau) reporting, lottery winnings, contempt actions.

What types of income cannot be withheld?
SSI, State employee retirement benefits.

What are the limits on income withholding?
None, other than the limits in the Consumer Credit Protection Act (CCPA).

When does support end?
21, unless child has been determined to be legally incapacitated.

Does support end if the child leaves home early?
No.

Can support be ordered beyond the age of majority?
Yes.

What is the time-limit for collecting past-due support?
10 years after age 18 or date of emancipation, whichever is earlier. 20 years for child support judgments.

Is interest charged on past-due support?
Yes, if requested, court may order up to 1.5% per month.

Addresses

Indiana Bar Association
230 East Ohio Street
4th Floor
Indianapolis, IN 46204
(317) 639-5465
(800) 266-2581

Child Support Bureau
402 West Washington Street
Room W360
Indianapolis, IN 46204
(317) 233-5437

Office of Child Support
Enforcement Region V
233 N. Michigan Avenue
Suite 400
Chicago, IL 60601
(312) 353-4237

Indiana Head Start
402 West Washington Street
Room W461
Indianapolis, IN 46204
(317) 233-6837

Admin. for Children and Families
Family & Social Services
Administration
Division of Family and Children
402 W. Washington Street
Room W-386
Indianapolis, IN 46204
(317) 232-4469

Iowa

Child Custody

What is the age of majority?
18.

How is custody divided?
Legal and physical separate.

Is mediation authorized?
Yes.

Will mediation be confidential?
Yes.

Is joint custody allowed?
Permitted despite one parent objecting.

Will a custody evaluation be required?
Not specified.

Are the child's preferences considered?
Yes.

Can the court appoint someone to represent my child?
Yes.

Paternity

Does marriage create a presumption of paternity?
Yes.

Does the father's name on the birth certificate establish paternity?
No.

Is genetic testing used to establish paternity?
Yes, 95% probability.

Child Abuse

Who must report child abuse besides professionals?
Film and photographic processors, employees of substance abuse programs.

Are there legally recognized exceptions to child abuse?
Yes, religious exemption.

How long are child abuse complaints kept?
Sealed 10 years after receipt of report. If a subsequent report is received involving any one of the parties within this 10 year period, the information is sealed 10 years after the subsequent report. Expunged 8 years after the information is sealed.

Child Support

What model is used?
Shared income variation. The noncustodial parent's net monthly income is compared to the custodial parent's net monthly income.

Whose income is used?
Both parents.

What methods are used to enforce a support order?
State income tax refund intercept, license revocation/

suspension, property seizure and sale, withholding of state funds or benefits, consumer credit (credit bureau) reporting, administrative seek work, garnishment, contempt of court, attachment of property.

What types of income cannot be withheld?
Those from federally exempt sources.

What are the limits on income withholding?
50% of disposable income on administrative IWO (entered by Iowa IV-D agency). Court-entered withholding can be up to the CCPA limits.

When does support end?
18, or as ordered by the court.

Does support end if the child leaves home early?
No.

Can support be ordered beyond the age of majority?
Yes.

What is the time-limit for collecting past-due support?
No statute of limitations after 7/1/97. Before that, 20 years from date of each child support installment.

Is interest charged on past-due support?
Yes, 10%. Not commonly enforced.

Addresses

Iowa Bar Association
521 East Locust
3rd Floor
Des Moines, IA 50309
(515) 243-3179
www.iowabar.org

Bureau of Collections
Department of Human Services
Hoover Building
5th Floor
Des Moines, IA 50319
(515) 242-5530

Office of Child Support
Enforcement Region VII
Federal Office Building
Room 276
601 E. 12th Street
Kansas City, MO 64106
(816) 426-3981

Iowa Head Start
Iowa Department of Education
Bureau of Children, Families, and Community Services
Grimes State Office Building
Des Moines, IA 50319
(515) 242-6024

Admin. for Children and Families
Department of Human Services
Division of Behavioral
Development & Protective
Services
Child Day Care Unit
Hoover State Office Building, 5th Floor
Des Moines, IA 50319
(515) 281-8746

Kansas

Child Custody

What is the age of majority?
18.

How is custody divided?
Legal and physical combined.

Is mediation authorized?
Yes.

Will mediation be confidential?
Yes.

Is joint custody allowed?
Available if both parents agree.

Will a custody evaluation be required?
Court ordered.

Are the child's preferences considered?
Yes.

Can the court appoint someone to represent my child?
No.

Paternity

Does marriage create a presumption of paternity?
Yes.

Does the father's name on the birth certificate establish paternity?
No.

Is genetic testing used to establish paternity?
Yes, 97% probability.

Child Abuse

Who must report child abuse besides professionals?
Firefighters, Juvenile intake and assessment workers.

Are there legally recognized exceptions to child abuse?
Yes, religious exemption.

How long are child abuse complaints kept?
Indefinitely.

Child Support

What model is used?
Shared Income.

Whose income is used?
Both parents.

What methods are used to enforce a support order?
State income tax refund intercept, license revocation/ suspension, property seizure and sale, withholding of state funds or benefits, consumer credit (credit bureau) reporting, garnishment and contempt.

What types of income cannot be withheld?
Any amounts exempted by law, including but not limited to disability, public assistance payments, unemployment insurance benefits.

What are the limits on income withholding?

None, other than the limits in the Consumer Credit Protection Act (CCPA).

When does support end?

Child support is automatically extended through June 30 of the school year (July 1 - June 30) during which the child turns 18, unless the court specifically orders otherwise. The court has the discretion to extend child support through the school year in which the child turns 19, but only if both parents participate or acquiesce in the decision that delayed completion of high school.

Does support end if the child leaves home early?

No.

Can support be ordered beyond the age of majority?

Yes.

What is the time-limit for collecting past-due support?

Generally, installments due after 7/1/81 are enforceable until 2 years after child is emancipated. With appropriate actions, enforcement may be extended indefinitely. Installments due before 7/1/81 may be enforceable, but require case by case determination. In a proceeding for arrearages, the statute of limitation under the laws of Kansas or of the state issuing the order, whichever is longer, applies.

Is interest charged on past-due support?

Yes, from the date of judgement.

Addresses

Kansas Bar Association
1200 SW Harrison
Topeka, KS 66612
(785) 234-5696
www.ksbar.org

Child Support Enforcement
Program
P.O. Box 497
Topeka, KS 66601
(785) 296-3237

Office of Child Support
Enforcement Region VII
Federal Office Building
Room 276
601 E. 12th Street
Kansas City, MO 64106
(816) 426-3981

Kansas Head Start
Kansas Department of Social and
Rehabilitation Services
Docking State Office Building
915 Southwest Harrison
Room 681 West
Topeka, KS 66612
(785) 368-6354

Admin. for Children and Families
Department of Health and
Environment
Curtis State Office Bldg
1000 SW Jackson
Suite 200
Topeka, KS 66612
(785) 296-1270

Kentucky

Child Custody

What is the age of majority?
18, 19 if attending high school.

How is custody divided?
Legal and physical combined.

Is mediation authorized?
Yes.

Will mediation be confidential?
Not specified.

Is joint custody allowed?
Available if both parents agree.

Will a custody evaluation be required?
Court ordered.

Are the child's preferences considered?
Yes.

Can the court appoint someone to represent my child?
Yes.

Paternity

Does marriage create a presumption of paternity?
Yes.

Does the father's name on the birth certificate establish paternity?
No.

Is genetic testing used to establish paternity?
Yes, 99% probability.

Child Abuse

Who must report child abuse besides professionals?
None.

Are there legally recognized exceptions to child abuse?
Yes, religious exemption.

How long are child abuse complaints kept?
Indefinitely.

Child Support

What model is used?
Shared Income.

Whose income is used?
Both parents.

What methods are used to enforce a support order?
State income tax refund intercept, license revocation/ suspension, property seizure and sale, withholding of state funds or benefits, consumer credit (credit bureau) reporting, income withholding, passport denial, vehicle booting, administrative subpoena, most wanted poster, delinquent listing of obligors.

What types of income cannot be withheld?
TANF, SSI, VA Disability.

What are the limits on income withholding?
None, other than the limits in the Consumer Credit Protection Act.

When does support end?
18, 19 if attending high school.

Does support end if the child leaves home early?
No.

Can support be ordered beyond the age of majority?
Yes.

What is the time-limit for collecting past-due support?
15 years after the last child emancipates.

Is interest charged on past-due support?
No.

Addresses

Kentucky Bar Association
514 West Main Street
Frankfort, KY 40601
(502) 564-3795
www.kybar.org

Division of Child Support
Enforcement
Cabinet for Human Resources
P.O. Box 2150
Frankfort, KY 40602
(502) 564-2285

Office of Child Support
Enforcement Region IV
61 Forsyth Street, S.W.
Suite 4M60
Atlanta, GA 30303
(404) 562-2900

Kentucky Head Start
Governor's Office of Early
Childhood Development
275 East Main Street
2W-E
Frankfort, KY 40621
(502) 564-8099

Admin. for Children and Families
Cabinet for Health Services
C.H.R. Building
275 East Main Street
5E-A
Frankfort, KY 40621
(502) 564-2800

Louisiana

Child Custody

What is the age of majority?
18.

How is custody divided?
Legal and physical combined.

Is mediation authorized?
Yes.

Will mediation be confidential?
Yes.

Is joint custody allowed?
Available if both parents agree.

Will a custody evaluation be required?
Not specified.

Are the child's preferences considered?
Yes.

Can the court appoint someone to represent my child?
No.

Paternity

Does marriage create a presumption of paternity?
Yes.

Does the father's name on the birth certificate establish paternity?
No.

Is genetic testing used to establish paternity?
Yes, 99.9% probability.

Child Abuse

Who must report child abuse besides professionals?
Film or photographic print processors, mediators.

Are there legally recognized exceptions to child abuse?
Yes, poverty, religious exemption.

How long are child abuse complaints kept?
Expunged 3 years after audit. Sealed during 3 years for audit purposes.

Child Support

What model is used?
Shared Income.

Whose income is used?
Both parents. The income of the child may be considered in certain circumstances.

What methods are used to enforce a support order?
State income tax refund intercept, license revocation/ suspension, property seizure and sale, withholding of state funds or benefits, consumer credit (credit bureau) reporting,

What types of income cannot be withheld?
Supplemental Security Income, VA Disability Benefits.

What are the limits on income withholding?
Withholding for child support cannot exceed 50% of disposable earnings.

When does support end?
Louisiana Revised Statue 9:309 (C) allows for child support to be paid for a child over the age of majority if the child is unmarried, a full time student in good standing in a secondary school, and a dependent of either parent.

Does support end if the child leaves home early?
No.

Can support be ordered beyond the age of majority?
Yes.

What is the time-limit for collecting past-due support?
10 years.

Is interest charged on past-due support?
No.

Addresses

Louisiana Bar Association
601 St. Charles Avenue
New Orleans, LA 70130
(800) 421-5722
(504) 566-1600
www.lsba.org

Support Enforcement Services
Office of Family Support
P.O. Box 94065
Baton Rouge, LA 70804
(225) 342-4780

Office of Child Support
Enforcement Region VI
1301 Young Street
Suite 914
Dallas, TX 75202
(214) 767-9648

Louisiana Head Start
412 4th Street
Room 105
Baton Rouge, LA 70802
(225) 219-4246

Admin. for Children and Families
Department of Social Services
2751 Wooddele Blvd.
P.O. Box 3078
Baton Rouge, LA 70821
(225) 922-0015

Maine

Child Custody

What is the age of majority?
18.

How is custody divided?
Legal and physical combined.

Is mediation authorized?
Yes.

Will mediation be confidential?
Not specified.

Is joint custody allowed?
Available if both parents agree.

Will a custody evaluation be required?
Not specified.

Are the child's preferences considered?
Yes.

Can the court appoint someone to represent my child?
Yes.

Paternity

Does marriage create a presumption of paternity?
Yes.

Does the father's name on the birth certificate establish paternity?
Yes.

Is genetic testing used to establish paternity?
Yes, 97% probability.

Child Abuse

Who must report child abuse besides professionals?
Guardians ad litem and CASAs, fire inspectors, film processors, homemakers.

Are there legally recognized exceptions to child abuse?
Yes, religious exemption.

How long are child abuse complaints kept?
Expunged after 18 months. Unsubstantiated cases may be retained for 5 years for audit purposes.

Child Support

What model is used?
Shared Income.

Whose income is used?
Both parents. In addition, the available income and financial contributions of the domestic associate or current spouse of each party and a child's financial resources may be reasons to justify deviating from the support guidelines.

What methods are used to enforce a support order?
State income tax refund intercept, license revocation/suspension, property seizure and sale, withholding of state funds or benefits, consumer credit (credit bureau) reporting, seek work orders.

What types of income cannot be withheld?
None specified.

What are the limits on income withholding?
None, other than the limits in the Consumer Credit Protection Act (CCPA).

When does support end?
18, or if the child gets married or becomes a member of the armed services. However, if the child is attending secondary school, then support continues until the child graduates, withdraws or is expelled from secondary school or attains 19 years of age, whichever occurs first.

Does support end if the child leaves home early?
No.

Can support be ordered beyond the age of majority?
Yes.

What is the time-limit for collecting past-due support?
None, but there is a presumption of payment after 20 years.

Is interest charged on past-due support?
No.

Addresses

Maine Bar Association
P.O. Box 788
Augusta, ME 04332
(207) 622-7523
www.mainebar.org

Division of Support Enforcement and Recovery
Bureau of Income Maintenance
Department of Human Services
State House Station
11 Whitten Road
Augusta, ME 04333

Office of Child Support Enforcement Region I
John F. Kennedy Federal Bldg.
Room 2000
Boston, MA 02203
(617) 565-10205

Maine Head Start
Office of Child Care and Head Start
Department of Human Services
State House Station II
Augusta, ME 04333
(207) 287-5060

Admin. for Children and Families
Bureau of Child & Family Services
221 State Street
State House, Station 11
Augusta, ME 04333
(207) 287-5060

Maryland

Child Custody

What is the age of majority?
18.

How is custody divided?
Legal and physical combined.

Is mediation authorized?
Yes.

Will mediation be confidential?
Yes.

Is joint custody allowed?
Available if both parents agree.

Will a custody evaluation be required?
Court ordered.

Are the child's preferences considered?
Yes.

Can the court appoint someone to represent my child?
Yes.

Paternity

Does marriage create a presumption of paternity?
Yes.

Does the father's name on the birth certificate establish paternity?
No.

Is genetic testing used to establish paternity?
Yes, 97.3% probability.

Child Abuse

Who must report child abuse besides professionals?
None.

Are there legally recognized exceptions to child abuse?
No.

How long are child abuse complaints kept?
Expunged within 5 years after referral or 7 years after entry on registry.

Child Support

What model is used?
Shared Income.

Whose income is used?
Both parents.

What methods are used to enforce a support order?
State income tax refund intercept, license revocation/suspension, property seizure and sale, withholding of state funds or benefits, consumer credit (credit bureau) reporting, passport denial, state lottery intercept, medical support withholding, contempt.

What types of income cannot be withheld?
Benefits from means-tested public assistance programs, including Temporary Cash Assistance (TCA), Supplementary Security Income (SSI), food

stamps, and transitional emergency, medical and housing assistance.

What are the limits on income withholding?
None, other than the limits in the Consumer Credit Protection Act (CCPA).

When does support end?
18.

Does support end if the child leaves home early?
No.

Can support be ordered beyond the age of majority?
Yes.

What is the time-limit for collecting past-due support?
12 years.

Is interest charged on past-due support?
No.

Addresses

Maryland Bar Association
520 W. Fayette St.
Baltimore, MD 21201
(410) 685-7878
(800) 492-1964
www.msba.org

Child Support Enforcement
Administration
Department of Human Resources
311 West Saratoga Street
Baltimore, MD 21201
(410) 767-7619

Office of Child Support
Enforcement Region III
150 S. Independence Mall West
Suite 864
Philadelphia, PA 19106
(215) 861-4000

Maryland Head Start
Governor's Office for Children,
Youth and Families
301 West Preston Street
15th Floor
Baltimore, MD 21201
(410) 767-4160

Admin. for Children and Families
Department of Human Resources
Child Care Administration
311 W. Saratoga Street
1st Floor
Baltimore, MD 21201
(410) 767-7805

Massachusetts

Child Custody

What is the age of majority?
18.

How is custody divided?
Legal and physical combined.

Is mediation authorized?
No.

Will mediation be confidential?
Not specified.

Is joint custody allowed?
Permitted despite one parent objecting.

Will a custody evaluation be required?
Not specified.

Are the child's preferences considered?
No.

Can the court appoint someone to represent my child?
Yes.

Paternity

Does marriage create a presumption of paternity?
Yes.

Does the father's name on the birth certificate establish paternity?
No.

Is genetic testing used to establish paternity?
Yes, 97% probability.

Child Abuse

Who must report child abuse besides professionals?
Drug and alcoholism counselors, probation and parole officers, clerks/magistrates of district courts, firefighters.

Are there legally recognized exceptions to child abuse?
No.

How long are child abuse complaints kept?
Expunged after one year; or when a child reaches 18; or one year after end of services, whichever occurs last.

Child Support

What model is used?
Percent of Income.

Whose income is used?
Noncustodial parent. In addition, Massachusetts Child Support Guidelines allow income of a new spouse to be considered.

What methods are used to enforce a support order?
State income tax refund intercept, license revocation/suspension, property seizure and sale, withholding of state funds or benefits, consumer credit

(credit bureau) reporting, insurance liens, contempt.

What types of income cannot be withheld?
Federally excluded sources only, no sources excluded by state law.

What are the limits on income withholding?
None, other than the limits in the Consumer Credit Protection Act (CCPA).

When does support end?
18.

Does support end if the child leaves home early?
No.

Can support be ordered beyond the age of majority?
Yes.

What is the time-limit for collecting past-due support?
None.

Is interest charged on past-due support?
Yes, 12%. Depending upon payments received, parents might not be assessed interest or might be eligible to apply for a waiver under certain circumstances.

Addresses

Massachusetts Bar Association
20 West Street
Boston, MA 02111
(617) 338-0500
(413) 731-5134
www.massbar.org

Child Support Enforcement Division
Department of Revenue
141 Portland Street
Cambridge, MA 02139
(617) 577-7200

Office of Child Support Enforcement Region I
John F. Kennedy Federal Bldg.
Room 2000
Boston, MA 02203
(617) 565-10205

Massachusetts Head Start
Executive Office of Health and Human Services
One Ashburton Place
#1109
Boston, MA 02108
(617) 727-7600

Admin. for Children and Families
Office of Child Care Services
One Ashburton Place
Room 1105
Boston, MA 02108
(617) 626-2000

Michigan

Child Custody

What is the age of majority?
18.

How is custody divided?
Legal and physical combined.

Is mediation authorized?
Yes.

Will mediation be confidential?
Yes.

Is joint custody allowed?
Permitted despite one parent objecting.

Will a custody evaluation be required?
Court ordered.

Are the child's preferences considered?
Yes.

Can the court appoint someone to represent my child?
Yes.

Paternity

Does marriage create a presumption of paternity?
Yes.

Does the father's name on the birth certificate establish paternity?
Yes.

Is genetic testing used to establish paternity?
Yes, 99% probability.

Child Abuse

Who must report child abuse besides professionals?
No one.

Are there legally recognized exceptions to child abuse?
Yes, religious exemption.

How long are child abuse complaints kept?
Expunged when alleged perpetrator dies.

Child Support

What model is used?
Shared Income.

Whose income is used?
Both parents.

What methods are used to enforce a support order?
State income tax refund intercept, license revocation/suspension, property seizure and sale, withholding of state funds or benefits, lottery intercept, contempt.

What types of income cannot be withheld?
Public Assistance.

What are the limits on income withholding?
None, other than the limits in the Consumer Credit Protection Act (CCPA).

When does support end?
18, but support may continue until 19 1/2 for completion of high school, or beyond 19 1/2 by agreement of the parties.

Does support end if the child leaves home early?
No.

Can support be ordered beyond the age of majority?
Yes.

What is the time-limit for collecting past-due support?
10 years after last obligation due, and affirmative defense.

Is interest charged on past-due support?
No, prejudgment arrears specifically excluded. By statute interest does not apply to child support debts. However, there is a surcharge applied to arrears twice a year at an annual rate of 8%.

Office of Child Support
Family Independence Agency
P.O. Box 30478
Lansing, MI 48909
(517) 373-7570

Office of Child Support
Enforcement Region V
233 N. Michigan Avenue
Suite 400
Chicago, IL 60601
(312) 353-4237

Michigan Head Start
Michigan Family Independence Agency
235 South Grand Avenue
Suite 1302
P.O. Box 30037
Lansing, MI 48909
(517) 373-2492

Admin. for Children and Families
Department of Consumer & Industry Services
7109 W. Saginaw
2nd Floor
P.O. Box 30650
Lansing, MI 48909-8150
(517) 373-8300

Addresses

Michigan Bar Association
306 Townsend Street
Lansing, MI 48933
(800) 968-1442
www.michbar.org

Minnesota

Child Custody

What is the age of majority?
18, or until age 20 if the child is still attending secondary school, whichever occurs later.

How is custody divided?
Legal and physical separate.

Is mediation authorized?
Yes.

Will mediation be confidential?
Yes.

Is joint custody allowed?
Permitted despite one parent objecting.

Will a custody evaluation be required?
Court ordered.

Are the child's preferences considered?
Yes.

Can the court appoint someone to represent my child?
Yes.

Paternity

Does marriage create a presumption of paternity?
Yes.

Does the father's name on the birth certificate establish paternity?
Yes.

Is genetic testing used to establish paternity?
Yes, 99% probability is the threshold. However, temporary child support orders prior to paternity adjudication can be obtained with a 92% or greater result.

Child Abuse

Who must report child abuse besides professionals?
No one.

Are there legally recognized exceptions to child abuse?
Yes, corporal punishment, religious exemption, cultural practices.

How long are child abuse complaints kept?
Maintained for 4 to 10 years.

Child Support

What model is used?
Percent of Income.

Whose income is used?
Noncustodial parent. If the noncustodial parent has subsequent children, the needs of the subsequent children are considered in determining support.

What methods are used to enforce a support order?
State income tax refund intercept, license revocation/suspension, property seizure and

sale, withholding of state funds or benefits, consumer credit (credit bureau) reporting.

What types of income cannot be withheld?

Any need based benefits received under Title IVA of Social Security Act or state public assistance such as TANF, foster care, medical assistance, and SSI. Also excluded are VA Disability, life insurance proceeds, military housing allowance, military separate rations, military basic allowance, military bonus, capital gains, in kind payments.

What are the limits on income withholding?

None, other than the limits in the Consumer Credit Protection Act (CCPA).

When does support end?

18, or until age 20 if the child is still attending secondary school, whichever occurs later.

Does support end if the child leaves home early?

No.

Can support be ordered beyond the age of majority?

Yes.

What is the time-limit for collecting past-due support?

No statute of limitations on the following actions: income withholding, state tax intercept, credit bureau reporting, license suspension, and contempt. Docketed judgments extend for 10 years. Judgments are renewable.

Is interest charged on past-due support?

Yes, If there is court ordered obligation to pay a portion of the retroactive support on a monthly basis, and the obligor does not pay, then the annual judgment rate plus 2% is charged. If there is no court ordered obligation to pay a portion of the retroactive support on a monthly basis, then interest is not charged.

Addresses

Minnesota Bar Association
600 Nicollet Mall
#380
Minneapolis, MN 55402
(612) 333-1183
(800) 882-6722

Office of Child Support Enforcement
Department of Human Services
444 Lafayette Road, 4th floor
St. Paul, MN 55155
(651) 296-2542

Office of Child Support Enforcement Region V
233 N. Michigan Avenue
Suite 400
Chicago, IL 60601
(312) 353-4237

Minnesota Head Start
Minnesota Department of Children, Families and Learning
1500 West Highway 36
Roseville, MN 55113
(651) 634-2203

Mississippi

Child Custody

What is the age of majority?
21.

How is custody divided?
Legal and physical separate.

Is mediation authorized?
Yes.

Will mediation be confidential?
Yes.

Is joint custody allowed?
Permitted despite one parent objecting.

Will a custody evaluation be required?
Not specified.

Are the child's preferences considered?
No.

Can the court appoint someone to represent my child?
Yes.

Paternity

Does marriage create a presumption of paternity?
Yes.

Does the father's name on the birth certificate establish paternity?
No.

Is genetic testing used to establish paternity?
98% or greater creates a rebuttable presumption of paternity.

Child Abuse

Who must report child abuse besides professionals?
Attorneys, ministers.

Are there legally recognized exceptions to child abuse?
Yes, corporal punishment, religious exemption.

How long are child abuse complaints kept?
Indefinite.

Child Support

What model is used?
Percent of adjusted gross income. The percentage determined by number of children.

Whose income is used?
Noncustodial parent.

What methods are used to enforce a support order?
State income tax refund intercept, license revocation/suspension, property seizure and sale, withholding of state funds or benefits, consumer credit (credit bureau) reporting, arrest for civil contempt, state criminal prosecution, federal prosecution.

What types of income cannot be withheld?
SSI.

What are the limits on income withholding?
None, other than the limits in the Consumer Credit Protection Act (CCPA).

When does support end?
21. However, if the support order does not specify per child, and there is more than one child, support may continue until the youngest child turns 21.

Does support end if the child leaves home early?
No.

Can support be ordered beyond the age of majority?
Yes.

What is the time-limit for collecting past-due support?
Seven years after the child reaches 21.

Is interest charged on past-due support?
Yes, if and when a payment is missed, usually 8%.

Addresses

Mississippi Bar Association
P.O. Box 2168
Jackson, MS 39225
(601) 948-4471
www.msbar.org

Division of Child Support Enforcement
Department of Human Services
P.O. Box 352
Jackson, MS 39205
(601) 359-4861

Office of Child Support Enforcement Region IV
61 Forsyth Street, S.W.
Suite 4M60
Atlanta, GA 30303
(404) 562-2900

Mississippi Head Start
Central High School Building
359 N. West Street
Jackson, MS 39205
(601) 359-5798

Admin. for Children and Families
Department of Health
Division of Child Care
P.O. Box 1700
Jackson, MS 39215
(601) 576-7613

Missouri

Child Custody

What is the age of majority?
18.

How is custody divided?
Legal and physical separate.

Is mediation authorized?
Yes.

Will mediation be confidential?
Yes.

Is joint custody allowed?
Permitted despite one parent objecting.

Will a custody evaluation be required?
Court ordered.

Are the child's preferences considered?
Yes.

Can the court appoint someone to represent my child?
Yes.

Paternity

Does marriage create a presumption of paternity?
Yes.

Does the father's name on the birth certificate establish paternity?
No.

Is genetic testing used to establish paternity?
Yes, 98% probability.

Child Abuse

Who must report child abuse besides professionals?
People who care for children, Christian Science practitioners, probation/parole officers, film processors.

Are there legally recognized exceptions to child abuse?
Yes, corporal punishment, religious exemption.

How long are child abuse complaints kept?
Expunged after 10 years if report from a mandated reporter; 2 years for other reports; or 10 years if unable to locate the child.

Child Support

What model is used?
Shared Income.

Whose income is used?
Both parents. A child's income may be considered when deviating from the presumed support amount. The child's income cannot be based on the child's special needs.

What methods are used to enforce a support order?
State income tax refund intercept, license revocation/

suspension, property seizure and sale, withholding of state funds or benefits, consumer credit (credit bureau) reporting, real and personal property liens, liens to financial institutions, liens on decedent's estate, liens on lawsuits, civil contempt and criminal non-support.

What types of income cannot be withheld?

TANF, SSI, prison inmate monthly allowance.

What are the limits on income withholding?

The statutory limitation is the limit described by the Consumer Credit Protection Act (CCPA). However, the state IV-D agency limits its withholding orders to 50% of disposable income.

When does support end?

Child support ends at 18 unless the child is in high school at 18, then support ends upon graduation from high school or age 21, whichever comes first. Enrollment in a GED program is also considered being enrolled in a "secondary school program of instruction," and support would terminate upon completion of the program or age 21, whichever comes first.

Does support end if the child leaves home early?

No.

Can support be ordered beyond the age of majority?

Yes.

What is the time-limit for collecting past-due support?

10 years from last payment on court record or other form of revival of order on court record.

Is interest charged on past-due support?

Yes, 1% per month simple interest once reduced to a lump-sum judgment. Obligee must compute and file computation with the circuit clerk to make interest collectible.

Addresses

Missouri Bar Association
P.O. Box 119
Jefferson City, MO 65102
(573) 635-4128
www.mobar.org

Department of Social Services
Division of Child Support
Enforcement
P.O. Box 2320
Jefferson City, MO 65102
(573) 751-4301

Office of Child Support
Enforcement Region VII
Federal Office Building
Room 276
601 E. 12th Street
Kansas City, MO 64106
(816) 426-3981

Missouri Head Start
University of Missouri-Columbia
Rock Quarry Center
1400 Rock Quarry Road
Columbia, MO 65211
(573) 884-0579

Montana

Child Custody

What is the age of majority?
18 or upon graduation from high school, whichever is later, but no later than 19.

How is custody divided?
Legal and physical combined.

Is mediation authorized?
Yes.

Will mediation be confidential?
Yes.

Is joint custody allowed?
Permitted despite one parent objecting.

Will a custody evaluation be required?
Not specified.

Are the child's preferences considered?
Yes.

Can the court appoint someone to represent my child?
Yes.

Paternity

Does marriage create a presumption of paternity?
Yes.

Does the father's name on the birth certificate establish paternity?
No.

Is genetic testing used to establish paternity?
Yes, 95% probability.

Child Abuse

Who must report child abuse besides professionals?
Guardians ad litem, clergy, religious healers, Christian Science practitioners.

Are there legally recognized exceptions to child abuse?
Yes, religious exemption, reasonable medical judgment.

How long are child abuse complaints kept?
Expunged within 30 days of the determination.

Child Support

What model is used?
Melson.

Whose income is used?
Both parents. Also, income of a child, new spouse, etc. may be considered as a variance on the guideline support amount.

What methods are used to enforce a support order?
State income tax refund intercept, license revocation/suspension, property seizure and sale, withholding of state funds or benefits, consumer credit (credit bureau) reporting.

What types of income cannot be withheld?

Any amounts by law exempted from judgment, execution, or attachment.

What are the limits on income withholding?

50% of wages and 100% of contract proceeds.

When does support end?

In the event of the child's death, the child's marriage, the child's enlistment in the US armed services, or the child's emancipation in a District Court proceeding.

Does support end if the child leaves home early?

No.

Can support be ordered beyond the age of majority?

Yes.

What is the time-limit for collecting past-due support?

10 years from date payment due for debt accrued prior to 10/1/93; 10 years after termination of obligation for payments due after 10/1/93 BUT the statute is tolled when the obligor is out of state and cannot be served with process; and the entire 10-year statute begins running anew when the obligor acknowledges the debt in writing or makes partial payment or a court or administrative action (including sending a demand letter) is taken to enforce the debt.

Is interest charged on past-due support?

No.

Addresses

Montana Bar Association
P.O. Box 577
Helena, MT 59624
(406) 442-7660
www.montanabar.org

Child Support Enforcement Division
Department of Public Health and Human Services
P.O. Box 202943
Helena, MT 59620
(406) 442-7278

Office of Child Support Enforcement Region VIII
1961 Stout Street
Room 924
Denver, CO 80294
(303) 844-2622

Montana Head Start
P.O. Box 202952
Helena, MT 59620
(406) 444-0589

Admin. for Children and Families
Department of Public Health and Human Services (DPHHS)
Quality Assurance Division (QAD)
P.O. Box 202953
Helena, MT 59620

Nebraska

Child Custody

What is the age of majority?
19, unless the child marries, dies, or is emancipated by the court.

How is custody divided?
Legal and physical combined.

Is mediation authorized?
No.

Will mediation be confidential?
Not specified.

Is joint custody allowed?
Permitted despite one parent objecting.

Will a custody evaluation be required?
Court ordered.

Are the child's preferences considered?
Yes.

Can the court appoint someone to represent my child?
Yes.

Paternity

Does marriage create a presumption of paternity?
Yes.

Does the father's name on the birth certificate establish paternity?
Yes.

Is genetic testing used to establish paternity?
Yes, 99% probability.

Child Abuse

Who must report child abuse besides professionals?
No one.

Are there legally recognized exceptions to child abuse?
No.

How long are child abuse complaints kept?
Expunged promptly or upon good cause shown.

Child Support

What model is used?
Shared Income.

Whose income is used?
Both parents.

What methods are used to enforce a support order?
State income tax refund intercept, license revocation/ suspension, property seizure and sale, withholding of state funds or benefits, consumer credit (credit bureau) reporting, state lottery offset, contempt, criminal non-support.

What types of income cannot be withheld?
SSI, VA Disability.

What are the limits on income withholding?
None, other than the limits in the Consumer Credit Protection Act (CCPA).

When does support end?
When the child reaches 19, marries, dies, or is emancipated by the court, unless the support order specifically extends support after such circumstances.

Does support end if the child leaves home early?
No.

Can support be ordered beyond the age of majority?
Yes.

What is the time-limit for collecting past-due support?
None.

Is interest charged on past-due support?
Yes, child support is considered a judgment. The interest rate on judgments is fixed at a rate equivalent yield of the average accepted auction price for the last auction of one-year Treasury bills, and takes effect two weeks after the publication of the auction price by the Secretary of the Treasury.

Nebraska Dept. of Health and Human Services
Child Support Enforcement Office
P.O. Box 94728
Lincoln, NE 68509
(402) 479-5555

Office of Child Support Enforcement Region VII
Federal Office Building
Room 276
601 E. 12th Street
Kansas City, MO 64106
(816) 426-3981

Nebraska Head Start
Nebraska Department of Education, Office of Children and Families
301 Centennial Mall South
P.O. Box 94987
Lincoln, NE 68509-4987
(402) 471-3501

Admin. for Children and Families
Department of Health and Human Services
Child Care
P.O. Box 95044
Lincoln, NE 68509
(402) 471-7763

Addresses

Nebraska Bar Association
635 South 14th St.
P.O. Box 81809
Lincoln, NE 68501
(402) 475-7091
www.nebar.com

Nevada

Child Custody

What is the age of majority?
18, but if the child is a student in high school who expects to graduate by age 19, then 19.

How is custody divided?
Legal and physical combined.

Is mediation authorized?
Yes.

Will mediation be confidential?
Yes.

Is joint custody allowed?
Available if both parents agree.

Will a custody evaluation be required?
Court ordered.

Are the child's preferences considered?
Yes.

Can the court appoint someone to represent my child?
Yes.

Paternity

Does marriage create a presumption of paternity?
Yes.

Does the father's name on the birth certificate establish paternity?
Yes.

Is genetic testing used to establish paternity?
Yes, 99% probability.

Child Abuse

Who must report child abuse besides professionals?
Clergy, religious healers, alcohol/drug abuse counselors, Christian Science practitioners, probation officers, attorneys.

Are there legally recognized exceptions to child abuse?
Yes, religious exemption.

How long are child abuse complaints kept?
Expunged at the conclusion of the investigation within 60 days after report filed. Sealed no later than 10 years after child is 18.

Child Support

What model is used?
Percent of Income.

Whose income is used?
Noncustodial parent. The gross monthly income of the noncustodial parent is used to compute the guideline support. Currently, for one child support is 18% of gross monthly income, for two children 25%, for three children 29%, for four 4 children 31%, and for each additional child, add two percent.

What methods are used to enforce a support order?

License revocation/suspension, property seizure and sale, withholding of state funds or benefits, consumer credit (credit bureau) reporting, creditor's claim against estate, U.S. Attorney referrals.

What types of income cannot be withheld?

Exempted funds such as TANF, SSI, VA disability.

What are the limits on income withholding?

None, other than the limits in the Consumer Credit Protection Act (CCPA).

When does support end?

18, but if the child is a student in high school who expects to graduate by age 19, then 19.

Does support end if the child leaves home early?

No.

Can support be ordered beyond the age of majority?

Yes.

What is the time-limit for collecting past-due support?

None if order exists, but if there is no order, retroactive support may be requested back 4 years.

Is interest charged on past-due support?

No.

Addresses

Nevada Bar Association
600 East Charleston Boulevard
Las Vegas, NV 89104
(702) 382-2200
www.nvbar.org

Child Support Enforcement
Program
Nevada State Welfare Division
2527 North Carson Street
Carson City, NV 89710
(775) 687-4744

Office of Child Support
Enforcement Region IX
50 United Nations Plaza
Room 450
San Francisco, CA 94102
(415) 437-8400

Nevada Head Start
Community Connections
Nevada Department of Human
Resources
3987 South McCarran Boulevard
Reno, NV 89502
(775) 688-2284

Admin. for Children and Families
Department of Human Resources
Division of Child and Family
Services
3920 E. Idaho Street
Elko, NV 89801
(775) 753-1237

New Hampshire

Child Custody

What is the age of majority?
18.

How is custody divided?
Legal and physical separate.

Is mediation authorized?
No.

Will mediation be confidential?
Not specified.

Is joint custody allowed?
Required unless health or safety compromised.

Will a custody evaluation be required?
Not specified.

Are the child's preferences considered?
Yes.

Can the court appoint someone to represent my child?
Yes.

Paternity

Does marriage create a presumption of paternity?
Yes.

Does the father's name on the birth certificate establish paternity?
No.

Is genetic testing used to establish paternity?
Yes, 97% probability.

Child Abuse

Who must report child abuse besides professionals?
Christian Science practitioners, clergy.

Are there legally recognized exceptions to child abuse?
Yes, religious exemption.

How long are child abuse complaints kept?
Retained from 3 to 7 years.

Child Support

What model is used?
Shared Income.

Whose income is used?
Custodial parent.

What methods are used to enforce a support order?
License revocation/suspension, property seizure and sale, withholding of state funds or benefits, consumer credit (credit bureau) reporting. Obligors have the right to either a court or administrative review for any administrative enforcement action.

What types of income cannot be withheld?
Public Assistance, including TANF, APTD, SSI, Food Stamps

and general assistance received
from a county or town.

What are the limits on income withholding?

None, other than the limits in the
Consumer Credit Protection Act
(CCPA).

When does support end?

When the child reaches 18 or
ends high school, whichever is
later, or becomes married or
becomes a member of the armed
services, or is declared legally
dependent beyond that age due
to mental or physical disability,
or a court has otherwise ordered
support to continue beyond age
18.

Does support end if the child leaves home early?

No.

Can support be ordered beyond the age of majority?

Yes.

What is the time-limit for collecting past-due support?

Pursuant to RSA 508:5 Once a
debt is a judgment the statute of
limitations is 20 years and
pursuant to RSA 458:17,VII,
support payments become
judgments when due and
payable by operation of law.

Is interest charged on past-due support?

No.

Addresses

New Hampshire Bar Association
112 Pleasant St.
Concord, NH 03301
(603) 224-6942
www.nhbar.org

Office of Child Support
Division of Human Services
Health and Human Services
Building
6 Hazen Drive
Concord, NH 03301
(603) 271-4427

Office of Child Support
Enforcement Region I
John F. Kennedy Federal Bldg.
Room 2000
Boston, MA 02203
(617) 565-10205

New Hampshire Head Start
New Hampshire Department of
Health and Human Services
Child Development Bureau
129 Pleasant Street
Concord, NH 03301
(603) 271-4454

Admin. for Children and Families
Department of Health and
Human Services
Office of Program Support
129 Pleasant Street
Concord, NH 03301
(603) 271-4624

New Jersey

Child Custody

What is the age of majority?
18, however attaining this age does not automatically emancipate the child.

How is custody divided?
Legal and physical separate.

Is mediation authorized?
Yes.

Will mediation be confidential?
Yes.

Is joint custody allowed?
Permitted despite one parent objecting.

Will a custody evaluation be required?
Court ordered.

Are the child's preferences considered?
Yes.

Can the court appoint someone to represent my child?
Yes.

Paternity

Does marriage create a presumption of paternity?
No.

Does the father's name on the birth certificate establish paternity?
Yes.

Is genetic testing used to establish paternity?
Yes, 95% probability.

Child Abuse

Who must report child abuse besides professionals?
No one.

Are there legally recognized exceptions to child abuse?
No.

How long are child abuse complaints kept?
Expunged upon determination.

Child Support

What model is used?
Shared Income.

Whose income is used?
Both parents.

What methods are used to enforce a support order?
State income tax refund intercept, license revocation/ suspension, property seizure and sale, withholding of state funds or benefits, consumer credit (credit bureau) reporting, incarceration.

What types of income cannot be withheld?
TANF, Food Stamps, General Assistance, Supplemental Security Income for the Aged, Blind or Disabled, Veterans' Disability payments.

What are the limits on income withholding?
None, other than the limits in the Consumer Credit Protection Act (CCPA).

When does support end?
Support ends when the child is emancipated, which is determined by the court on a case by case basis.

Does support end if the child leaves home early?
No.

Can support be ordered beyond the age of majority?
Yes.

What is the time-limit for collecting past-due support?
None.

Is interest charged on past-due support?
Yes.

Addresses

New Jersey Bar Association
New Jersey Law Center
One Constitution Square
New Brunswick, NJ 08901
(732) 249-5000
www.njsba.com

Division of Family Development
Department of Human Services
Bureau of Child Support and
Paternity Programs CN 716
Trenton, NJ 08625
(609) 588-2915

Office of Child Support
Enforcement Region II
26 Federal Plaza
Room 4114
New York, NY 10278
(212) 264-2890

New Jersey Head Start
DHS Office of Early Care and
Education
P.O. Box 700
Trenton, NJ 08625
(609) 984-5321

Admin. for Children and Families
Division of Youth and Family
Services
P.O. Box 717
Trenton, NJ 08625
(609) 292-1018

New Mexico

Child Custody

What is the age of majority?
18, unless the child is still in
High School, then up to 19.

How is custody divided?
Legal and physical combined.

Is mediation authorized?
Yes.

Will mediation be confidential?
Not specified.

Is joint custody allowed?
Required unless health or safety
compromised.

**Will a custody evaluation be
required?**
Court ordered.

**Are the child's preferences
considered?**
Yes.

**Can the court appoint someone
to represent my child?**
Yes.

Paternity

**Does marriage create a
presumption of paternity?**
Yes.

**Does the father's name on the
birth certificate establish
paternity?**
No.

**Is genetic testing used to
establish paternity?**
Yes, 99% probability.

Child Abuse

**Who must report child abuse
besides professionals?**
Judges.

**Are there legally recognized
exceptions to child abuse?**
Yes, religious exemption.

**How long are child abuse
complaints kept?**
Expunged 2 years after final
release from legal custody and
supervision; or if 2 years have
elapsed since entry of any other
judgement not involving legal
custody or supervision.

Child Support

What model is used?
Shared Income

Whose income is used?
Both parents.

**What methods are used to
enforce a support order?**
State income tax refund
intercept, license revocation/
suspension, property seizure and
sale, withholding of state funds
or benefits, consumer credit
(credit bureau) reporting,
passport denial and gaming/
lottery reporting.

What types of income cannot be withheld?
Public assistance, required withholdings.

What are the limits on income withholding?
50%.

When does support end?
18, unless the child is still in High School, then up to 19.

Does support end if the child leaves home early?
No.

Can support be ordered beyond the age of majority?
Yes.

What is the time-limit for collecting past-due support?
14 years.

Is interest charged on past-due support?
Yes, at the court's discretion.

Addresses

New Mexico Bar Association
P. O. Box 25883
Albuquerque, NM 87125
(505) 797-6000
www.nmbar.org

Child Support Enforcement
Bureau
Department of Human Services
P.O. Box 25109
Santa Fe, NM 87504
(505) 476-7040

Office of Child Support
Enforcement Region VI
1301 Young Street
Suite 914
Dallas, TX 75202
(214) 767-9648

New Mexico Head Start
Department of Children, Youth
and Families
P.O. Drawer 5160
Sante Fe, NM 87502
(505) 827-7499

Admin. for Children and Families
PERA Building
Room 111
P.O. Drawer 5160
Santa Fe, NM 87502
(505) 827-4185

New York

Child Custody

What is the age of majority?
21.

How is custody divided?
Legal and physical combined.

Is mediation authorized?
No.

Will mediation be confidential?
Not specified.

Is joint custody allowed?
Available if both parents agree.

Will a custody evaluation be required?
Not specified.

Are the child's preferences considered?
Yes.

Can the court appoint someone to represent my child?
Yes.

Paternity

Does marriage create a presumption of paternity?
Yes.

Does the father's name on the birth certificate establish paternity?
Yes.

Is genetic testing used to establish paternity?
Yes, 95% probability.

Child Abuse

Who must report child abuse besides professionals?
Alcoholism/substance abuse counselors, District Attorneys, Christian Science practitioners.

Are there legally recognized exceptions to child abuse?
No.

How long are child abuse complaints kept?
Sealed upon investigation. Expunged 10 years after youngest child named in report is 18, or upon successful challenge by subject.

Child Support

What model is used?
Shared Income.

Whose income is used?
Both parents. Under limited circumstances, new spouse's incomes can be considered.

What methods are used to enforce a support order?
State income tax refund intercept, license revocation/suspension, property seizure and sale, consumer credit (credit bureau) reporting, lottery intercept, federal tax refund offset process, property executions, medical support executions, issuance of money judgments, cash undertakings, criminal prosecution.

What types of income cannot be withheld?

Public assistance benefits paid pursuant to the social services law and federal supplemental security income.

What are the limits on income withholding?

Amounts deducted for arrears payments capped at 40% of disposable income.

When does support end?

21.

Does support end if the child leaves home early?

No.

Can support be ordered beyond the age of majority?

Yes.

What is the time-limit for collecting past-due support?

20 years from date of default in payment regardless of whether or not the past due has been reduced to a judgment for support orders entered after 8/7/87; 6 years for default in payment on orders entered on or before 8/7/87; 20 years for all defaults in payment which have been granted as a money judgment.

Is interest charged on past-due support?

No.

Addresses

New York Bar Association
1 Elk St.
Albany, NY 12207
(518) 463-3200
www.nysba.org

Office of Child Support
Enforcement
Department of Social Services
P.O. Box 14
Albany, NY 12260
(518) 474-9081

Office of Child Support
Enforcement Region II
26 Federal Plaza
Room 4114
New York, NY 10278
(212) 264-2890

New York Head Start
New York State Council on
Children and Families
5 Empire State Plaza
Suite 2810
Albany, NY 12223
(518) 474-6294

Admin. for Children and Families
NY State Department of Family
assistance
Office of Children and Family
Services
Bureau of Early Childhood
Services
52 Washington Street
Riverview Center 6th Floor
Rensselaer, NY 12144
(518) 474-9454

North Carolina

Child Custody

What is the age of majority?
18, unless the child is attending secondary school full time or up to age 20 whichever comes first.

How is custody divided?
Legal and physical combined.

Is mediation authorized?
Yes.

Will mediation be confidential?
Yes.

Is joint custody allowed?
Available if both parents agree.

Will a custody evaluation be required?
Not specified.

Are the child's preferences considered?
Yes.

Can the court appoint someone to represent my child?
No.

Paternity

Does marriage create a presumption of paternity?
Yes.

Does the father's name on the birth certificate establish paternity?
Yes.

Is genetic testing used to establish paternity?
Yes, 97% probability.

Child Abuse

Who must report child abuse besides professionals?
Any institution.

Are there legally recognized exceptions to child abuse?
No.

How long are child abuse complaints kept?
Indefinitely.

Child Support

What model is used?
Shared Income.

Whose income is used?
Noncustodial parent.

What methods are used to enforce a support order?
State income tax refund intercept, license revocation/suspension, property seizure and sale, withholding of state funds or benefits, consumer credit (credit bureau) reporting, increase in income withholding, work requirement, work release, bond.

What types of income cannot be withheld?
AFDC, SSI, federal, payments under Federal Tort Claims Act, federal grants, fellowships, VA

disability, VA Educational Assistance, refunds from erroneous payment or overpayment of federal income tax, and ROTC.

What are the limits on income withholding?
None, other than the limits in the Consumer Credit Protection Act (CCPA).

When does support end?
18.

Does support end if the child leaves home early?
No.

Can support be ordered beyond the age of majority?
Yes.

What is the time-limit for collecting past-due support?
10 years.

Is interest charged on past-due support?
No.

Addresses

North Carolina Bar Association
P.O. Box 3688
Cary, NC 27519
(919) 677-0561
www.barlinc.org

Child Support Enforcement Section
Division of Social Services
Department of Human Resources
100 East Six Forks Road
Raleigh, NC 27609
(919) 571-4114

Office of Child Support Enforcement Region IV
61 Forsyth Street, S.W.
Suite 4M60
Atlanta, GA 30303
(404) 562-2900

North Carolina Head Start
Division of Child Development
319 Chapanoke Road
2201 Mail Service Center 27699-2201
Raleigh, NC 27603
(919) 662-4543

Admin. for Children and Families
Division of Child Development
2201 Mail Service Center
Raleigh, NC 27699
(919) 662-4499
(919) 662-4527

North Dakota

Child Custody

What is the age of majority?
18.

How is custody divided?
Legal and physical combined.

Is mediation authorized?
Yes.

Will mediation be confidential?
Yes.

Is joint custody allowed?
Not specified.

Will a custody evaluation be required?
Court ordered.

Are the child's preferences considered?
Yes.

Can the court appoint someone to represent my child?
No.

Paternity

Does marriage create a presumption of paternity?
Yes.

Does the father's name on the birth certificate establish paternity?
No.

Is genetic testing used to establish paternity?
Yes, 95% probability.

Child Abuse

Who must report child abuse besides professionals?
Clergy, religious healers, addiction counselors.

Are there legally recognized exceptions to child abuse?
No.

How long are child abuse complaints kept?
Indefinitely.

Child Support

What model is used?
Percent of Income.

Whose income is used?
Noncustodial parent.

What methods are used to enforce a support order?
State income tax refund intercept, license revocation/suspension, property seizure and sale, withholding of state funds or benefits, consumer credit (credit bureau) reporting, income withholding, contempt of court, criminal non-support statutes.

What types of income cannot be withheld?
Public assistance benefits administered under state law.

What are the limits on income withholding?
None, other than the limits in the Consumer Credit Protection Act.

When does support end?

18. If the child is enrolled and attending high school and resides with a person to whom duty of support is owed, the court can extend the child support obligation until the child is 19 or graduates from high school, whichever occurs first.

Does support end if the child leaves home early?

No.

Can support be ordered beyond the age of majority?

Yes.

What is the time-limit for collecting past-due support?

Effective 4/2/99, past-due child support is no longer subject to statute of limitations. Past-due child support which had been affected by the statute of limitations prior to 4/2/99, is not revived, however, application of the statute of limitations, while it serves to bar certain judicial enforcement remedies, does not extinguish the debt.

Is interest charged on past-due support?

Yes, 12% per year simple.

Addresses

North Dakota Bar Association
515 1/2 East Broadway
Suite 100
Bismarck, ND 58501
(701) 255-1404
www.sband.org

Department of Human Services
Child Support Enforcement
Agency
P.O. Box 7190
Bismarck, ND 58507
(701) 328-3582

Office of Child Support
Enforcement Region VIII
1961 Stout Street
Room 924
Denver, CO 80294
(303) 844-2622

North Dakota Head Start
North Dakota Department of
Human Services
Children and Family Services
Division #325
600 East Boulevard Avenue
Bismarck, ND 58505
(701) 328-1711

Admin. for Children and Families
Department of Human Services
Early Childhood Services
600 East Boulevard
State Capitol Building
Bismarck, ND 58505
(701) 328-4809

Ohio

Child Custody

What is the age of majority?
18.

How is custody divided?
Legal and physical separate.

Is mediation authorized?
Yes.

Will mediation be confidential?
Yes.

Is joint custody allowed?
Permitted despite one parent
objecting.

**Will a custody evaluation be
required?**
Court ordered.

**Are the child's preferences
considered?**
Yes.

**Can the court appoint someone
to represent my child?**
Yes.

Paternity

**Does marriage create a
presumption of paternity?**
Yes.

**Does the father's name on the
birth certificate establish
paternity?**
No.

**Is genetic testing used to
establish paternity?**
Yes, 99% probability.

Child Abuse

**Who must report child abuse
besides professionals?**
Attorneys, religious healers.

**Are there legally recognized
exceptions to child abuse?**
Yes, corporal punishment,
religious exemption.

**How long are child abuse
complaints kept?**
Indefinitely.

Child Support

What model is used?
Shared Income.

Whose income is used?
Both parents. In addition, new
spouse's or child's income may
be considered by the court in a
request for a deviation, however,
the guidelines worksheets do not
include any incomes other than
the parents' income.

**What methods are used to
enforce a support order?**
State income tax refund
intercept, license revocation/
suspension, property seizure and
sale, withholding of state funds
or benefits, consumer credit
(credit bureau) reporting, a
variety of income type intercepts
including lottery winnings and

other lump sums, criminal non-support including both misdemeanor and felony penalties, contempt, withholding of prisoner earnings.

What types of income cannot be withheld?
Benefits from means-tested public assistance programs or benefits for any service connected disability.

What are the limits on income withholding?
None, other than the limits in the Consumer Credit Protection Act (CCPA).

When does support end?
18, or as long as the child attends high school on a full time basis, or a court order requires support to continue. Unless specified in the court order, support does not extend beyond 19.

Does support end if the child leaves home early?
No.

Can support be ordered beyond the age of majority?
Yes.

What is the time-limit for collecting past-due support?
There is no statute of limitations on collection of child support.

Is interest charged on past-due support?
No.

Addresses

Ohio Bar Association
1700 Lake Shore Drive
Columbus, OH 43204
(800) 282-6556
www.ohiobar.org

Office of Child Support
Enforcement
Department of Human Services
30 East Broad Street - 31st Floor
Columbus, OH 43266
(614) 752-6561

Office of Child Support
Enforcement Region V
233 N. Michigan Avenue
Suite 400
Chicago, IL 60601
(312) 353-4237

Ohio Head Start
Office of Early Childhood
Education
Ohio Department of Education
25 East Front Street
3rd Floor
Columbus, OH 43215
(614) 466-0224

Admin. for Children and Families
Ohio Department of Job &
Family Services
Bureau of Child Care and
Development
255 East Main Street
3rd Floor
Columbus, OH 43215
(614) 466-1043

Oklahoma

Child Custody

What is the age of majority?
18.

How is custody divided?
Legal and physical combined.

Is mediation authorized?
No.

Will mediation be confidential?
Not specified.

Is joint custody allowed?
Permitted despite one parent
objecting.

**Will a custody evaluation be
required?**
Not specified.

**Are the child's preferences
considered?**
Yes.

**Can the court appoint someone
to represent my child?**
No.

Paternity

**Does marriage create a
presumption of paternity?**
Yes.

**Does the father's name on the
birth certificate establish
paternity?**
No.

**Is genetic testing used to
establish paternity?**
Yes, 95% probability. If the
results of genetic testing
establish paternity at 98% or
higher, it is considered
conclusive.

Child Abuse

**Who must report child abuse
besides professionals?**
Film and photographic
processors.

**Are there legally recognized
exceptions to child abuse?**
Yes, religious exemption,
corporal punishment.

**How long are child abuse
complaints kept?**
Indefinitely.

Child Support

What model is used?
Shared Income.

Whose income is used?
Both parents.

**What methods are used to
enforce a support order?**
State income tax refund
intercept, license revocation/
suspension, property seizure and
sale, withholding of state funds
or benefits, consumer credit
(credit bureau) reporting.

What types of income cannot be withheld?
None.

What are the limits on income withholding?
None, other than the limits in the Consumer Credit Protection Act (CCPA).

When does support end?
18 or as long as the child is a dependent and is still in high school.

Does support end if the child leaves home early?
No.

Can support be ordered beyond the age of majority?
Yes.

What is the time-limit for collecting past-due support?
None.

Is interest charged on past-due support?
Yes, 10% per year.

Addresses

Oklahoma Bar Association
P.O. Box 53036
1901 N. Lincoln Blvd.
Oklahoma City, OK 73152
(405) 416-7000
www.okbar.org

Department of Human Services
P.O. Box 53552
Oklahoma City, OK 73125
(405) 522-5871

Office of Child Support
Enforcement Region VI
1301 Young Street
Suite 914
Dallas, TX 75202
(214) 767-9648

Oklahoma Head Start
OACAA
2915 Classen Suite 215
Oklahoma City, OK 73106
(405) 524-4124

Admin. for Children and Families
Department of Human Services
Office of Child Care
P.O. Box 25352
Oklahoma City, OK 73125
(405) 521-3561

Oregon

Child Custody

What is the age of majority?
18.

How is custody divided?
Legal and physical combined.

Is mediation authorized?
Yes.

Will mediation be confidential?
Yes.

Is joint custody allowed?
Available if both parents agree.

Will a custody evaluation be required?
Not specified.

Are the child's preferences considered?
Yes.

Can the court appoint someone to represent my child?
Yes.

Paternity

Does marriage create a presumption of paternity?
Yes.

Does the father's name on the birth certificate establish paternity?
No.

Is genetic testing used to establish paternity?
Yes, 99% probability.

Child Abuse

Who must report child abuse besides professionals?
Attorneys, clergy, firefighters, CASAs.

Are there legally recognized exceptions to child abuse?
Yes, corporal punishment.

How long are child abuse complaints kept?
Indefinitely.

Child Support

What model is used?
Shared Income.

Whose income is used?
Both parents.

What methods are used to enforce a support order?
State income tax refund intercept, license revocation/suspension, property seizure and sale, withholding of state funds or benefits, consumer credit (credit bureau) reporting, income withholding, contempt, criminal non-support, security deposit intercept.

What types of income cannot be withheld?
Supplemental Security Income (SSI), Veteran's Benefits.

What are the limits on income withholding?
Withholding plus fee may not

exceed 50% of disposable income unless by court order, but still may not exceed Consumer Credit Protection Act (CCPA) limits. Arrears-only cases must retain income equal to 160 hours multiplied by the federal minimum wage rate before withholding occurs.

When does support end?
18. Support may be extended to 21 if the child is attending school half-time or more.

Does support end if the child leaves home early?
No.

Can support be ordered beyond the age of majority?
Yes.

What is the time-limit for collecting past-due support?
Prior to 1/1/94, each overdue payment was a judgment that expired 10 years from the date of accrual if not renewed. Any arrears unexpired on 1/1/94 and any child support judgment entered after that date expires 25 years from the date of the original child support judgment.

Is interest charged on past-due support?
Yes, 9%. Interest is added only if a party requests and provides an accounting that includes a calculation of accrued interest. Periodic updates must be provided in order for a case to reflect ongoing interest accrual.

Addresses

Oregon Bar Association
5200 SW Meadows Road
Lake Oswego, OR 97035
(503) 620-0222
www.osbar.org

Department of Justice
Division of Child Support
1495 Edgewater N.W.
Suite 290
Salem, OR 97304
(503) 986-5950

Office of Child Support
Enforcement Region X
2201 Sixth Avenue
Blanchard Plaza
Suite 600
Seattle, WA 98121
(206) 615-2547

Oregon Head Start
Oregon Department of Education
Public Service Building
255 Capitol Street, NE
Salem, OR 97310
(503) 378-3600

Admin. for Children and Families
Employment Department
Child Care Division
875 Union Street, NE
Salem, OR 97311
(503) 947-1400

Pennsylvania

Child Custody

What is the age of majority?
18.

How is custody divided?
Legal and physical separate.

Is mediation authorized?
Yes.

Will mediation be confidential?
Not specified.

Is joint custody allowed?
Available if both parents agree.

Will a custody evaluation be required?
Court ordered.

Are the child's preferences considered?
Yes.

Can the court appoint someone to represent my child?
Yes.

Paternity

Does marriage create a presumption of paternity?
Yes.

Does the father's name on the birth certificate establish paternity?
No.

Is genetic testing used to establish paternity?
Yes, 99% probability.

Child Abuse

Who must report child abuse besides professionals?
Funeral directors, Christian Science practitioners, clergy.

Are there legally recognized exceptions to child abuse?
Yes, poverty, religious exemption.

How long are child abuse complaints kept?
Expunged within 120 days after one year after report is received by the department, or when child turns 23, or upon good cause shown.

Child Support

What model is used?
Percent of Income. However, this model is not followed if the custodial parent's income exceeds $15,000/month.

Whose income is used?
Custodial parent.

What methods are used to enforce a support order?
License revocation/suspension, property seizure and sale, withholding of state funds or benefits, consumer credit (credit bureau) reporting, imprisonment, fine, probation.

What types of income cannot be withheld?
Non-periodic Income, Public Assistance Supplemental Social

Security, and court-ordered Alimony Payments.

What are the limits on income withholding?

None, other than the limits in the Consumer Credit Protection Act (CCPA). However, local courts have discretionary authority to place limits on income withholding.

When does support end?

18 or graduation from high school unless the child has a disability (mental, developmental or physical), in which case the court can order support to continue. It does not occur automatically.

Does support end if the child leaves home early?

No.

Can support be ordered beyond the age of majority?

Yes.

What is the time-limit for collecting past-due support?

None.

Is interest charged on past-due support?

No.

Addresses

Pennsylvania Bar Association
100 South Street
P.O. Box 186
Harrisburg, PA 17108
(717) 238-6715
www.pabar.org

Bureau of Child Support Enforcement
Department of Public Welfare
P.O. Box 8018
Harrisburg, PA 17105
(717) 783-5184

Office of Child Support Enforcement Region III
150 S. Independence Mall West
Suite 864
Philadelphia, PA 19106
(215) 861-4000

Pennsylvania Head Start Center for Schools and Communities
1300 Market Street
Suite 12
Lemoyne, PA 17043
(717) 763-1661

Admin. for Children and Families
Department of Public Welfare,
Bureau of Child Day Care
Office of Children, Youth & Families
Bertolino Bldg., 4th Floor
P.O. Box 2675
Harrisburg, PA 17105
(717) 787-8691

Rhode Island

Child Custody

What is the age of majority?
18.

How is custody divided?
Legal and physical combined.

Is mediation authorized?
Yes.

Will mediation be confidential?
Yes.

Is joint custody allowed?
No statutes.

Will a custody evaluation be required?
Not specified.

Are the child's preferences considered?
Yes.

Can the court appoint someone to represent my child?
Yes.

Paternity

Does marriage create a presumption of paternity?
Yes.

Does the father's name on the birth certificate establish paternity?
No.

Is genetic testing used to establish paternity?
Yes, 97% probability.

Child Abuse

Who must report child abuse besides professionals?
No one.

Are there legally recognized exceptions to child abuse?
No.

How long are child abuse complaints kept?
Expunged 3 years after final determination.

Child Support

What model is used?
Shared Income.

Whose income is used?
Both parents.

What methods are used to enforce a support order?
State income tax refund intercept, license revocation/ suspension, property seizure and sale, withholding of state funds or benefits, consumer credit (credit bureau) reporting, contempt referral to the Attorney General and U.S. Attorneys office.

What types of income cannot be withheld?
Veterans benefits.

What are the limits on income withholding?
None, other than the limits in the Consumer Credit Protection Act.

When does support end?
No automatic termination.

**Does support end if the child
leaves home early?**
Yes.

**Can support be ordered beyond
the age of majority?**
Yes.

**What is the time-limit for
collecting past-due support?**
None.

**Is interest charged on past-due
support?**
Yes, 12%.

Addresses

Rhode Island Bar Association
115 Cedar St.
Providence, RI 02903
(401) 421-5740
www.ribar.com

Rhode Island Child Support
Services
Department of Human Services
77 Dorrance Street
Providence, RI 02903
(401) 222-2847

Office of Child Support
Enforcement Region I
John F. Kennedy Federal Bldg.
Room 2000
Boston, MA 02203
(617) 565-10205

Rhode Island Head Start
Department of Human Services
Louis Pasteur Building
600 New London Avenue
Cranston, RI 02920
(401) 464-3071

Admin. for Children and Families
Rhode Island Department of
Children, Youth, and Families
101 Friendship Street
Providence, RI 02903
(401) 528-3624

South Carolina

Child Custody

What is the age of majority?
18.

How is custody divided?
Legal and physical combined.

Is mediation authorized?
Yes.

Will mediation be confidential?
Not specified.

Is joint custody allowed?
Available if both parents agree.

Will a custody evaluation be required?
Not specified.

Are the child's preferences considered?
Yes.

Can the court appoint someone to represent my child?
Yes.

Paternity

Does marriage create a presumption of paternity?
Yes.

Does the father's name on the birth certificate establish paternity?
Yes.

Is genetic testing used to establish paternity?
Yes, 95% probability.

Child Abuse

Who must report child abuse besides professionals?
Judges, funeral home employees, Christian Science practitioners, film and photographic processors, religious healers, substance abuse treatment staff.

Are there legally recognized exceptions to child abuse?
Yes, corporal punishment.

How long are child abuse complaints kept?
Expunged immediately upon determination or 7 years after services are terminated.

Child Support

What model is used?
Shared Income.

Whose income is used?
Custodial parent.

What methods are used to enforce a support order?
State income tax refund intercept, license revocation/suspension, property seizure and sale, withholding of state funds or benefits, consumer credit (credit bureau) reporting.

What types of income cannot be withheld?
None.

What are the limits on income withholding?

None, other than the limits in the Consumer Credit Protection Act (CCPA).

When does support end?

A court order is necessary to end child support.

Does support end if the child leaves home early?

No.

Can support be ordered beyond the age of majority?

Yes.

What is the time-limit for collecting past-due support?

None.

Is interest charged on past-due support?

No.

Addresses

South Carolina Bar Association
950 Taylor St.
Columbia, SC 29202
(803) 799-6653
www.scbar.org

Department of Social Services
Child Support Enforcement
Division
P.O. Box 1469
Columbia, SC 29202
(803) 898-9341

Office of Child Support
Enforcement Region IV
61 Forsyth Street, S.W.
Suite 4M60
Atlanta, GA 30303
(404) 562-2900

South Carolina Head Start
South Carolina Department of
Health and Human Services
1801 Main Street
10th Floor
Columbia, SC 29201
(803) 898-2550

Admin. for Children and Families
Department of Social Services
P.O. Box 1520
Room 520
Columbia, SC 29202
(803) 898-7345

South Dakota

Child Custody

What is the age of majority?
18.

How is custody divided?
Legal and physical combined.

Is mediation authorized?
Yes.

Will mediation be confidential?
Not specified.

Is joint custody allowed?
Permitted despite one parent objecting.

Will a custody evaluation be required?
Court ordered.

Are the child's preferences considered?
Yes.

Can the court appoint someone to represent my child?
No.

Paternity

Does marriage create a presumption of paternity?
Yes.

Does the father's name on the birth certificate establish paternity?
No.

Is genetic testing used to establish paternity?
Yes, 99% probability.

Child Abuse

Who must report child abuse besides professionals?
Chemical dependency counselors, religious healers, parole or court services officers, employees of domestic abuse shelters.

Are there legally recognized exceptions to child abuse?
No.

How long are child abuse complaints kept?
Expunged upon successful challenge by subject, no longer than 3 years.

Child Support

What model is used?
Shared Income.

Whose income is used?
Custodial parent.

What methods are used to enforce a support order?
License revocation/suspension, property seizure and sale, withholding of state funds or benefits, consumer credit (credit bureau) reporting, lien against estate and settlements, lottery offset, order to show cause hearings.

What types of income cannot be withheld?

Supplemental Security Income (SSI), VA Benefits, Work Release Earnings of inmates of the State Penitentiary, State Retirement Funds, Census Bureau Earnings, Work Study.

What are the limits on income withholding?

The total amount of arrearage may be withheld from personal property, money and credits, or other income not listed. However, withholding is limited to 50% of wages, salaries, commissions, bonuses, compensation as an independent contractor, workers compensation, unemployment compensation or disability benefits.

When does support end?

18, or until 19 years of age, if the child is a full-time student in a secondary school.

Does support end if the child leaves home early?

No.

Can support be ordered beyond the age of majority?

Yes.

What is the time-limit for collecting past-due support?

20 years from date support is due.

Is interest charged on past-due support?

Yes, 1% per month.

Addresses

South Dakota Bar Association
222 East Capitol Avenue
Pierre, SD 57501
(605) 224-7554
(800) 952-2333
www.sdbar.org

Office of Child Support
Enforcement
Department of Social Services
700 Governor's Drive
Pierre, SD 57501
(605) 773-3641

Office of Child Support
Enforcement Region VIII
1961 Stout Street
Room 924
Denver, CO 80294
(303) 844-2622

South Dakota Head Start
South Dakota Department of
Education and Cultural Affairs
(DECA)
700 Governors Drive
Pierre, SD 57501
(605) 773-4640

Admin. for Children and Families
Department of Social Services
Child Care Services
Kneip Building
700 Governors Drive
Pierre, SD 57501
(605) 773-4766

Tennessee

Child Custody

What is the age of majority?
18.

How is custody divided?
Legal and physical combined.

Is mediation authorized?
No.

Will mediation be confidential?
Not specified.

Is joint custody allowed?
Available if both parents agree.

Will a custody evaluation be required?
Not specified.

Are the child's preferences considered?
Yes.

Can the court appoint someone to represent my child?
Yes.

Paternity

Does marriage create a presumption of paternity?
Yes.

Does the father's name on the birth certificate establish paternity?
Yes.

Is genetic testing used to establish paternity?
Yes, 99% probability.

Child Abuse

Who must report child abuse besides professionals?
Judges, neighbors, relatives, friends, religious healers.

Are there legally recognized exceptions to child abuse?
No.

How long are child abuse complaints kept?
Indefinitely.

Child Support

What model is used?
Percent of Income.

Whose income is used?
Noncustodial parent.

What methods are used to enforce a support order?
License revocation/suspension, property seizure and sale, withholding of state funds or benefits, consumer credit (credit bureau) reporting, genetic testing.

What types of income cannot be withheld?
None.

What are the limits on income withholding?
The amount withheld must not exceed 50% after FICA, withholding taxes and health insurance, which covers the child.

When does support end?
18. However, if the child is still in high school, support ends when the child graduates from high school or when the class the child is in when he/she reaches 18 graduates.

Does support end if the child leaves home early?
No.

Can support be ordered beyond the age of majority?
Yes.

What is the time-limit for collecting past-due support?
None.

Is interest charged on past-due support?
No.

Addresses

Tennessee Bar Association
221 Fourth Avenue North
Suite 400
Nashville, TN 37219-2198
(615) 383-7421
www.tba.org

Child Support Services
Department of Human Services
Citizens Plaza Building
12th Floor
400 Deadrick Street
Nashville, TN 37248
(615) 313-4880

Office of Child Support
Enforcement Region IV
61 Forsyth Street, S.W.
Suite 4M60
Atlanta, GA 30303
(404) 562-2900

Tennessee Head Start
Andrew Johnson Tower, 7th Floor
710 James Robertson Parkway
Nashville, TN 37243
(615) 741-4849

Admin. for Children and Families
Department of Human Services
Child Care Services Unit
Citizens Plaza
14th Floor
400 Deaderick Street
Nashville, TN 37248
(615) 313-4778

Texas

Child Custody

What is the age of majority?
18.

How is custody divided?
Legal and physical separate.

Is mediation authorized?
Yes.

Will mediation be confidential?
Not specified.

Is joint custody allowed?
Available if both parents agree.

Will a custody evaluation be required?
Not specified.

Are the child's preferences considered?
Yes (age 12).

Can the court appoint someone to represent my child?
Yes.

Paternity

Does marriage create a presumption of paternity?
Yes.

Does the father's name on the birth certificate establish paternity?
Yes.

Is genetic testing used to establish paternity?
Yes, 99% probability.

Child Abuse

Who must report child abuse besides professionals?
Juvenile probation officers, employees or clinics that provide reproductive services.

Are there legally recognized exceptions to child abuse?
Yes, corporal punishment.

How long are child abuse complaints kept?
Indefinitely.

Child Support

What model is used?
Percent of Income. Adjusted for obligations to other children.

Whose income is used?
Noncustodial parent.

What methods are used to enforce a support order?
License revocation/suspension, property seizure and sale, withholding of state funds or benefits, consumer credit (credit bureau) reporting, lottery intercept.

What types of income cannot be withheld?
Return of principal or capital, accounts receivable, public assistance payments.

What are the limits on income withholding?
None, other than the limits in the

Consumer Credit Protection Act (CCPA).

When does support end?
18 or until the child graduates high school.

Does support end if the child leaves home early?
No.

Can support be ordered beyond the age of majority?
Yes.

What is the time-limit for collecting past-due support?
If any arrears are owed, the court retains jurisdiction to take enforcement action until the arrears are paid in full.

Is interest charged on past-due support?
Yes, interest accrues from the date the Texas order is rendered at the rate of 6% simple per year.

Addresses

Texas Bar Association
1414 Colorado
Austin, Texas 78701
(512) 463-1463
(800) 204-2222
www.texasbar.com

Office of the Attorney General
State Office
Child Support Division
P.O. Box 12017
Austin, TX 78711-2017
(512) 460-6000

Office of Child Support
Enforcement Region VI
1301 Young Street
Suite 914
Dallas, TX 75202
(214) 767-9648

Texas Head Start
Office of the Governor
7000 Fannin Street
Suite 2355
Houston, TX 77030
(713) 500-3835

Admin. for Children and Families
P.O. Box 149030
M.C. E-550
Austin, TX 78714-9030
(800) 862-5252
(512) 438-3267

Utah

Child Custody

What is the age of majority?
18.

How is custody divided?
Legal and physical separate.

Is mediation authorized?
Yes.

Will mediation be confidential?
Yes.

Is joint custody allowed?
Permitted despite one parent
objecting.

**Will a custody evaluation be
required?**
Court ordered.

**Are the child's preferences
considered?**
Yes.

**Can the court appoint someone
to represent my child?**
Yes.

Paternity

**Does marriage create a
presumption of paternity?**
Yes.

**Does the father's name on the
birth certificate establish
paternity?**
No.

**Is genetic testing used to
establish paternity?**
Yes, 99.33% probability.

Child Abuse

**Who must report child abuse
besides professionals?**
No one.

**Are there legally recognized
exceptions to child abuse?**
No.

**How long are child abuse
complaints kept?**
Expunged from one to 10 years.

Child Support

What model is used?
Shared Income.

Whose income is used?
Both parents. In addition, new
spouse's income may be
included.

**What methods are used to
enforce a support order?**
State income tax refund
intercept, license revocation/
suspension, property seizure and
sale, withholding of state funds
or benefits, consumer credit
(credit bureau) reporting,
automated annual notice of past-
due support (super notice).

**What types of income cannot
be withheld?**
Means tested income (i.e. IV-A,
SSI).

What are the limits on income withholding?
50% of disposable income after mandatory deductions. Up to 65% in some cases to meet all current support obligations.

When does support end?
For orders issued after 7/1/94, support ends when the child reaches 18 or the child's normal and expected year of graduation from high school, which ever occurs later. For orders issued prior to 7/1/94, child support automatically ends when the child reaches 18.

Does support end if the child leaves home early?
No.

Can support be ordered beyond the age of majority?
Yes.

What is the time-limit for collecting past-due support?
The age of majority of the last child in the order plus 4 years, unless a sum-certain judgment has been taken (support has been reduced to a judgment and the eight year statute of limitations allow collection for a longer time period).

Is interest charged on past-due support?
No.

Addresses

Utah Bar Association
645 South 200 East
Salt Lake City, UT 84111
(801) 531-9077
www.utahbar.org

Bureau of Child Support Services
Department of Human Services
P.O. Box 45011
Salt Lake City, UT 84145
(801) 536-8500

Office of Child Support
Enforcement Region VIII
1961 Stout Street
Room 924
Denver, CO 80294
(303) 844-2622

Utah Head Start
Utah Department of Health,
Division of Community and
Family Health Services
Child, Adolescent and School
Health Program (CASH)
P.O. Box 142001
Salt Lake City, UT 84114
(801) 538-9312

Admin. for Children and Families
Department of Health
Child Care Unit
P.O. Box 142003
Salt Lake City, UT 84114
(801) 538-9299

Vermont

Child Custody

What is the age of majority?
18.

How is custody divided?
Legal and physical combined.

Is mediation authorized?
No.

Will mediation be confidential?
Not specified.

Is joint custody allowed?
Available if both parents agree.

Will a custody evaluation be required?
Not specified.

Are the child's preferences considered?
No.

Can the court appoint someone to represent my child?
Yes.

Paternity

Does marriage create a presumption of paternity?
Yes.

Does the father's name on the birth certificate establish paternity?
No.

Is genetic testing used to establish paternity?
Yes, 98% probability.

Child Abuse

Who must report child abuse besides professionals?
Camp counselors, probation officers.

Are there legally recognized exceptions to child abuse?
Yes, religious exemption.

How long are child abuse complaints kept?
Expunged if no court proceeding initiated within one year, or when child reaches age of majority, or when youngest sibling reaches age of majority.

Child Support

What model is used?
Shared Income.

Whose income is used?
Both parents.

What methods are used to enforce a support order?
State income tax refund intercept, license revocation/ suspension, property seizure and sale, withholding of state funds or benefits, consumer credit (credit bureau) reporting, administrative wage withholding, administratively increasing the withholding in order to collect arrearages, issuing administrative garnishment orders, civil remedies, trustee process, assets in escrow, contempt, work search.

What types of income cannot be withheld?
Needs based income: TANF, SSI, VA benefits.

What are the limits on income withholding?
None, other than the limits in the Consumer Credit Protection Act (CCPA).

When does support end?
18, or when the child completes his or her secondary education, whichever is later.

Does support end if the child leaves home early?
No.

Can support be ordered beyond the age of majority?
Yes.

What is the time-limit for collecting past-due support?
In cases with an order but no adjudicated arrearage, an action to adjudicate arrears must be taken within 6 years after the youngest child reaches 18. In cases in which arrearages have been previously adjudicated, the limit is 8 years after the last adjudication.

Is interest charged on past-due support?
No.

Addresses

Vermont Bar Association
35-37 Court Street
P.O. Box 100
Montpelier, VT 05601
(802) 223-2020
www.vtbar.org

Office of Child Support
103 South Main Street
Waterbury, VT 05671
(802) 241-2313

Office of Child Support
Enforcement Region I
John F. Kennedy Federal Bldg.
Room 2000
Boston, MA 02203
(617) 565-10205

Vermont Head Start
Agency of Human Services
103 South Main Street
Waterbury, VT 05671
(802) 241-2705

Admin. for Children and Families
Department of Social
Rehabilitation Services
Child Care Services Division
103 S. Main Street
Waterbury, VT 05671-2901
(802) 241-2158
(802) 241-3110

Virginia

Child Custody

What is the age of majority?
18.

How is custody divided?
Legal and physical separate.

Is mediation authorized?
Yes.

Will mediation be confidential?
Yes.

Is joint custody allowed?
No statutes.

Will a custody evaluation be required?
Court ordered.

Are the child's preferences considered?
Yes.

Can the court appoint someone to represent my child?
Yes.

Paternity

Does marriage create a presumption of paternity?
Yes.

Does the father's name on the birth certificate establish paternity?
No.

Is genetic testing used to establish paternity?
Yes, 98% probability.

Child Abuse

Who must report child abuse besides professionals?
Mediators, Christian Science practitioners, probation officers, CASAs.

Are there legally recognized exceptions to child abuse?
Yes, religious exemption.

How long are child abuse complaints kept?
Expunged from Department records after one year which are kept separate from the Central Registry.

Child Support

What model is used?
Shared Income.

Whose income is used?
Both parents. Monthly gross income of both parents' is considered when calculating child support.

What methods are used to enforce a support order?
State income tax refund intercept, license revocation/suspension, property seizure and sale, withholding of state funds or benefits, consumer credit (credit bureau) reporting, income withholding, lottery intercept, orders to withhold and deliver, passport denial.

What types of income cannot be withheld?

Public assistance payments, SSI, college work study, annuities to survivors of federal judges, benefits for victims of crime, burial contracts, proceeds from industrial sick benefits insurance, benefits from group life insurance policies, and growing crops not severed.

What are the limits on income withholding?

None, other than the limits in the Consumer Credit Protection Act (CCPA).

When does support end?

Support will continue for any child that is a full-time high school student, not self-supporting, and living in the home of the parent, until the child reaches 19 or graduates high school, whichever comes first. Support terminates when the child turns 18 if the child is not in high school.

Does support end if the child leaves home early?

No.

Can support be ordered beyond the age of majority?

Yes.

What is the time-limit for collecting past-due support?

None.

Is interest charged on past-due support?

Yes, 8% per year.

Addresses

Virginia Bar Association
707 E. Main Street
Suite 1500
Richmond, VA 23219
(804) 775-0500
www.vsb.org

Division of Support Enforcement
Department of Social Services
730 East Broad Street
Richmond, VA 23219
(804) 692-1428

Office of Child Support
Enforcement Region III
150 S. Independence Mall West
Suite 864
Philadelphia, PA 19106
(215) 861-4000

Virginia Head Start
Norfolk State University
700 Park Avenue
Norfolk, VA 23504
(757) 823-8322

Admin. for Children and Families
Department of Social Services
730 E. Broad Street
7th Floor
Richmond, VA 23219
(800) 543-7545

Washington

Child Custody

What is the age of majority?
18.

How is custody divided?
Legal and physical combined.

Is mediation authorized?
Yes.

Will mediation be confidential?
Yes.

Is joint custody allowed?
Available if both parents agree.

Will a custody evaluation be required?
Court ordered.

Are the child's preferences considered?
Yes.

Can the court appoint someone to represent my child?
Yes.

Paternity

Does marriage create a presumption of paternity?
Yes.

Does the father's name on the birth certificate establish paternity?
No.

Is genetic testing used to establish paternity?
Yes, 98% probability.

Child Abuse

Who must report child abuse besides professionals?
Any adult with whom a child resides, responsible living skills program staff.

Are there legally recognized exceptions to child abuse?
Yes, corporal punishment, physical disability, Christian Science treatment.

How long are child abuse complaints kept?
Expunged 6 years after receipt of the report.

Child Support

What model is used?
Shared Income.

Whose income is used?
Any other household income.

What methods are used to enforce a support order?
State income tax refund intercept, license revocation/ suspension, property seizure and sale, withholding of state funds or benefits, consumer credit (credit bureau) reporting.

What types of income cannot be withheld?
TANF, SSI, VA disability, work release earnings from state, federal work-study grants, non-obligated spouse.

What are the limits on income withholding?
50% of disposable income.

When does support end?
18, unless there is an administrative order and the child is a full-time student expected to graduate before age 19.

Does support end if the child leaves home early?
No.

Can support be ordered beyond the age of majority?
Yes.

What is the time-limit for collecting past-due support?
For orders entered after 7/22/89, 10 years after emancipation of youngest child; for orders entered before 7/23/89, 10 years after a payment becomes delinquent.

Is interest charged on past-due support?
Yes, but only if reduced to or included in judgement.

Addresses

Washington Bar Association
2101 Fourth Avenue
Suite 400
Seattle, WA 98121
(800) 945-WSBA
(206) 443-WSBA

Division of Child Support
Department of Social and Health Services
P.O. Box 9162
Olympia, WA 98507
(360) 664-5000

Office of Child Support Enforcement Region X
2201 Sixth Avenue
Blanchard Plaza
Suite 600
Seattle, WA 98121
(206) 615-2547

Washington Head Start
Division of Child Care and Early Learning
Department of Social and Health Services
P.O. Box 45480
Olympia, WA 98504
(360) 413-3330

Admin. for Children and Families
Division of Child Care and Early Learning
Economic Services Administration
Department of Social and Health Services
P.O. Box 45480
Olympia, WA 98504
(360) 413-3209

West Virginia

Child Custody

What is the age of majority?
18.

How is custody divided?
Legal and physical separate.

Is mediation authorized?
Yes.

Will mediation be confidential?
Not specified.

Is joint custody allowed?
Available if both parents agree.

Will a custody evaluation be required?
Not specified.

Are the child's preferences considered?
Yes.

Can the court appoint someone to represent my child?
No.

Paternity

Does the father's name on the birth certificate establish paternity?
Yes.

Does marriage create a presumption of paternity?
Yes.

Is genetic testing used to establish paternity?
Yes, 98% probability.

Child Abuse

Who must report child abuse besides professionals?
Clergy, religious healers, judges, family law masters or magistrates, Christian Science practitioners.

Are there legally recognized exceptions to child abuse?
Yes, poverty, exemption to state compulsory education.

How long are child abuse complaints kept?
Expunged 6 years after their preparation.

Child Support

What model is used?
Shared Income.

Whose income is used?
Both parents.

What methods are used to enforce a support order?
State income tax refund intercept, license revocation/suspension, property seizure and sale, withholding of state funds or benefits, consumer credit (credit bureau) reporting.

What types of income cannot be withheld?
TANF, SSI, VA Disability.

What are the limits on income withholding?

The total amount withheld shall not exceed 125% of the current month's support. In addition, the amount withheld may be increased up to $100.00 when an obligor's total support arrears meet certain "triggering" criteria, such as the total arrearages is more than $8000.00, or support has not been paid for 12 consecutive months. Tax refund intercepts cannot be included in the 12-month period.

When does support end?

18.

Does support end if the child leaves home early?

No.

Can support be ordered beyond the age of majority?

Yes.

What is the time-limit for collecting past-due support?

10 years from and after date of judgment.

Is interest charged on past-due support?

Yes, 10% simple per year.

Addresses

West Virginia Bar Association
2006 Kanawha Boulevard, East
Charleston, WV 25311
(304) 558-2456
www.wvbar.org

Child Support Enforcement
Division
Department of Health & Human
Resources
1900 Kanawha Boulevard East
Capitol Complex, Building 6,
Room 817
Charleston, WV 25305
(304) 558-3780

Office of Child Support
Enforcement Region III
150 S. Independence Mall West
Suite 864
Philadelphia, PA 19106
(215) 861-4000

West Virginia Head Start
Governor's Cabinet on Children
and Families
1900 Kanawha Boulevard East
Building 5, Room 218
Charleston, WV 25305
(304) 558-4638

Admin. for Children and Families
Department of Health and
Human Resources
P.O. Box 2590
Fairmont, WV 26555
(304) 363-3261

Wisconsin

Child Custody

What is the age of majority?
18.

How is custody divided?
Legal and physical separate.

Is mediation authorized?
Yes.

Will mediation be confidential?
Yes.

Is joint custody allowed?
Permitted despite one parent objecting.

Will a custody evaluation be required?
Court ordered.

Are the child's preferences considered?
Yes.

Can the court appoint someone to represent my child?
Yes.

Paternity

Does marriage create a presumption of paternity?
Yes.

Does the father's name on the birth certificate establish paternity?
Yes.

Is genetic testing used to establish paternity?
Yes, 99% probability.

Child Abuse

Who must report child abuse besides professionals?
Alcohol or drug abuse counselors, mediators, financial and employment planners, CASAs.

Are there legally recognized exceptions to child abuse?
Yes, poverty.

How long are child abuse complaints kept?
Indefinitely.

Child Support

What model is used?
Percent of Income.

Whose income is used?
Noncustodial parent.

What methods are used to enforce a support order?
State income tax refund intercept, license revocation/ suspension, property seizure and sale, withholding of state funds or benefits, administrative subpoenas and denial of grants and loans, i.e., grants and loans for higher education, contempt, warrants, bonds, criminal nonsupport, Children First (a court-ordered work program).

What types of income cannot be withheld?

Veteran's disability benefits, Supplemental Security Income benefits, and Public Assistance payments.

What are the limits on income withholding?

None, other than the limits in the Consumer Credit Protection Act (CCPA).

When does support end?

18 unless the child is still in high school or pursuing a course of education designed to lead to a high school diploma or its equivalent, in which case support continues until 19.

Does support end if the child leaves home early?

No.

Can support be ordered beyond the age of majority?

No.

What is the time-limit for collecting past-due support?

20 years. However, there is conflicting authority as to whether it is 20 years after the children reach the age of majority or 20 years from the date the arrearage accrued.

Is interest charged on past-due support?

Yes, 1% per month.

Addresses

Wisconsin Bar Association
5302 Eastpark Blvd.
Madison, WI 53718
(608) 257-3838
(800) 728-7788
www.wisbar.org

Division of Economic Support
P.O. Box 7935
Madison, WI 53707
(608) 266-9909

Office of Child Support
Enforcement Region V
233 N. Michigan Avenue
Suite 400
Chicago, IL 60601
(312) 353-4237

Wisconsin Head Start
Wisconsin Department of
Workforce Development
201 E. Washington Avenue
Madison, WI 53707
(608) 261-4596

Admin. for Children and Families
Division of Children & Family
Services
1 West Wilson Street
P.O. Box 8916
Madison, WI 53708
(608) 266-9314

Wyoming

Child Custody

What is the age of majority?
18.

How is custody divided?
Legal and physical combined.

Is mediation authorized?
No.

Will mediation be confidential?
Not specified.

Is joint custody allowed?
Available if both parents agree.

Will a custody evaluation be required?
Not specified.

Are the child's preferences considered?
Yes.

Can the court appoint someone to represent my child?
Yes.

Paternity

Does marriage create a presumption of paternity?
Yes.

Does the father's name on the birth certificate establish paternity?
No.

Is genetic testing used to establish paternity?
Yes, 99% probability.

Child Abuse

Who must report child abuse besides professionals?
No one.

Are there legally recognized exceptions to child abuse?
Yes, religious exemption.

How long are child abuse complaints kept?
Expunged upon completion of the investigation or upon good cause shown.

Child Support

What model is used?
Percent of Income.

Whose income is used?
Noncustodial parent.

What methods are used to enforce a support order?
License revocation/suspension, property seizure and sale, withholding of state funds or benefits, consumer credit (credit bureau) reporting, federal/administrative offset, income withholding.

What types of income cannot be withheld?
Pell grants, SSI benefits, Welfare benefits.

What are the limits on income withholding?
Not less than 35% nor more than 65% of gross income after

deducting federal taxes (following 15 U.S.C. 1673).

When does support end?
18, unless the child is emancipated by becoming self supporting, legally married, active in the armed services, or successfully petitions the court for a Declaration of Emancipation.

Does support end if the child leaves home early?
No.

Can support be ordered beyond the age of majority?
Yes.

What is the time-limit for collecting past-due support?
None.

Is interest charged on past-due support?
Yes, 10% charged on amount reduced to judgement after 7/1/90.

Addresses

Wyoming Bar Association
500 Randall Avenue
P.O. Box 109
Cheyenne, WY 82003
(307) 632-9061
www.wyomingbar.org

Child Support Enforcement
Department of Family Services
Hathaway Building
2300 Capital Avenue, 3rd Floor
Cheyenne, WY 82002
(307) 777-6948

Office of Child Support
Enforcement Region VIII
1961 Stout Street
Room 924
Denver, CO 80294
(303) 844-2622

Wyoming Head Start
University of Wyoming
1465 North 4th Street
Suite 111
Laramie, WY 82072
(307) 766-2452

Admin. for Children and Families
Department of Family Services
Division of Juvenile Services
Hathaway Building
Room 343
2300 Capitol Avenue
Cheyenne, WY 82002
(307) 777-6285

Glossary

A

Ability to earn. What a parent is capable of earning.

Ability to pay. What a parent actually earns.

Abuse. Behavior that causes physical, mental, or emotional harm.

Acknowledged father. A biological father who has admitted paternity.

Action. A legal proceeding in a court of law.

Adjudication. The act of pronouncing a judgment after evidence has been submitted.

Adjusted gross income. Gross income after making certain adjustments.

Admissible. Evidence that may be introduced.

Adulterine bastard. A child born to a married woman when she is not married to the father.

Adversary system. The system of resolving disputes where the two sides compete instead of cooperate.

Affidavit. A written statement made under oath and filed with the court.

Allegations. The claims made by one side in a lawsuit.

Alternative Dispute Resolution (ADR). A collection of techniques that settle a dispute without a trial.

Answer. A response to allegations made in a complaint.

Appeal. A request to a higher court to review a decision made by a lower court.

Appellant. The person initiating the appeal.

Appellate court. A court that can review the decisions of another court.

Appellee. The person against whom the appeal is filed.

Arbitration. A form of alternative dispute resolution where the two sides submit the dispute to a third party, who makes the decision.

Arrearage. A past due debt.

Attorney. A person who can represent you.

Award. Compensation given by the court.

B

Bailiff. A person who keeps order in the courtroom

Bench trial. A trial conducted by a judge without a jury.

Best interests of the child. The legal standard used to guide decisions about child custody and child support.

Bias. An inability of the judge to make an impartial decision.

Brief. A written statement containing facts and law that support an argument in a case.

Burden of proof. The standard by which a case is decided. The duty to prove a fact in dispute.

C

Calendar. The list of cases with the day and time to be heard.

Caption. The heading on a court paper. The caption contains the names of the parties, the name of the court, the case number, and the title of the document.

Case law. Law based on prior decisions.

Case-in-chief. The main body of evidence presented during a trial.

Case. A legal dispute.

Cause of action. The facts or legal theories that form the basis for the lawsuit.

Certiorari. An order allowing an appeal.

Chambers. The judge's office.

Change of venue. The act of moving a lawsuit to another court in the same county or district.

Child care credit. A credit for parents who pay someone to care for their child so they can work or look for work.

Child custody. The right to raise the child and/or to decide how the child is raised.

Child support. The money one parent pays the other for the care and welfare of the children.

Child support guidelines. A mathematical formula used to calculate how much money one parent should pay the other.

Citation. A reference to a legal source, such as a case, statute, or treatise.

Claim. An assertion made by the person who is suing.

Complainant. The person who initiates the lawsuit. Also, petitioner or plaintiff.

Complaint. The first document in a lawsuit that states what the plaintiff is suing for.

Conciliation. A form of alternative dispute resolution where a neutral person helps the parties settle their dispute.

Contempt of court. Behavior intended to obstruct a court order.

Contingency fee. A legal fee based on the outcome of the case.

Continuance. The act of postponing a legal proceeding to a later date.

Counsel. An attorney.

Counterclaim. A complaint made by the defendant against the plaintiff.

Count. A statement in a complaint or petition claiming a specific legal violation or injury.

Clerk. A court employee who may maintain the record of court proceedings, file documents, or assist the judge.

Court costs. Additional expenses in a lawsuit beyond those charged by a lawyer.

Court papers. Papers filed with the court related to the lawsuit.

Court reporter. An official who records the discussions and proceedings in a hearing, deposition, or trial.

Court rule. Rules created by the court to handle administrative details.

Cross-examination. The questioning of a witness by the opposing side.

Custodial parent. The parent who is primarily responsible for raising the children.

D

Decision. A judgment made by the court.

Decree. A decision or order of the court.

Deductions. Expenses that are subtracted from gross income.

Default judgment. The judgment made when the defendant fails to respond.

Defendant. A person being sued.

Dependent. A person supported by someone else.

Dependent exemption. A tax deduction for a dependent.

Deposed. The act of being questioned under oath.

Deposition. An oral statement made under oath.

Direct examination. The questioning of a witness by the party who called the witness.

Discovery. The process of gathering information to present at a hearing or trial.

Dispute. The conflict that the court is being asked to resolve.

Divorce. A legal decision that ends a marriage

Docket. A record containing the list of the court proceedings.

Due process. The administration of law through the court system.

E

Earned income. All the income you get from working.

Emancipation. When a minor child demonstrates freedom from parental control, and the parents have no more obligations to the child.

Equitable parent. A parent who is not the biological or adoptive parent, but who nevertheless may be granted custody or visitation.

Equitable relief. A remedy meant to make amends for an injury.

Evidence. Proof presented to the court that supports allegations.

Ex parte. A procedure that allows only one side in a dispute to address the court.

Exemptions. A tax deduction for a person.

Exhibit. Physical evidence used to prove a point.

Expert. A person who is a recognized authority. An expert witness is allowed to give his or her opinion in court.

F

Fact finder. In a bench trial, the role of the judge to decide what evidence will be accepted.

Family law. The body of law involving marriage, separation, custody, support, and so on.

Family support. A taxable form of support combining child support and spousal support into one payment.

Federal Parent Locator Service (FPLS). A service run by the Office of Child Service Support Enforcement (OCSE) to help locate parents who owe child support.

Filing status. The category of tax filer you are.

Financial statement. A court paper containing a parent's income and expense information.

Finding. A decision made by a judge.

Full faith and credit. The legal principle requiring a judge in one state to enforce a decision made by a judge in another state.

G

Garnishment. A proceeding in which a debtor's money or property is seized to pay a debt.

Gross income. Generally, all the money you receive.

Guardian. A person appointed by the court to be responsible for a child.

Guardian ad litem. A person appointed by the court to represent a child in a legal matter.

Guideline. A standard method for determining child support.

H

Hardship. When a person suffers extreme losses.

Head of household. The filing status of a person who maintains a home for a dependent and is not married.

Hearing. Any court proceeding where testimony is given or arguments are heard.

Hearsay. An out-of-court statement offered to prove something.

Hostile witness. A witness who is antagonistic to the party who called him.

I

Illegitimate child. A child born to parents who are not married.
Impeachment. The act of undermining the credibility of a witness.
In camera. A private discussion in the judge's office.
Inadmissible. Evidence that is not allowed to be introduced.
Injunction. An order requiring someone to do something, or preventing someone from doing something.
Interlocutory. Temporary orders.
Interrogatories. Written questions one side asks the other.
Issue. The items being disputed.
IV-D agency. A government agency that handles child support enforcement.

J

Joint custody. An arrangement allowing for mutual sharing of the children. Joint legal custody involves shared decision making, and joint physical custody allows for equal time with the children.
Judge. The official who presides over a courtroom.
Judgment. The official decision of a court.
Jurisdiction. A court's authority to hear a case.

L

Lawsuit. A legal proceeding that settles a private dispute between two people.
Leading question. A question that suggests how a witness should answer.
Legal custody. The right to make major decisions for the child.
Legal father. A man recognized by law as the father.
Lien. A claim against property designed to stop a sale of transfer until the debt is paid.
Litigant. A person involved in a lawsuit.
Litigation. The process of pursuing a lawsuit.

M

Material evidence. Evidence that is relevant to the dispute.
Mediation. A form of alternative dispute resolution where the two sides meet with a third person who tries to help them resolve the dispute.
Memoranda of law. A written argument that supports a motion.
Memorandum of understanding. A document that identifies the

decisions reached in negotiation.

Mental health professional. A psychiatrist, psychologist, marriage counselor, or licensed social worker.

Merits. The essential issues in a case.

Modification. When a court revises an existing order.

Motion. A formal request to a court for an order or ruling.

N

Neglect. Ignoring a child's needs.

Negotiation. The attempt to resolve a dispute through discussion.

Net income. Gross income minus allowable expenses.

New mate. A new spouse or partner.

Noncustodial parent. A parent who is not responsible for raising the children.

Notice. The official notification that a lawsuit has been filed.

Notice of appeal. A court document that indicates a party is appealing the decision.

Notice to produce. A court document that requires the other party to deliver evidence.

O

Objection. The act of protesting a statement made in court. Objections are sustained or overruled.

Obligation. A requirement to pay money.

Obligee. The person who is owed the money.

Obligor. The person who must pay the money.

Office of Child Support Enforcement (OCSE). A government agency that helps locate absent parents, establishes paternity, and establishes and enforces child support obligations.

Officer of the court. A court official. Judges, court clerks, and lawyers are all officers of the court.

Offset. Money deducted from a person's income tax refund to pay a court judgment.

Opinion. The written explanation of a court decision.

Oral argument. The time when a party can verbally summarize the dispute to the judge.

Order. Instructions from the court.

Order of protection. An order forbidding one person from harming another.

P

Paralegal. Someone other than an attorney with legal skills.

Parties. The people in a lawsuit.

Paternity action. A lawsuit designed to identify the father.

Perjury. A false statement made under oath.

Personal exemption. A tax deduction you may claim for yourself.

Personal jurisdiction. The authority of the court to make orders involving someone.

Petition. A court document requesting something.

Petitioner. The person who files a lawsuit. Also, plaintiff.

Physical custody. The right to have the children live with you.

Plaintiff. The person who files a lawsuit. Also, petitioner.

Pleading. A court document that outlines the issues in a dispute.

Prayer. The part of a petition that describes what the person wants the court to do.

Precedent. The decision in a case that influences future cases that are similar.

Prejudice. When a judgment is made with prejudice, the issues cannot be relitigated. When a judgment is made without prejudice, the issues may be retried.

Prejudicial error. A mistake made in a decision that by a court that justifies a reversal by an appellate court.

Preponderance of the evidence. The standard used to decide civil disputes.

Presumed correct. The guideline amount of child support assumed to be correct.

Presumed father. A man assumed to be the father unless he proves otherwise.

Pretrial conference. A meeting before trial between the judge and the attorneys.

Primary caretaker. The parent who provides most of the daily care for the child.

Propria persona. Pro per and pro se are Latin terms that describe individuals who represent themselves.

Q

Quash. A decision to void or cancel a court order or judgment.

R

Rebuttal. Arguments or evidence used to disprove.

Record. All papers filed with the court, including documents, evidence, and transcripts.

Recusal. When a judge removes himself from a case.

Redirect examination. The questioning that follows cross-examination.

Relevant. Evidence which directly addresses an issue.

Remand. When a higher court returns a case back to a lower court.

Remedy. The way a court can make amends for an injury.

Rent-a-judge. A private judge hired by the parties to resolve the dispute.

Reply. The response to a pleading.

Res judicata. A question that has already been settled and cannot be relitigated.

Residence. Where someone lives.

Respondent. The person being sued.

Response. A court document that answers the allegations made in a complaint.

Retainer. Money paid to a lawyer for future work.

Reverse. When a higher court cancels a lower court's decision.

Rules of evidence. Legal standards that establish what type of evidence can be heard.

S

Sanction. A penalty for violating a court order.

Service. The official delivery of a legal document.

Settlement. When the two sides come to an agreement without a trial.

Settlement agreement. A written agreement between the two sides.

Show cause. An order requiring someone to appear in court.

Significant change of circumstance. The minimum requirement for changing an existing court order.

Single. The filing status of a person who is not married and has no dependents.

Sole custody. An arrangement where the children are raised by only one of their parents.

Split custody. An arrangement where the time with the children is divided between the two parents.

Standard of living. The relative comfort the children were accustomed to before the parents separated.

Standing. The right to sue or join a lawsuit.

Statute. A law created by the legislature.

Stay. A court order that stops the enforcement of a court order.

Stipulation. An agreement between the two sides in a lawsuit.

Strike. An order to remove improper evidence from the court record.

Subject-matter jurisdiction. The authority of the court to decide a particular type of case.

Subpoena. A court order requiring someone to appear and give testimony.

Subpoena Duces Tecum. A court order requiring someone to provide documents or evidence.

Summary judgment. An order that decides a case before the trial begins.

Summons. The notice informing someone that he or she is being sued, the location of the court, and when the matter will be heard.

T

Taxable income. Your income after reducing it by claiming various exemptions, credits, and deductions.

Temporary restraining order (TRO). An order that prohibits someone from doing something until a hearing can be held.

Testimony. A statement made under oath.

Transcript. A written record of court proceedings.

Trial. A court hearing when a judge listens to evidence and decides issues in dispute.

Trial memorandum. A document that presents the facts and arguments in a case.

U

Uniform Child Custody Jurisdiction Act (UCCJA). A uniform law that has been adopted in all states the prevents two states from making simultaneous child custody orders.

Uniform Interstate Family Support Act (UIFSA). A uniform law that strengthens child support enforcement across state lines by preventing the second state from altering the amount of support ordered by the home state.

Unwed father. A father who is not married to the mother.

V

Venue. A place where a trial can be held.

Visitation. The time a noncustodial parent spends with the children.

W

Wage assignment. An automatic deduction from wages to pay a debt, such as child support. Also wage withholding.

Weight of evidence. The preponderance of credible evidence.

Witness. A person who testifies under oath.

Writ. A court order requiring someone to do something.

Index

K

L

M

About the Author

Webster Watnik lives outside of Los Angeles. After earning a Master's at USC, he began a technical writing career. Soon after, he was drawn into a custody battle over his son, Wyeth.

To reach the author, please contact:

Single Parent Press
P.O. Box 1298
Claremont, CA 91711
(909) 624-6058 phone
(909) 624-2208 fax
www.SingleParentPress.com